THE LIFE AND WORKS OF SIMON DIGBY
VOLUME III

Sufis in the Life of Medieval India

Simon Digby (1932–2010)
Photo courtesy: Nandita Mahajan

THE LIFE AND WORKS OF SIMON DIGBY
VOLUME III

Sufis in the Life of Medieval India

SIMON DIGBY

edited by
DAVID LUNN

with an Introduction by
NILE GREEN

PRIMUS BOOKS

PRIMUS BOOKS
An Imprint of Ratna Sagar P. Ltd.
Virat Bhavan
Mukherjee Nagar Commercial Complex
Delhi 110 009

Offices at

CHENNAI LUCKNOW
AGRA AHMEDABAD BANGALORE COIMBATORE
DEHRADUN GUWAHATI HYDERABAD JAIPUR JALANDHAR
KANPUR KOCHI KOLKATA MADURAI MUMBAI
PATNA RANCHI VARANASI

First published 2025

ISBN: 978-93-6883-198-3 (Hardback)
ISBN: 978-93-6883-367-3 (PoD)

Published by Primus Books

Typeset by Manmohan Kumar
manmohankumar2015@gmail.com

The Life and Works of Simon Digby is intended to bring most of Simon Digby's publications, together with a large body of work left unpublished at his death, to new and wider audiences. The series stands as testimony to his extraordinary scholarship.

Publication of this series has been made possible by the Simon Digby Memorial Charity (SDMC). Registered in the Channel Island of Jersey where Digby was based, the SDMC was established to further the study of subjects that were of particular interest to Simon Digby. The SDMC has donated much of his collection to Oxford University's Ashmolean Museum and Bodleian Library, to the British Museum, and to other museums across the globe. It has funded the production of this series through a postdoctoral fellowship at SOAS University of London, aided in the publication of a volume on Digby's historical method, and continues to fund projects in fields associated with his research.

THE LIFE AND WORKS OF SIMON DIGBY
Edited by David Lunn

I. *Against the Mughals: Dreams and Wars of Dattū Sarvānī, a Sixteenth-Century Indo-Afghan Soldier*
II. *Encounters with Jogīs in Indian Sūfī Hagiography*
III. *Sufis in the Life of Medieval India*
IV. *Tales, Translations, Trajectories*
V. *War-Horse and Elephant in the Dehli Sultanate: Revised Edition with Supplementary Materials*
VI. *The North Indian Sultanates: Studies and Stories*
VII. *Sufis and Soldiers in Awrangzeb's Deccan I: New Revised Edition*
VIII. *Sufis and Soldiers in Awrangzeb's Deccan II: A Historian's Handbook*
IX. *Indian Art and Numismatics*
X. *Overseas and Far Horizons I: Essays and Documents on Indo-Persian Perceptions in the Age of the Europeans*
XI. *Overseas and Far Horizons II: Travel Accounts, from Pilgrims to Princes*

Contents

Editor's Note and Acknowledgements

David Lunn

The essays in this volume represent a significant part of the late Simon Digby's writings on one of his greatest passions: the Sufis of medieval India. All have been previously published, but their collection here not only fulfils the intention of the Simon Digby Memorial Charity to make his occasionally inaccessible writings available to new audiences, but also completes in part an intended project of Simon Digby's—to bring these writings on Sufis and Sufism together. Other volumes in this series also touch on similar and related themes: volume I expands upon his 1965 examination of the Sufi anecdotes of Dattū Sarvānī; volume II is a book-length version of his never-published (though oft-cited) 1970 paper on encounters with *Jogīs* in Sufi hagiography; volume VII is a new edition of his magisterial translation of the *Malfūẓāt-i Naqshbandiyya*; and volume VIII is his substantial commentary on and companion to that translation, never previously published.

The essays in this volume were published over the period 1975–94 in a diverse array of journals and edited volumes. The conventions regarding spelling, formatting, and transliteration naturally differed between them. I have not attempted to harmonize these systems absolutely among the essays here, preferring to retain the original schemes, and so beg the reader's indulgence for the resulting inconsistencies—shaykh, shaikh, and sheikh; Delhi, Dehli, and Dehlī; and so on. I have, however, presumed (or attempted) to apply a consistent rule for the transliteration of the names of the great Chishtī shaykhs who are the subject of so much of this volume, as well as the major primary sources. Other editorial interventions have in the main been restricted to applying a consistent referencing style, and correcting obvious orthographic and typographic errors in the original versions, while endeavouring to avoid adding more of my own.

Speaking of corrections, Simon's archive consists in substantial part of off-prints of his various articles and chapters, many of which contain annotations in his hand—corrections, emendations, and updates to reflect his subsequent publishing activities. These have been inserted without comment in the essays here. Other updated references to *The Life and Works*, to his collection of manuscripts (now in the Bodleian Library, University of Oxford, donated there by the trustees of the Simon Digby Memorial Charity in 2015), occasional rephrasing of 'this century' to compensate for the twenty-first-century context of this edition, and any other more significant interventions are clearly marked in square brackets and, where appropriate, signed '~DL'.

Readers may be confused at the apparent omission of Simon's important 1998 article 'Before the Bābās Came to India: A Reconstruction of the Earlier Lives of Bābā Sa'īd Palangpōsh and Bābā Muḥammad Musāfir in "Wilāyat"' on the Sufis in the Deccan. Simon Digby had expanded this essay and included it along with other details and an extensive commentary on Shāh Maḥmūd Awrangābādī's *Malfūẓāt-i Naqshbandiyya*, which he had translated and published. *The Life and Works of Simon Digby* includes a new edition of that translation and his commentary or 'historian's handbook' to it, of which the aforementioned essay forms a considerable part, so it is not included here.

Finally, let me acknowledge some of the many people who have been involved in this project. First and foremost, my thanks go to the Trustees of the Simon Digby Memorial Charity—Richard Harris, Colin Perchard, and Dr Dominic Omissi—for their vision in this quest to see Simon's works reach new audiences, and for their support, enthusiasm, and patience throughout. An extra word of thanks goes to Lis Perchard for her warm welcome to Jersey in the early days of this project. I also thank most sincerely Francesca Orsini, Shahid Amin, and the late Sunil Kumar for their support of this project, as well as Nile Green for his scholarly introduction to this volume. I would also like to express my thanks and admiration to Prasun Chatterjee and his colleagues at Primus Books for their enthusiasm for this project from the very beginning. And as I put the finishing touches to copyedited files in the disappointing London summer, I want to thank particularly and effusively Jess Hayton and Rocco Brunori, the dearest of friends, who have gone above and beyond; perhaps Frank and Agata deserve a mention too.

Many others—too many to name—have shared their memories of Simon Digby and his life and works with me over the years since I began this project, and their obvious respect, appreciation, and sense of loss at his passing gave extra impetus to the task at hand. I hope this volume—and this series—meets their expectations, and stands as a fitting testimony to Simon Digby and his scholarship.

The Editor and the Trustees of the Simon Digby Memorial Charity would like to thank the various publishers—listed below with corresponding copyright notices—for permission to republish the respective chapters. Additionally, our thanks go to Harrassowitz Verlag for their prompt and courteous assistance in confirming the reversion of copyright of Chapter 6, and to Professor Yohanan Friedmann for his kind help.

- 'The Sufi Shaikh as a Source of Authority in Medieval India', *Puruṣārtha*, vol. 9, 1986, pp. 57–77, © L'École des Hautes Études en Sciences Sociales;
- 'The Sufi Shaykh and the Sultan: A Conflict of Claims to Authority in Medieval India', *Iran*, vol. 28, 1990, pp. 71–81, and 'Anecdotes of a Provincial Sufi of the Dehlī Sultanate, Khwāja Gurg of Kara', *Iran*, vol. 32, 1994, pp. 99–109, © British Institute of Persian Studies, reprinted by permission of Informa UK Limited, trading Taylor & Francis Group, https://www.tandfonline.com on behalf of British Institute of Persian Studies;
- '*Tabarrukāt* and Succession among the Great Chishtī Shaykhs of the Dehli Sultanate', Robert Eric Frykenberg, ed., *Delhi through the Ages*, Delhi: Oxford University Press, 1986, pp. 62–103, © Oxford University Press;
- 'Early Pilgrimages to the Graves of Mu'īn al-Dīn Sijzī and other Indian Chishtī Shaykhs', Milton Israel and N.K. Wagle, ed., *Islamic Society and Culture: Essays in Honour of Professor Aziz Ahmad*, New Delhi: Manohar, 1983, pp. 95–100, © Manohar;
- 'Qalandars and Related Groups: Elements of Social Deviance in the Religious Life of the Dehlī Sultanate of the Thirteenth and Fourteenth Centuries', Yohanan Friedmann, ed., *Islam in Asia, Volume 1: South Asia*, Jerusalem: The Hebrew University, 1984, pp. 60–108, © Truman Institute for the Advancement of Peace;
- 'The *Tuḥfa i naṣā'iḥ* of Yūsuf Gadā: An Ethical Treatise in Verse from the Late-Fourteenth-Century Dehlī Sultanate', Barbara Daly Metcalf, ed., *Moral Conduct and Authority: The Place of Adab in South Asian Islam*, Berkeley: University of California Press, 1984, pp. 91–123, © The Regents of the University of California.

Introduction

The Sufi Histories of Simon Digby

Nile Green

The Sufi literature which Simon Digby spent a lifetime studying was replete with paradoxes. So, it is perhaps fitting to begin by declaring that Digby was a pioneer because he was an outsider, and he was an outsider because he was a pioneer.

Though he occasionally made appearances at conferences and knew the Bodleian Library collections better than most, the seminar room was not his habitual environment; nor for that matter was the university library or classroom. Instead, he studied India through India; more specifically, he studied Indian Sufism through the legacy of the tradition itself. Which is to say he based his research on *traditio* in its core sense of 'what was handed down'. And this meant not only the Indo-Persian manuscripts in which he immersed himself, but also the shrines, ceremonies, spoken tales, and sheer tangible stuff of Sufism: objects, relics, and ritual paraphernalia. He was as at home in museum storerooms and auction houses as he was at libraries, with the latter more likely to be private collections in the provinces of India than the British Library and Indian National Archives from whose Anglophone collections his academic contemporaries were creating a historiographical behemoth from the colonial past. By contrast, his vocation was for the medieval period, an era that, like Marc Bloch, he saw as bequeathing analysable imprints on the present. The past was alive, back then as now, and Digby's interest was always in lived religion rather than the abstractions of Sufi theory or the lofty summits of its literature on which earlier generations of Western scholars had focused. For that reason, he was a historian rather than an Orientalist; and the reason he was not an Orientalist was precisely because he was interested in historical processes.

With his concern for geography and architecture, written record and folktale, object and ritual, we might be tempted to classify Digby's oeuvre as an exercise in what Bloch and his colleague Lucien Febvre called *histoire totale*. But while Digby maintained a lifelong commitment to the social history that Bloch and Febvre prioritized—presumably instilled as part of his history degree at Cambridge in the 1950s—he was ever suspicious of academic fashions. As an outsider, he could afford to eschew them; and remaining an academic outsider was perhaps the price he paid for doing so. The same sceptical suspicions made him steer clear of explicit theorization and, still more, of sacrificing his research on the altar of political commitment. The result was limpid, readable prose which, as academic fashions and political priorities change, will stand the test of time.

Yet what makes Digby's work endure is not merely his prose style, with its tone of infectious enthusiasm. The enduring value of his essays lies in their proximity to his source materials. A close reader, he stayed similarly close to his sources in his writing. Before the avalanche of French literary theory swept across Anglo-American then Indian academia, he showed remarkable sensitivity in his reading of Persian texts; sensitivity both to language, with its varying registers and idiolects, and to writing, with its genres and (what others would call) their intertextuality.

Hence, in reading Simon Digby, we in turn never lose sight of those medieval manuscripts, with their unfamiliar ways of classifying experience, their alien priorities for the lived human life, their curious criteria for what was worth recording, and their distinctive modes of organizing ideas. So, as an homage to Digby, the remaining sections of this introduction adopt a central feature of the Sufi texts he interpreted for us: the *fā'ida*. Meaning 'beneficial anecdote' or simply 'benefit', the *fā'ida* was effectively an edifying precursor to the paragraph that formed the organizing principle of classic works, such as the *Fawā'id al-Fu'ād* ('Benefits for the Inner Heart')—cited frequently in the following chapters. And like this introduction, the *fā'ida* sought to encapsulate the teachings of a master.

ف

Following his source texts, Digby was attentive to paradigms, and likewise to paradigmatic figures, from the medieval world he studied. The two most prominent such figures form the focus of the first two chapters in this volume, namely the Sufi saint and the sultan. For Sufi writers, they served as visible and living paradigms in the sense of exemplars of different aspects of eternal and temporal realities. The saint and the sultan were a pair; and Sufis—drawing on the dichotomous terminology of the Quran—used many such pairs in their teachings. Hence, the saint and the sultan represented *dīn* (religion, eternal truth) and *dunyā* (the world, transitory matters), which in turn represented the *zāhirī* (visible, exoteric) and *bātinī* (invisible, esoteric) dimensions of existence.

However, as a historian, while recognizing the importance of this dichotomy, Digby was primarily interested in the former dimension of Sufi life: the visible and tangible: the politically and socially manifest. His scholarly paradigms were those of the social historian, which prompted him to extrapolate sociological paradigms from his source texts, and in turn examine such classic Weberian questions as the construction of authority (in Chapter 1); the articulation of rival forms of authority (in Chapter 2); and the challenges of succession to charismatic authority (in Chapter 3).

Yet he was never willing to misrepresent his sources to make them fit with larger theories. Thus, in Chapter 1, he declared,

> The concept of the transmission of *baraka* (charisma) through a *ṭarīqa* or *silsila* of Sufi Shaikhs is strongly held, but examples of all three of Spencer Trimingham's groupings may be found at one and the same time, and the structures are to some extent reversible or interchangeable.[1] Moreover claims to the inheritance of authority were not always accompanied by an identity of practice.

While here he used Weber's 'charisma' to translate the key term *baraka* (more often rendered as 'blessing power' or simply 'blessing'), he was unwilling to overlook the variations he found in his sources. So, while maintaining a Weberian taste for typologies, Digby offered up his own that more accurately reflected the paradigms *qua* patterns he found in Indo-Persian texts. For example, in examining challenges to authority by way of narrative 'strategies of prestige' (in Chapter 6), he provided a fivefold typology of 'anecdotal patterns' that featured in tales about holy men who rode either tigers or miraculously moving walls. Yes: his sober prose dealt with many strange things, for he never considered any miraculous testament—nor anything in his sources—beyond the pale of serious study.

ف

[1] Here Digby refers to the highly influential schema proposed in J.S. Trimingham, *The Sufi Orders in Islam*, Oxford: Oxford University Press, 1971.

With such tales of supernatural contests, here Digby was working with the typologies of folklore studies as much as social history (as he would again in an essay on hawk and dove motifs in other tales of Sufi rivalry).[2] For his use of interpretive models was eclectic, picking them up according to questions that caught his interest, and putting them aside when their purpose was served. We see this again in Chapter 1, where he borrows the concept of Sanskritization developed by the Indian sociologist M.N. Srinivas (1916–99) as an analogy for 'Islamization': a parallel process of positional mobility that Digby defined as 'the quest or maintenance of high social status [that] leads to a stricter conformity of belief and observance'. But he had little interest in such abstractions in themselves, and could be scornful of their over-simplifications. Hence, in Chapter 6, he dismisses the model of Great and Little Traditions propounded by the American anthropologist Robert Redfield (1897–1958) as a 'crude conceptual formulation'.

Instead, Digby would stay true to his sources, taking seriously their own conceptual terminology—such as *wilāyat* (territorial spiritual jurisdiction)—and use those emic ideas to probe such social historical problems as how the Chishtī order first rose to prominence, then how such eminence was manifested, maintained, transferred, and challenged. These questions demanded that he also pay special attention to the concept of *karāmāt*, which he variously translated as 'graces', 'abnormal powers', or 'miraculous powers'. For such miracles were not only a perpetual topic of medieval Indo-Persian texts, whether composed at the 'courts' (*dargāhs*) of the Sufis or the sultans, thereby intrinsically demanding his attention. In their narrative elaboration, *karāmāt* stories

[2] S. Digby, 'Hawk and Dove in Sufi Combat', in *Pembroke Papers 1: Festschrift for P.W. Avery*, ed. C. Melville, Cambridge: Pembroke College, 1990 [incorporated in *L&WSD* II].

also provided him with evidence for how authority was conceived, expressed, and publicized in medieval milieux in which oral communication far outstripped (and also shaped) its written counterparts that survived as manuscripts for modern historians to study. The miracle, then, was the visible demonstration of a Sufi's status as a saintly friend of God; or alternatively, a demonstration of divine approval of a would-be Sultan's seizure of power. The *karāma* was, in other words, a paradigm that functioned in the core sense of the Greek verb *paradeiknumi*, 'to exhibit or expose' what was not otherwise apparent or visible.

For medieval Indian Muslims, this meant to expose the invisible realm of God: to briefly tear the veil between the hidden (*bātin*) and manifest (*zāhir*) dimensions of reality: to display *dīn* in the *dunyā*. Simon Digby's skill was to recognize that, for the social historian, the miracle story could serve as a narrative paradigm. Whether in hagiographies written by the disciples of a given Sufi, or in courtly chronicles written by the supporters (or, more rarely, critics) of a particular sultan, the miracle story was the visible—or, in written form, at least legible—social testament of the claim to authority.

ف

Digby was not only a master of Persian texts. His work in the Department of Eastern Art at Oxford's Ashmolean Museum exposed him to the artistic and material legacy of Muslim South Asia, as did his regular visits to London auction houses, to museums and private collections in India, and his friendships with art historians such as Robert Skelton (1929–2022), an authority on Sultanate and Mughal painting and decorative arts who served as curator of the Indian department of the Victoria and Albert Museum, and Mark Zebrowski (1945–99), a London-based American specialist on Indo-Muslim metalwork. Moreover, Digby's understanding of the Indian past was not based on merely being born and raised there, but more importantly on his repeated travels across the subcontinent that continued till the very end of his life. These were targeted travels, taking in many provincial and sometimes remote sites that fed into his scholarship, and occasionally undertaken with perspicacious friends such as Skelton, further training each other's gaze.[3] In short, another of Digby's *fawā'id* was his attention to objects and places.

Chapter 3 builds on his interest in the visible social manifestation of Sufi authority—and the process of its inheritance—through a study of the material relics of prominent Chishtī shaykhs. On the one hand, this was a textual study: his sources were not so much medieval sacred objects themselves but written accounts of them. But on the other hand, it was his recognition of the significance of physical objects that prompted him to reconstruct their medieval social functions. The inheritance of religious authority was not primarily a textual matter, he realized, even though *waṣīyat-nāmas* and *khilāfat-nāmas* might play supporting roles. Rather, the process of succession was based on 'the gift of the private and personal insignia or articles of common use of the Shaykh, which by their nature were not multipliable except by fraudulent claims.' Whereas talk was cheap, and texts could be fabricated, objects offered medieval communities more reliable—because tangible, visible, and less 'multipliable'—proof of who had inherited a shaykh's authority, even though it was invisible and intangible.

ف

[3] S. Digby, 'Travels with Robert', in *Arts of Mughal India: Studies in Honour of Robert Skelton*, ed. R. Crill et al., London: Victoria and Albert Museum/Ahmadabad: Mapin, 2004.

As described in such texts as the *Siyar al-awliyā'*, these material *tabarrukāt* ('blessed things', which Digby glossed as 'symbols of office') comprised eight objects: the staff (*'aṣā*); the prayer-carpet (*muṣallā* or *sajjāda*); the robe (*khirqa* or *jāma*); the begging bowl (*kāsa*)—these were the most important—supplemented sometimes by the shaykh's turban (*dastār*); finger-ring (*angushtarī*); rosary (*tasbīḥ*); and most rarely—pointing again to the importance of objects over texts—his Qur'ān.

Such relics were quite familiar to Digby: in his book *Sufis and Soldiers in Awrangzeb's Deccan*, he included photographs of the *tabarrukāt* of Shāh Musāfir (d.1126/1715) taken at the latter's Sufi lodge in Aurangabad.[4] During his travels he had seen many other such relics in shrines and ceremonies, as well as the ascetic paraphernalia and outlandish clothes of the Qalandars and other antinomian dervishes whose forebears he traces in Chapter 7. It seems likely that such observations inspired his search for their historical precedents, because anecdotes of on-the-spot observations (as at the Gulbarga *'Urs* in 1963) were a regular feature of his writing, plainly reported for what they were worth and never aggrandized as 'fieldwork' with navel-gazing theory.

By the time Chapters 3 and 7 were first published in the mid-1980s, he had gained a deep professional familiarity with Indo-Muslim material culture. Thirty years earlier, during a year of study at what was then still called the Prince of Wales Museum in Bombay, he had written one of his first articles about medieval copper and brass items, and he would continue to write on Indo-Muslim metalware (and painting) throughout his career, always with that rare

[4] S. Digby, *Sufis and Soldiers in Awrangzeb's Deccan*, New Delhi: Oxford University Press, 2001 [*L&WSD* VII].

methodological ability to move between texts and objects, with each shedding light on the other.[5]

ف

Digby would not deracinate the objects he scrutinized from their spatial contexts in settings which he would in turn situate the texts he studied in another echo of Bloch and Febvre's *histoire totale*.

This engagement with place took myriad forms in his writings. There was the conceptual dimension of space, as expressed in the notion of saintly *wilāyat* and its manifold implications, as explored in Chapters 1, 2, 6, and 9. There was the infrastructural dimension of space by way of his various enquiries into historical geography by way of routes and roads, pilgrimage sites, and hospices. Thus, in Chapter 4, he draws on the *Fawā'id al-Fu'ād* to reconstruct the existence by the 1320s of a Sufi infrastructure of interlinked *khānqāhs* that in turn connected Hindustan to the wider pilgrimage networks of the Arabian Hadramawt and Hijaz. In Chapter 4, we also learn about the more quotidian hardships faced by those who would travel across northern India to see Nizām al-Dīn at a time when such journeys involved the threat of murderous bandits, terrifying lions, excruciating hunger, and the lack of a common language with the locals one met. Similarly, Chapters 4 and 5 shed light on the organization of the trade caravans, or *qāfilas*, on which such pilgrimages depended. For Digby also had much to say about the economic past which, like social history, continued to preoccupy his Indian contemporaries after their Anglo-

5 S. Digby, 'Some Notes Towards the Classification of Muslim Copper and Brass Work in the Museum', *Bulletin of the Prince of Wales Museum of Western India, Bombay*, vol. 5, 1955–7 [*L&WSD* IX.6].

American counterparts had taken linguistic and theoretical 'turns'. Hence, the inscriptions, insignia, and circulation of coins under the Delhi sultans was another of his longstanding interests on which he published repeatedly.[6]

Then there were the processual dimensions of space through which the architecture of mosques and *khānqāhs* combined with the imported organizations of the Sufi orders and with the Persian hagiographies that linked these buildings to the *silsilas* and their saintly paragons. The result of this spatial process was what in Chapter 1 he describes as the 'Islamic sanctification of the new homeland'. This interest in historical geography would later blossom into such mature masterpieces as 'Before the Babas Came' and especially 'Before Timur Came'.[7] But the essays in this volume already widened the spatial ambit of Indian history, taking us to such provincial outposts of the Delhi Sultanate as the little town of Kara on the Ganges and the dustier likes of Rudawli, Shahabad, and Gangoh under the aegis of the Lodi Afghans. Occasionally, we are even led out into the wilds in the company of ʿAbd al-Quddūs Gangohī (d. 950/1543–4), whose 'rambles in the jungle lasted for two or three days'. In such distant places, the old Indo-Persian saying that '*hanūz Dihlī dūr ast*' ('Delhi is yet far off'), attributed to Nizām al-Dīn Awlīyā (d. 725/1325), was all too literally true.

[6] See for example S. Digby, 'The Broach Coin-Hoard as Evidence of the Import of Valuta across the Arabian Sea during the 13th and 14th and Centuries', *Journal of the Royal Asiatic Society*, vol. 2, 1980 [*L&WSD* IX.17] and S. Digby, 'Coinage in the Reign of Sultan Feroz Tughluq: A Literary Reference', *Numismatic Digest*, vol. 4, no. 2, 1980 [*L&WSD* IX.18].

[7] S. Digby, 'Before the Babas Came to India: A Reconstruction of the Earlier Lives of Baba Saʿid Palangposh and Baba Musafir in "Wilayat"', *Iran*, vol. 36, 1998 [incorporated in *L&WSD* VII] and S. Digby. 'Before Timur Came: The Provincialization of the Delhi Sultanate through the Fourteenth Century', *Journal of the Economic and Social History of the Orient*, vol. 47, no. 3, 2004 [*L&WSD* VI.4].

Not that medieval life in the provinces was so bad that everyone wanted to flee it for the metropole. A case in point is the aforementioned town of Kara, which is brought alive for us in Chapter 9. There Digby recounts for us the anecdotes recorded in the hagiographical *Asrār al-majdhūbīn* ('Secrets of the God-Intoxicated') about the deeds of the mysterious 'wolf master', Khwāja Gurg (d.700/1301). For as Digby repeatedly points out, both Khwāja Gurg and his hagiographer Muḥammad Ismā'īl showed much 'local feeling' for life in Kara, of whose educational amenities and even sanctity they were proud (albeit perhaps with the provincial's hope of approval by readers in distant Delhi). On one occasion, when Khwāja Gurg was invited to visit the capital by 'Alā' al-Dīn Khaljī, he turned down the invitation and composed a poem to send in reply:

dihlī u samarqand u bukhārā u 'irāq
har chār turā bād u marā bād kara

Dehlī and Samarqand and Bukhara and 'Irāq,
You can take them all and leave me Kara!

It took a brave or foolhardy man to turn down the notoriously temperamental Sultan 'Alā' al-Dīn, who not only faced off the Mongols but in 1291 crushed a rebellion by Kara's governor, Malik Chajju. But then, as Digby reminds us, Khwāja Gurg was a *majdhūb*, a holy fool, and he was inordinately fond of his hometown. As he declared more simply on a different occasion, 'There is no place like Kara (*hamchū maqām-i kara jā'ī nēst*)!'

ف

Khwāja Gurg is only one of many fascinating figures we encounter over the following chapters. He was certainly a complex character, and a contradictory one too; or at least, a personage who confounds modern expectations of what a medieval Muslim saint would be like. Digby delighted in such figures, and it is probably fair to say that no other historian of premodern India has brought to light so many colourfully complicated lives.

One reason for this is Digby's unrivaled technical skill: he could parse precise details and local nuances from manuscripts and lithographs that otherwise lay forgotten. But the other, driving reason was his interest in people, his novelist-like pursuit of the foibles, intricacies, and follies of human character. After half a century of postmodernism, few historians would nowadays believe—or at least admit—they could glimpse a genuine human life through the distorting mirrors of medieval genres. We are probably the poorer for such radical skepticism, and in any case, Digby was himself a scrupulous critical comparer of textual evidence. But he was convinced that there was a social, and human, reality that could still be reached through such sources. Hence, back in 1975, when Chapter 10 was first published, he could confidently claim to have descried the 'personality and attitudes' of 'Abd al-Quddūs Gangohī.

And what a personality he was! No moralist like Yūsuf Gadā, the author of the didactic treatise discussed in Chapter 8, 'Abd al-Quddūs was known for his states of spiritual intoxication, of *sukr u mastī*, during which he would make ecstatic utterances known as *shaṭḥ*. In one such utterance, he declared: 'I do not say [this]: with my tongue God says "I".' This was daring stuff. For as every Indian Sufi knew, back in 'Abbasid-era Baghdad, the great Manṣūr al-Ḥallāj (d. 309/922) had been put to death for making similar declarations during his states of ecstasy. 'Abd al-Quddūs remained unperturbed, even in his more rational states of mind. Digby informs us that on one occasion while visiting Delhi, 'Abd al-Quddūs publicly defended Ḥallāj in an argument with a shaykh from Jawnpur.

Khwāja Gurg was associated with another, more literal kind of drunkenness, for his hometown of Kara—despite its many merits—apparently had 'a problem of lower-class urban alcoholism'. Gurg greatly enjoyed his country liquor too (given his moniker, one is tempted to say he wolfed it down). In his hagiography we hear of him 'drinking wine with sixteen other people from the mid-morning prayer to the afternoon prayer'. But this is no mundane boozing session with his cronies, because miraculously the wine never runs out. Such, as Digby was wont to show, was the complex morality, the supernatural strangeness, and the comical humanity, of Muslim life in medieval India.

ف

Digby was captivated by other such rule-breakers, not least the brigades of *bē-shar'* ('beyond the sharia') Qalandars, Abdāls, Juwāliqs, and Ḥaydarīs, who roamed the subcontinent with monkeys and bears for companions, with a fondness for disrupting the assemblies of more legally observant fellow Sufis. In Chapter 7, he pores over his Persian sources to provide us with descriptions of their outlandish appearance. In the *Khayr al-majālis*, he found a depiction of a band of Qalandars who wore only iron chains, fragments of blanket, and loincloths. Other accounts portrayed them wearing leather garments, displaying an ostracizing taste for polluting materials that prompted fleeing bystanders to invent *chiram-pōsh* ('wearer of leather') as a synonym for Qalandar.

As for the paraphernalia of these roving antinomians, aside from their insignia of a banner and drum, they carried only a razor for shaving their hair and beards in defiance of the Sunna, and a large needle known as a *juwāl-dōz* for sewing the course red cloth called a *juwāl* or *duwāl* that lent them another name, Juwāliqs. Like Khwāja Gurg, they too were fond of spiritual and literal drunkenness, though we learn their intoxicants of choice were 'drugs of the *ḥashīsh* family'.

Yet amid this historiographical revelry, there is always a serious purpose in Digby's investigations. Building on the pressing public concern with what was called 'social deviance' at the time it was written, Chapter 7 ponders the social process of recruitment into the counter-society of the Qalandars whom he compared with the hippy movement of the 1960s. Not that such dropouts were ever the sole focus of his scholarship: Chapter 8 examines a moralizing advice text whose author propounded the punctiliously proper *adab*, or etiquette, of every aspect of behaviour for a male Muslim youth in the Delhi Sultanate's more respectable circles. Whether eating, dressing, or marrying; whether entering fatherhood, finding employment, or purchasing a concubine—everything had its correct *adab*. It is fitting that his essay on this advice text is positioned here between chapters on figures who flaunted their defiance of such pious Islamic norms, while at the same time claiming to be 'God's unruly friends' (as the Turkish scholar Ahmet Karamustafa memorably labelled the Qalandars).[8] For as Digby well knew, it is only by recognizing the social power of such protocols that the rule-breaking transgressions of the Qalandars make sense.

As rich a human panoply as it was, Digby was not only concerned with Muslim life in medieval India. Many other communities and counter-communities enter the pages of this volume, whether Nāth Yogis, Vajrayāna Buddhist *siddhas*, or Maharashtrian Nātha-panthīs. He teaches us about interactions between these different religious groups without ever lapsing into anachronistic back-projections of the 'composite culture' thesis promoted by Indian secular

[8] A.T. Karamustafa, *God's Unruly Friends: Dervish Groups in the Islamic Later Middle Period, 1200–1550*, Salt Lake City: University of Utah Press, 1994.

nationalists. Digby does not gloss over cultural differences, social distance, or even occasional conflict. But he also recognizes continuities and shared customs and idioms. Thus, in an exercise in comparative folklore, we learn in Chapter 6 how the followers of many different holy men—Hindu, Buddhist, and Muslim (as well as Sikh and Eastern Christian)—shared the same story of the tiger- and wall-rider. And in Chapter 10, we are told about the attitudes of 'Abd al-Quddūs to his 'Indian environment', including his interactions with the doctrines of yoga.

Then there are the more ordinary folk who flit through the pages of the following chapters: the everyday disciples, the Afghan soldiers, the dancers, the traders, the tribal people. Their cameo appearances in saintly hagiographies saved them from the oblivion of time, allowing Digby to briefly register their existence once again and to position them, beside their saintly protectors, in our picture of the medieval past. Like many of the forgotten authors over whose manuscripts he pored, he was (to use a word of which he was fond) a remembrancer.

ف

Finally, we must turn to the texts that were the foundation of Digby's scholarship. His métier was Persian; or rather that more lexically capacious literary vehicle he called 'Indo-Persian'. Still, he also worked with the emergent vernaculars that occasionally appeared in Persian texts under the label 'Hindawī' or simply 'Hindī', as well as with the later Urdu language that furnished him with many studies by modern Indian and Pakistani scholars.

Whereas Persian remained his prime focus, he worked with many of its different genres, from the *tadhkira* (hagiography) and *malfūzāt* (recorded conversation) to the *tārīkh* (chronicle) and *naṣīḥat-nāma* (advice book), along with various forms of poetry, lyrical and narrative. Some of the sources he used, such as the *Siyar al-awliyā'* and *Tārīkh-i Firūz Shāhī*, were already well known to specialists, though Digby would bring new questions to them and read them with characteristic exactitude. Other texts were his own rare finds, including the focus of Chapter 8: the versified *Tuḥfa-i naṣā'iḥ* ('Present of Counsels') that the moralist Yūsuf Gadā had written for his son. Though Digby made no grand claims to its value as literature—some of it 'verges on doggerel'—its significance was instead historical by adding another text to the small Indian corpus of Sufi texts written before 1400. Indeed, in being completed in 1393, it was written just prior to that major watershed: five years 'before Timur came'. Placing the text before a modern public, Digby deployed the techniques of classic textual scholarship, comparing different manuscripts and, as so often in his essays, positioning its contents in relation to the many other texts he knew intimately.

A similarly rare find was Chapter 9's *Asrār al-majdhūbīn*, of which he modestly remarked, '[t]he work has previously been known only from the rare lithographic printing of the Nasīm-i Hind Press, Fathpur Haswa, 1893'. As in Chapter 8's study of Yūsuf Gadā's *Tuḥfa-i naṣā'iḥ*, he offers painstakingly close readings of these works, subjecting even individual words to scrutiny. One case is his reconstruction of the name of Khwāja Gurg, whose moniker had, with the passing of centuries, been phonologically corrupted and then semantically misconstrued as Kaṛak, connoting a 'crack' of thunder rather than a 'wolf'. For such orthographic peculiarities of premodern Persian manuscripts as the absence of a second stroke to distinguished *gāf* from *kāf* could lead to misreadings that his experienced eye avoided. A quarter-century before his study of Khwāja Gurg, Digby conducted a similar investigation into the correct rendering of the name of the sultan formerly known as Iltutmish.[9] These were not mere exercises in pedantry, though. They were expressions of fascination with north India's languages, in all their amorphous forms. One can sense his glee when he tells us that the Qalandars 'developed a special vocabulary or patois of their own'.

ف

Glimpses of these tangential and subcultural linguistic worlds that surrounded the Persian-using literati occasionally registered in Indo-Persian texts and, along with Simon Weightman, Digby was among the earliest researchers to seize on these scraps of evidence.[10] In the last section of Chapter 10, having surveyed eighteen works produced by 'Abd al-Quddūs Gangohī in the early 1500s, he turns to the *dohras*, *caupads*, and *sarods* that the shaykh composed in Hindi and inserted in his *Rushd-nāma* ('Book of Guidance'). Digby digs out the following *dohra*—interposed between refined Persian prose and verse—for our contemplation:

jidhara dekhun he sakkhi tidhara aur na koi
dekha bujha bicari main sabahi apan soi

Wherever I look, O friend, there is none other:
after reflecting I realised that everything was Himself.

[9] S. Digby, 'Iletmish or Iltutmish? A Reconsideration of the Name of the Delhi Sultan', *Iran*, vol. 8, 1970 [*L&WSD* VI.1].

[10] Together with the late Aditya Behl (1966–2009)—who, like Digby, was born in Jabalpur—Weightman would later make an elegant literary translation of an important sixteenth-century Hindawī poetic allegory. See Mīr Sayyid Manjhan Shattārī, *Madhumālatī: An Indian Sufi Romance*, tr. A. Behl and S. Weightman with S. Manohar Pandey, Oxford: Oxford University Press, 2000.

Written by 'Abd al-Quddūs under his yogi-like pen-name Alakhdas ('Servant of the Invisible'), this little poetic gem reflects the essence of Sufi thought—and shows how deep the seams of Sufism lie in the cultural soil of the subcontinent. As such, the verse is a fitting *fā'ida*, or utterance of spiritual benefit, with which to end this introduction to Digby's work and move on to the essays of the master himself, in which he excavates many more treasures from the rich mine of India's Muslim past.

SUFIS IN THE LIFE OF MEDIEVAL INDIA

1

The Sufi Shaikh as a Source of Authority in Medieval India

The Historical Background

The period of the greater Dehlī Sultanate began with the events of AD 1192, when the upper Gangetic plain with the site of Dehlī itself was permanently wrested from Hindu Rajput control by a victorious Muslim army, whose commanders and functionaries were of immigrant Central Asian background. The Muslim conquest of Sind had taken place at the hands of the Arabs in the eighth century, and Lahore and Multan had been attached to the Ghaznavid Kingdom of the Afghan plateau for a century and a half. After the new breakthrough of AD 1192 a great military camp was established on the site of Dehlī; and within a few years Muslim arms swept across the vast Gangetic plain of eastern India, destroying the great Buddhist monasteries and putting an end to the Hindu dynasty of the Sena rulers of Bengal. Circumstances a few decades after the initial conquests not only gave the Dehlī sultans independence; they also forced them to struggle to maintain the newly founded state without outside aid. Quṭb al-Dīn Aibak, the slave general of the Ghorid rulers of what is now Afghanistan, became the first independent sultan of the new realm in AD 1206; less

* Originally published in *Puruṣārtha*, vol. 9, 1986, pp. 57–77.

than two decades later Ghor, Ghazni, and the Khurasani homelands had been overwhelmed and engulfed by the Mongol confederacy of Cinggiz Khan, a horde of unknown invaders, seemingly invincible and as yet un-Islamicized and un-Persianized. In these Asian lands, as in Europe, they appeared to be a manifestation of the Wrath of God.

For the following 180 years the Sultanate of Dehlī survived as the dominant military power of northern India. It repelled numerous and formidable Mongol invasions from the north-west, and it expanded by plundering and sometimes annexing the Hindu kingdoms of the south and east. This was a pan-Indian realm, which at one time or another exercised control over an expanse of the subcontinent comparable to the realms of Ashoka and of the Mughal emperors in their heyday and only exceeded by the British colonial unification. The expansion of the Dehlī Sultanate was only limited by the tendency, which grew stronger with time, for the remote areas of Muslim conquest to break away and form independent sultanates, and by occasional regroupings of Hindu resistance after the shock of the initial conquest.[1] Thus, Bengal, the Deccan, and Ma'bar (the southern Coromandel coast) were lost to Dehlī long before the debacle of AD 1398. In the north, local Rajput dynasties, not wholly subdued, tended to recover some of their power and regain lost frontier territories in moments of weakness of the Dehlī Sultanate; and the southern Deccan witnessed the emergence in the late fourteenth century of the new and powerful Hindu state of Vijayanagar. The debacle of AD 1398 was the invasion of Amīr Timur, the Tamerlane of European history, who had reorganized the Central Asian tribal confederacies and brought them to devastate the established civilized economies.

[1] A.B.M. Habibullah, *The Foundation of Muslim Rule in India*, Allahabad: Central Book Depot, 1961, pp. 142–60.

By this time the city, or perhaps one should say the cities of Dehlī, which were of enormous extent, were sacked.[2] Many of their inhabitants were taken into captivity and slavery and the surviving army of the sultanate was destroyed. This event perhaps only set the seal on a rapid recent decline of the administration and of the capital city, which was already the scene of civil war within the gates. Through the fifteenth century we witness a different political scene. The provinces of Muslim conquest, Bengal, Jaunpur, Gujarat, Malwa, and the Deccan, developed as independent sultanates. They contended among themselves for mastery, and consolidated the cultural and administrative traditions, transported from the Persian speaking lands of eastern Islam, which they had inherited from the Dehlī Sultanate.[3]

The Islamic Sanctification of the New Homeland

At the close of the twelfth Christian century, when the victorious army of Islam entered its new domain, the military camp of the invaders was established near a Hindu fort of moderate dimensions, in a good strategic situation for the consolidation of power over the conquered territories; and the need for symbolic legitimation and sanctification of the Muslim presence in this still alien land was felt. Immediate plans were made and the foundations were laid for the building of a mosque and a minaret on a most ambitious scale.[4]

[2] For the extent of the cities of Dehlī, see J. Burton-Page in *Encyclopedia of Islam*, 2nd edn., s.v. *Dihlī*.

[3] For a general outline of the history of this period, see M. Habib and K.A. Nizami, ed., *A Comprehensive History of India*, vol. V: The Delhi Sultanat, A.D. 1206–1526, Delhi: People's Publishing House, 1970.

[4] J.A. Page, *An Historical Memoir on the Qutb, Delhi*, Calcutta: Government of India, Central publication branch, 1926.

There were many earlier Middle Eastern Islamic precedents for the appropriation, after conquest, of non-Muslim edifices or building materials to create mosques for Muslim worship. Here in Dehlī the inscription at the eastern entrance of the mosque records not only the initiation of the project by the general in command but also the estimated building cost of the twenty-seven Hindu and Jain temples from which materials had been plundered for the new structure.[5] At the same time the great arched screen to the prayer hall and a huge freestanding minaret (known today as the Quṭb Minār) were begun. Hindu temple stonemasons and sculptors—the latter doubtless instructed to avoid un-Islamic figural representation—were employed to construct in stone a semblance of what the conquerors remembered of the brick monuments of Ghazni and Khurasan.

The mosque of Qubbat al-Islām ('The Pinnacle of Islam') was also embellished with objects which were symbols of the domination of Islam in these new territories. The great fourth-century iron column of Chandragupta, its Hindu deity lopped off above the capital, was placed beneath the central arch of the mosque screen.[6] Later, at the close of the thirteenth century, large bronze idols from the conquest of Malwa were smashed and carried back to bury before the threshold of the mosque.[7]

The re-use of carved Hindu pillars and masonry set a pattern for subsequent spoliations during the initial phases of conquest and colonization in Gujarat and the Deccan. The richness of the materials is only matched in the other

[5] Ibid., p. 29.

[6] Y.D. Sharma, *Delhi and its Neighbourhood*, New Delhi: Archaeological Survey of India, 1964, pp. 48–9.

[7] Amir Khusrau, *Miftāḥ al-futūḥ*, quoted in H.M. Elliot and J. Dowson, *The History of India as Told by its Own Historians*, vol. III, London: Trübner and Co., 1871, p. 542.

great monument of the initial decades of the Dehlī Sultanate, the early thirteenth-century mosque at Ajmer known as the *Arhā'ī din kā jhōṅprā*. There the finely carved temple columns, placed one on top of another, are surmounted by cusped arches, creating an even more elegant effect.[8]

In the early decades of the thirteenth century, the Muslim outpost at Ajmer confined the Chauhans and their Rajput allies from an attempt at the reconquest of Dehlī. In the subsequent historical image of the Muslim colonization, there is a polarity between the capital city and the perilous outpost. Ajmer is a town cradled in rocky hills, down whose precipitous slopes run the lines of ancient fortifications. There are great rocks and springs and lakes and at the summit of the hill are the graves of Muslim martyrs who died in frays against the infidel.[9] These are the picturesque and sentimental adjuncts to the legend of Mu'īn al-Dīn Chishtī, called 'the Deputy of the Prophet in India',[10] the Sufi shaikh whose presence is thought to guard the welfare of Muslims throughout the Indian subcontinent.

A programme of mosque-building was not in itself sufficient to satisfy the longing for the sanctification of a land where, a single generation after the conquest, the Muslim population grew up in the shadow of the loss of the immediate homeland of their fathers. This need also inspired the provision made by the sultans, their great officers and other people of means, of stipends for those who called to prayer or otherwise officiated in the mosques which were being built, of *qāḍīs* to administer Islamic law, and of '*ulamā*', experts in the traditional Islamic sciences.

[8] Percy Brown, *Indian Architecture: The Islamic Period*, 2nd edn., Bombay: Taraporevala, 1946, pp. 12–13.

[9] For a general description, see H.B. Sarda, *Ajmer: Historical and Descriptive*, Ajmer: Fine Art Printing Press, 1941.

[10] Amīr Khwurd, *Siyar al-awliyā'*, ed. Chiranjī Lāl, Dehli: Muhibb-i Hind Press, AH 1302/AD 1885, p. 45.

However, such measures provided meagre spiritual fare for a community of Muslim believers which came to include a growing number of *assimilés* living within a political and cultural system which was novel in the environment. An easier path of devotion, of mediation and guidance in the sometimes arid landscape of mandatory Muslim beliefs and observances seemed to be at hand in a tradition of holy men, the tradition of the Ṣūfīs, which was introduced in the evolved state to which it had developed in Khurasan and elsewhere in the lands of Islam by the time of the creation of the Dehlī Sultanate. This tradition provided a channel of intercession with the Deity which might procure benefits in this world or the next, which might even lead to heights of mystical experience. What it certainly provided was a local Muslim identity which bound the newly formed community to the land where they dwelt.

Sufism as Imported into the Dehlī Sultanate

In the eleventh and twelfth Christian centuries there was a vigorous Sufi tradition in Khurasan (the north-east of modern Iran together with most of modern Afghanistan). It was characterized by 'Orders' (*ṭarīqa* or *silsila*) of quite recent historical development, but the strictly linear chronological development propounded by J. Spencer Trimingham, from *khānqāh* (the hospice of a Sufi shaikh or teacher) through *ṭarīqa* ('path', in this usage synonymous with *silsila*, 'chain') to *ṭā'ifa* ('group'—seldom used in this sense in the Indo-Persian literature) is not found in Khurasan. The concept of the transmission of *baraka* (charisma) through a *ṭarīqa* or *silsila* of Sufi shaikhs is strongly held, but examples of all three of Spencer Trimingham's groupings may be found at one and the same time, and the structures are to some extent reversible or interchangeable. Moreover, claims to the inheritance of authority were not always accompanied by an identity of practice.[11]

However, patterns of the holy life and of Sufi organization were transmitted from Khurasan to the Dehlī Sultanate. Among the substrata of what was transmitted were traits which are often ignored by modern writers describing in a pietistic tradition the activities of Sufi shaikhs of the Dehlī Sultanate: an uncompromising arrogance despite professions of humility in the advancement of personal claims to spiritual eminence, and examples of the display of *jalāl* ('splendour'), but in practice the 'wrath' which led to the discomfiture, misery, and often death of those who presumed to oppose the shaikh. Here, the character of the shaikh too often approached that of the *darwīsh* in Persian folklore, a disagreeable and terrifying figure, exercising his supernatural powers with malignance.[12]

Such traits are visible among other strands of sentiment, belief, and practice in Indo-Persian hagiographical literature; and they also recur in the non-Muslim collections of biographical narratives of later date, modelled on the Sufi *tadhkiras*, in the vernacular literatures of northern India.[13] This substratum of malignance rather than benevolence, combined with supernatural powers acquired magically by the practice of austerities, has ancient Indian parallels, but here appears to be a re-importation from a wide Central Asian milieu, partly Turkish and replete with practices

[11] J. Spencer Trimingham, *The Sufi Orders in Islam*, Oxford: Oxford University Press, 1971; review by S. Digby, *Bulletin of the School of Oriental and African Studies*, vol. 36, no. 1, 1973, pp. 136–9.

[12] L. Elwell-Sutton, 'The *Darvīsh* in Persian Folklore', *Proceedings of the Twenty-sixth International Congress of Orientalists, New Delhi, 1964*, Poona: Bhandarkar Oriental Research Institute, 1968, pp. 200–3.

[13] S. Digby, review of W.H. McLeod, *Guru Nanak and the Sikh Religion*, Oxford, 1968, in *The Indian Economic and Social History Review*, vol. 7, no. 2, 1970, p. 305.

described by modern writers as Shamanistic, thinly disguised by some centuries of superimposed Islamic piety.

Some of the wilder, less 'orthodox' or approved practices among ecstatic Sufis which make their appearance in the Indian conquered territories in the thirteenth century appear ultimately to derive from the extended and culturally alloyed late Indo-Buddhist culture of Central Asia. Even if this was submerged under the apparatus of traditional Islamic learning, it was a part of the mental stock-in-trade of the Sufis which particularly commended them not only to the immigrant Turkish soldiers of the armies of the sultanate, but also to a considerable portion of the non-Muslim population of the north Indian plains. Vaishnava *bhaktamālas*, Sikh *janamsākhīs*, and other *vitae* of non-Muslim men of religion repeat the emphasis and structure of Sufi anecdotes, particularly regarding contests of superiority, magical displays, and a general lack of charity towards opponents and doubters.[14]

The Attributes of a Sufi Shaikh

As the present writer has stated elsewhere, a detailed study of a medieval Sufi shaikh will often reveal inconsistencies of attitude, character, and behaviour. Acceptance of a Sufi in his lifetime as a great shaikh depended on the recognition that he possessed, to an impressive degree, qualities which showed that he was the recipient of Divine grace. The balance of these qualities in a single shaikh might vary, just as a winning hand at cards may be stronger in some suits than in others. Descent from the Prophet, his Companions, or other *ashrāf*; connection with a Sufi *silsila* of already established prestige; a reputation for strict orthodoxy;

[14] Ibid., p. 306.

austerities sometimes of a more and sometimes of a less orthodox character; a mastery of Islamic doctrinal or Sufi texts, or an abundance of literary compositions; the working of miracles together with a careful avoidance of vulgar display of them; a reputation for inaccessibility and of dislike of human society, often combined with a care for disciples and accepted hangers-on (as well as strangers and visitors); visible ecstasy, often of a Shamanistic type and often also linked to a refined sensibility to (mainly Persian) poetry and to music—all these qualities were held to be evidence of the especially close relations of the shaikh with the Deity, and all contributed to his prestige and the winning of devotees.[15]

Not all of these attributes were wholly reconcilable with one another, and Sufi shaikhs were confronted with certain problems of choice in the lifestyles they adopted.[16] An obvious division was between Sufi claimants who were described as *bā-shar‘*, whose behaviour was in conformity with Islamic law as they understood it, and those who were *bē-shar‘*, who considered themselves in some way excused from its observance.[17] This was a division which increasingly came to resemble, among the hierarchies and the devotees of Sufi cults and shrines, the division between the pure and impure Hindu castes, among Indian Muslims between the *ashrāf* (the 'noble' or perhaps we should say the respectable)

[15] S. Digby, "Abd al-Quddūs Gangōhī (1456–1537 A.D.): The Personality and Attitudes of a Medieval Indian Sufi Shaykh', *Medieval India, a Miscellany*, vol. III, Aligarh: Aligarh Muslim University, 1975, pp. 17–18 [*L&WSD* III.10; this volume, pp. 330–2].

[16] S. Digby, 'Qalandars and Related Groups: Elements of Social Deviance in the Religious Life of the Dehlī Sultanate', in *Islam in Asia*, vol. I, ed. Y. Friedman, Jerusalem: Hebrew University of Jerusalem, 1984, pp. 72–6 [*L&WSD* III.7; this volume, pp. 203–8].

[17] M. Titus, *Islam in India and Pakistan*, 2nd edn., Calcutta: YMCA Publishing House, 1959, p. 131.

and the *ajlāf* or *ardhāl* (the 'base').[18] The *ashrāf* are prone to a process of 'Islamization' (using this term on the analogy of Srinivasan's 'Sanskritization') in which the quest for or maintenance of high social status leads to a stricter conformity of belief and observance of the propositions of Muslim doctors and jurists of the 'classical' period. Such strictness can be advanced as a claim to authority on the part of a Sufi shaikh or a *silsila* of such shaikh. The last of the great Chishtī shaikhs of the Dehlī Sultanate advances the claims of the religious law in conjunction with his own claims to authority:

People keep on saying that *ḥaqīqat* ['Truth', the mystical Sufi perception of God] is the Divine secret; but I Muḥammad Ḥusainī say that *sharī'at* [the observance of Muslim law] is the Divine secret: because I have also heard talk of *ḥaqīqat* from Ḥaidarīs, Qalandars, Mulḥids and Zindīqs; nay, I have even heard of it from the mouths of Jōgīs, of Brahmans, and of Gurūs: but talk of the *sharī'at* I have not heard from anyone's mouth than the people of true faith and belief [i.e. Sunni Muslims]. From this it is evident that *sharī'at* is the Divine secret.[19]

Immediately after this statement the shaikh (Sayyid Muḥammad Gēsūdarāz) put forward his own claims to authority—learning and orthodoxy in conjunction with descent from the Prophet and his own rank as a Sufi shaikh: 'There are few men who are at once a *Faqīh* [jurist], a *Ṣūfī*, a *Sunnī*, and a *Sayyid*. All these four qualities are present in me.'[20]

[18] M. Gaborieau, 'Les orders mystiques dans le sous-continent Indien: un point de vue ethnologique', in *Les orders mystiques de l'Islam: ceminement et situation actuelle*, ed. A. Popovic and G. Veinstein, Paris: EHESS, 1986, pp. 105–34.

[19] 'Abd al-'Azīz b. Shēr Malik, *Ta'rīkh-i ḥabībī*, Urdu tr., Hyderabad, Deccan: n.p., n.d. [c. 1920], p. 36.

[20] Ibid.

In addition to the symbols of authority which Sayyid Muḥammad Gēsūdarāz claimed to have inherited from his predecessor in the Chishtī order,[21] we may note another claim to authority as a shaikh: that God had preserved him to an extreme old age in order to vindicate him from an assertion that he was too young to have had authority transmitted to him at the time when he claimed that this event had occurred.[22]

Somewhat distant from orthodox Islamic belief and observance is another well-attested source of prestige. This is a poetic sensibility, which extended also to the music of sung or chanted verse. The popular appeal of this characteristic during the period usually outweighed deprecations from the point of view of Islamic orthodoxy. Such a sensibility was shared by all the great Chishtī shaikhs of the Dehlī Sultanate, although some may have possessed it in greater measure than others,[23] and we lack detailed information in the case of the founder of the lineage in India. The second shaikh of the *silsila* there, Quṭb al-Dīn Bakhtyār Kākī, is alleged to have expired after four days of violent ecstasy at the recital of a Persian *bait* (couplet):

kushtagān-i khanjar-i taslīm-rā
har zaman az ghaib jān-i dīgar ast

For those slain by the dagger of belief
Every time from the Unseen there is new life.[24]

[21] Muḥammad Akbar Ḥusaynī, *Jawāmi‘ al-kalim*, Hyderabad, Deccan: Taḥqīqātī Akāḍmī, Faṣlī 1356/AD 1946, p. 240; Muḥammad ‘Alī Sāmānī, *Siyar-i Muḥammadī*, Allahabad: Yūnānī Davalkhānah, AH 1347/AD 1928, pp. 17–19.

[22] ‘Alī Sāmānī, *Siyar-i Muḥammadī*, p. 5.

[23] Bruce B. Lawrence, *Notes from a Distant Flute*, Tehran: Imperial Iranian Academy of Philosophy, 1978, pp. 29–31.

[24] Amir Hasan ‘Alā’ Sijzī, *Fawā’id al-fu’ād*, ed. Muḥammad Latīf Malik, Lahore: Malik Sirāj al-Dīn and Sons, AH 1386/AD 1966, p. 246; Khwurd, *Siyar al-awliyā’*, p. 55.

This event is said to have occurred in AD 1235. Down to the twentieth century there have been attested examples of death in ecstasy at *samāʿ* or audition parties. In the Persian-speaking world of the medieval period the connections between poetic sensibility and Sufism are almost inseparable. The verse of the greatest of Persian poets, Saʿdī and Ḥāfiẓ, as well as that of many of their predecessors, contemporaries, and successors, would often have been unintelligible without some knowledge of Sufi concepts and practice. Even when the poet himself had worldly connections and employment, and did not live the life of a Sufi shaikh or full-time disciple, he had strong claims to admission to their companionship. This was the case of Amīr Khusraw (AD 1253–1325), the greatest of the Indo-Persian poets, who was an intimate companion of Shaikh Niẓām al-Dīn of Dehlī; and of his rival Amīr Ḥasan, author of a record of the conversations of the same shaikh.[25]

As suggested above, the hand of cards held by different Sufi shaikhs in their bids for allegiance would be stronger in some suits than others. The hagiographies composed by their followers are likely to resort to myth and invention in order to explain away potential deficiencies or weak suits. The Chishtī shaikhs in India were mostly unable or unwilling to travel beyond the territories of the Dehlī Sultanate, although subsequent sources credited them with wider ranges of travel.[26] By the end of the thirteenth century conditions of travel to the central lands of Islam had become easier as a result of the diminution of the ferocity of the Mongol attacks and the annexation of Gujarat. Explanations might therefore be sought why a major shaikh like Niẓām al-Dīn

[25] The connection of the two poets with Niẓām al-Dīn is discussed below.
[26] P.M. Currie, *The Shrine and Cult of Muʿīn al-Dīn Chishtī of Ajmer*, New Delhi: Oxford University Press, 1989, maps showing places associated with Muʿīn al-Dīn in the *Siyar al-awliyā'*, *Siyar al-ʿārifīn*, *Siyar al-aqṭāb* and *Hasht bahisht*, pp. 57, 69, 148, 353.

had not performed the Muslim duty of *ḥajj*, pilgrimage to the Holy Places of Mecca and Medina. An explanation current within decades of his death is that a camel used to arrive at his *khānqāh* on Friday eve, to transport him through the air to Mecca, where he was observed at the congregational prayers by a trustworthy witness.[27] The same story is told in another fourteenth-century source about a less reputable contemporary of Niẓām al-Dīn, the *majdhūb* or madman Khwāja Gurg, and the identical story or close analogues are related about other Sufi figures down to the present day.[28]

Belief in the Miraculous and Supernatural

Modern writers, when they make use of the hagiographical literature of the Dehlī Sultanate as historical evidence, often ignore and pass over in silence frequent mentions of the appearance of supernatural beings and narratives of the exercise of supernatural powers. In a dated and unquestionably authentic narrative of individual conversations of the great Shaikh Niẓām al-Dīn we find a succession of anecdotes of a preacher in a mosque who was so transported by his own eloquence that he flew away from the pulpit (*mimbar*) to a neighbouring wall;[29] of meetings in deserted places with Khwāja Khiḍr who has everlasting life;[30] and of various 'fairy people'—of the *abdāls* who physically fly above the

[27] Khwurd, *Siyar al-awliyā'*, pp. 143–4.

[28] Muḥammad Ismā'īl Lahaurī, *Asrār al-majdhūbīn*, Digby MS 10, folio 4b; S. Digby, 'The Waterseller's Pilgrimage', *Lycidas*, vol. III, Oxford: Wolfson College, 1974–5, pp. 20–1; S. Digby, 'Anecdotes of a Provincial Sufi of the Dehlī Sultanate: Khwāja Gurg of Kara', *Iran*, vol. XXXII, 1994, p. 106 [*L&WSD* III.9; this volume, p. 304].

[29] 'Alā' Sijzī, *Fawā'id al-fu'ād*, pp. 83–4.

[30] 'Alā' Sijzī, *Fawā'id al-fu'ād*, pp. 211–13; cf. Khwurd, *Siyar al-awliya'*, p. 51.

territories which they protect from harm,[31] of a holy man circling around the vault of the chief mosque at Dehlī through the night till the dawn,[32] and of the *mardān-i-ghaib*, 'men of the Unseen' who appear and disappear, and sometimes call away a mortal to join them.[33] Shaikh Niẓām al-Dīn and his successor at Dehlī Shaikh Naṣīr al-Dīn Maḥmūd shared these folk-beliefs with their followers.

A strong, often crude, belief in the miraculous pervaded all sections of society, including the learned and the powerful. *Karāmāt* ('graces', in fact miracles) were proofs to the devotees of a Sufi shaikh that he had attained the status which they attributed to him. The shaikh's interventions in the ordinary course of nature (*kharq-i 'ādat*) extended from the trifling affairs of individuals, to whom they supplied amulets,[34] to an influence over major political events. In the opinion of their followers they held powers for the making and unmaking of kings and kingdoms.[35]

The Territorial *Wilāyat* of the Shaikh

The *Kashf al-maḥjūb* of 'Alī Hujwērī, written at Lahore before the beginning of our period, provides a theoretical basis for this large assumption of supernatural powers:

> God has saints (*awliyā'*, pl. of *walī*) whom he has especially distinguished by his friendship and whom He has chosen to be the governors of His kingdom ... He has made the saints the governors

[31] 'Alā' Sijzī, *Fawā'id al-fu'ād*, pp. 3–4.
[32] Ibid., p. 19.
[33] Ibid., pp. 24–5; but cf. p. 343.
[34] Ibid., p. 336.
[35] S. Digby, 'The Sufi Shaykh and the Sultan: A Conflict of Claims to Authority', *Iran*, vol. 28, 1990, pp. 75–8 [*L&WSD* III.2; this volume, pp. 61–76].

of the universe ... Through the blessing of their advent the rains fall from heaven and through the purity of their lives the plants spring up from the earth and through their spiritual influence Muslims gain victories over unbelievers ...[36]

Above the authority of mundane rulers there is ordained a hierarchy of those with supernatural powers, perpetually watchful over the welfare of all the regions of the world. The lowest rank of these, the *abdāls* ('substitutes') are also *walīs* ('friends [of God]'); through the Arabic triliteral root *walia* a conceit is pursued and elaborated, identifying *walāya* or *wilāya* (Divine 'friendship') with *wilāya* (Persian *wilāyat*, 'governance') which comes to be used for spiritual jurisdiction over a specific territory.[37]

Such claims to the *wilāyat* of a specific territory were actively and vigorously pursued by shaikhs in Khurasan in the eleventh and twelfth centuries, and the concept is very common in fourteenth-century and later Indian Sufi literature. In the Dehlī Sultanate this notion of the territorial *wilāyat* of a shaikh led, at the beginning of the fourteenth century, to the common identification of Shaikh Niẓām al-Dīn of the Chishtī *silsila* with the well-being and fortunes of the capital city of Dehlī and the realm over which it held sway. In his lifetime the question arose in people's minds whether such *wilāyat* was personal, or passed away at his death. A quarter of a century after this the poet 'Iṣāmī, writing in the new secessionist Muslim state of the Deccan, maintained that power and prosperity passed away from Dehlī at Niẓām al-Dīn's death:

36 Al-Hujwīrī, *Kashf al-maḥjūb*, tr. R.A. Nicholson, Leiden: Brill and London: Luzac and Co., 1911, p. 213.

37 'Alā' Sijzī, *Fawā'id al-fu'ād*, p. 22; Ashraf Jahāngīr Simnānī, *Makhtūbāt-i Ashrafī*, British Library MS Or. 267, folio 109a; Ḥusaynī, *Jawāmi' al-kalim*, p. 164; 'Iṣāmī, *Futūḥ al-salāṭīn*, ed. A.S. Usha, Madras: University of Madras, 1948, pp. 455–6.

> He was one of the friends of God
> Through whom the realm of Hindostan was maintained.
> First that man of wise dominion
> Set out from Dehlī to another kingdom [the next world];
> After this that city and country were ruined;
> Discord prevailed in that realm.[38]

With this concept of territorial jurisdiction, it was difficult for a locally established shaikh to tolerate the presence of another shaikh of powerful charisma in his vicinity. Bahā' al-Dīn Zakariyā' at Multan, we are told, laid out the shoes of the Chishtī shaikh Quṭb al-Dīn Bakhtyār, indicating that he should set out towards Dehlī.[39] Niẓām al-Dīn mentions that his predecessor Farīd al-Dīn considered that his own *wilāyat* extended a certain distance from Ajodhan towards Multan, and was replaced at that frontier by that of Shaikh Bahā' al-Dīn Zakariyā'. He himself could give protection to a traveller only up to that frontier.[40]

The dominance of Niẓām al-Dīn at this place and moment of time, in Dehlī at the apogee of the power of the sultanate, has permanently affected the historical consciousness of Muslims of the subcontinent and has furthered the notion of an especial position of the Chishtī *silsila* in the establishment of the enduring Muslim presence in India. Yet this local pre-eminence was not achieved without struggle and rivalry, nor was it unquestioned in its day by those who put forward rival claims to authority—representatives of other Sufi lineages, upholders of Muslim law and traditional sciences,

[38] 'Iṣāmī, *Futūḥ al-salāṭīn*, p. 456.

[39] Khwurd, *Siyar al-awliyā'*, p. 61; K.A. Nizami, *The Life and Times of Shaikh Farid-u'd-din Ganj-i Shakar*, Aligarh: Aligarh Muslim University, 1955, p. 17.

[40] 'Alā' Sijzī, *Fawā'id al-fu'ād*, p. 236; Jamālī, *Siyar al-'ārifīn*, Dehlī: Maṭba'-i Riẓvī, AH 1311/AD 1893, p. 115; cf. 'Afīf, *Ta'rīkh-i Fērōzshāhī*, Calcutta: Bibliotheca Indica, 1891, p. 61.

and the sultans themselves, who held material sway over the territories whose spiritual jurisdiction was assigned in popular estimation to the Shaikh.

Conflict and Accommodation within the *Silsilas*

The rivalry between the Suhrawardī *silsila*, with its centre of power in Multan, and the Chishtīs, influential in Dehlī and the lands of the new conquests, was conducted amicably, possibly because all the Chishtī shaikhs in India used manuals of Sufi practice, such as the *'Awārif al-ma'ārif*, which had been compiled or transmitted in the Suhrawardī environment. By contrast, no early hagiographical work regarding the lives of the great Suhrawardī shaikhs of Multan entered the mainstream of the hagiographical tradition; and no such work is accessible to us. In consequence we are exclusively dependent on sources which present the Chishtī view of the relations between the two *silsilas*.

The Chishtī sources emphasize the virtue of the rule of poverty (*faqr*) as practised by the shaikhs of the order, who did not accept land grants which would have yielded an assured income, and distributed before nightfall the *futūḥāt* (offerings) which were presented to them. This is contrasted with the accumulation of wealth and property by Bahā' al-Dīn Zakariyā' and his successors at Multan.[41] Early in the thirteenth century a *khalīfa* (deputy) of Mu'īn al-Dīn Chishtī at Ajmer, Ḥamīd al-Dīn Suwālī of Nagaur in Rajasthan, sent epistles to Bahā' al-Dīn Zakariyā' criticizing

[41] K.A. Nizami, *Some Aspects of Religion and Politics in India during the Thirteenth Century*, Aligarh: Aligarh Muslim University, 1961, pp. 185–229; K.A. Nizami, 'Early Indo-Muslim Mystics and their Attitude towards the State', *Islamic Culture*, vols. 22–4, 1948–50.

his departure from the Sufi rule of *faqr*.[42] Yet during the same period a Suhrawardī *khalīfa*, also called Qāḍī Ḥamīd al-Dīn Nāgaurī, was on terms of intimacy with the other Chishtī *khalīfa* of Mu'īn al-Dīn at Dehlī, Quṭb al-Dīn Bakhtyār Kākī, enthusiastically participating with him in *samā'* (listening to music).[43] Neither of these two shaikhs maintained a *khānqāh* (hospice). The considerably later sources possibly exaggerate the extent of the influence of Quṭb al-Dīn and Qāḍī Ḥamīd al-Dīn upon the pious Sultan Shams al-Dīn Iltutmish and upon the urban population of Dehlī.[44]

In early thirteenth-century Dehlī the principal religious conflicts of authority of which records remain concerned the question of the lawfulness of *samā'*, and the arraignment on an accusation of adultery of the migrant Suhrawardī *khalīfa* Jalāl al-Dīn Tabrīzī. The Chishtī and the Suhrawardī shaikhs were on the same side, and their main opponent was the *Shaikh al-Islām*, Najm al-Dīn Ṣughrā. Our Chishtī sources record that he received appropriate retribution for his attempt to humiliate Jalāl al-Dīn Tabrīzī. The latter, sitting by the banks of a river, saw by clairvoyance the death of Najm al-Dīn Ṣughrā. He invited those present to participate in funeral prayers, remarking: 'If the *Shaikh al-Islām* sent me out of Dehlī, my *Shaikh* sent him out of the world.'[45]

By the early fourteenth century, when the influence of Niẓām al-Dīn in Dehlī was at its height and he had established a considerable *khānqāh* there, Rukn al-Dīn, grandson of Bahā' al-Dīn Zakariyā', came on a visit to the city from Multan. A whole section of our principal source,

[42] Khwurd, *Siyar al-awliyā'*, p. 158.

[43] 'Alā' Sijzī, *Fawā'id al-fu'ād*, p. 315, 407–8; Khwurd, *Siyar al-awliyā'*, p. 149.

[44] Khwurd, *Siyar al-awliyā'*, pp. 53–5; Nizami, *Some Aspects of Religion and Politics*, p. 189; the hostile Firdausī source implies the reality of that influence, see below, note 49.

[45] 'Alā' Sijzī, *Fawā'id al-fu'ād*, p. 245.

the *Siyar al-awliyā'*, is devoted to anecdotes of the mutual courtesy and the consideration which the Chishtī and the Suhrawardī shaikhs extended to one another. When Rukn al-Dīn was received by Niẓām al-Dīn, he was presented with a silken purse through which the glitter of the red-gold coins could be seen, a detail which sheds a curious light on the actual practice of *faqr* and the distribution of *futūḥāt* at the *khānqāh* at this period. Rukn al-Dīn disclaimed any intention of setting up his own *khalīfa* in rivalry to Niẓām al-Dīn in the capital city, even though (or perhaps because) this was the suggestion of the reigning sultan. At the death of Niẓām al-Dīn, Rukn al-Dīn led the funeral prayers.[46]

There is a real contrast between earlier Chishtī and Suhrawardī practice in the matter of the acceptance of land grants and the accumulation of treasure, even if the difference has been exaggerated by the Chishtī sources. This difference of practice may have been dictated by the differing political conditions which prevailed at Multan, when compared to Dehlī and the inner territories of the Dehlī Sultanate. Multan was in an exposed position on the insecure western frontier. It was at different times under the control of the Dehlī sultans and of the Chaghatayid Mongols of Transoxania, or of provincial satraps serving both sides. To maintain the Suhrawardī *khānqāh* through periods of adversity required a prudent conservation of resources. This suggestion is supported by the fortress-like site of the *khānqāh* at Multan, on an ancient inhabited site on the crest of the two hills (possibly 'tells') of Multan; and by the mediatory political roles played by the Suhrawardī shaikhs acting on behalf of the inhabitants of Multan.[47] Similar circumstances may

[46] Khwurd, *Siyar al-awliyā'*, pp. 135–41; 'Abd al-Ḥaqq, *Akhbār al-akhyār*, Dehlī: Mujtabā'ī Press, AH 1309/AD 1892, p. 65.

[47] 'Alā' Sijzī, *Fawā'id al-fu'ād*, pp. 206–7; Khwurd, *Siyar al-awliyā'*, p. 579; Sīrhindī, *Ta'rīkh-i Mubārakshāhī*, Calcutta: Bibliotheca Indica, 1931,

have dictated the abandonment in the fourteenth century of the rule against the acceptance of land grants at the border Chishtī *khānqāh* of Ajodhan (Pakpattan).[48]

The amicable relations which existed between the Chishtīs and the Suhrawardīs contrast with those of which we have fragmentary record between the Chishtī shaikhs in the capital city and a group of successors of the Khwarazmian Shaikh Najm al-Dīn Kubrā (d. AD 1221) who later became known as the Firdausī *silsila.* As his name suggests, the *Shaikh al-Islām* Najm al-Dīn Ṣughrā belonged to this group. In a Firdausī source he is predictably described as *mardē buzurg ṣāḥib-i wilāyat* ('a holy man, possessor of *wilāyat*'). The same source sharply criticizes Quṭb al-Dīn Bakhtyār for the hold he had acquired over the population of Dehlī by the display of miraculous powers.[49]

The hostility between the Chishtīs and the Firdausīs is well illustrated by an unpleasant incident which occurred in the early fourteenth century. This is worthy of extended notice, both as an example of the attribution of not wholly beneficent supernatural powers to Sufi shaikhs, and as a demonstration of the tendency, even when there are two accounts written within the same hagiographical tradition by partisans of the same shaikhs, for a conflict either of memory or of veracity to occur.

The anecdote occurs in its simpler form in the *Siyar al-awliyā'*, although this is the later of the two nearly contemporary sources:

The writer of these words [has heard] that Shaikh Rukn al-Dīn, who was not too sincerely attached to [Niẓām al-Dīn] had come

---

p. 100; K.A. Nizami, 'The Suhrawardi Silsila and its Influence on Medieval Indian Politics', *Medieval India Quarterly*, vol. III, 1957, pp. 109–49.

[48] See below, p. 27, and notes 60–1.

[49] Shaikh Shu'aib Manērī, *Manāqib a-aṣfiyā'*, Calcutta: Nūr al-Afāq Press, AH 1313/AD 1895, pp. 121–2.

outside the city and had also made a residence on the banks of the river Jamuna at the limit of Kilokhrī; and had set up as a Shaikh [i.e. he had set up a *khānqāh*, deliberately not called such by our source, in proximity and rivalry to that of Niẓām al-Dīn]. His sons were adolescent, and his *Murīds* were impertinent towards the servants of Niẓām al-Dīn ['servants' is a polite periphrasis]. Time and again, riding in a boat, they used to pass the house of the Shaikh [Niẓām al-Dīn] in *samā'* [music] and *raqṣ* [ecstatic dancing]. One day, a little after the midday prayer, in a body and performing *samā'* and *raqṣ* they passed before the house of the Shaikh in this manner. The Shaikh himself was seated on the roof of the *Jamā'at-Khāna* [congregational hall], and he was sitting 'occupied' [*mashgūl*; i.e. in the performance of *dhikr*]. The father of the author of this account was present standing in the gathering. When they came into view of the Shaikh, in their boat and making excessive noise with their *samā'*, he remarked: 'Praise be to God! It is years since [I] have drunk my heart's blood and offered my soul in this Path. Others are growing boys and say, "Who are you that we are not?"' He raised his blessed hand towards them and said: 'Now go away!'

The moment that the boat of Shaikh Rukn al-Dīn's sons arrived below their home with all that noise, they came out of it and wished to perform their ablutions; but as soon as they went into the water they were instantly drowned. The author [Amīr Khwurd] has heard this story from his uncle … Sayyid Ḥusain.[50]

The same incident is recorded in the *Khair al-majālis*, directly from the lips of Niẓām al-Dīn's successor at Dehlī, Naṣīr al-Dīn Maḥmūd. A new comb had been brought to him by a young Arab. He recalled how Niẓām al-Dīn had been relating an anecdote regarding the latter's *pīr*, Farīd al-Dīn. A *darwīsh* (with the insolent behaviour characteristic of Qalandars) had insistently demanded a comb from Farīd al-Dīn. Just as Niẓām al-Dīn was telling this story, some 'friends' (*yārān*, i.e. devotees) arrived in the shaikh's

[50] Khwurd, *Siyar al-awliyā'*, p. 147.

assembly and announced: 'We were present at the invitation of the Ṭūsīs, in that gathering the sons of 'Imād Firdausī were present. They said something [abusive] about the servants [polite periphrasis] of the Shaikh.'

In the continuation of the anecdote which Niẓām al-Dīn was telling when their conduct was reported to him, the *darwīsh* finally stated that *barakat* would accrue from the gift of the comb, but Farīd al-Dīn terminated the interview by saying: 'We have sent that *barakat* down the river (*ān barakat-rā dar āb ravān kardīm*)!'

The *darwīsh* was a traveller and he came to a river near the settlement (of Ajodhan) which was fordable. He went into the river to perform his ablutions and vanished from sight.

According to Naṣīr al-Dīn Maḥmūd's relation, which is recorded in the *Khair al-majālis*, after Niẓām al-Dīn had finished telling this anecdote:

> There immediately arose from the direction of Kilokhrī a clamour that the sons of 'Imād Firdausī had drowned. The question was asked how they had drowned. The reply was that they had come from the *Khānqāh* of the Ṭūsīs. In a boat they had passed below the *Khānqāh* of the Shaikh [Niẓām al-Dīn] and had arrived at Kilokhrī. The *langar* [charitable kitchen] of Maulānā 'Imād Firdausī was there. They had got out of their boat and had taken off their clothes and gone into the water to wash their bodies. One brother had begun to drown and called out to the other: 'Take hold of my hand!'
>
> He grasped his hand, but could not come up. At this time the water flowed strongly and both were drowned. The cry rose that both the *Shaikhzādas* [sons of 'Imād] had been drowned in the river, until in time this news reached the Shaikh [Niẓām al-Dīn].

It was then ascertained that these were the two sons who had abused Niẓām al-Dīn at the celebration of the Ṭūsīs, and that the drowning had occurred just at the time when Niẓām al-Dīn was telling the story of the *darwīsh* who had vanished (or drowned) in the river after Farīd al-Dīn's parting remark. The compiler of the *Khair al-majālis*, Ḥamīd Qalandar, concludes his record with a 'cheer for the miracles of miracles in miracles' of Farīd al-Dīn and Niẓām al-Dīn.[51]

It is obvious that both these accounts describe the same incident, and they have certain details in common. One account is an immediate record from apparently first-hand testimony, while the other purports to be what the compiler's uncle told him about an event of which the compiler's father was a witness. Apart from the variation in the name of the Firdausī shaikh (*'Imād* and *Rukn* both meaning 'pillar' and therefore easily confused), they have totally different accounts of how Niẓām al-Dīn was occupied and what he said at the time of the drowning. The second anecdote from the *Khair al-majālis* is of a more elaborate structure, implying foreknowledge by Niẓām al-Dīn that the news of the misconduct of the sons of the Firdausī shaikh was about to be brought to him; it makes clear that the fate which was about to befall them would resemble that which had befallen someone who had been equally disrespectful to Niẓām al-Dīn's own *pīr*.

A hagiographer of the Firdausī *silsila*, writing only a few decades later, was familiar with both these sources, which he cites on other occasions. He only refers obliquely to the incident, but his statement is indicative of the hostility between the *silsilas*:

> The Shaikhs of the age were envious of [Rukn al-Dīn Firdausī's] upbringing and *ṭarīqa*. Shaikh Niẓām al-Dīn was too pure to show malevolence, but malevolence was characteristic of his *Murīds* and devotees. They were watching for calamities and accidents. If anything of temporal misfortunes befell Khwāja Rukn al-Dīn, they loosed their tongues and said: 'This calamity or this accident of Khwāja Rukn al-Dīn has occurred from the pronouncement (*nafas*) of Shaikh Niẓām al-Dīn or from his heaviness of heart!'

[51] Ḥamīd Qalandar, *Khair al-majālis*, Aligarh: Aligarh Muslim University, 1959, pp. 202–3.

> It is well known that all the people of Dehlī were devoted to Shaikh Niẓām al-Dīn. They all dared to wish harm to Khwāja Rukn al-Dīn.[52]

The Firdausīs, with their enduring tradition of hostility to the Chishtīs appear to have achieved little success in the capital city of Dehlī, but in the middle of the fourteenth century their influence was established in Bihar through the activities and writings of Sharaf al-Dīn Aḥmad bin Yaḥyā of Maner. Paradoxically, this success may be a consequence of their failure in Dehlī.

The hagiographical tradition of the Firdausīs is embodied in the *tadhkira Manāqib al-aṣfiyā'*. This was written shortly after the sack of Dehlī in AD 1398, and in it there are signs of an enduring tradition of hostility to those in power in the capital city. The establisher of the *silsila* in eastern India had initially been the pupil of Maulānā Ashraf al-Dīn Tawwāma. Regarding him we are told that 'in the days when the country of Bengal was subject to the King of Dehlī', the ruler, who is not named, had exiled Ashraf al-Dīn to Sunargaon, because 'from the excess of the obedience of the population [to him], the King feared that he might seize the realm'. After a stay with Ashraf al-Dīn Tawwāma at Sunargaon, Sharaf al-Dīn went to Dehlī, where he observed the shaikh of the time with deprecation. 'If this is Shaikhhood, then I am a Shaikh!' He attended upon Niẓām al-Dīn, who did not accept him as a disciple, but turned him away with a courteous phrase and a leaf of *tambūl* (betel). However, when he appeared before Khwāja Najīb al-Dīn Firdausī (*khalīfa* of Rukn al-Dīn) he felt an awe (*dahshat*) which he had not felt before Niẓām al-Dīn, and he became his *murīd*.[53]

The links of the *silsila*, at the time when it spread to Bihar, with the capital city were further embittered by an incident

[52] Manērī, *Manāqib a-aṣfiyā'*, p. 124.
[53] Manērī, *Manāqib a-aṣfiyā'*, pp. 131–2; cf. Jamālī, *Siyar al-'ārifin*, p. 84.

which occurred late in the reign of Fērōz Shāh Tughluq (r. AD 1351–88) and not long before the death of Sharaf al-Dīn (d. AD 1381). Two of the Shaikh's followers, Aḥmad Bihārī and 'Izz Kākawī, one described as mad (*dīwāna*) and both at the wilder end of the Sufi spectrum, went to Dehlī, where their 'open words about the mysteries of Union' were heard by the people of Dehlī, who accused them before the sultan. The sultan held an inquest (*maḥḍar*) with all the notables of the city, and the poor wretches (*miskīnān*) were put to death. 'There were many Shaikhs of *ṭarīqa*; not one of them by a defence of madness or the like of this caused them to be spared.'[54]

The (possibly spurious) *apologia* of the sultan has a sharply differing account of 'a group … who made *Murīds* and spoke words of *kufr* [infidelity]. The leader of those who had gone astray was called Aḥmad Bihārī, and a faction from Bihar called him God (*khudā*).… One of his disciples said, "In Dehlī God has arisen!"'[55]

When the news of the two executions reached Sharaf al-Dīn, we are told that he remarked (with predictable consequences) that 'it would be strange if the city should continue to flourish, where the blood of such as these had been spilt!' These words reached the sultan, who once more called together the *'ulamā'* and notables and was persuaded by them to despatch a *farmān* summoning the shaikh to Dehlī. He was persuaded to rescind the order when he found that the noted Suhrawardī shaikh who was then visiting Dehlī, Sayyid Jalāl al-Dīn Bukhārī ('Makhdūm-i jahāniān') had been in retreat reading the epistles (*maktūbāt*) which Sharaf al-Dīn had sent to him.[56]

[54] Manērī, *Manāqib a-aṣfiyā'*, pp. 130, 137.
[55] Feroz Shāh Tughluq, *Futūḥāt-i Fērōzshāhī*, ed. S. Abdur Rashid, Aligarh: Aligarh Muslim University, 1954, p. 8.
[56] Manērī, *Manāqib a-aṣfiyā'*, pp. 137–8.

Precept and Practice among Sufi Shaikhs

In this period there was an unavoidable conflict between professed aims and necessary practice in the pursuit of the role of a great shaikh. This is visible in the hagiographical literature, and thrown into sharper relief if other evidence is taken into consideration. The Chishtī shaikhs were committed to a lifestyle of personal austerities, poverty or even deliberate indebtedness, inaccessibility, avoidance of cities and of contact with worldly people—and especially of avoidance of contact with the rich and powerful—and to the concealment of *karāmāt* (miraculous powers). Their charisma largely derived from the widespread conviction that they possessed these qualities, but for this charisma to be recognized they had often to proceed in exactly the opposite way. Prestige also depended on the ability to construct, extend, and organize a *khānqāh*; to feed, accommodate, and attend to the material and spiritual needs of disciples and often numerous dependants; and to accommodate travellers according to Muslim precept and the expectations of hospitality. The principal means to support such necessarily extensive establishments were likely to be offerings from the wealthy and powerful, sometimes by a system of monasterial labour. Such offerings implied the accessibility of the *khānqāh* and of the shaikh himself, contrary to the ideal of inaccessibility and avoidance of worldly contacts.

The fond descriptions, which passed from the record of Niẓām al-Dīn's conversations into later hagiographical literature, of Farīd al-Dīn's *khānqāh* at Ajodhan embody many memorable and striking circumstantial details—the shaikh and his disciples going out to gather firewood and unappetizing fruits of the jungle, Farīd's own mother eaten by a wild beast a short distance away from the road, female descendants of the Prophet washing the soiled clothes of the disciples who had walked the long way to Ajodhan, the thatched huts and the rustic fare—the details and anecdotes in this vein suggest a remote idyll of rural simplicity and holy poverty.[57] Nevertheless, the *khānqāh* lay on a major route between the populous cities of Dehlī and Multan, along which trade and travellers constantly passed. It had a stable for the horses and it stands, like the Suhrawardī *khānqāh* at Multan, in a commanding position at the height of what is probably an ancient 'tell', dominating the small walled town.[58]

According to the hagiographical tradition, in the early days after the foundation of the *khānqāh*, Farīd al-Dīn was visited here by Ulugh Khān, the future Sultan Balban who was then in command of the western marches of the Dehlī Sultanate.[59] An offer of a grant of villages was rejected by Farīd, but in the following century such grants appear to have been accepted from the Tughluq sultans of Dehlī by his descendants.[60] Ibn Baṭṭūṭa remarked that the town of Ajodhan belonged to the shaikh. Himself a traveller of high social status, he commented unfavourably on the manners and arrogance of the incumbent shaikh, in fact a grandson of Farīd.[61]

There is the same visible conflict between precept and practice in the location and organization of the *khānqāh* of

[57] For a modern presentation with an abundance of details, see Nizami, *The Life and Times of Shaikh Farid-u'd-din Ganj-i-Shakar.*

[58] A.M. Stow, 'The Road between Delhi and Multan', *Journal of the Punjab Historical Society*, vol. 3, no. 1, 1914–15, pp. 26–37; S. Digby, 'Sufis and Travellers in the Early Dehli Sultanate: The Evidence of the *Fawā'id al-fu'ād*', in *Socio-Cultural Impact of Islam on India*, ed. Attar Singh, Chandigarh: University of the Punjab, 1976, pp. 171–7 [*L&WSD* III.4; this volume].

[59] Khwurd, *Siyar al-awliyā'*, pp. 79–80.

[60] Baranī, *Ta'rīkh-i Fērōzshāhī*, Calcutta: Bibliotheca Indica, 1862, p. 543; Richard M. Eaton, 'The Political and Religious Authority of the Shrine of Bābā Farīd', in *Moral Conduct and Authority: The Place of* Adab *in South Asian Islam*, ed. B.D. Metcalf, Berkeley: University of California Press, 1984, pp. 339–40.

[61] Ibn Baṭṭūṭa, *Riḥla*, vol. III, Paris: Societé Asiatique, 1855, p. 135; cf. Khwurd, *Siyar al-awliyā'*, pp. 193, 195.

Niẓām al-Dīn, located in the area of southern New Delhi known as Hazrat Nizamuddin. If, as is claimed by the hagiographic sources, the *khānqāh* was established on this site in order that the shaikh might reside there free from the distractions of urban life, it was also conveniently accessible from the city or denser urban areas of Dehlī, a suburb to which all classes of people could throng.

Those who did resort to the *khānqāh* included the ill-fated royal princes Shādī Khān and Khiḍr Khān, sons of Sultan 'Alā' al-Dīn Khaljī. They are stated to have built the *Jamā'at-khāna,* a building which served both as a communal residence hall and as a mosque. On its roof the shaikh spent a part of his time (as mentioned in an anecdote quoted above). If it is the present building, which stylistically can hardly date from later than the early fourteenth century, this is one of the grandest of the red sandstone monuments of its period in Dehlī.[62] Many court officials as well as humbler members of the urban population came to profess their devotion at the *khānqāh*; it was a centre of the literary life of the capital. One has an uneasy impression that 'everyone who was anyone', despite the shaikh's professed desire for solitude, came to Niẓām al-Dīn's *khānqāh* and were received with courtesies appropriate to his station in life. The exception was the reigning monarch, the sultan.

At an early stage in the establishment of the Chishtī *silsila* in Dehlī, meetings took place between Quṭb al-Dīn Bakhtyār and the pious Sultan Iltutmish.[63] The events which had led to the putting to death of Sīdī Muwallih, as well as the ascendancy and recognition which Niẓām al-Dīn had achieved, necessitated a careful proclamation by the shaikh of his freedom from worldly ties and of his

[62] Khwurd, *Siyar al-awliyā'*, p. 74; cf. Zafar Hasan, *A Guide to Nizamu-d Din*, Calcutta: Archaeological Survey of India, 1922, p. 14.

[63] Khwurd, *Siyar al-awliyā'*, p. 53; Jamālī, *Siyar al-'ārifīn*, p. 20; Ḥusaynī, *Jawāmi' al-kalim*, p. 207.

lack of concern with the administration of the sultanate.[64] Total avoidance of either attendance upon the sultan at his court or of reception of the sultan at the *khānqāh* prevented a potentially disastrous confrontation of incompatible claims to secular and spiritual governance over the same territory:

> In every realm although there is a ruler (*Amīr*)
> He is under the protection of a *Faqīr*;
> Although the rulers may be at the head of the kingdom,
> The *Faqīrs* are the drinkers [averters] of disaster of the kingdom.[65]

Confrontations between Niẓām al-Dīn and the ruler were narrowly averted in the reigns of each of the three Khaljī sultans (AD 1290–1320).[66] The apparent subjection of the shaikh by Sultan Giyāth al-Dīn Tughluq terminated with the death of both figures within months of one another in AD 1325.[67] The coercion of Sufi shaikhs by Muḥammad bin Tughluq (r. AD 1325–51) was a part of a developing feud of the sultan with the majority of the educated and possessing classes of his capital city and realm.[68] Just as he sought to employ foreigners and 'new men' in high administrative posts, he found an external legitimation of his authority in the mandate of the 'Abbāsid caliph in Egypt. In the Sufi

64 Khwurd, *Siyar al-awliyā'*, p. 134; for Sīdī Muwallih's death, see Digby, 'Qalandars and Related Groups', pp. 67–8, and references there given [this volume, pp. 189–90].
65 'Iṣāmī, *Futūḥ al-salāṭīn*, p. 456, referring to Niẓām al-Dīn.
66 Khwurd, *Siyar al-awliyā'*, pp. 132–5, 151–2; Jamālī, *Siyar al-'ārifīn*, p. 75.
67 Khwurd, *Siyar al-awliyā'*, pp. 526–32; Jamālī, *Siyar al-'ārifīn*, pp. 88–90; Baranī, *Ta'rīkh-i Fērōzshāhī*, pp. 96–7; Badā'ōnī, *Muntakhab al-tawārīkh*, Calcutta, 1868, I, p. 225.
68 Ibn Baṭṭūṭa, *Riḥla*, III, pp. 294–311; Khwurd, *Siyar al-awliyā'*, pp. 215–18.

hagiographical tradition, Amīr Khwurd explains his death, on the distant campaign of Thattha, as a consequence of his having summoned Niẓām al-Dīn's *khalīfa* Naṣīr al-Dīn Maḥmūd from Dehlī to join him, and of not having treated him as he should have done (*ka-mā ḥaqquhu*).[69] Sultan Fērōz Shāh Tughluq (r. AD 1351–88) sought the approval of a number of Sufi shaikhs;[70] and the death of Naṣīr al-Dīn Maḥmūd in AD 1356 left the capital city without any shaikh exercising a predominant authority. A composition of a follower of Naṣīr al-Dīn Maḥmūd in the last decade of the century reveals strong hostility to the sultan and his court.[71] In the fifteenth century, conflicts of authority between sultans and Sufi shaikhs were to recur in the Deccan and in Gujarat.[72]

The Rise to Pre-eminence of the Chishtī Shaikhs

How is it that the Chishtīs, from a relatively obscure lineage outside India, attained their position of dominance in the

[69] Khwurd, *Siyar al-awliyā'*, p. 246.

[70] 'Afif, *Ta'rīkh-i Fērōzshāhī*, pp. 27–9.

[71] S. Digby, 'The *Tuḥfa i naṣā'iḥ* of Yūsuf Gadā: An Ethical Treatise in Verse from the Late-fourteenth century Dehlī Sultanate', in *Moral Conduct*, ed. B.D. Metcalf, Berkeley: University of California Press, 1984, pp. 107, 118–19 [*L&WSD* III.8; this volume, pp. 263, 276–9].

[72] Firishta, *Ta'rīkh*, vol. I, Bombay: Government College Press, 1831, pp. 633–5; ibid., Kanpur, 1290/1874, pp. 328–9; Ṭabāṭabā'ī, *Burhān-i ma'āthir*, Hyderabad: Maṭba' Jami'ah, 1955, pp. 166–7; Sikandar b. Muḥammad, *Mir'āt-i Sikandarī*, ed. S.C. Misra and M.L. Rahman. Baroda: Maharaja Sayajirao University, 1961, pp. 86–93; Sir E.C. Bayley, *The Local Muhammadan Dynasties: Gujarat*, London: W.H. Allen and Co., 1886, pp. 153–60. Cf. Digby, 'The Sufi Shaykh and the Sultan' [this volume, pp. 42–76]. See also Aziz Ahmad, 'The Sufi and the Sultan in pre-Mughal Muslim India', *Der Islam*, vol. 38, no. 1–2, 1962, pp. 142–53.

Dehlī Sultanate, which has in turn led to their legends, their tombs and shrines exercising so great an influence on the historical imagination of South Asian Muslims for several centuries down to the present day?

Answers to such historical questions are necessarily personal assessments which are not susceptible to proof. The decisive factor, I suggest, is neither the possession in abundance and variety of the qualities which contributed to the charisma of a great shaikh nor the number of devotees in their lifetimes. The historical advantage which the Chishtīs in India have possessed is rather that of ascendancy at a particular moment in the development of the capital city of a great kingdom, whose literary, cultural and institutional traditions spread to the farthest areas of the subcontinent. At that moment the ideologues and the writers (some of whose works were transmitted to posterity) recognized a pre-eminence of charisma in a particular shaikh and embodied that opinion in their literary records.

This occurred around the first decade of the fourteenth century, when the two principal Persian poets of their time and place, Amīr Khusrau and Amīr Ḥasan, expressed allegiance to Niẓām al-Dīn, and were joined by their younger contemporary, the historian of the Dehlī Sultanate Ḍiyā' al-Dīn Baranī.[73] In this context the importance of Amīr Ḥasan was not as a poet, though his poetry was esteemed and read by posterity, but as the author of a valuable and striking historical record of the conversations of Niẓām al-Dīn.

This record, the *Fawā'id al-fu'ād*, was begun in AD 1308 and finished nearly fourteen years later. Like Baranī's history, the *Ta'rīkh-i Fērōzshāhī*, it was evidently circulated in parts

[73] Khwurd, *Siyar al-awliyā'*, pp. 301–5, 308, 312–13, 346–7; Baranī, *Ta'rīkh-i Fērōzshāhī*, pp. 359–60; M.W. Mirza, *The Life and Works of Amir Khusrau*, Lahore: Panjab University Press, 1962, pp. 116–19; Amīr Ḥasan Sijzī, *Dīwān*, ed. M.A. Maḥvī, Hyderabad: Maktabah-i Ibrāhīmiyah, AH 1352/AD 1933, Introduction, pp. 1–14.

before the whole was completed.[74] It enjoyed contemporary popularity and was in demand in the capital city.

According to the historian Baranī, a furore of piety was inspired in the capital city by the presence of Niẓām al-Dīn during the reign of Sultan 'Alā' al-Dīn Khaljī. This was expressed in the performance of obligatory and supererogatory prayers and fasts, and in demands for works of Muslim learning and manuals of Sufi instruction, the *Iḥyā' al-ulūm*, *Qūt al-qulūb*, *'Awārif al-ma'ārif* and others; and also for copies of Amīr Ḥasan's *Fawā'id al-fu'ād*.[75] One may suspect that only the last work was perused with understanding and enthusiasm. A further testimony to the popularity of this work is that it inspired a whole series of fabricated *malfūẓāt* (recorded conversations) of Niẓām al-Dīn's predecessors in the Chishtī *silsila*.[76] By internal evidence and references, as well as traces of their influence on the genuine collections of *malfūẓāt* and *tadhkiras* of the second half of the fourteenth century, these fabrications were produced in Dehlī in imitation of the *Fawā'id al-fu'ād*, probably in response to the immediate popular demand which that work had created. The fabrications were filled with even more credulous anecdotes than those found in the genuine hagiographical works and with examples of even cruder popular levels of superstition. They were not generally recognized as spurious (as they so obviously are), and they

[74] Baranī's reference (p. 346, see note 75 below) implies that it was in circulation by AD 1315. For the contemporary circulation of portions of Baranī's own work, see S. Digby, 'Muhammad bin Tughluq's Last Years in Kathiavad and His Invasions of Thattha', in *Sind Through the Centuries*, ed. H. Khuhro, Karachi: Oxford University Press, 1981, pp. 133–4 [*L&WSD* VI.3].

[75] Baranī, *Ta'rīkh-i Fērōzshāhī*, pp. 343–6, 360; cf. Khwurd, *Siyar al-awliyā'*, pp. 308, 346–7, quoting from Baranī's lost *Ḥasrat-nāma*.

[76] M. Habib, 'Chishtī Mystic Records of the Sultanate Period', *Medieval India Quarterly*, vol. 1, no. 3, pp. 1–42.

were copied and lithographed until modern times. To this day Urdu translations of them are sold at Sufi festivals and in ordinary booksellers.

The contemporary popularity of Amīr Ḥasan's work had therefore brought into being a corpus of literature which, however trivial or worthless the contents, continued to circulate as evidence of the singular importance of the Chishtī shaikhs in general and of Niẓām al-Dīn in particular. This advantage was denied to shaikhs of rival *silsilas*. The literary contributions of Amīr Khusrau and of Ḍiyā' al-Dīn Baranī to the pre-eminence of Niẓām al-Dīn were of different kinds.

Amīr Khusrau has remained from his own day through subsequent centuries the most famous and widely read of the Persian poets of India. His *mathnavīs* or longer narrative or didactic poems, following the model of those of Niẓāmī of Ganja, usually contain a section devoted to the praise of a Sufi *pīr* following the *na't* of the Prophet and preceding the poet's submission to the reigning sultan. In Amīr Khusraw's case the *pīr* is Niẓām al-Dīn, sometimes with a mention of his predecessors Quṭb al-Dīn and Farīd al-Dīn.[77] Thus, every reader of Amīr Khusrau's *mathnavīs*, whether in his own day or later, was made familiar with the spiritual gifts of Niẓām al-Dīn. No other Indian Sufi shaikh possessed a comparable panegyrist.

The allegiance of the historian Baranī had a similar effect. The Dehlī Sultanate was, as we have suggested, a key period in the development of Indo-Muslim culture. The historical record for a large portion of the period, from the mid-thirteenth to the mid-fourteenth century, is more

[77] Amīr Khusrau, *Matla' al-anwār*, Kanpur: Naval Kishor, AH 1302/AD 1884, pp. 17–20; *Laylā Majnūn*, Aligarh: Maṯba'-yi Insṭīṭiyūṭ-i 'Alīgaṛh, 1917, pp. 13–14; *Shīrīn u Khusrau*, Moscow: Izd-vo vostochnoi lit-ry, 1961, pp. 15–16; *Ā'īna-i Iskandarī*, Aligarh: Maṯba'-yi Insṭīṭiyūṭ, 1917, pp. 11–14; *Dawal Rānī Khiḍr Khān*, Aligarh: Maṯba'-yi Insṭīṭiyūṭ, 1917, pp. 15–16; *Nuh sipihr*, Calcutta: Asiatic Society, 1948, pp. 23–8.

dependent upon Baranī's narrative than upon any other source. Even when the testimony of this somewhat devious recorder is suspect, subsequent historians, whether they wrote in Persian in the sixteenth century or are writing in English at the present day, must reproduce, even when they question, Baranī's assertions. In this case Baranī testifies to the unique position of Niẓām al-Dīn in the religious life of the capital and the sultanate.[78] Once again, no rival shaikh had a comparable publicist as disciple.

From the late period of his life when Niẓām al-Dīn had founded his hospice and was receiving the allegiance and offerings of a large body of supporters in the royal court and the city, one may project the story of the rise of the *silsila* backwards. Niẓām al-Dīn had the advantage of a scholarly education before he enrolled as a disciple of Farīd. He was also a *Sayyid*, and he was brought up in Badā'on, one of the principal subsidiary Muslim settlements of the Doab after the main conquest of AD 1192. He had strong claims to have inherited the mantle of Farīd al-Dīn (d. AD 1265) many decades before he set up his *khānqāh*.[79]

Farīd al-Dīn is a key figure in the rise of the Chishtī *silsila*, without whose precursory activities Niẓām al-Dīn could not have achieved his ascendancy. A detailed picture of his personality emerges from the numerous anecdotes which Niẓām al-Dīn related about him. He was the offspring of a line of Muslim *'ālims*, previously connected with the Ghaznavid and Ghorid rulers of Khurasan, but long settled in the Punjab. He had a formal Islamic education, and from adolescence displayed a mania for austerities, as well as an abundance of human and poetic sensibilities. After receiving his license

[78] Baranī, *Ta'rīkh-i Fērōzshāhī*, pp. 343–6, 360.

[79] Khwurd, *Siyar al-awliyā'*, pp. 99–116; M. Habib, *Ḥaḍrat Niẓām al-Dīn Auliyā': ḥayāt aur ta'līmāt*, Delhi: Shu'bah-yi Urdū, Dehlī Yunīversitī, 1970.

from Quṭb al-Dīn, having acquired some reputation in the capital, and after an intervening period at Hansi, he set up his *khānqāh* at Ajodhan, situated as we have seen on a major route between Dehlī and Multan.[80] Reports of the personality of the shaikh and of the ideal poverty of the hospice were carried by travellers; they served to spread and enhance the reputation of the *silsila*, and to emphasize its connection with the still fragile power of the Sultanate of Dehlī.[81] When Niẓām al-Dīn received his leave from Farīd al-Dīn and finally moved back from Ajodhan to Dehlī, there must have been those in the metropolitan population who looked forward to a time when he might establish his own hospice.

The personalities of the predecessors of Farīd al-Dīn are less well remembered in a mere handful of anecdotes in the *Fawā'id al-fu'ād* and the *Siyar al-awliyā'*. Quṭb al-Dīn's ecstatic sensibilities, his practice of *samā‘* and his manner of death entered popular folk-memory. He was evidently held in some esteem by the pious Sultan Iltutmish, and the hostile Firdausī tradition maintains that he had an unequivocal reputation for the display of *karāmāt* (abnormal powers).[82] Possibly his utterance regarding the ground where he wished to be buried at Dehlī had some part in strengthening popular faith in the connection of the *silsila* with the capital.[83] Subsequently the presence of his grave as a place of pilgrimage strengthened this link.[84]

The historical facts which can be established regarding Mu‘in al-Dīn are few indeed. 'He emerges from the clouds

[80] Nizami, *The Life and Times*, pp. 10–11, 15–16, 21–3, 36ss.

[81] 'Alā' Sijzī, *Fawā'id al-fu'ād*, pp. 252–3; Digby, 'Sufis and Travellers', pp. 171–7 [this volume, pp. 130–7].

[82] See notes 44, 63 above.

[83] 'Alā' Sijzī, *Fawā'id al-fu'ād*, p. 425; Khwurd, *Siyar al-awliyā'*, p. 55.

[84] 'Alā' Sijzī, *Fawā'id al-fu'ād*, pp. 132, 315; Khwurd, *Siyar al-awliyā'*, pp. 50–1, 126, 264; Qalandar, *Khair al-majālis*, p. 57.

of legend as an obscure *Darwīsh*: either contemporary writers were ignorant of his existence, or they found little in it to interest them.'[85] Yet for the legend of the Chishtīs, the presence of this lineal predecessor in Ajmer in the first days of the Muslim conquest was a powerful link with the destinies of the Muslim community on Indian soil.

We have noted the need of the newly established, part immigrant, part convert or *assimilé* population of the Sultanate of Dehlī, for a Muslim sanctification of their land. The Chishtī shaikhs appealed, and their shrines continue to appeal, to Indian Muslims in search of a sanctification of their native land. All of the great Chishtī shaikhs of Dehlī, including Sayyid Muḥammad Gēsūdarāz (who at one point boasted of a connection with Dehlī extending back twelve generations) were of *ashrāf* Muslim families established in the subcontinent from the early days of the conquest of Dehlī or from the earlier Muslim conquests of the Punjab.[86] Their graves stood as symbols of their presence and they were observers of the practice of *ziyārat*, visiting the graves of the pious dead, even when, as we have noted, their deficiency in performing *ḥajj* to Arabia was a matter of concern for their hagiographers.[87]

From Living Shaikhs to Tomb-cults: The Growth of the Legend of Mu'īn al-Dīn at Ajmer

With the decay and eclipse of the Dehlī Sultanate in northern India, the power and prestige of living Chishtī shaikhs came to an end, and representatives of lineages at Dehlī

[85] Currie, *The Shrine and Cult of Mu'īn al-Dīn*, p. 4.

[86] Nizami, *The Life and Times*, pp. 10–11; 'Abd al-Ḥaqq, *Akhbār al-akhyār*, p. 54; Qalandar, *Khair al-majālis*, Intro. by K.A. Nizami, p. 39; Shēr Malik, *Ta'rīkj-i ḥabībī*, pp. 7–8.

[87] See pp. 12–13 and note 28, above.

ceased to exercise a wide charisma. Later Chishtī shaikhs who sometimes resided at Dehlī—'Abd al-Quddūs of the Chishtī Ṣābirī line in the early sixteenth century, Shāh Kalīm Allāh in the revived seventeenth-century capital of Shahjahanabad, and Maulānā Fakhr al-Dīn at Mehrauli at the end of the eighteenth century—were all incomers from distant areas.[88] At Pakpattan (Ajodhan) the numerous descendants of Shaikh Farīd al-Dīn came to exercise leadership over the rural tribes of that area of the Punjab.[89] In the Deccan Sayyid Muḥammad Gēsūdarāz founded a powerful Chishtī *wilāyat*, part of the appeal of which lay in the historical connection of the immigrant Deccani Muslims, their language and culture with the expansion and eclipse of the Dehlī Sultanate. This was a second cycle of expansion followed by loss of the original homeland, like that which had overtaken the Dehlī Sultanate after its foundation in the early thirteenth century.

The image of the activities of the earlier Chishtī shaikhs remained potent, even when shaikhs from other *silsilas*, often staking their claims on different sources of prestige (one of which was that they were but newly arrived in India from the older and holier lands of Islam) established networks of influence in the subcontinent in the fifteenth and sixteenth centuries. Dehlī in the early sixteenth century was thinly populated. It was considered a city of the hallowed dead, in which holy men would assemble and hold discourse on successive days of the week at different sanctified places.[90] The Lōdī sultans of Dehlī, although they held court at Agra, were buried in royal tombs close to the hospice of Niẓām al-

[88] Digby, "Abd al-Quddūs Gangōhī', pp. 10, 25–7 [this volume, pp. 320, 342–3]; K.A. Nizami, *Ta'rīkh-i mashā'ikh Chisht*, Delhi: Idarah-i Adabiyat, 1953, pp. 369–85, 460–71.

[89] Eaton, 'The Political and Religious Authority', pp. 341–53.

[90] Rizq Allāh Mushtāqī, *Waqi'āt-i Mushtāqī*, British Library MS Add. 11,633, f. 31a; British Library MS Or. 1929, f. 31b.

Dīn.[91] The alien conqueror Bābur, when he took possession of the city in AD 1526, in the course of a day's sightseeing visited the tombs of two of the three great Chishtī shaikhs buried there, Quṭb al-Dīn Bakhtyār and Niẓām al-Dīn.[92]

Among the tombs of the early Chishtī shaikhs, that of the founder of the lineage in India, Mu'īn al-Dīn Chishtī at Ajmer had the greatest potential appeal. Although little was remembered about his activities and possibly less committed to writing during the fourteenth century, his burial place provided an appropriate mythopoeic setting for the greatest tomb-cult of Indian Muslims. In the later fourteenth century Amīr Khwurd briefly adumbrated the development of the territorial legend of Mu'īn al-Dīn. The Muslim presence in India itself is listed as a *karāmāt* ('miracle', 'grace') of Mu'īn al-Dīn. The land of Hindostan was a country, the whole of which as far as the sunrise was (full of) unbelief, idols, and idol worship, and its disobedient people were polytheists who bowed down before stones and clods, beasts and cattle and their excrement:

> By the arrival of the blessed footsteps of 'that Sun of the People of Belief' ... the darkness of this land was illuminated by Islam.... Whoever will become a Musalmān in this land, enduring to the Day of Resurrection, as well as their offspring as they are engendered who will be Musalmāns; and those who will be brought from infidel territory (*dār-i ḥarb*) to the land of Islam [i.e. slaves taken from unconverted Hindu territories and converted]—until the day of Resurrection the recompenses of these are added to the lofty court (*bārgāh*) ... [of Mu'īn al-Dīn] ... in obedience to him.[93]

Thus, his *wilāyat* extends over all India. His blessed tomb was in Ajmer. 'The pure earth of the grave of this saint is

[91] S. Digby, 'The Tomb of Bahlūl Lōdī', *Bulletin of the School of Oriental and African Studies*, vol. 38, no. 3, 1975, pp. 553–4 [*L&WSD* VI.8].
[92] *Bābur-nāma*, Leiden: Brill, 1905, ff. 267b–268a; tr. Beveridge, London: Luzac, 1921, vol. II, p. 475.
[93] Khwurd, *Siyar al-awliyā'*, p. 47.

medicine for the hearts of those in pain. May (they) obtain the good fortune of pilgrimage (*ziyārat*)!'[94]

The site of the grave was neglected in the period immediately after Mu'īn al-Dīn's death, though if it was where the present tomb is located, with a massive excavated tank (reservoir) behind it, it is probably, as the legends and local traditions suggest, a Hindu site of some importance which has been taken over by the adherents of the new cult.[95]

The practice of visiting tombs (*ziyārat*) was popular in the fourteenth century and considered by the Chishtī shaikhs commendable and efficacious. Mu'īn al-Dīn's tomb at Ajmer was visited by Sultan Muḥammad bin Tughluq and at least two important Chishtī *khalīfas* in the fourteenth century.[96] In the decline of the early fifteenth century Ajmer passed altogether out of Muslim hands, a fact which emphasized the 'frontier' appeal of the site. In the later fifteenth century the sultans of Malwa, apparently inspired by the legend of Mu'īn al-Dīn, gained control of Ajmer as an outpost of their own dominions, and the shrine was recolonized by alleged descendants of the shaikh from Malwa.[97]

The pilgrimages of the emperor Akbar on foot to Ajmer between the years AD 1562 and 1579 are testimony of the popular reputation of the shrine and cult;[98] and the emperor's visits doubtless added to that reputation. By the beginning

[94] Ibid., p. 48.

[95] Currie, *The Shrine and Cult of Mu'īn al-Dīn*, pp. 151–2; Sarda, *Ajmer*, p. 90.

[96] S. Digby, 'Early Pilgrimages to the Graves of Mu'īn al-Dīn and other Chishtī Shaikhs', in *Islamic Society and Culture*, ed. M. Israel and N.K. Wagle, New Delhi: Manohar, 1983, pp. 95–100 [*L&WSD* III.5; this volume, pp. 138–43]; Khwurd, *Siyar al-awliyā'*, p. 264; 'Abd al-Ḥaqq, *Akhbār al-akhyār*, p. 91.

[97] 'Abd al-Ḥaqq, *Akhbār al-akhyār*, p. 177; Currie, *The Shrine and Cult of Mu'īn al-Dīn*, p. 170.

[98] A.L. Srivastava, *Akbar the Great*, vol. I, Agra: Shiva Lal Agarwala, 1962, pp. 61, 246.

of the seventeenth century Ajmer attracted, apart from visitors of distinction, large numbers of pilgrims from distant areas of India who congregated on the occasion of the *'urs* (commemoration of the date of the shaikh's death).[99] The fullest and most highly embroidered literary exposition of Mu'īn al-Dīn's legend dates from this period, the *Siyar al-aqṭāb* of Ilāhdiyā Chishtī. It provides a fantastic narrative of how Mu'īn al-Dīn vanquished local material and spiritual powerholders by his magical powers, and gained possession of this sacred site—an emblem for Indian Muslims of their tenures in the subcontinent.[100] It also describes in the same style the election of the person of Mu'īn al-Dīn and of the *topos* of Ajmer to fulfil this role among Indian Muslims:

It is related that the Shaikh was 52 years old when he received the gifts (*tabarrukāt*) of his *pīr* [and set out on his own mission]. Everywhere he went he customarily lived in cemeteries, and wherever his reputation spread he tarried no longer, but secretly departed from there. After some days he came to the House of the *Ka'ba* and stayed there for some days. Then he went to Medina the Illuminated, and performed the pilgrimage to the Holy Tomb of the Lord of the World [the Prophet Muḥammad]. He stayed there for a while, until one day from inside the pure and blessed Tomb a cry came: 'Send for Mu'īn al-Dīn!' The servitor of the Tomb called out the name, and from several places heard the reply: 'I am here for Thee!'

The servitor went back and stood before the door of the radiant and holy Tomb, and again the cry came forth: 'Send for Mu'īn al-Dīn Chishtī!'

[99] *Jahangir's India: The* Remonstrantie *of Francisco Pelsaert*, tr. W.H. Moreland and P. Geyl, Cambridge: Heffer, 1925, p. 70; *Travels of Peter Mundy*, ed. R.C. Temple, London: Hakluyt Society, 1914, vol. II, p. 244.

[100] Ilāhdiyā Chishtī, *Siyar al-aqṭāb*, Kanpur: Naval Kishor, 1889, pp. 125–31; S. Digby, 'Encounters with *Jogīs* in Indian Sūfī Hagiography', Seminar on aspects of religion in South Asia, SOAS University of London, January 1970 [*L&WSD* II].

The servitor came forward and told what he had been ordered, and at that moment a strange ecstasy, such as cannot be described, came over the *Khwāja* [Mu'īn al-Dīn]. Weeping and crying and invoking blessings, he came to the door of the Tomb and stood there. The voice cried: 'Enter, O Polestar (*Quṭb*) of Shaikhs!'

Lost to self and intoxicated, the *Khwāja* went in and was exalted by the sight of the world-adorning beauty of that Presence; and he beheld that Presence speak to him: 'Mu'īn al-Dīn, you are the essence of my faith, yet you must go to Hindostan. There is a place called Ajmer, to which one of my sons [descendants] went for a holy war. Now he has become a martyr and the place has passed again into the hands of the infidels. By the grace of your footsteps Islam shall once more be manifest there, and the infidels punished by God's wrath.'

Then the Prophet—on whom be Blessings and Peace—gave a pomegranate into the hands of the *Khwāja* and said: 'Look into this, so that you may see and know where you have to go!'

At his command the *Khwāja* looked into the pomegranate, and he saw all that exists between the east and the west; and he looked well at Ajmer and its hills. He humbly offered prayers and sought help from that *Dargāh* ('Court') which is the envy of the heavens. Then he set out for Hindostan.[101]

From this wholly legendary recital we may note how, as a result of the historical circumstances by which the shaikhs of the Chishtī *silsila* attained an ascendancy in the Dehlī Sultanate, a devotional legend of lasting appeal had gained currency among Indian Muslims. The *'urs* or festival of the anniversary of the death of Mu'īn al-Dīn is today the greatest pilgrimage festival of Muslims of the Indian subcontinent, with the annual number of pilgrims in the 1970s reaching 300,000.[102]

[101] Chishtī, *Siyar al-aqṭāb*, pp. 123–4.

[102] Currie, *The Shrine and Cult of Mu'īn al-Dīn*, pp. 196–7.

2

The Sufi Shaykh and the Sultan

A Conflict of Claims to Authority in Medieval India

The claims of Sufi shaykhs to be sources of authority in medieval India, and in particular in the greater Delhi Sultanate of the thirteenth and fourteenth Christian centuries, have been surveyed elsewhere by the present writer, but space prevented a detailed examination of the relations between Sufi shaykhs on whose behalf a claim of territorial *wilāyat* was advanced and the Muslim rulers or de facto power holders of the same regions.[1]

The Sufi Shaykh's *Wilāyat* in Contemporary Sources

The territorial *wilāyat* of the Sufi shaykh was believed to have a direct influence on the political events and material destiny of the realm over which it was exercised.[2] Thus, the prosperity of the reign of Sultan 'Alā' al-Dīn Khaljī (r. 1296–1316) might be attributed to the influence of the unbounded

* Originally published in *Iran*, vol. 28, 1990, pp. 71–81; reproduced here with only minor corrections.

[1] S. Digby, 'The Sufi Shaikh as a Source of Authority in Mediaeval India', *Puruṣārtha*, vol. 9, 1986, pp. 57–77 [*L&WSD* III.1].

[2] See ibid., pp. 62–3 [this volume, pp. 14–17].

blessings of 'the King of *Shaykhs*' Niẓām al-Dīn Awliyā'.[3] Equally, the decline in the fortunes of the sultanate might be attributed to the removal of such spiritual protection. 'Iṣāmī, writing some twenty-five or thirty years after the event in a new secessionist Muslim state in the Deccan, maintained that the power and prosperity passed away from Delhi with the death of Shaykh Niẓām al-Dīn:

> He was one of the friends of God
> Through whom the realm of Hindōstān was maintained.
> First that man of wise dominion
> Set out from Dehlī to another kingdom;[4]
> After this that city and country were ruined;
> Discord prevailed in that realm.[5]

This belief in the ability of Sufi shaykhs to exercise, through their spiritual strength, a decisive influence on the outcome of material events is well illustrated by a number of references in the conversations of Shaykh Niẓām al-Dīn himself to the ever-present menace of attacks of the Mongols:

1. When the Mongols besieged Multan, Shaykh Quṭb al-Dīn Bakhtyār one night gave an arrow into the hands of the ruler Qubācha, with instructions to loose it in the darkness against the army of the unbelievers. In the morning the besieging host had vanished.[6]

[3] Baranī, *Ta'rīkh-i Fērōzshāhī*, Calcutta: Bibliotheca Indica, 1862, p. 325; Badāyūnī, *Muntakhab al-tawārīkh*, vol. I, Calcutta: Asiatic Society, 1868, p. 266. Cf. also Baranī's remarks on the protective influence of Niẓām al-Dīn's predecessor Shaykh Farīd al-Dīn, and of other great shaykhs during the reign of Sultan Balban (1266–87): Baranī, *Ta'rīkh*, p. 112.

[4] I.e. the next world.

[5] 'Iṣāmī, *Futūḥ al-salāṭīn*, ed. A.S. Usha, Madras: University of Madras, 1948, p. 456.

[6] Amīr Ḥasan 'Alā' Sijzī, *Fawā'id al-fu'ād*, Lahore: Malik Sirāj al-Dīn and Sons, 1966, p. 185.

2. In the year when the *wilāyat* of Shaykh Farīd al-Dīn (Niẓām al-Dīn's predecessor) was removed by death, the Mongols came and devastated the Panjab.[7]
3. When in Khwārazm the great Shaykh Najm al-Dīn Kubrā had pronounced that the Khwārazmshāh and his whole kingdom were the blood-price (*diyat*) for the murder of one of his disciples, the shaykh added: 'O that I had not spoken this word (*āh nafas-i khwudrā bērūn na-mēāwurdam!*)'. Such spoken words (*nafas*, 'breath') of a shaykh had an especial force which the shaykh himself would be powerless to reverse. In this case, the consequence of Shaykh Najm al-Dīn's words were that Khwārazm was overrun in Chinggiz Khān's first western campaign.[8]

The sultan could recruit, as objects of his bounty and clients of his patronage, Sufis with lesser claims than the great shaykhs, who were obliged by their own pretensions to reject such patronage. Thus, Sufi shaykhs are stated to have been put in charge of 120 *khānaqāhs* endowed by Sultan Fērōz Shāh Tughluq (r. 1351–88) in the capital city of Delhi. With the three days' hospitality at each stop prescribed by Muslim tradition, Muslim travellers might spend 360 days or a whole year in the capital city.[9] But if a major Sufi shaykh

[7] Ibid., p. 374.

[8] Amīr Khwurd, *Siyar al-awliyā'*, Delhi: Muhibb-i Hind Press, AH 1302/ AD 1885, p. 518.

[9] 'Afīf, *Ta'rīkh-i Fērōzshāhī*, Calcutta: Bibliotheca Indica, 1891, pp. 330–1. Regarding the establishment of such official *khānaqāhs*, Sayyid Jalāl al-Dīn remarked that he had been appointed *Shaykh al-Islām* of Sind-Sīwistān by Sultan Muḥammad b. Tughluq and had been given charge of forty *khānaqāhs*; but he went on *Ḥajj* and spent six years in the Holy Places (Ḥaramayn): 'Alā' al-Dīn Ḥusayni, *Khulāṣat al-alfāẓ*, Digby MS 11, ff. 481b–482a [now in the Bodleian Library, University of Oxford, MS. S. Digby Or. 8 ~DL]; Ghulām Sarwar, *Kazīnat al-aṣfiyā'*, vol. II, Lucknow: Naval Kishor, 1914, p. 58.

laid claims to *wilāyat* or spiritual rule over a territory which the sultan held by the force of his arms and ordered through the civil administration, he could ill afford to be seen to be under the sultan's patronage, as indicated by such gestures as accepting largesse, alms or grants directly from the sultan; or attending upon the sultan at his court, which would involve the observance of court etiquette designed to emphasize the supremacy of the sovereign over all who attended; or even willingly permitting the sultan to visit his own *khānaqāh*, with the shaykh receiving the sultan with the same politeness as was the lot of other visitors.

From the point of view of the sultan, the failure of the shaykh to perform such gestures might constitute a threat to his authority, because of the visible independence of the shaykh from that authority and the possibility that the shaykh's *khānaqāh* might provide a refuge and a rallying point for dissidents and plotters against it.[10] Some sultans may not have taken Sufi claims to *wilāyat* seriously, even though these are referred to in nearly contemporary chronicles as well as hagiographic sources. Nevertheless, such claims remained a source of vague and recurrent unease. That they could constitute a real threat to the power of a reigning sultan was demonstrated by the conspiracy with the Shaykh Sīdī

[10] That such ascetics, retired from the world and disclaiming worldly ambitions, should be a focus for the plots of those disaffected towards the ruler is taken for granted in an anecdote of the *Kitāb al-Tāj* of pseudo-Jāḥiẓ, composed in Baghdad under the 'Abbāsids. We are told that the Sasanian monarch Khusraw Parwīz caused a foster-brother to set up as such a holy man, in order to act as *agent-provocateur* towards those disaffected against the monarch's rule; see Ch. Pellat, tr., *Le livre de la couronne*, Paris: Société d'édition 'Les belles lettres', 1954, pp. 125–7. Cf. Digby 'The Sufi Shaikh', pp. 66–7 [this volume, p. 24] for fears said to have been expressed by an unnamed Sultan of Delhi regarding Mawlānā Ashraf al-Dīn Ṭawwāma that 'from the excess of the obedience of the population ... he might seize the realm.'

Muwallih as its figurehead in the reign of Jalāl al-Dīn Fērōz Khaljī (r. 1290–6)[11] and by examples from later Indo-Muslim history and from elsewhere in the Islamic world.[12]

[11] Baranī, *Ta'rīkh*, pp. 209–12; 'Iṣāmī, *Futūḥ al-salāṭīn*, pp. 215–17. Among modern secondary works, see S.H. Hodivala, *Studies in Indo-Muslim History*, vol. I, Bombay: Popular Book Depot, 1939, pp. 267–8; K.A. Nizami, *Some Aspects of Politics and Religion in India During the Thirteenth Century*, Aligarh: Aligarh Muslim University, 1961, pp. 288–91; Simon Digby, 'Qalandars and Related Groups: Elements of Social Deviance in the Religious Life of the Delhī Sultanate of the Thirteenth and Fourteenth Centuries', in *Islam in Asia*, vol. I, ed. Y. Friedmann, Jerusalem: Hebrew University of Jerusalem, 1984, pp. 67–8 [*L&WSD* III.7; this volume, pp. 195–7]. Even in this case, the sultan's treatment of the shaykh was thought by near-contemporaries to have had dire consequences for the realm. We are told that a black wind arose on the day of Sīdī Muwallih's death, and both Baranī and 'Iṣāmī attribute the subsequent drought and famine in Delhi and in neighbouring areas to his death. Baranī also ascribes the subsequent troubles of the realm of the Khaljī Sultans to the misfortune of his death.

[12] Examples outside India of Sufi lineages assuming royal powers include the Ṣafavids of Iran, descendants of Shaykh Ṣafī al-Dīn Ardabīlī, the Naqshbandī *khwājas* who displaced the Khāns of the Eastern Horde in eastern Turkistan in the seventeenth century, and the Qaramanlus of Anatolia in the thirteenth century (see Neshrī, *Cihannuma*, vol. I, Ankara: Türk Tarih Kurumu Basımevi, 1949, p. 42). In the middle of the nineteenth century, the Ākhond dynasty rose to power in Swat. Among unsuccessful Sufi contenders for thrones one may cite: the *faqīr* Shaydā in Bengal in the mid-fourteenth century, see Ibn Baṭṭūṭa, *Riḥla*, tr. M. Hussain, Baroda: Oriental Institute, 1953, p. 237; Shāh Jalāl Gujarātī, put to death for his royal pretensions by a sultan of Bengal in the fifteenth century, see 'Abd al-Ḥaqq Dehlavī, *Akhbār al-akhyār*, Delhi: Mujtabā'ī Press, AH 1309/AD 1892, p. 168; and the late eighteenth-century *sajjāda-nashīns* of Farīd al-Dīn Chishtī at Pakpattan, who fought the Sikh *misls* at the head of their own levies of tribal devotees, see S.M. Latif, *History of the Punjab*, Lahore: Civil and Military Press, 1892, p. 313, and Richard M. Eaton, 'The Political and Religious Authority of the Shrine of Baba Farid', in *Moral Conduct and Authority: The Place of* Adab *in South Asian Islam*, ed. B. Metcalf, Berkeley: University of California Press, 1984, p. 350.

Niẓām al-Dīn 'Awliyā'' Chishtī (d. 1325), the most powerful shaykh of the capital city at the time when the power of the Delhi Sultanate itself had attained its greatest extent at the beginning of the fourteenth century, was given by his followers the honorific of *Sulṭān al-mashā'ikh* ('the Sultan of shaykhs'). This regal imagery is pursued in a famous encomium on the shaykh by the poet Amīr Khusraw:

> An emperor in a *faqīr*'s cell,
> A 'Refuge of the World' for the heart of the world,
> A King of Kings without throne or crown,
> With kings in need of the dust of his feet.[13]

It is accordingly no matter of surprise that the conflict between royal and Sufi claims of authority in the period of the Delhi Sultanate centred around the person of Shaykh Niẓām al-Dīn. Four anecdotes in the *Siyar al-awliyā'*, a biographical source regarding Niẓām al-Dīn compiled within a generation of his death, illustrate the tensions which arose between the shaykh and successive sultans of Delhi.

The reign of Sultan Fērōz Shāh Khaljī preceded the period of Niẓām al-Dīn's greatest influence in the capital city. Knowing the reluctance of the shaykh to meet him, the sultan conspired with the poet Amīr Khusraw, who was both a *murīd* (disciple) of the shaykh and *muṣḥafdār* (keeper of the Qur'ān) of the sultan himself. The sultan planned to go in the company of the poet and pay an unexpected call upon the shaykh. Amir Khusraw felt bound secretly to inform the shaykh of this plan. Niẓām al-Dīn left

[13] Amīr Khusraw Dehlavī, *Majnūn Laylā*, ed. M. Habīb al-Raḥmān Khān, Aligarh: Maṭba'-yi Instīṭiyūṭ, 1917, p. 13; Amīr Khusraw Dehlavī, *Khamsa*, ed. A.A. Ashrafī, Tehran: Šaqāyiq, 1362 Shamsī/1983 AD, p. 150; quoted by Amīr Khwurd at the head of his notice of 'the coming of the Kings of the time as beggars to the court of the Sultan of Shaykhs Niẓām al-Dīn': Khwurd, *Siyar al-awliyā'*, p. 130.

Delhi immediately for a visit to the resting place of his *pīr* (predecessor) at Ajodhan.[14]

In the reign of 'Alā' al-Dīn Khaljī the influence of Niẓām al-Dīn had reached its apogee and '*'ulamā'*, *shaykhs*, *maliks* and *amīrs* were his servants'. Envious people (*ḥāsidān*) described the lavishness of the hospitality which the shaykh dispensed and brought such reports about him as led the sultan, who (we are told) had a suspicious and vengeful nature, to fear that the shaykh would bring injury to his rule, of the same kind as 'others of this group (*ṭā'ifa*)' had brought to rulers in the past.[15]

The sultan accordingly devised a ruse to ascertain whether the shaykh had intentions of seizing power. He indited a letter to him to the effect that, since the shaykh was the 'Lord of Mankind' by whom people's needs were fulfilled and since God had given temporal power to the writer (the sultan), it would be appropriate for him to submit to the shaykh's judgement in matters arising in the kingdom.[16]

[14] Khwurd, *Siyar*, p. 135. For the transmission of authority in the Chishtī *silsila* of the Delhi Sultanate, see Simon Digby, '*Tabarrukāt* and Succession among the Great Chishtī Shaykhs of the Delhi Sultanate', in *Delhi Through the Ages*, ed. R.E. Frykenberg, Delhi: Oxford University Press, 1986, pp. 63–103 [*L&WSD* III.3]; and Digby, 'The Sufi Shaikh', pp. 69–71 [this volume, pp. 30–6].

[15] This appears to be an oblique reference to the conspiracy around Sīdī Muwallih in the previous reign. *Ṭā'ifa* is not used in the specific sense assigned to it in the historical scheme of J. Spencer Trimingham, *The Sufi Orders in Islam*, Oxford: Oxford University Press, 1971; for animadversions on this scheme, see Digby's review in *Bulletin of the School of Oriental and African Studies*, vol. 36, 1973, pp. 136–7. The *maliks* and *amīrs* of the quotation above were major and minor grades of officers of the sultanate, in theory commandants of 1,000 and 100.

[16] An anecdote narrated by Baranī indicates that 'Alā' al-Dīn had some faith in the paranormal powers of Shaykh Niẓām al-Dīn. The sultan, not having had news for forty days of the fate of the army which he had despatched in the autumn of 1309 to Warangal in the eastern Deccan

The sultan sent the letter by the hand of his son Khiżr Khān, who was a *murīd* of the shaykh and was not aware of the background to its dispatch. The shaykh took the letter in his hand and remarked without studying it: 'What business have *darwēshs* with the doings of kings? I am a *darwēsh* who has made a retreat from the city, and I am occupied in praying for the king and for Muslims. If the king says anything further I will leave this place also.'[17]

The Sultan 'Alā' al-Dīn was much pleased with the answer that the prince brought back, and he remarked that he knew that all this had nothing to do with 'the Sultan of Shaykhs' (i.e. with Niẓām al-Dīn himself), adding that this would have caused the ruin of his realm.

After this the sultan announced his intention of visiting the shaykh, who sent a message back that 'there is no need to come'. He himself was occupied with 'prayer in absentia'

---

under his slave-general Malik Nā'ib (Malik Kāfūr), sent two of his high officials to Niẓām al-Din to find out how they had fared from the shaykh's powers of discovery (*kashf u karāmāt*). The shaykh prophesied their victorious return, and further victories thereafter: Baranī, *Ta'rīkh*, pp. 330–2. A lengthier account of this consultation of the shaykh by the sultan, with the names of intermediaries and other apparently circumstantial details, is given by Jamālī, *Siyar al-'ārifīn*, Delhi: Maṭba'-i Riẓvī, AH 1311/AD 1893, pp. 78–9. For Jamālī's credibility, see notes 21, 25, 51 below.

Another incident shows amicable relations between Sultan 'Alā' al-Dīn and the shaykh. When there was grave trouble from the Mongols (*malā'īn*, 'the accursed ones'), Sultan 'Alā' al-Dīn sent a messenger to Niẓām al-Dīn, telling him to come within the city walls of Delhi, and the shaykh is shown as about to move into the city on the morrow or the day after that: Ḥamīd Qalandar, *Khayr al-majālis*, ed. Nizami, Aligarh: Aligarh Muslim University, 1959, pp. 261–2. The most likely occasion for this incident is just before the battle of Kili in 1299.

17 'This place also' refers to Niẓām al-Dīn's previous removal from the city to the suburb of Ghiyāthpūr, not far distant; see Digby, 'The Sufi Shaikh', p. 68 [this volume, pp. 27–8].

(*du'ā-yi ghaybat*) and such prayer had peculiar efficacy. When after this message the sultan continued to press him, the shaykh pronounced: 'The house of this weak one has two doors. If the Sultan enters by one door, I will go out by the other!'[18]

According to the *Siyar al-awliyā'*, the youthful son and successor of 'Alā' al-Dīn Khaljī, Sultan Quṭb al-Dīn Mubarak (r. 1316–20) was hostile to Shaykh Niẓām al-Dīn for two reasons. The first was that the sultan had built a congregational mosque (*masjid-i jāmi'*) at Sīrī (the most recent 'New City' of Delhi).[19] On the first Friday (after its completion) he summoned all the shaykhs and *'ulamā'* to offer their prayers there. Niẓām al-Dīn sent back an answer that he had a mosque close to him, and that it was more fitting that he should offer his prayers there.

The second reason was that all the *imāms*, shaykhs, and other men of religion used to assemble on the first day of the month to offer their greetings to the sultan. Shaykh Niẓām al-Dīn did not go, but used to send his servant Iqbal. This afforded an opportunity for 'the envious' (*ḥāsidān*) to stir up trouble. The young sultan in his pride said that if Niẓām al-Dīn did not come on the first of the month he would have him brought forcibly.[20]

[18] Khwurd, *Siyar al-awliyā'*, pp. 132–5; cf. Jamālī, *Siyar al-'ārifīn*, p. 74.

[19] This reference suggests that the completion of the large Begampuri mosque at Sīrī, traditionally dated to the later fourteenth century, should be dated to this reign.

[20] Khwurd, *Siyar al-awliyā'*, pp. 150–1. Baranī gives a more general account of the growth of the hostility of the sultan towards the shaykh. The prospect of the downfall of the sultan, he remarks, became as clear as day to observers when he began to abuse Shaykh Niẓām al-Dīn and to forbid the *maliks* of his court to visit Niẓām al-Dīn at Ghiyāthpūr. Time and again in diverse forms of intoxication, he said with the tongue of recklessness that he would give a thousand *tankas* of gold to the man who brought the head of Niẓām al-Dīn. Then he met Shaykh Niẓām al-Dīn at the recitation on the third day after death in the enclosure of Shaykh

Niẓām al-Dīn went to the tomb of his mother, who was buried in Delhi, and stated that the sultan desired to injure him. If before the end of the month 'his business was not settled' (*kār-i ū ba-kifāyat na-rasad*), he would not come to visit her then. The first of the month (it is explained) was the anniversary of the shaykh's mother's death. After his return from this visit, as the first of the month drew near, Niẓām al-Dīn's followers became increasingly concerned; but the shaykh, deriving assurance from his submission of the matter to his mother, sat waiting for what the future had in store. On the last night before the beginning of the new month, Khusraw Khān, the favourite of the sultan, treacherously cut off his head, throwing the sultan's body down from the roof of the palace and setting the head on top of a lance to display it to the populace.[21]

Żiyā' al-Dīn Rūmī, where the sultan did not show courtesy towards the shaykh nor acknowledge his salutation. Wishing to pick a quarrel with the shaykh, he took as a companion the *Shaykhzāda* of Jām, who was an enemy of Niẓām al-Dīn, and summoned the *Shaykh al-Islām* Rukn al-Dīn of Multan to the capital city: Baranī, *Ta'rīkh*, p. 396. The Baranī variant has a briefer account of the Sultan's hostility to Niẓām al-Dīn, the 'Pole-star of the world and Ka'ba of its inhabitants'; Digby MS 57, f. 144 [now in the Bodleian Library, University of Oxford, MS S. Digby Or. 54 ~DL]. Ibn Baṭṭuṭa gives the name of the *Shaykhzāda* of Jām as Shaykh Shihāb al-Dīn, with a lengthy account of his imprisonment and death at the hands of Muḥammad bin Tughluq; Ibn Baṭṭūṭa, *Riḥla*, vol. III, pp. 293–8; tr. Gibb, vol. III, pp. 697–700. This *Shaykhzāda* must therefore be distinguished from the *Shaykhzāda* Ḥusām al-Dīn who a few years later played a part in the proceedings against Niẓām al-Dīn before Sultan Ghiyāth al-Dīn Tughluq; see note 24 below.

[21] Khwurd, *Siyar al-awliyā'*, p. 151. For other accounts of relations between Sultan Quṭb al-Dīn Mubārak and Shaykh Niẓām al-Dīn, see Qalandar, *Khayr al-majālis*, p. 258; Jamālī, *Siyar al-'ārifīn*, pp. 74–5, 75–8. Jamālī tells the same story of the conflict between sultan and shaykh with the same outcome, at greater length with circumstantial details, some of which conflict with those of the earlier source; cf. notes 16, 25, 51.

The conflict between Shaykh Niẓām al-Dīn and Sultan Ghiyāth al-Dīn Tughluq (r. 1320–5) has passed into folk tradition.[22] The background to the quarrel is not adequately explained in our earliest main source, the *Siyar al-awliyā'*, but the account of the early sixteenth-century *Siyar al-'ārifīn* (whose author Jamālī customarily devotes more attention than his predecessor to the topic of the maintenance of *khānaqāhs*) is plausible.

After the murder of Sultan Quṭb al-Dīn Mubārak, his usurping successor Khusraw Khān distributed large sums to *darwēshs* in the city. Three shaykhs of note refused to receive these but Niẓām al-Dīn took the 5 lakhs of *tankas* which he had been sent, and shared this sum out among the *faqīrs* and the deserving poor of the city. Other shaykhs who had received such sums from Khusraw Khān kept them in trust. After Ghiyāth al-Dīn Tughluq defeated Khusraw Khān and ascended the throne, he sought to recover the donations which had left the treasury depleted. Niẓām al-Dīn argued that the sum he had received was from the *bayt al-māl* (the public treasury of Muslim believers) and he had therefore distributed it to the deserving, keeping nothing for himself. The sultan was silenced by this reply, but his heart was turned against Niẓām al-Dīn.[23]

The sequel to this was that, at the instance of a hostile group motivated by envy (*ḥasad*), Sultan Ghiyāth al-Dīn allowed proceedings to be instituted in which Niẓām al-Dīn had to defend the legitimacy, according to Muslim law, of his practice of *samā'* (listening to music). The accusers were

[22] See below, p. 68.

[23] Jamālī, *Siyar al-'ārifīn*, p. 88. For the theory of the *bayt al-māl* or public treasury and of distribution to the needy from it, see N.P. Aghnides, *Mohammedan Theories of Finance*, repr., Lahore: Premier Book House, 1961, pp. 431–79; cf. I.H. Qureshi, *The Administration of the Sultanate of Delhī*, 4th edn., Karachi: Pakistan Historical Society, 1958, pp. 241–2, quoting 'Afīf.

led, according to Amīr Khwurd in the *Siyar al-awliyā'*, by an immigrant *shaykhzāda* called Ḥusām al-Dīn, who had originally received hospitality from Shaykh Niẓām al-Dīn; and by Qażī Jalāl al-Dīn, who held the office of *Nā'ib Ḥākim* (Deputy Governor of the city).[24]

Shaykh Niẓām al-Dīn was obliged to appear in person before a large gathering presided over by the sultan himself. Amīr Khwurd says that this took place at the sultan's palace (*dar-i sarāy-i bādshāh*), but Jamālī adds the detail that this was in the sultan's new fortress of Tughluqābād in south Delhi.[25] The case was that *samā'* was unlawful according to the opinion of Imām Abū Ḥanīfa. Arguments turned on whether *ḥadīths* of the Prophet could be accepted which were not recognized by the Ḥanafī school of law. Evidence was given by Mawlānā 'Alam al-Dīn, a grandson of the great Shaykh Bahā' al-Dīn Zakariyyā' of Multan. 'Alam al-

[24] Another early source mentions as leaders of the faction who compiled the *maḥżar* (legal judgement) the grandson of Qāżī Minhāj (the thirteenth-century historian Jūzjānī, compiler of the *Ṭabaqāt-i Nāṣirī*) and the *Shaykh al-Islām*; Ashraf Jahāngīr Simnānī, *Makhtūbāt i-Ashrafī*, British Library MS Or. 267, f. 129b. With regard to the part played by this immigrant *Shaykhzāda*, the title itself is faintly derogatory though evidently current at the sultan's court, cf. Ibn Baṭṭūṭa, *Riḥla*, tr. Husain, pp. 71, 89, 173; cf. also note 20 above. It is evident from Ibn Baṭṭūṭa's narrative of his Indian travels, and from the conversations of Sayyid Muhammad Gēsūdarāz and from other references, that hostility existed between the numerous foreigners from the lands of Islam who sought their fortunes at the court of the fourteenth-century Delhi sultans and the old established Muslim families of the capital city; see Ibn Baṭṭūṭa, *Riḥla*, tr. Husain, p. 107, and note 1; Baranī, *Ta'rīkh*, pp. 461–2; Sayyid Muḥammad Akbar Ḥusaynī, *Jawāmi' al-kalim*, Kanpur/Hyderabad: Intiẓāmī Press, 1352 Faṣlī, p. 136; Sīrhindī, *Ta'rīkh-i Mubārakshāhī*, p. 107.

[25] Jamālī, *Siyar al-'ārifīn*, pp. 88–9. This is not improbable, but Jamālī is inclined to fill out from imagination or conjecture rather than from another tradition the details of anecdotes from earlier sources; see Digby, 'Qalandars and Related Groups', p. 93 [this volume, pp. 230–1].

Dīn had written a treatise on the topic of the lawfulness of *samā'* and had travelled to 'Baghdād and Shām and Rūm.' He testified that *samā'* was practised by the shaykhs of those lands without prohibition. The sultan then complied with Niẓām al-Dīn's request and refused to make a pronouncement upon the subject. According to a 'less trustworthy source' also mentioned but not named by Amīr Khwurd, the sultan pronounced *samā'* lawful for Niẓām al-Dīn, but not for others 'like the group (*ṭā'ifa*) of the Qalandars and Ḥaydarīs'.[26]

The effective outcome of the last incident was a check on the pretensions of the shaykh. Niẓām al-Dīn had been compelled to appear at the sultan's judicial inquest (*maḥżar*) and to submit to judgement. The humiliation was evidently mitigated by the sultan's prudent consideration that the shaykh and his followers should not be pressed to an extreme confrontation. One of the principal attackers, Qāżī Jalāl al-Dīn, had in the course of the proceedings uttered a threat that, if Niẓām al-Dīn continued to hold *samā'*, he would intervene by virtue of his office of *Nā'ib Ḥākim*. The shaykh had replied that he should (i.e. would) be retired from that office. According to Amīr Khwurd, he was relieved of it twelve days later; this author adds that he soon 'went on a journey' (i.e. died).[27] According to Jamālī, just after Niẓām al-Dīn had returned to his *khānaqāh* the news reached him that the sultan was much ashamed, and had dismissed the Qāżī from his post as *Ḥākim*.[28]

[26] Khwurd, *Siyar al-awliyā'*, pp. 526–30. For the Qalandars and Haydarīs and the problems posed by them, see Digby, 'Qalandars and Related Groups', especially pp. 72–7 [this volume, pp. 203–9].

[27] Khwurd, *Siyar al-awliyā'*, pp. 528–9. Simnānī, *Maktūbāt-i Ashrafī*, f. 129b, states that the enemies of the shaykh 'fell ill in that very assembly, and in two or three days most of the accusers took their baggage to the caravan of the Last Day.'

[28] Jamālī, *Siyar al-'ārifīn*, p. 90. The *qāżī*'s name is there given as Rukn al-Dīn.

In this Sufi ideology, the imposition of the will of the sultan against that of the shaykh was unacceptable. For if the sultan could act thus with impunity, the *wilāyat* of the shaykh was cast into doubt in the minds of his followers. In the four accounts, surveyed above, of Niẓām al-Dīn's relations with four different sultans of Delhi, the shaykh's desire to avoid a meeting prevailed without a contest in the first two instances over the importunities of Jalāl al-Dīn Fērōz Khaljī and 'Alā' al-Dīn Khaljī. In the third case, the threat of compulsion by Quṭb al-Dīn Mubārak leads to the brutal and exemplary death of the sultan. But in the fourth case the shaykh was in fact compelled to attend the sultan's summons and hear his judgement. What would be the consequences of this?

Possibly, in an attempt to avert further trouble, the *Nā'ib Ḥākim*, who had been told by the shaykh that he would be retired from his post, was so retired. Thus, the *nafas* (pronouncement) of the shaykh was not discredited.[29] Yet this retirement was not in itself a sufficiently momentous consequence of the flouting of the shaykh's authority to satisfy his devotees.

Predictably, the *Siyar al-awliyā'* reproduces remarks of the shaykh after the conclusion of the inquest (*maḥżar*). Surprisingly, they are said to be taken from a now lost work of the main contemporary historian of the Delhi Sultanate, the *Ḥasrat-nāma* ('Book of Regret') of Żiyā' al-Dīn Baranī. After the shaykh had returned home, he summoned Baranī together with Mawlānā Muḥyī al-Dīn Kāshānī and the poet Amīr Khusraw at the time of the midday prayer. He said that the men of learning were filled with envy and enmity, and had found the field open. In 'our city' (Delhi) the narrations of *fiqh* had been preferred to *ḥadīth*; and *ḥadīth* of the Shāfi'ī school had been ignored. What would be the fate of a city where such insolence was committed? How could it flourish?

29 See the anecdote of the undoing of the Khwārazmshāh, quoted above.

It would be strange if it was not reduced to a pile of bricks! As a result of the wickedness of the unsound faith of the *'ulamā'*, upon the city there would rain from heaven calamity and exile, famine, and plague.

In the view of the writer, the comminations of the shaykh were amply fulfilled. Within four years of the event, all the *'ulamā'* who were in that *maḥżar*, and others because of them, were exiled to Devgīr (Dawlatābād). Most of them set out for Devgīr, and a mortal famine and epidemic appeared in the city (of Delhi).[30] These calamities were not at an end at the time of writing.[31] Every word that had been spoken

[30] Two years after the death of Niẓām al-Dīn, the transfer of the population of Delhi to Devgīr or Dawlatābād was initiated in 1327. The date of the move, which has been contested, is confirmed by the variant recension of Baranī, *Ta'rīkh*, Digby MS 57, f. 160; Bodleian MS 173, f. 191; Bihāmad Khānī, *Ta'rīkh-i Muḥammadī*, British Library MS Or. 137, ff. 399–400. The mention of famine and plague (*wabā*) appears to refer to the period of the return of Muḥammad bin Tughluq to Delhi with an army bearing the disease (possibly the great bubonic plague of the Black Death) after his Warangal expedition; see Baranī, *Ta'rīkh*, pp. 481–2; Digby MS 57, f. 161; Bodleian MS 173, ff. 194–5; 'Iṣāmī, *Futūḥ al-salāṭīn*, pp. 469–71. The standard recension of Baranī is specific on famine around Delhi at the time of the sultan's return, while the variant mentions the gradual drifting back of the population from Dawlatābād which preceded this. 'Iṣāmī is clear that the epidemic still affected the army when the sultan marched from Dawlatābād to Delhi; and Gēsūdarāz describes its ravages in Delhi around 1337, see Ḥusaynī, *Jawāmi' al-kalim*, p. 293. A.M. Husain gives a date of January 1335 to July 1337 for 'the Emperor's journey from Delhi to Warangal and back', but advances no reasons for his conjecture; see A.M. Husain, *Tughluq Dynasty*, Calcutta: Thacker Spink & Co., 1963, p. 657.

[31] The question arises whether these words are part of the quotation from the lost *Ḥasrat-nāma* of Baranī, or a remark of Amīr Khwurd himself. If they were the latter, they could date from as late as *c.*1400, when the latest additions to the text of the *Siyar al-awliyā'* appear to have been made. This is improbable in view of the tranquillity and partial return to prosperity of the early decades of the reign of Fērōz Shāh Tughluq. If, as is likely, the words are those of the *Ḥasrat-nāma*, it is unlikely that they

by the blessed tongue of *Ḥaẓrat Sulṭān al-mashā'ikh* (Niẓām al-Dīn) had come to pass.[32]

The *Siyar al-awliyā'*, which includes this notice of the fate of the *'ulamā'* who participated in the *maḥẓar* and of the city of Delhi itself, has no mention of the fate which befell Sultan Ghiyāth al-Dīn Tughluq. He was killed by the collapse of a pavilion of welcome after a victorious campaign, one stage away from the capital to which he was returning. The pavilion was erected by his son and successor Muḥammad bin Tughluq, and some contemporaries considered that its collapse was not accidental.[33] The silence of the *Siyar al-awliyā'* regarding this event may have been a politic one, as the work was mostly written in the reign of a sovereign of the dynasty who honoured the memory of his kinsman and predecessors.[34]

The death of Sultan Ghiyāth al-Dīn Tughluq gave rise to one of the best-known stories regarding Shaykh Niẓām al-

---

were written at the same time as the accounts by Baranī in his *Ta'rīkh-i Fērōzshāhī* of Muḥammad bin Tughluq's reign. The first of these was evidently completed in 1354, and the revised version two years later. In these there is no mention of Niẓām al-Dīn's displeasure among the causes of the disasters, which are there ascribed to the waywardness of the Sultan Muḥammad. It would therefore seem likely that the *Ḥasrat-nāma* is a composition from an earlier phase of Baranī's thought, probably written between 1335 and 1340.

[32] Khwurd, *Siyar al-awliyā'*, pp. 531–2.

[33] The accusation is openly voiced by Ibn Baṭṭūṭa, whose account was recorded, out of range of the wrath of the Tughluqs, in the distant Maghrib: Ibn Baṭṭūṭa, *Riḥla*, vol. III, pp. 212–13; tr. Gibb, vol. III, pp. 654–5.

[34] Cf. the efforts of Fērōz Shāh to procure letters of satisfaction (*khuṭūṭ-i khwushnūdī*) from the heirs of those whom Sultan Muḥammad had killed or mutilated; Feroz Shāh Tughluq, *Futūḥāt-i Fērōzshāhī*, ed. S.A, Rashid, Aligarh: Aligarh Muslim University, 1954, p. 16; tr. in H.M. Elliot and J. Dowson, *The History of India as Told by its Own Historians*, London: Trübner and Co., 1872, vol. IV, p. 385.

Dīn, and to a popular proverb of which the Urdu translation is still current: 'Delhi is yet far away! (*hanōz Delhī dūr ast*)'. The sultan, on his return from a victorious campaign in the east was threatening a further reckoning with the shaykh, who is said to have made this pronouncement (*nafas*). The earliest clear reference to the shaykh uttering the sentence is in the chronicle of Sīrhindī, written just over a century later.[35] Ibn Baṭṭūṭa, who was in Delhi a decade after the event, ascribes the statement to astrologers, but he reports that Niẓām al-Dīn in an ecstasy had already bestowed the kingdom on Muḥammad bin Tughluq. It is possible that the association of the shaykh with the sentence had already been made, but Ibn Baṭṭūṭa, as elsewhere, had misunderstood or misremembered the narrative of his informant.[36]

In spite of this anecdote of Niẓām al-Dīn's premature approval of the new ruler, relations between Sufi shaykhs and the reigning Sultan of Delhi reached a nadir in the reign of Muḥammad bin Tughluq (1325–51). Muḥammad bin Tughluq's harsh treatment of shaykhs, some examples of which are vividly described by Ibn Baṭṭūṭa, continued for many years without injury to himself;[37] but in the opinion

[35] Sīrhindī, *Ta'rīkh-i Mubārakshāhī*, p. 97. A calque of this story, set in the Deccan some fifty years later, displays the Bahmanī sultan Mujāhid Shāh (r. 1375–78) struck down by the sword of an African slave as he returned from the siege of Adhoni for a reckoning with Shaykh Sirāj al-Dīn Junaydī; see Muḥammad Sulṭān, *Armughān-i Sulṭānī*, Agra: Maṭba'-i Mufīd-i 'Ām, 1902, p. 167.

[36] Ibn Baṭṭūṭa, *Riḥla*, vol. III, pp. 212–13. For the bestowal of the kingdom by Sufi shaykhs and this instance, see below.

[37] Ibn Baṭṭūṭa, *Riḥla*, vol. III, pp. 293–311; tr. Gibb, vol. III, pp. 697–706; for the sultan's quarrel with the shaykhs, see M. Habib, 'Shaikh Nasiruddin Mahmud Chiragh-i Delhi as a Great Historical Personality', repr. in *Politics and Society During the Early Medieval Period: Collected Works of Professor Mohammad Habib*, ed. Nizami, Delhi: People's Publishing House, 1974, pp. 367–73.

of the author of the *Siyar al-awliyā'*, it ultimately led to his comfortless death in a distant land.

Amīr Khwurd observes that at the beginning of the Sultan's rule, when the kingdom of Hindostan attained a great expansion, he caused injuries to Shaykh Naṣīr al-Dīn Maḥmūd (Shaykh Niẓām al-Dīn's *khalīfa* or successor at Delhi), who 'in the opinion of everybody' was the shaykh of his age, and was obeyed by the whole population. Naṣīr al-Dīn Maḥmūd, following the example of his *pīrs* (the great Chishtī shaykhs), thought it proper to endure all this and did not strive for retribution, until the time when this king, at the end of his life, went to Thattha, which is 1,000 *karōhs* away from Delhi, on the campaign against the rebel Ṭāghī.[38] From there he summoned Shaykh Naṣīr al-Dīn Maḥmūd together with *'ulamā'* and holy men (from the capital of Delhi) to join him, and he did not show to them the respect that they deserved. Transporting them thus brought the king from the throne (*takht*) of sultanate to the planks (*takhta*) of the bier on which he was borne back to the city (of Delhi).[39]

Devout contemporaries sought for explanations of the lack of immediate retribution upon Sultan Muḥammad bin Tughluq for his persecution of Sufi shaykhs and in particular for his coercion of Shaykh Naṣīr al-Dīn Maḥmūd, 'the lamp of Delhi'. The shaykh himself, it is recorded, saw the sultan's persecution as God's punishment for some undisclosed fault of his own. 'There was a matter between me and God. For

[38] See Digby, 'Muḥammad bin Tughluq's Last Years in Kathiavad and his Invasions of Thatha', in *Sind Through the Centuries*, ed. Khuhro, Karachi: Oxford University Press, 1981, pp. 130–8 [*L&WSD* VI.3], and references there given.

[39] Khwurd, *Siyar al-awliyā'*, pp. 245–6. More correctly, the sultan summoned Shaykh Naṣīr al-Dīn Maḥmūd and other notables of Delhi to Kathiawar before his army crossed the Rann of Kacch to Thattha in Sind.

that I suffered this.'[40] The view of a fellow-*khalīfa* of Niẓām al-Dīn, the aged Shaykh Burhān al-Dīn at Dawlatābād, was that the lack of divine retribution upon the sultan was the result of Naṣīr al-Dīn Maḥmūd's mild and forgiving character:

When [Burhān al-Dīn Gharīb] heard of the impolitenesses (*bē-adabīhā*) which Sultan Muḥammad had committed against the Shaykh he wept and said: 'What can I do? Khond Mawlānā Maḥmūd [Naṣīr al-Dīn Maḥmūd] is mild and generous. At this time if he wishes he could bring down the whole of the army and the people and the horses and elephants, not arousing grief.'[41]

Half a century later and from the point of view of a hagiographer of the rival Firdawsī *silsila*, it was the misconduct of Fērōz Shāh Tughluq (r. 1351–88) and of the shaykhs, '*ulamā*', and population of the city of Delhi in putting to death two disciples of Shaykh Sharaf al-Dīn Manērī which brought about the sequence of events leading to the downfall of the greater Delhi Sultanate.[42] When the news of the execution of his disciples reached Sharaf al-Dīn (in Bihār), he said: 'In a city where they have shed the blood of such holy men—it would be strange if such a city continued to flourish!'

It happened as he said. The ruin began in Fērōz Shāh's lifetime. For all his pomp, the Sultan lost control in the city itself. The son of the Sultan [i.e. Prince Muḥammad Shāh] fought with the *Wazīr* Khān-i Jahān. Many Muslims were killed in the incident and the city faced ruin. Then the royal slaves seized Delhi and fought with the son of the Sultan. After this, the Mughals [i.e. Amīr Timur with his army] came and turned Delhi upside down.[43]

[40] Ibid., p. 246. Cf. Qalandar, *Khayr al-majālis*, Nizami's introduction, p. 58.
[41] Ḥusaynī, *Jawāmi' al-kalim*, p. 240.
[42] For the hostility between the Chishtī and Firdawsī *silsilas*, see Digby, 'The Sufi Shaikh', pp. 63–7 [this volume, pp. 17–25].
[43] Shaykh Shu'ayb, *Manāqib al-aṣfiyā'*, Calcutta: Nur al-Afaq Press, 1895, p. 130.

Though one may reject the explanation of the cause of the débâcle as being Shaykh Sharaf al-Dīn's displeasure, this is an accurate brief summary of the course of events in the capital city of Delhi in the years from 1387 to 1398.[44]

Sufis and Kingmaking: The Shaykh as the Bestower of the Sultan's Good Fortune in the Delhi Sultanate

The corollary of the belief repeatedly visible in the narratives quoted above, that an offence against a Sufi shaykh will lead to the downfall of a ruler, is the belief that such shaykhs also had the power to bestow kingship upon individuals they encountered, or to foresee the attainment of a throne by such men. Such a belief is more likely to flourish in a society where there is no strong tradition of primogeniture or hereditary rule, and usurpations of power are common. This power attributed to Sufi shaykhs is one of the stock images of Persian poets of the period, among them Ḥāfiẓ:

> *dalq-i gadā-yi 'ishq-rā ganj buvad dar āstīn zūd ba-salṭanat rasad harki buvad gadā-yi tu*[45]

> The cloak of the beggar of love has a treasure in its sleeve;
> Anyone who is your beggar swiftly attains sovereignty.

[44] See K.S. Lal, *Twilight of the Sultanate*, Bombay: Asia Publishing House, 1963, pp. 1–15, 27–31; substantially reinterpreted by Simon Digby, *War-Horse and Elephant in the Dehlī Sultanate*, Oxford: Orient Monographs, 1971, pp. 74–82 [*L&WSD* V].

[45] *Dīwān-i Ḥāfiẓ*, ed. M. Qazwīnī and A. Ghanī, Tehran: Zavvār, 1320 Shamsī/AD 1941, no. 411, p. 284. Cf. ibid., no. 49, *bayt* 7, p. 35:

> Kings are the direction of prayer of the world, and yet
> Its reason is service of the presence of *darvēshs*.

In India, during the Delhi Sultanate and later, recorded examples of the bestowal of kingship by Sufis are numerous. The earliest anecdote is of the first decade of the thirteenth century. Ḥusām al-Dīn ʻAważ Khaljī, who overran Bengal in the aftermath of the initial conquest of Delhi, while he was travelling with a laden ass in the hilly region of modern Afghanistan between Zawulistan and Ghor, was told by two *faqīrs*: 'O Chief, go to Hindōstān! We give you the country as far as Islam has spread!'[46] Such good fortune was less impressive if it was bestowed upon a prince who could claim to be legitimate heir to a throne. In recollection and in folk tradition, such anecdotes were particularly liable to be attached to slaves who rose to the throne; and this was the condition of the *mamlūk* or 'Slave Sultans' of thirteenth-century Delhi. Jūzjānī, the chronicler who related the previous anecdote, records an anecdote of the second independent Sultan of Delhi, Shams al-Dīn Iltutmish (r. 1210–35). Jūzjānī states that he heard the story from a trustworthy witness who had heard it from the lips of the Sultan himself:

> As a boy-slave at Bukhara, the future Sultan was sent out to purchase grapes. In the street he lost the money and started to cry. A *faqīr* took his hand, bought some grapes, and told him: 'When you attain rule and dominion, take care that you show respect to *faqīrs* and holy folk!'
>
> The Sultan added: 'I swore this to him, and the good fortune and rule that I have attained, I have attained from the glance of that *darwēsh*!'[47]

A fourteenth-century source relates an alternative bestowal of kingship upon the same sultan. When Qāżī

[46] Minhāj-i Sirāj Jūzjānī, *Ṭabaqāt-i Nāṣirī*, Calcutta: College Press, 1864, pp. 160–1.
[47] Ibid., p. 167.

Ḥamīd al-Dīn Nagawrī (the Suhrawardi friend of the Chishti shaykh Quṭb al-Dīn Bakhtyār Kākī) came to Delhi, he was in *samā‘* day and night, until the *‘ulamā’* arraigned him and made Sultan Iltutmish ask him for justification. Qāżī Ḥamīd stated that he and the sultan used to be in the same assemblies in Baghdad, with the Qāżī all night in *samā‘* and *raqṣ* (dancing). The sultan was the little slave-boy who stood all night by the lamp with a pair of scissors to trim the wick.

darān shab turā mulk-i Hindōstān
bidādand z-ān chākarī ‘ārifān

On the night for that service the ‘knowers’ (*‘ārifān*, mystics) gave you the kingdom of Hindōstān.[48]

Yet another story of a bestowal of tidings of future kingship upon Iltutmish exists in four differing versions of varying degrees of elaborateness. The earliest exists in the conversations of Shaykh Niẓām al-Dīn, told by him in 1319. The incident must be presumed, from the personages, to have been set in Baghdad like the conferral recorded by ‘Iṣāmī reproduced above.[49] Shaykh Niẓām al-Dīn's previous remarks in his conversation had been about Sultan Shams al-Dīn Iltutmish. After that he made another remark about him: 'He had met with Shaykh Shihāb al-Dīn Suhrawardī

[48] ‘Iṣāmī, *Futūḥ al-salāṭīn*, p. 119; cf. Nizami, *Some Aspects*, pp. 302–3.

[49] The earliest anecdote, recorded by Jūzjānī with a more than fair semblance of historicity, is set in Bukhara. In the late twelfth century, a boy-slave could have been brought from Bukhara to Baghdad, but this diminishes the likelihood of him subsequently becoming a slave-élite soldier in the Ghorid army of India. For the purpose of this anecdote and those which follow, Baghdad had a much greater Sufi charisma in this period; and the future ruler's transfer there would have been necessary for his encounter with some of the shaykhs mentioned. See also notes 50, 52 below.

and Shaykh Awḥad Kirmānī, and one of them had said to him, "You will be a King!"'[50]

In the early sixteenth century, Jamālī sought to attach this information to another anecdote related by Jūzjānī of the purchase of Iltutmish by the trader Khwāja Jamāl al-Dīn, who took him to sell in India. At the age of fifteen, when he had discretion, the future Sultan passed before the *khānaqāh* of Shaykh Shihāb al-Dīn Suhrawardī, and his gaze fell upon the Shaykh. Awḥad al-Dīn Kirmānī was also present. The boy entered the *khānaqāh* and offered some broken pieces (of precious metal) from his waistband, asking for a recitation of the *Fātiḥa*. After the recitation, Shihāb al-Dīn said: 'I see the light of sultanate shining in the face of this fellow!' Awḥad al-Dīn added: 'From your *baraka* during his worldly rule his faith will remain intact.'[51]

Long before Jamālī's embellishments, another hagiographical tradition had transferred the credit of this bestowal to the first of the Chishti shaykhs in India, Mu'īn al-Dīn. The transfer is first made by a less scrupulous source, one of the spurious collections of *Malfūẓāt* of the line of Chishti shaykhs produced in direct and almost immediate imitation of the *Fawā'id al-fu'ād*.[52] The narration is (falsely)

[50] 'Alā' Sijzī, *Fawā'id al-fu'ād*, p. 358; conversation of 13 Safar 719/5 April 1319. [The Hijri date here, and the Gregorian date in the main text ('1309'), were mistranscribed in the original publication. Cf. Bruce B. Lawrence, *Nizam Ad-din Awliya: Morals for the Heart*, New York: Beacon Books, 1991, p. 318. ~DL] The association of Shihāb al-Dīn Suhrawardī and Awḥad al-Dīn Kirmānī in Baghdad is well attested: see the early anonymous *Manāqib-i Awḥad al-Dīn*, ed. B. Furuzanfar, Tehran: Bungāh-i Tarjumah va nashr-i Kitāb, 1347 Shamsī/AD 1969, passim.

[51] Jamālī, *Siyar al-'ārifīn*, pp. 112–13. As elsewhere, Jamālī has tidied up the anecdote as found in his source and adorned it with picturesque details giving it a bogus but attractive circumstantiality.

[52] M. Habib first recognized the character of such spurious collections of Chishtī *Malfūẓāt*, and he also noted the evidence for their circulation before the middle of the fourteenth century; see Habib, 'Shaikh

attributed to Quṭb al-Dīn Bakhtyār Kākī who has figured in previous anecdotes:

Shaykh Mu'īn al-Dīn Ḥasan Sijzī, Shaykh Awḥad Kirmānī, Shaykh Shihāb al-Dīn Suhrawardī and I myself were sitting together and we were telling tales of past saints. Sultan Shams al-Dīn—may God illuminate his proofs—was then twelve years old and at that moment passed by with a cup in his hand. The glance of those holy men fell upon him, and straightaway a pronouncement (*nafas*) came out from the tongue of Shaykh Mu'īn al-Dīn Hasan Sijzī: 'This child will be King of Delhi. God will not take him from the world till he reaches kingship.'

Then the *khwāja* [Quṭb al-Dīn] remarked: 'The tidings (*nafas*) of holy men are a fine thing!'[53]

We may note that the author of this narrative (pseudo-Farīd al-Dīn) has made the recipient more of a child (*kōdak*), three years younger than the youthful warrior with some savings to offer the Shaykh as he appears in Jamālī's version. To achieve kingship at this period he needs must have been a slave, and the cup (*kāsa*) in his hand would indicate that he was employed as a youthful cupbearer (*sāqī*).

The seventeenth-century Chishti hagiography *Siyar al-aqtāb* also gives the credit for these 'tidings' to Mu'īn al-Dīn:

Nasiruddin Mahmud Chiragh-i Delhi', pp. 402, 410–11; cf. Qalandar, *Khayr al-majālis*, pp. 52–3. Further evidence for this dating is provided by citations of the *malfūẓ-i Khwāja Quṭb al-Dīn* in the (genuine) *Malfūẓāt* of Sharaf al-Dīn Manērī, *Mukhkh al-ma'ānī*, Digby MS 8, ff. 27a, 45b [now in the Bodleian Library, University of Oxford, MS S. Digby Or. 6 ~DL]. The presence of Mu'īn al-Dīn in this company at Baghdad is at best doubtful; see Digby, 'The Sufi Shaikh', p. 62 [this volume, p. 13]; P.M. Currie, *The Shrine and Cult of Mu'īn al-Dīn*, Delhi: Oxford University Press, 1989, map on front endpaper of places associated by successive hagiographers with the travels of the shaykh.

53 Pseudo-Farīd al-Dīn, *Fawā'id al-sālikīn*, Delhi: Mujtabā'ī Press, 1311/1892, p. 16.

One day Mu'īn al-Dīn was sitting in the company of Awḥad al-Dīn Kirmānī and Shihāb al-Dīn 'Umar Suhrawardī. Suddenly the future Sultan passed by with a bow and arrow in his hand.

'My friends!', Mu'īn al-Dīn observed, 'this child will be Sultan of Delhi, for I have seen in the tablet [of the heavens] that he will not leave the world until he becomes Sultan of Delhi.'[54]

This anecdote has added a touch of grandeur to its predecessor, with the shaykh looking at the 'preserved tablet' of the heavens, while the bow and arrow, substituted for the cup in the preceding source, suitably prefigure a military career.

In the case of the next slave to attain the throne of Delhi, Sultan Ghiyāth al-Dīn Balban (r. 1266–87), two accounts of the bestowal of kingship resemble those related with regard to the choice by *faqīrs* of Iltutmish in his boyhood. In Delhi or in Bukhara the boy-slave Balban made an offering to a *faqīr*, who then bestowed the realm of Hindōstan upon him. The offering was a copper coin and the place of the incident was Delhi, according to the story told to Ibn Baṭṭūṭa in Delhi itself in the third decade of the fourteenth century.[55] It was in Bukhara, and the gift was a pomegranate according to the verse chronicle of 'Isāmī, who wrote in the Deccan some twenty years after the Arab traveller heard the story in Delhi.[56]

A third account, also recorded in the fourteenth century, regarding the bestowal of kingship on Balban, when the latter was not a slave-boy but a powerful and ambitious general, is found in the *Siyar al-awliyā'*. The incident is historically

[54] Ilāhdiyā Chishtī, *Siyar al-aqṭāb*, p. 134. Ilāhdiyā is drawing upon Pseudo-Farīd quoted above, affording an identifiable instance of the travelling of a visibly falsified anecdote from a less reputable source into a more honest, if credulous, compilation.

[55] Ibn Baṭṭūṭa, *Riḥla*, vol. III, p. 171; tr. Husain, p. 36.

[56] 'Iṣāmī, *Futūḥ al-salāṭīn*, pp. 123–4.

plausible and is an indication of the growing influence of the Chishti *silsila* in the period in which it is set, the middle of the thirteenth century. The account is of the future sultan's visit to Shaykh Farīd al-Dīn at Ajodhan. Balban, then known by the title of Ulugh Khān, was defending the western marches of the Delhi Sultanate against the incursions of the Mongols. He cherished an ambition to succeed the reigning sultan, his father-in-law Naṣīr al-Dīn Maḥmūd. Ulugh Khān offered the shaykh a sum of silver and the grants (*mithāl*) of four villages. Farīd accepted the silver but not the grants. Balban then demanded some statement of 'what the Shaykh had in mind'. Farīd al-Dīn replied with a suitably oracular pronouncement. He recited two couplets of Persian verse, which might be interpreted as an injunction to the inquirer to rule well should he attain to power in spite of evident imperfections of character ('he was no angel'). According to the *Siyar al-awliyā'*, this answer appears to have pleased the future usurper.[57]

Perhaps the most powerful of all the sultans of Delhi was 'Alā' al-Dīn Khaljī (r. 1295–1316), who murdered his uncle and usurped the throne. The fourteenth-century verse chronicle of 'Iṣāmī, which draws a significant amount of its material from folk tradition, records that he received two nominations to sovereignty from the wilder *bē-shar'* end of the spectrum of Sufi behaviour. 'Iṣāmī's first anecdote is of a madman known (possibly in mockery) as Qāżī 'Ālam, who was in the habit of throwing stones from a balcony in the same town of Karra, an important southern frontier town close to modern Allahabad [now Prayagraj], and of wandering through the bazaar there with an African servant cracking a whip. He proffered a ring to 'Alā' al-Din who was

[57] Khwurd, *Siyar al-awliyā'*, pp. 79–80. The story of the visit of Ulugh Khān, without mention of the inquiry and prophecy, is told in 'Alā' Sijzī, *Fawā'id al-fu'ād*, p. 171, and again in Khwurd, *Siyar al-awliyā'*, p. 250.

passing by, and proclaimed that the realm of Hindōstan was bestowed upon him.[58] The gesture of this *darwēsh* seems to be a remote reminiscence of the divine investiture of the Sasanian rulers of Iran by the bestowal of a ring or wreath;[59] a similar gesture by a *darwēsh* is also recorded in eleventh-century Iran.[60] The second bestowal was from the *majdhūb* or madman known as Khwāja Gurg ('Wolf'), also of the town of Karra. Gurg greeted the future sultan as he rode up to the shop-platform where he was seated, remarking that God had made him the rider of Fortune (*dawlat*, also the power of the state).[61]

Sultan Ghiyāth al-Dīn Tughluq is said in a contemporary poem to have been nominated to the throne by an unnamed *pīr* whom he saw in a dream. It may have been politic of Amīr Khusraw not to name the *pīr*.[62] In the modern oral tradition of the Panjab, 'Bābā' Farīd al-Dīn is said to have nominated this monarch, evidently many decades before the fulfilment of the prophecy.[63] Regarding Ghiyāth al-Dīn's

[58] 'Iṣāmī, *Futūḥ al-salāṭīn*, pp. 225–6. The name of this man, which can be inferred from p. 225, line 2, and p. 226, line 5, is given in the rubric on p. 224. He is described as from Damascus.

[59] For depictions of the divine bestowal on Sasanian monarchs, see F. Sarre, *Die Kunst des alten Persien*, Berlin: B. Cassirer, 1922, pp. 37–8, 42, pl. 70, 71, 78, 81. For the survival of this symbolism in the Islamic world, see Ernest J. Grube, 'Fostat Fragments', in *Islamic Painting and the Arts of the Book*, ed. B.W. Robinson, London: Faber and Faber, 1976, p. 35.

[60] For Bābā Ṭāhir's bestowal of a ring from the top of his waterpot (*ibrīq*) on the Seljuk Sultan Ṭughril Beg, see Rāwandī, *Rāḥat al-ṣudūr*, London: Luzac, 1921, p. 99.

[61] 'Iṣāmī, *Futūḥ al-salāṭīn*, p. 229. That the name of the *majdhūb* was Gurg, and not Karak as remembered in modern times, is evident from his recorded remarks and verses; see Digby, 'Qalandars and Related Groups', n. 116 [this volume, p. 236, n. 115].

[62] Amīr Khusraw, *Tughluq-nāma*, Hyderabad/Awrangabad: Maṭba' Urdū, AH 1352/AD 1933, pp. 72–3, lines 1373–4.

[63] S.M. Ikrām, *Āb-i Kawthar*, Lahore: Ferozesons, 1965, p. 395. Both this folk tradition and Amīr Khusraw's unnamed *pīr* of note 62 probably refer

son and successor Muḥammad bin Tughluq, Ibn Baṭṭūṭa, a contemporary foreign observer, records the belief that Shaykh Niẓām al-Dīn while in a state of ecstasy had said: 'We have given him the kingdom!'[64]

At the time when Ibn Baṭṭūṭa was in Delhi, the worst troubles between Sultan Muḥammad bin Tughluq and the Sufi shaykhs were just beginning. It is not surprising that this anecdote is not found in later Chishtī sources.[65]

Nominations to sovereignty by Sufi shaykhs continue in the period from the later fourteenth century to the sixteenth century. In the case of the last major ruler of the greater Delhi Sultanate, Sultan Fērōz Shāh Tughluq, the panegyrical historian of his reign, Shams-i Sirāj 'Afīf, presents the sultan himself in the guise of a holy man. 'Afīf provides a predictably ornate version of the bestowal of kingship on his subject. He derives the ascent of the throne by Sultan Fērōz

---

to Shaykh Farīd al-Dīn's grandson and successor, 'Alā' al-Dīn 'Mawj-i Daryā'. The connection of the Tughluq family with this shaykh dated from before they attained the throne. Muḥammad b. Tughluq erected the tomb of the shaykh which is still standing, and appointed his son Mu'izz al-Dīn to high office in Gujarāt; see Khwurd, *Siyar al-awliyā'*, p. 196. For Ghiyāth al-Dīn and his next two successors being given sovereignty by this shaykh, see 'Afīf, *Ta'rīkh*, p. 27, translated below. Cf. also 'Afīf, *Ta'rīkh*, p. 371; Baranī, *Ta'rīkh*, p. 543; Hodivala, *Studies in Indo-Muslim History*, vol. I, pp. 334–5.

64 Ibn Baṭṭūṭa, *Riḥla*, vol. III, p. 211; tr. Gibb, vol. III, p. 652. Niẓām al-Dīn died shortly (probably some months) afterwards, and Ibn Baṭṭūṭa mentions that the future sultan carried the bier of the shaykh on his shoulder, a detail which is corroborated by another contemporary Arabic source: Ibn Baṭṭūṭa, *Riḥla*, vol. III, p. 211; tr. Gibb, III, p. 654; see Hodivala, *Studies in Indo-Muslim History*, vol. I, p. 292. Understandably, mention of this, like the shaykh's words of bestowal, has been omitted from the accounts of the burial of Niẓām al-Dīn by Amīr Khwurd and later hagiographers; cf. the account of his funeral in Khwurd, *Siyar al-awliyā'*, p. 155.

65 Cf. the explanation of the cause of the same sultan's death in ibid., pp. 245–6, cited above.

Shāh from the 'tidings' (*bashārāt*) spoken by four different Sufi shaykhs. This multiplicity itself perhaps reflects the vogue among later fourteenth-century Sufis for acquiring a plurality of spiritual lineages, becoming a 'gatherer of the threads' (*jāmi' al-salāsil*).[66] The structure of each of the four anecdotes given by 'Afīf has analogues elsewhere in the corpus of Sufi anecdotal literature. 'Afīf sets their patterns beside one another with the somewhat ingenuous artistry which is characteristic of his whole composition.

The Tidings of Shaykh 'Alā' al-Dīn, Grandson of Shaykh Farīd al-Dīn

When Sultan Ghiyāth al-Dīn Tughluq [uncle of Fērōz Shāh] was *muqṭa'* (governor) of Dīpālpūr, he went to meet Shaykh 'Alā' al-Din (at Ajodhan). The shaykh had in front of him a roll of unsewn cloth. He tore four-and-a-half yards (*gaz*) from the cloth and gave it to Sultan Tughluq, telling him to tie it around his head. He gave twenty-seven yards to Sultan Muḥammad and forty yards to Sultan Fērōz, to be tied around their heads. As a result of the pronouncements of the shaykh, they each ruled for the corresponding number of years. After this, as the shaykh had given the whole of the remainder of the roll to Sultan Fērōz, the kingdom came to an end with him. 'After his departure [death], this city of Delhi came to an end, that is to say, it was sacked.'

The Tidings Heard from the Tongue of Shaykh Sharaf al-Dīn (Bū 'Alī Qalandar) of Panipat

When the same three members of the Tughluq dynasty went to meet Shaykh Sharaf al-Dīn, the Shaykh ordered his

[66] Notable examples among shaykhs in India who were the sultan's contemporaries are Sayyid Jalāl al-Dīn 'Makhdūm-i Jahāniyān' and Sayyid Ashraf Jahāngīr Simnānī.

servitors (*khādimān*) to bring food in a bowl (*kāsa*). When all three of his visitors put their hands into the bowl, Shaykh Sharaf al-Dīn said: 'Three kings are eating from one bowl!'

The Tidings from the Tongue of Niẓām al-Dīn

In the days when Sultan Fērōz was a little boy, he went to kiss the shaykh's feet (i.e. to pay his respects to the shaykh) in Ghiyāthpūr. The shaykh was much pleased by the greeting of Fērōz.

'My boy (*bābā*), what's your name?' the Shaykh asked.

'Kamāl al-Dīn', the future sultan replied.

Sultan Fērōz had the *laqab* [honorific name] Kamāl al-Dīn ['Perfection of the Faith']. When the shaykh heard this, he immediately pronounced: 'Life to perfection [i.e. a long life]! Fortune (*dawlat*, implying sovereignty) to perfection! Grace (*ni'mat*) to perfection!'[67]

The Tidings from Shaykh Naṣīr al-Dīn Maḥmūd

When Sultan Muḥammad was pursuing the rebel Ṭaghī to Thattha in Sind,[68] he took Shaykh Naṣīr al-Dīn Maḥmūd in his entourage. After Sultan Muḥammad's death in Thattha, Sultan Fērōz ascended the throne. Shaykh Naṣīr al-Dīn Maḥmūd sent him a message, asking him if he was going to rule his people justly. Otherwise, another ruler would be requested from God [i.e. by the prayers of the shaykh]. Sultan Fērōz sent the reply that he would observe clemency

[67] There is some similarity to Ḥamīd Qalandar's anecdote of why he himself had taken the name and garb of Qalandar, see *Khayr al-majālis*, pp. 10–11; Digby, 'Qalandars and Related Groups', pp. 71–2 [this volume, pp. 202–3]. Both anecdotes show Niẓām al-Dīn taking a benevolent interest in small boys attending his *khānaqāh*, impelled by their name or behaviour to make a prophecy regarding their future.

[68] See above, and notes 37, 38.

(*ḥilm*) and act with the consensus (*ittifāq*). When the shaykh heard this, he sent an answer that, if the sultan behaved with such humanity towards the people, he would ask for forty years [of life and rule] for him from God.

'Afīf here notes that some people told the story that Shaykh Naṣīr al-Dīn Maḥmūd sent thirty-nine dates to the Sultan (i.e. one for each year of future rule beyond the current year). His notice concludes: 'Hurrah for tidings upon tidings!'[69]

This last anecdote anticipates a trend, visible in the following century and later, of shaykhs participating in the public acknowledgement or enthronement of Sultans.

Among the successor states to the greater Delhi Sultanate we have evidence of traditions of such nominations. Sufi shaykhs and their actual or alleged bestowals of kingship also played a considerable part in determining the rise to power of the new ruling dynasties and the succession among their members.

In Bengal, the first area to break away from the control of the Delhi sultans in the fourteenth century, 'Alī Mubārak, the future Sultan 'Alā' al-Dīn 'Alī-Shāh (r. in West Bengal 1339–46) saw Shaykh Jalāl al-Dīn Tabrīzī, who promised him rule over 'the province of Bang' if he should build him a *khānaqāh* at Pandwa.[70]

The chronicles of fifteenth-century Gujarāt mention the nomination of the founder of the ruling house, Ẓafar Khān, by the Suhrawardī Bukhārī shaykh from Ucch, Jalāl al-Dīn

[69] 'Afīf, *Ta'rīkh*, pp. 27–9. 'Afīf consciously imitates accounts of *manāqib* (virtues, eminent deeds of Sufis or other good Muslims). The close of the notice again suggests an influence of Ḥamīd Qalandar's *Khayr al-majālis* as a model; cf. Digby, 'Qalandars and Related Groups', pp. 71–2 [this volume, pp. 202–3]. 'Afīf's account of these tidings is reproduced in Makkī, *Ẓafar al-wālih*, ed. E. Denison Ross as *An Arabic History of Gujarat*, vol. III, London: J. Murray, 1910–28, pp. 893–4.

[70] Salīm, *Riyāż al-salāṭīn*, Calcutta: Asiatic Society of Bengal, 1890, p. 94.

'Makhdūm-i Jahāniyān', a prominent Sufi of the latter years of Fērōz Shāh Tughluq's reign.[71] In the course of the fifteenth century, some of Jalāl al-Dīn's descendants settled in Gujarāt and intermarried with the ruling family. According to one possibly partial source, among these descendants of Jalāl al-Dīn, Shāh 'Ālam of Sarkhej played a decisive part in the events which led to the succession in 1458 of Maḥmūd Begaṛhā, the greatest of the Gujarāt sultans. Maḥmūd Begaṛhā was both a nephew by marriage and a stepson of this shaykh.[72] The 'Bukhārī Sayyids', descendants of Jalāl al-Dīn, participated in a rite of enthronement. Thus in 1554 Sayyid Mubārak Bukhārī, a descendant of 'Makhdūm-i Jahāniyān', led the boy king Aḥmad III up to the throne.[73]

In the Deccan, the mid-fourteenth century founder of the Bahmanī dynasty, Ḥasan Kāngū, is said to have received 'tidings' of his future sovereignty from Shaykh Niẓām al-Dīn of Delhi. The shaykh had given a general invitation to a feast at the *khānaqāh*, in which the future Sultan Muḥammad bin Tughluq had shared. As he left the shaykh pronounced: 'A Sultan has gone and a Sultan is coming!'[74]

[71] Sikandar b. Muḥammad 'urf Manjhū, *Mir'āt-i Sikandarī*, ed. S.C. Misra and M.L. Rahman, Baroda: Oriental Institute, 1961, pp. 10–11. Significant details include the bestowal of a leopard-skin by the shaykh on Ẓafar Khān, and the prophecy that rule in Gujarāt would remain in Ẓafar Khān's house for a number of generations corresponding to the number of dates that he had offered to the shaykh: 'Some say the number of those dates was twelve or thirteen, and some say more.' Cf. the number of dates symbolizing the number of years of the reign of Fērōz Shāh Tughluq in the fourth of 'Afīf's 'tidings' above.

[72] Manjhū, *Mir'āt-i Sikandarī*, pp. 86–91; Sir E.C. Bayley, *The Local Muhammadan Dynasties: Gujarat*, London: W.H. Allen and Co., 1886, pp. 153–5.

[73] Manjhū, *Mir'āt-i Sikandarī*, p. 389.

[74] This anecdote, like the anecdote in 'Afīf of the three sultans of the Tughluq dynasty eating from the bowl of Sharaf al-Dīn Pānīpatī, emphasizes the point that kings are supplicants at the courts of the Sufi shaykh. See the verses of Amīr Khusraw quoted above and the rubric of Amīr Khwurd cited in note 13.

The shaykh then ordered his servitor to bring in a man standing at the gate. After hesitating when he saw his shabby clothes, the servitor brought in Ḥasan Kāngū. As the food of the feast had already been distributed, Niẓām al-Dīn gave him a round of bread which he pronounced to be an umbrella (*chatr*) of sovereignty which would long endure.[75]

Other sources ascribe the promotion of Ḥasan Kāngū to the *baraka* of a *shaykh* established in the western Deccan, Shaykh Sirāj al-Dīn Junaydī, whose *murīd* Ḥasan became.[76] Sirāj al-Dīn is said to have placed his turban in Ḥasan's hands, and when the latter placed it upon his own head, the shaykh said that he would wear a royal crown. He also revealed the site of a buried treasure, instructing Ḥasan to raise an army with it.[77] Sirāj al-Dīn's successors at Gulbarga claimed that their lineage had conferred sovereignty on the Bahmanī sultans.[78] Following the example of their ancestor they invested successive sultans with a turban, a tunic, and

[75] Tabāṭabā'ī, *Burhān-i ma'āthir*, Delhi/Hyderabad: Maṭba' Jami'ah, 1936, p. 12; Firishta, *Ta'rīkh*, vol. I, Bombay: Government College Press, 1832, p. 520; vol. I, Kanpur, 1874, p. 274; Makkī, *Ẓafar al-wālih*, vol. I, p. 159. For Shaykh Niẓām al-Dīn bestowing a round (*qurṣ*) of bread, cf. Qalandar, *Khayr al-majālis*, p. 10.

[76] Muḥammad Sulṭān, *Armughān-i Sulṭānī*, p. 157, citing Rafī' al-Dīn Shīrāzī, *Tadhkirat al-mulūk*.

[77] Muḥammad Sulṭān, *Armughān-i Sulṭānī*, p. 158. The story of the buried treasure probably has a common origin with Firishta's tale of Ḥasan Kāngū discovering a treasure in the vicinity of Delhi; Firishta, *Ta'rīkh*, vol. I, p. 519. H.K. Sherwani states that 'Alā' al-Dīn Ḥasan Kāngū was crowned by Shaykh Sirāj al-Dīn Junaydī in the enthronement ceremony at Dawlatābād in 1347, but the references which he gives do not support this assertion, and the shaykh's name is absent from the list of participants in the enthronement mentioned by 'Iṣāmī, a contemporary witness; see Sherwani, *The Bahmanis of the Deccan*, Hyderabad: Manager of Publications, 1953, pp. 37 and 46, note 83; Firishta, *Ta'rīkh*, vol. I, Bombay, 1832, p. 528; vol. I, Kanpur, 1874, p. 277; 'Iṣāmī, *Futūḥ al-salāṭīn*, pp. 554–8.

[78] Muḥammad Sulṭān, *Armughān-i Sulṭānī*, p. 177.

a girdle of coarse (*khādī*) cloth.[79] When the garments of investiture were treated with disrespect by Sultan Maḥmūd Bahmanī (r. 1482–1518), the last powerful ruler of the dynasty, these are said to have been bestowed by the incumbent shaykh on Yūsuf ʻĀdil Shāh, founder of the new ruling house of the sultans of Bījāpūr.[80]

Following the sack of Delhi in 1398, the last great Chishti shaykh of the Delhi sultanate, Sayyid Muḥammad Gēsūdarāz, came to settle in the Bahmanī capital of Gulbarga and played a decisive role in the succession of Shihāb al-Dīn Aḥmad Shāh Bahmanī (Aḥmad I) in 1422.[81] The latter monarch, in order to support his authority, within a few years imported from Iran the heirs of another shaykh of similar attributes and powerful reputation, Shāh Niʻmat Allāh of Māhān. The historical record is clear that it was largely through the support of Gēsūdarāz that Aḥmad I was victorious over his brother the reigning Sultan Fērōz, and set aside the claims of his nephew Ḥasan; but Aḥmad later claimed that his elevation to the throne had been preceded by a dream in which Shāh Niʻmat Allāh Walī of Kirman had with his own hands offered to him the royal crown. The dream was followed (probably years later) by a letter of investiture from this shaykh.[82] Sultan Aḥmad himself claimed the Sufi rank of *Walī*, and his heirs retained

[79] Ibid., pp. 164–5. The investiture of Mujāhid Shah by Sirāj al-Dīn himself is mentioned.

[80] Muḥammad Sulṭān, *Armughān-i Sulṭānī*, p. 178.

[81] Tabāṭabā'ī, *Burhān-i ma'āthir*, p. 48; cf. ibid., pp. 46–7, for an account of Sayyid Muḥammad Gēsūdarāz's alienation from the Sultan's brother and predecessor, Fērōz Shāh Bahmanī.

[82] ʻAbd al-ʻAzīz b. Shēr Malik Wāʻiẓī, *Risāla dar siyar-i Shāh Niʻmat Allāh Walī*, in *Matériaux pour la biographie de Shah Niʻmatullah Kermani*, ed. J. Aubin, Tehran/Paris: Adrien-Maisonneuve, 1956, pp. 316–17. As was the case between the sultans of Gujarāt and the descendants of Jalāl al-Dīn Bukhārī, intermarriage took place in the Deccan kingdom, with the Bahmanīs giving daughters to the family of Niʻmat Allāh; see Tabāṭabā'ī, *Burhān-i ma'āthir*, p. 68.

this title down to the end of the dynasty.[83] As was the case with the Muslim ruling house of Gujarāt, Sufi shaykhs played a prominent part in the enthronement ceremony of the Bahmanī sultans of the Deccan.[84]

[83] Some confusion has been created by the late sixteenth-century historian Ṭabāṭabā'ī, who, when describing the alleged encounter of Ḥasan Kāngū with Shaykh Niẓām al-Dīn, refers to the future Sultan by the anachronistic title of al-Walī al-Bahmanī: Tabāṭabā'ī, *Burhān-i ma'āthir*, p. 12. Sherwani compounds this confusion with some errors of his own; see *The Bahmanis of the Deccan*, pp. 37, 46, n. 82. Only the title al-Bahmanī is found on the coinage of Sultan Shihāb al-Dīn Aḥmad I, the immediate *khalīfa* of Shāh Ni'mat Allāh; see A. Wali Khan, *Bahmani Coins*, Hyderabad: Govt. of Andhra Pradesh, 1964, p. 78. However, al-Walī al-Bahmanī is found in the painted inscriptions of his tomb, thought to be nearly contemporary; one may also note among his titles given there *afżal khalīfati'llāh fi'l-'ālamīn* (sic); see G. Yazdani, *Bidar: Its History and Monuments*, Oxford: Oxford University Press, 1947, p. 125. The strict contemporaneity of this inscription is put in doubt by the fact that the date of death, given as 839/1436, conflicts not only with Firishta as noted by Yazdani, *Bidar*, but also with numismatic evidence which supports AH 838. The use of the title by Aḥmad I is also attested by 'Abd al-'Azīz b. Sher Malik, writing in the following reign; see Aubin, *Matériaux pour la biographie de Shah Ni'matullah Kermani*, p. 316. The title al-Walī joined to al-Bahmanī is first found on the coinage in the reigh of 'Alā' al-Dīn Aḥmad II, with earliest recorded date 838/1434–35 and it is last recorded on an undated gold coin of Maḥmūd Shāh (r. 1482–1518); see Khan, *Bahmani Coins*, pp. 87, 148. But the regnal name of Maḥmūd's grandson Walī Allāh (r. 1522–24) would indicate that the spiritual claim was maintained to the end of the dynasty.

[84] Tabāṭabā'ī, *Burhān-i ma'āthir*, pp. 75, 96, 107. It is perhaps significant that no shaykh from the great family of Gēsūdarāz appears to have assisted at these enthronements. The descendants of Gēsūdarāz and the tombs at Gulbarga remained a major focus for the devotions of the population of the Deccan down to the present day. By contrast, the unconvincing claims to sanctity of the Bahmanī ruling house were in later times represented by a Lingayat *jangam* assuming the garb and style of a Sufi *pīr* on the occasion of the annual *'urs* at the tomb of Aḥmad Shāh I; see Yazdani, *Bidar*, p. 116 and Pl. LXXV.

3

Tabarrukāt and Succession among the Great Chishtī Shaykhs of the Dehli Sultanate

A line of Ṣūfī shaykhs of the Chishtī order enjoyed a pre-eminence in the Dehli Sultanate of the thirteenth and fourteenth centuries AD. This pre-eminence over other Ṣūfī orders in the capital city was probably established by the 1230s, when, if hagiographical sources more than a century later are to be trusted, Shaykh Quṭb al-Dīn Bakhtyār Kākī enjoyed the allegiance of the reigning sultan, Iltutmish, and of the urban population. The prestige of the Chishtī shaykhs grew in the time of his successor Farīd al-Dīn, and perhaps reached its apogee after Niẓām al-Dīn established an extensive *khānqāh* at Dehli in the late thirteenth century. The prestige of the living Chishtī shaykhs continued until the destruction of the capital city by Amīr Timur in AD 1398. The principal heir of the Chishtī prestige migrated very shortly before this disaster to the territories and capital of the Bahmanī Sultanate of the Deccan, where in AD 1422 he played the role of kingmaker.

The fourteenth century also saw the beginnings of the exaltation of the first of the Chishtī shaykhs in India, Mu'īn al-Dīn Sijzī, in popular estimation to the position of being the pioneer saint of the Muslim presence in India—'the

* Originally published in Robert Eric Frykenberg, ed., *Delhi through the Ages*, Delhi: Oxford University Press, 1986, pp. 62–103.

Representative of the Prophets and Saints in India' (*nā'ib rasūlī'llāh fi'l-hind*) in the words of the late fourteenth-century hagiographer Amīr Khwurd.[1] By this time the legend existed that by his spiritual powers he had delivered the Hindu ruler Prithvirāja into the hands of the victorious armies of Islam led by Sultan Mu'izz al-Dīn Muḥammad bin Sām.

The historical memory of these six great Chishtī shaykhs has ensured that they are much revered by the majority of Indian Muslims today. Around the graves of four of the six, the most widely attended Muslim rituals of pilgrimage in the Indian subcontinent take place.

All these six Chishtī shaykhs had a connection with the capital city of Dehli. The slightest connection perhaps is that of Mu'īn al-Dīn, about whom we have so little indubitably genuine historical information. There is however no reason to doubt that Mu'īn al-Dīn came to Dehli on a visit from Ajmer around AD 1235; he sought the intervention of the sultan in a dispute between the *muqta'* or governor of Ajmer and his own sons, who had brought into cultivation some barren land. Quṭb al-Dīn lived in Dehli during the latter part of his life and carefully sought a place for his own tomb there—the earliest recorded example, barring the founding inscriptions of the Qubbat al-Islām mosque, of a declaration that the earth of the capital city was hallowed by the Muslim presence. Farīd al-Dīn came from a family long established in the Muslim townships of the Panjab; Niẓām al-Dīn from the important Muslim settlement of Badā'on (later Bulandshahr) some two days' distance away from Dehli; and Naṣīr al-Dīn Maḥmūd from Awadh. Farīd al-Dīn came to Dehli to receive instruction from his Pīr, though he evidently had no liking for the capital and eventually established his *khānqāh* elsewhere, Niẓām al-Dīn and Naṣīr

[1] Amīr Khwurd, *Siyar al-awliyā'*, ed. Chiranji Lal, Dehli: Muhibb-i Hind Press, AH 1302/AD 1885, p. 45.

al-Dīn Maḥmūd passed the greater part of their lives in the suburbs of the capital, and established their *khānqāhs* there; like Quṭb al-Dīn, they are also buried in Dehli. The last of the six great Chishtī shaykhs surveyed in this paper, Sayyid Muḥammad Gēsūdarāz, was born in Dehli and claimed to come from a family which had been established there since the days of the original Muslim conquest. As a very young child he was taken to Dawlatabad on the forced migration ordered by Sulṭān Muḥammad bin Tughluq; but he returned to Dehli as a student, and passed over half a century of his long life there, before the disorders of the late Dehli Sultanate made him turn back to the Deccan in his old age.

The problems of how authority was transmitted in this lineage of Chishtī shaykhs are examined in this paper. The principal conflict is between the claims of the kin of the shaykh to succeed to this and the conviction that it should pass to the most worthy successor, designated by the dying shaykh. A subsidiary conflict often also occurs between intimate disciples of the shaykh, each of whom might feel that his individual claims for preferment were pre-eminent. In almost every transference of authority, the hagiographical tradition provides evidence of conflict; on several occasions we possess a conflict of evidence, which is examined in an attempt to establish which account is likely to be nearest to the truth.

The maintenance of claims to succession in spiritual authority, while apparently wholly dependent on the dying shaykh's testament, could not in fact remain uninfluenced by the role which a great shaykh had played in the society of the Dehli Sultanate. In spite of the often-expressed desire by the Chishtī shaykhs for solitude and their injunctions to seek it, the role of a great shaykh, on which his prestige depended, demanded unremitting attention to the spiritual needs, hopes, and aspirations of devotees of every social class and occupation. If the shaykh adequately fulfilled these functions, he was held by his followers to be the true principal heir of the *baraka* of his predecessor, and his hagiographers would be strongly inclined to believe that he had received from the latter the appropriate and unique *tabarrukāt* or symbols of office. The nature of these, as well as the occasions of their bestowal, are discussed later in this chapter.

The charisma wielded by Ṣūfī shaykhs in the medieval Islamic world clearly reflects the role they were performing in mediating between God and the secular societies of their period and locality. By the middle of the thirteenth century the lineage of the Chishtī shaykhs, in the person of Farīd al-Dīn Ganj-i Shakar, appears to have established an ascendancy over all other purveyors of *baraka* in the central domains of the Dehli Sultanate. However, the rational historical explanations for the authority they wielded do not correspond with the theories current at the time regarding its transmission. We are here concerned with contemporary beliefs as to how and to whom the *baraka* of a Ṣūfī shaykh descended when he took his departure from the mortal world.

By the thirteenth century the cult of graves and pilgrimages to local sites was well established in the Islamic world. A portion of the shaykh's *baraka*, of his spiritual and mediatory authority over the *wilāyat* or territory in which this was supposed to prevail, survived in the tomb of the shaykh, to which those who required his intercession would resort. By the ordinary Muslim process of inheritance, the *khānqāh* or hospice which he had founded and his grave within it would devolve to his children or nearest kin. Yet a powerful alternative system of transmission existed in the relationship between the shaykh or *pīr* and his *murīds* (disciples). The disciples might have profited more greatly than the shaykh's own kin from his spiritual instruction, and thereby acquired greater sanctity. Among his disciples, those who were wholly occupied with the Ṣūfī way of life and had absorbed all the teachings which he could impart to them, could receive his licence as *khalīfas* or deputies, fully proficient to act in a similar role to his own as Ṣūfī shaykhs. Yet one among these *khalīfas* might be considered by the shaykh and designated by him as a principal heir to his teaching and authority. Such a designation was symbolized not by a *Khilāfat-nāma* indicating unspecific competence to practise as a Ṣūfī shaykh approved by his teacher, but by the gift of the private and personal insignia or articles of common use of the shaykh, which by their nature were not multipliable except by fraudulent claims.

We have therefore two conflicting systems of inheritance which came into operation at the death of a shaykh. A portion of his spiritual authority could be claimed by the custodians of his grave, among whom his immediate kin would have strong claims; but another claim to the whole of his authority might descend to a designated heir among his favoured disciples, who could exhibit the articles of intimate personal use of his shaykh, which had been given to him, as proof of his claims to the spiritual inheritance.

At the time of the establishment of the Dehli Sultanate, the problem of the inheritance of *baraka* existed among Ṣūfīs in the Ghaznavid domains. One of the earliest recorded anecdotes of Shaykh Niẓām al-Dīn Awliyā' refers to the competition of interests between the children and the designated heir of a Shaykh:

There was a Pīr in Ghaznīn [Ghazni] who had a slave called Zīrak. This Zīrak was exceedingly sincere and worthy. When that holy Pīr was on his deathbed, his disciples asked, 'Who will sit in your place?' 'Zīrak,' he replied. Zīrak said, 'O Khwāja, your sons will not permit me to sit in your place. They will make strife with me in every way.' 'Sit there with untroubled heart,' the Pīr replied. 'If they oppose you, I shall avert their wickedness from you!'

So when the Pīr joined the precinct of God's mercy, Zīrak sat in his place. The sons of the Pīr began to oppose him, [declaring] that, 'You are one of our slaves. Have you the bile to sit in our father's place?'

When their contumaciousness had waxed great, Zīrak came to the head of the Pīr's grave and said, 'O Khwāja, you stated that if your sons molested me, you would avert their wickedness. Now they are out to injure me: you must fulfil your promise!'

He said this and returned to his own place. Within a few days the Kāfirs [i.e. the Mongols] assaulted the environs of Ghaznīn. The populace went out to fight them. All four sons of the Pīr also went forth and joined the battle; and they all attained martyrdom.[2]

Set forth in this anecdote is the conflict of claims between the kin of the *pīr* as legitimate heirs of his material property and those of the chosen heir of his spiritual authority, not a blood-relation and in this case even a slave. Here the slave takes all, the intercession of the dead *pīr* having brought about an honourable death for his own children. Unlike many anecdotes of confrontation, it does not end in the degradation of the wicked but rather a suitable end for those who have a reasonable claim. Though on more than one occasion we see a conflict between the family of the *pīr* and a disciple of his who could put forward a claim to be principal heir of his *baraka*, in no case among the Chishtī shaykhs do we find an attempt to displace the kin as guardians of the tomb or as administrators of the *khānqāh* or hospice which the shaykh had founded.

Though Niẓām al-Dīn supported the claims of the slave in the anecdote which he related, the rise of the Chishtī shaykhs to their widely accepted position of spiritual dominance in the Dehli Sultanate was favoured by a reasonable accommodation between conflicting claims regarding the descent of spiritual authority. Their popular prestige was based on their early presence in the Dehli Sultanate after

[2] Amīr Ḥasan 'Alā' Sijzī, *Fawā'id al-fu'ād*, ed. M.L. Malik, Lahore: Malik Sirāj al-Dīn and Sons, 1966, pp. 5–6.

its first establishment, which gave them a historic identity among the Muslim presence in the Indo-Gangetic plain, and upon their early victory over rival claimants to spiritual authority; but their lineage derived from the relatively obscure dynasty of the *pīrs* of Chisht, where succession to *baraka* was among the founder's kin.

The *pīrs* of Chisht exercised not uncontested authority over a limited area to the north of Herat in modern west Afghanistan. With the reflected prestige of their representatives in the Dehli Sultanate to aid them in the later thirteenth and fourteenth centuries, a *khānqāh* and the graves of their ancestors remained in their possession from the ninth century AD for at least eleven generations to around AD 1400. The tombs of the *pīrs* of Chisht have been deserted and ruined probably for some hundreds of years, but the descendants of their pre-Indian-conquest lineage survive in South Asia, a notable modern example being the Pakistani religious theorist and politician Mawlānā Abu'l-'Alā' Mawdūdī.[3]

Contacts with the *pīrs* of Chisht were maintained, obviously tenuously, by the Chishtī shaykhs of the Dehli Sultanate. There is no reference to the *pīrs* of Chisht in the conversation of Shaykh Niẓām al-Dīn Awliyā' recorded by Amīr Ḥasan in the *Fawā'id al-fu'ād*; but there are records of contacts in the much fuller *Siyar al-awliyā'*, possibly because the family of its author, Amīr Khwurd, late thirteenth-century aristocratic immigrants from Iran, attained initial

[3] Sayyid Ashraf Jahāngīr Simnānī, *Maktūbāt-i Ashrafī*, British Library MS Or. 267, ff. 119–21, affords evidence of the contacts between the Khwājas of Chisht and the shaykhs of the Dehli Sultanate at the close of the fourteenth century. It is clear that there was a considerable *khānqāh* at Chisht during this period. By contrast I have not found any evidence that the *khānqāh* continued to function through the fifteenth century. There is no mention of it in the descriptions of the topography of the Herat area in Khwandamīr, *Makārim al-Akhlāq*, ed. T. Gandjeï, London: Trustees of the E.F.W. Gibb Memorial, 1979.

acceptance and later high administrative position in the *khānqāh* of Niẓām al-Dīn after a previous *bay'at* (profession of allegiance) to the Sajjāda-nashīn (heir) at Chisht; and later were anxious to promote connections between the shrines at Dehli and at Chisht.

On two points the examples of the *pīrs* of Chisht may have exercised influence on problems of succession among the Chishtī shaykhs of the Dehli Sultanate. In the reign of Sulṭān Ghiyāth al-Dīn Balbān at Dehli (AD 1266–87) a dispute occurred with regard to the succession at Chisht. An elder member of the family had migrated to Dehli and, according to the testimony of Amīr Khwurd, was greatly cherished and esteemed by the Dehli sultan. At Chisht a party supported the claims of a minor, Khwāja Quṭb al-Dīn, and others at Chisht opposed these claims. A mission was then sent from Chisht to ascertain the views of Khwāja 'Alī, who had migrated to Dehli. The two representatives bore the dubiously literate names of Khwāja Zūr and Khwāja Ghūr. Khwāja 'Alī at Dehli indicated that he did not want to become the Sajjāda-nashīn at Chisht, and he supported the candidacy of Khwāja Quṭb al-Dīn. The two delegates travelled back from Dehli to Chisht via Ajudhan, where they were fêted by Shaykh Farīd al-Dīn. Farīd al-Dīn arranged for the *kullāh-i irādat* ('cap of profession') to be bestowed on two of his sons, who had not previously been shaved (*maḥlūq*) and made a profession of Ṣūfī allegiance. The transaction had elements of mutual acknowledgement and legitimation. The caps were selected and provided by Farīd al-Dīn himself and put on the heads of his sons by the two travelling members of the house of Chisht.[4]

There is no record that *khānqāhs* were established by the two earlier major Chishtī shaykhs of the Dehli Sultanate, Mu'īn al-Dīn at Ajmer or Quṭb al-Dīn at Dehli. Equally there

[4] Khwurd, *Siyar al-awliyā'*, pp. 188–9.

is no evidence that their kin thought of being maintained as servitors at their tomb. The problems of succession to a hospice and pilgrimage cult appear to have arisen at the death of Farīd al-Dīn at Ajudhan in AD 1265. Possibly Farīd's elder sons did not want to undertake this task and the succession devolved to his third son, Shaykh Badr al-Dīn Sulaymān. In this situation the example of the *pīrs* of Chisht would probably have been recalled and possibly Farīd al-Dīn himself, when the two members of that family had come to visit him over their dispute about inheritance, may have visualized the contingency. Yet a modern historian overstates the case when he writes that Shaykh Badr al-Dīn Sulaymān was given the office of Sajjāda-nashīn 'directly from the Chishtī elders in Chisht, western Afghanistan'. What his source, Amīr Khwurd, in the *Siyar al-awliyā'* states, is that two sons of Farīd were given the *kullāh-i irādat* by the representatives of the *pīrs* of Chisht. One of these—Shaykh Shihāb al-Dīn—became an *'ālim ba 'amal* (an Islamic man-of-learning who put his theological knowledge into practice), and the other—Shaykh Badr al-Dīn Sulaymān—became the Sajjāda-nashīn of Shaykh Farīd al-Dīn at Ajudhan.[5]

On another point the procedure at Chisht (as reported by an author of the Dehli Sultanate) is relevant to the struggle for power among the Chishtī shaykhs of the Dehli Sultanate. According to Amīr Khwurd, when the two-man delegation from Chisht returned to record Khwāja 'Alī's refusal of the office of Sajjāda-nashīn from Dehli, a contest ensued between

[5] R. Eaton, 'The Political and Religious Authority of the Shrine of Baba Farid in Pakpattan, Punjab', paper presented at the seminar on Adab and Moral Authority among the Muslims of South Asia, University of California, Berkeley, June 1979, p. 5, n. 10 [subsequently published as Richard M. Eaton, 'The Political and Religious Authority of the Shrine of Bābā Farīd', in *Moral Conduct and Authority: The Place of* Adab *in South Asian Islam*, ed. B.D. Metcalf, Berkeley: University of California Press, 1984, pp. 339–40 ~DL]; Khwurd, *Siyar al-awliyā'*, pp. 188–9, 289.

the remaining rivals at Chisht, presided over by the local ruler, Malik Shams al-Dīn Kart. The principal tomb in which the *pīrs* of Chisht were buried was locked, and in it were kept the prayer-carpet (*sajjāda*) and staff (*'aṣā*) which had been passed from one generation to another at the shrine. Khwāja Quṭb al-Dīn was a child and was brought forward by his attendant. As he approached the tomb, the lock miraculously opened and the two leaves of the door swung apart. At this, Quṭb al-Dīn's claims were acknowledged.[6] The anecdote demonstrates the importance attached to the personal insignia of the shaykh (*tabarrukāt*) as symbols of his accession to his authority. In the Dehli Sultanate, struggles between the kin of Chishtī shaykhs and their designated successors centred upon the possession of these insignia.

In the transference of authority among the Chishtī shaykhs of the Dehli Sultanate an important concession was the *Khilāfat-nāma* or *Ijāzat-nāma*, a licence of competence to teach and practise as a Ṣūfī shaykh, often with the injunction that the recipient should leave his master's *khānqāh* and dwell at a suitable distance. If it was granted to a new initiate, it might provoke resentment among the older *murīds* of the shaykh at the *khānqāh*, who, even if the shaykh considered them less spiritually developed, saw themselves as better entitled to this recognition. However, it was widely assumed that the main burden of the shaykh's authority was passed on to a single especially chosen disciple. This transfer of authority could be accomplished by a *waṣīyat*, or death-bed testament, whether written or oral. However, such a testament might be disputed or fabricated. In these circumstances, the *tabarrukāt*, objects of daily use or insignia of the devotional life of the deceased shaykh, became evidence of the validity of his successor's claim. In the anecdote discussed above regarding the succession of

[6] Khwurd, *Siyar al-awliyā'*, pp. 212–13.

Khwāja Quṭb al-Dīn at Chisht, the locked door which guards these heirlooms miraculously flies open at the presence of a worthy heir, and his authority is recognized. This chapter attempts to scrutinize the hagiographical evidence regarding the transmission of *tabarrukāt* in the succession of the six major Chishtī shaykhs of the Dehlī Sultanate—Mu'īn al-Dīn Sijzī, Quṭb al-Dīn Bakhtyār Kākī, Farīd al-Dīn Ganj-i Shakar, Niẓām al-Dīn Awliyā', Naṣīr al-Dīn Maḥmūd Chirāgh-i Dehlī, and Sayyid Muḥammad Gēsūdarāz.

In all, our sources mention seven objects as *tabarrukāt*, the first four being of greater importance. These are:

1. The staff (*'aṣā*). A symbol both of the wielding of authority and the venerability of age;
2. The prayer-carpet (*muṣallā* or *sajjāda*). In the usage of the period *sajjāda* came to be applied to the carpet on which the shaykh presided in his assemblies;
3. The robe or garment (*khirqa, jāma*). To be distinguished from the ordinary *khirqa* given to those who received a *khilāfat-nāma* from the shaykh. Often considered to be an heirloom passed down from the Prophet Muḥammad himself;
4. The begging bowl (*kāsa*);
5. The turban (*dastār*);
6. The finger-ring (*angushtarī*). Mentioned only in the testamentary dispositions of Gēsūdarāz;
7. A rosary (*tasbīḥ*). Mentioned in the implausible sixteenth-century account by Jamālī of the transmission from Niẓām al-Dīn to Naṣīr al-Dīn Maḥmūd, examined below;
8. A Qur'ān. Mentioned only in a nineteenth-century account of the transmission from Mu'īn al-Dīn to Quṭb al-Dīn which is demonstrably untrue, examined below.

None of the authentic accounts of *malfūẓāt* (accounts of the conversations of Ṣūfī shaykhs) contains a reference to the transference of *tabarrukāt* from the first Chishtī shaykh in India, Mu'īn al-Dīn, to his successor Quṭb al-Dīn Bakhtyār.

Such a reference is found in the inauthentic but early *Fawā'id al-sālikīn.*[7] This states that Quṭb al-Dīn was absent at the time of Mu'īn al-Dīn's death, and that the *khirqa* and *sajjāda* were despatched to Quṭb al-Dīn. It occurs in a passage describing the transmission in the following generation, from Quṭb al-Dīn to Farīd al-Dīn, which is directly modelled on the account of the genuine collection of Niẓām al-Dīn's *malfūẓāt, Fawā'id al-fu'ād.*[8]

A late nineteenth-century narrative (possibly deriving from a seventeenth-century original) shows the hagiographer's view of what ought to have happened:

[Khwāja Mu'īn al-Dīn] told Shaykh 'Alī Sanjarī [*sic*][9] to compose a *farman*[10] and *khilāfat-nāma* to the effect that: I give my Khilāfat and Sajjādagī [office of Sajjāda-nashīn] to Quṭb al-Dīn Bakhtyār. His place is in Dehli. Haẓrat Khwāja Quṭb al-Dīn relates that 'When the document had been composed and he had adorned it with his own signature, he gave it to me. Then he said, "Come near to me!"

'When I was close he put a cap and a turban on my head, and he gave the staff of Khwāja 'Uthmān[11] into my hand. Bestowing the cloak of the Prophet Muḥammad upon me, that is to say the cloak which was the gift of the Protector of the World, together with an ancient Holy Qur'ān, a prayer-carpet and a pair of sandals, he said, "These are a legacy from the true Prophet, upon whom be blessing and peace, which has come down to my elders, and I give them to you. As the Khwājas of Chisht have performed his works, so you should perform them!"

[7] *Fawā'id al-sālikīn*, Dehli: Mujtabā'ī Press, AH 1311/AD 1892, p. 35.

[8] 'Alā' Sijzī, *Fawā'id al-fu'ād*, p. 315.

[9] The *nisba* Sanjarī, almost universally applied in the subcontinent to Mu'īn al-Dīn, is a misreading for Sijzī—i.e. from Sijistan/Sīstān. An identical corruption of the *nisba* has occurred in the case of Amīr Hasan, poet and compiler of the *Fawā'id al-fu'ād.*

[10] The loose usage of *farmān* for a non-royal document is further evidence of the late date of this fabrication.

[11] Khwāja 'Uthmān Hārvanī, the *pīr* of Mu'īn al-Dīn; the *nisba* is corrupted to Hārūnī in modern pronunciation.

'Taking these pure gifts, I again saluted him and kissed the ground of service.

'"Go", he then said. "I have entrusted you to God!"

'Having recited for me the Fātiḥa he then said: "Wherever you abide, be the Man!"

'Then I saluted again, and I left there and came back to Dehli and dwelt there. Forty days had passed when a man came from Ajmer, and told me that twenty days after I had returned the Khwāja had set from this perishable world.'[12]

Both this account and the earlier narrative of the *Fawā'id al-sālikīn* are demonstrably unhistorical, as Quṭb al-Dīn Bakhtyār died in AD 1235, pre-deceasing his *pīr* Mu'īn al-Dīn, who died in March 1236, by a few months.[13]

With regard to the next stage in the transmission of *tabarrukāt*, we have a verbatim account of only one generation later:

Then he [Shaykh Niẓām al-Dīn] said:

'When the time of the departure of Shaykh Quṭb al-Dīn was near, the name of a *buzurg* [shaykh] was mentioned who now rests at the feet of Shaykh Quṭb al-Dīn, and had the ambition that he should sit in the place of the Shaykh [Quṭb al-Dīn] after him. Shaykh Badr al-Dīn Ghaznavī also…[had that ambition]. However in the *samā'* [musical session] in which Shaykh Quṭb al-Dīn was about to pass away, he ordered that his garment and staff and prayer-mat and wooden sandals should be given to Shaykh Farīd al-Dīn.'

'I have seen that staff and garment,' Niẓām al-Dīn said. 'It was a garment of fine cloth, embroidered. So, the night when Khwāja

[12] Munshī Qurbān 'Alī 'Bismil', *Sacchī sawāniḥ-i 'umri kalān, ma'hu malfūẓāt-i Khwāja Ajmērī*, Dehli: Raḥmānī Press, n.d., pp. 20–1.

[13] The date of Mu'īn al-Dīn's death is not given in Khwurd, *Siyar al-awliyā'*; see 'Abd al-Ḥaqq Muḥaddith Dehlavī, *Akhbār al-akhyār*, Dehli: Mujtabā'ī Press, AH 1309/AD 1892, p. 22. For the date of Quṭb al-Dīn's death, Khwurd, *Siyar al-awliyā'*, p. 56. As the 'Urs festival depended on the date of decease, this is a detail on which hagiographic sources are least likely to be in error.

Quṭb al-Dīn passed away, Shaykh Farīd al-Dīn was in Hansi ... That very night Shaykh Farīd al-Dīn saw his *pīr* in a dream, calling him into his presence. On the next day he left Hansi and on the fourth day he reached the town [Dehli].[14] Qāẓī Ḥamīd al-Dīn Nāgawrī was still alive, and he brought the garment to Shaykh Farīd al-Dīn.... The Shaykh performed two prostrations of prayer, put on the garment and came into the house where ... Quṭb al-Dīn had been. He was not more than three days there, or, according to another account, seven days, before he again set out for Hansi.'[15]

This passage requires a commentary at several points. The *buzurg* later buried at Quṭb al-Dīn's feet, who aspired to succeed to his authority, may have been Qāẓī Ḥamīd al-Dīn Nāgawrī, who is buried there, but who also conveyed the *tabarrukāt* in this anecdote to Farīd al-Dīn. It could also be a reference to the only surviving son of Quṭb al-Dīn, whom Niẓām al-Dīn regarded with disapproval.[16] It is curious that Niẓām al-Dīn states that he had seen the staff and garment passed on by Quṭb al-Dīn, as this would imply that they were not in Niẓām al-Dīn's own possession. In other references Niẓām al-Dīn was quite clear that his own staff was that which had been passed on by Quṭb al-Dīn to Farīd al-Dīn. There also seems to be no doubt, from his careful description, that the garment (*jāma*) was not in his own possession.

[14] *Shahr*, 'city', frequently refers to the capital city in the colloquial usage of the Dehli Sultanate.

[15] 'Alā' Sijzī, *Fawā'id al-fu'ād*, p. 315; reproduced verbatim in Khwurd, *Siyar al-awliyā'*, pp. 72–3.

[16] As the name of Badr al-Dīn Ghaznavī has been mentioned earlier in the anecdote, it is possible that the second name may have been omitted not through reticence by Niẓām al-Dīn but by the negligence of the recorder. On the other hand, this may be a reference to the only surviving son of Quṭb al-Dīn, whom Niẓām al-Dīn regarded with disapproval, remarking once that this son bore no likeness to his father, and Quṭb al-Dīn's true offspring was Farīd al-Dīn. This unnamed son may be conjectured not to have sought any portion of his father's authority as a Ṣūfī shaykh.

Certainly no *khirqa* alleged to be an heirloom of the Prophet had been passed on to him.

This anecdote is paraphrased in the inauthentic *Fawā'id al-sālikīn*,[17] and it is reproduced verbatim in the *Siyar al-awliyā'*, which appends it to another anecdote of this stage of the transmission of the *tabarrukāt*:

It is related that ... Shaykh Farīd al-Dīn said: 'Once I was seated with Shaykh Quṭb al-Dīn.... I rose up with the intention of setting out for Hansi. Shaykh Quṭb al-Dīn's blessed glance fell upon me. His eyes filled with tears and he said: "Mawlānā Farīd al-Dīn, I know that you are going to go away!" "Whatsoever you command," I remarked. "Go!" he said. "Fate has decreed that at the moment of my last journey you should not be with me."

'He turned to those who were present, and said: "For an increase of the comforts of the faith and the world and holy poverty (*faqr*), let us intone the Fātiḥa and the Sūra Ikhlās for this Darvish."

'They all recited this and also bestowed a prayer. Then he gave me his special prayer-mat (*muṣallā-yi khāṣṣ*), together with his staff, and he said: "I will give in trust your legacy, that is to say the prayer carpet (*sajjāda*) and cloak and turban and sandals to Qāẓī Ḥamīd al-Dīn. Five days afterwards he will convey them to you. My place is your place!"

'The moment that Shaykh Quṭb al-Dīn said this, a cry burst forth in the assembly, and everyone offered.'[18]

In this passage the *muṣallā* and *sajjāda* appear as separate objects, the 'special' *muṣallā* possibly indicating the mat actually used for the shaykh's devotions and *sajjāda* (in spite of its etymology) being applied to another mat on which the shaykh sat in his assemblies. Apart from the additional objects not mentioned in the previous anecdote, the staff is here said to have been bestowed on Farīd al-Dīn on his last

[17] *Fawā'id al-sālikīn*, pp. 34–5.

[18] Khwurd, *Siyar al-awliyā'*, pp. 72–3.

meeting with his living *pīr*, while in the previous anecdote it was handed over to Farīd al-Dīn after Quṭb al-Dīn's death by Qāẓī Hamīd al-Dīn Nāgawrī.

A third differing account of this transmission in a fourteenth-century source was related by Shaykh Naṣīr al-Dīn Maḥmūd. It bears only a vague general relationship to the anecdote as recorded from the lips of his own *pīr*, Niẓām al-Dīn:

> When Shaykh ... Farīd al-Dīn came from Hansi to visit the blessed tomb of Shaykh Quṭb al-Dīn, Shaykh Badr al-Dīn Ghaznavī came to visit Shaykh Farīd. He was a Khalīfa of Shaykh Quṭb al-Dīn. [Farīd al-Dīn] asked him: 'What testament (*waṣīyat*) did the Shaykh make at the time of his passing away?'
>
> 'The testament was "Give my *sajjāda* to Mas'ūd!"'
>
> Shaykh Farīd al-Dīn's name was Mas'ūd. After that he said: 'Offer him my wife.'
>
> 'I cannot accept this,' Shaykh [Farīd] said.
>
> After that he gave the *sajjāda* of the Shaykh [Quṭb al-Dīn] to Shaykh Farīd. Crowds began to come and he was inconvenienced.
>
> 'I cannot be about my work in this city,' the Shaykh said. He told no one, and left quietly and went to Hansi.[19]

Badr al-Dīn Ghaznavī has here taken the place of Qāẓī Hamīd al-Dīn Nāgawrī as the intermediary, and there is but one object mentioned in place of the six of the previous anecdote. There is no suggestion of the dream which had summoned Farīd from Hansi to Dehli. The detail of his refusal to take Quṭb al-Dīn's wife is not found in either of the other anecdotes; and the tale of his departure back to Hansi is again rather different. An event of about 90 to 120 years before from which they inherited their own authority was remembered with considerable vagueness by two of the great Chishtī shaykhs.

[19] Hamīd Qalandar, *Khayr al-majālis*, ed. K.A. Nizami, Aligarh: Aligarh Muslim University, 1958, pp. 88–9.

For the next stage in the transmission of the *tabarrukāt*, from Farīd al-Dīn to Niẓām al-Dīn, we have the recorded testimony of the recipient, with references to the previous transfer. Once again there is a conflict of evidence as regards the details of the transfer in the earliest sources. Niẓām al-Dīn's own narration, which may be accepted as historically the more accurate, maintains that the staff of his *pīr* was given to him by Farīd al-Dīn in his lifetime. This corresponds with the account of the previous transmission from Quṭb al-Dīn to Farīd al-Dīn in Amīr Khwurd's *Siyar al-awliyā'*. However, regarding this transmission, Amīr Khwurd includes the staff among the *tabarrukāt* conveyed from Farīd al-Dīn to Niẓām al-Dīn after the death of the elder shaykh, a transaction in which he maintains that his grandfather Sayyid Muḥammad Kirmānī had played an important part. Niẓām al-Dīn's own account of the gift of the staff, as recorded in the *Fawā'id al-fu'ād* is moving and circumstantial:

There was a staff which he had received from Shaykh Quṭb al-Dīn. They used to bring this and lay it at the head of his bed [*khaṭ*, Anglo-Indian 'cot']. The Shaykh used to lean back on that staff and lie at ease, and every time he used to take down the staff with his hand and kiss it.[20]

After describing further circumstances of Farīd's terminal illness, Niẓām al-Dīn related how his shaykh gave the staff to him:

He [Farīd al-Dīn] turned towards me and said: 'I have asked from God that whatsoever you ask from Him you shall find from Him.' After this he gave the staff to me.

At this moment I [i.e. Amīr Hasan, the compiler of the *Fawā'id al-fu'ād*] asked: 'Were you not there at the time of the Shaykh's death?'

[20] 'Alā' Sijzī, *Fawā'id al-fu'ād*, pp. 87–8.

[Niẓām al-Dīn's] eyes filled with tears, and he said: 'No, in the month of Shawwāl he sent me to Dehli. His death was on the night of the fifth of Muḥarram [i.e. about three months later]. As he lay dying he remembered me and said: "Such a one is in Dehli." And he added, "At the time of Shaykh Quṭb al-Dīn's death I also was not present; I was in Hansi."'

The Khwāja [Niẓām al-Dīn] told this story and he wept, so that all who were present were affected.

A similar pattern of transfer has been established in the last two transmissions in that the heir is absent at the death bed, subsequently falsely recorded in the transmission of the preceding generation from Mu'īn al-Dīn to Quṭb al-Dīn. Amīr Khwurd's account in the *Siyar al-awliyā'*—though it may magnify the role of his own grandfather, Sayyid Muḥammad Kirmānī, in the transmission, and though it is also not to be preferred against Niẓām al-Dīn's own testimony regarding the gift of the staff in Farīd al-Dīn's own lifetime—is circumstantially convincing in its description of the opposition of Farīd al-Dīn's family to the transfer of *tabarrukāt* to Niẓām al-Dīn:

The author [Amīr Khwurd] has heard from his father, Sayyid Mubārak Kirmānī, that while Shaykh [Farīd al-Dīn] was ill from the illness through which he was to pass from this world to the next, Sayyid Muḥammad Kirmānī, the author's grandfather, arrived at Ajudhan from the city of Dehli. He saw that the Shaykh was lying on his cot within his room (*ḥujra*) and that his sons and devotees were sitting in front of the door of the room, in discussion about his authority (*maqam*) and succession (*sajjāda*).

In the midst of this Sayyid Muḥammad Kirmānī wanted to go into the room to kiss the feet of the Shaykh, but his sons forbade him, saying that this was not the time for it. Sayyid Muḥammad Kirmānī could bear it no longer. He opened the door of the room, went inside and fell at the feet of the Shaykh. The great Shaykh opened his eyes and said: 'How are you, Sayyid? And when did you come?'

'I have arrived at this very moment', said Sayyid Muḥammad Kirmānī.

Then he desired to kiss the feet of the Shaykh. He wondered whether if in these circumstances he began to mention [Niẓām al-Dīn], Farīd al-Dīn would truly bestow his favour upon him. This would not please the sons of the Shaykh.

First he began to convey the salutations and inquiries [after Farīd al-Dīn's health] of the Shaykhs who in those days were in the city [of Dehli. i.e. of Niẓām al-Dīn and his circle at Dehli]. The Shaykh heard these with satisfaction. When [Sayyid Muḥammad Kirmānī] wanted to mention [Niẓām al-Dīn], he said: 'Mawlana Niẓām al-Dīn, the slave of Your Lordship, has conveyed his submission and the kissing of your feet. He passes his time in the recollection of the prayer of the Shaykh of Shaykhs of the world.'[21]

This would appear to be a reference to Farīd al-Dīn's prayer described in the incident related by Niẓām al-Dīn himself, and is a reminder that Farīd al-Dīn had already chosen him as an especial successor. The account continues:

Shaykh Farīd showed favour to Niẓām al-Dīn and asked: 'How is he? Is he well?'

Then he said, 'Give him this garment (*jāma*) and prayer-mat (*muṣallā*) and staff.'

In the previous anecdote we have noted that Niẓām al-Dīn had already received a prayer-mat and staff. The quarrel with the kin of the shaykh then reached a head:

When this matter reached the ears of the sons of the Shaykh, they grew angry and came forward, hostile and quarrelsome, saying: 'You have done this, and caused what we desired to be given to another!'

'What could I do?' said Sayyid Muḥammad Kirmānī. 'I did not make any special mention of him. I conveyed the salutations which had been entrusted to me from the Shaykhs of Dehlī, and

[21] Khwurd, *Siyar al-awliyā'*, pp. 121–2.

in the course of these I also mentioned his name. When God ... out of His grace gives something to a Man, what power have I that I should prevent that good fortune?'

When the news of the death of Shaykh Farīd al-Dīn reached Shaykh Niẓām al-Dīn, he set out for Ajudhan. When he had performed the pilgrimage to Shaykh Farīd's tomb, Mawlānā Badr al-Dīn Isḥāq [an important Khalīfa of Shaykh Farīd al-Dīn] conveyed to him the garment and prayer-mat and staff. He mentioned Sayyid Muḥammad Kirmānī: 'The Sayyid performed what was necessary for the obligations of [Farīd al-Dīn's] love for you in your absence.'

Niẓām al-Dīn embraced Sayyid Muḥammad, and the bond of love between these two *buzurgs* grew greater.

This account illustrates both the rivalries and the mutual obligations which evolved in branches of a Ṣūfī order. The sons of Shaykh Farīd al-Dīn were hostile to Shaykh Niẓām al-Dīn's claims of succession to their father's spiritual authority, and what must be regarded as material considerations made them make an ugly scene at the death of their father, when the symbols of authority were transferred to him. Yet, one of Farīd al-Dīn's prolific family came to dwell at Niẓām al-Dīn's *khānqāh* at Dehli and was treated with much honour as the leader of the shaykh's prayers; his descendants were a leading family at the *khānqāh* with a claim to a share in its income. Possibly as a result of the transaction recorded above, the claims of the family of Sayyids from Kirmān to which the hagiographer Amīr Khwurd belonged were also established.

The following stage in the transmission of the *tabarrukāt*, from Shaykh Niẓām al-Dīn Awliyā' to Shaykh Naṣīr al-Dīn Chirāgh-i Dehlī, is of particular interest as it is in a period in which the witnesses were contemporary observers. The received tradition on the transmission is represented by the twentieth-century historian K.A. Nizami's statement, in the detailed biography of Shaykh Naṣīr al-Dīn Maḥmūd which precedes his critical text of the *malfūẓāt* of the shaykh, *Khair al-majālis*, that Shaykh Naṣīr al-Dīn 'succeeded his master as head of the Chishtī Silsila'.[22] K.A. Nizami's principal source for this statement is the early sixteenth-century *tadhkīra*, *Siyar al-'ārifīn*. According to this source, when Niẓām al-Dīn lay ill upon his death bed, he ordered the distribution of any property which had been retained in his *khānqāh*. The claims of a prominent Khalīfa in the Deccan were recognized. A turban, shirt (*payrāhan*), prayer-mat and robe of honour (*khil'at*, not *khirqa*), and a document of authority (*mithāl*) were despatched to Mawlānā Burhān al-Dīn Gharīb in the Deccan; similar presents, without the *khil'at* and *mithāl* were despatched to Shaykh Ya'qūb in Gujarat and a scholar of *Ḥadīth*, Shams al-Dīn Yaḥyā. The credibility of this account is injured by the fact that Burhān al-Dīn's migration to the Deccan was a result of Muḥammad bin Tughluq's decision to establish a new capital at Devgir/Dawlatabad in the years following the death of Shaykh Niẓām al-Dīn. Jamālī's account of the subsequent transmission of the *tabarrukāt* received from Niẓām al-Dīn's Pīr Farīd is as follows:[23]

On the day when [Niẓām al-Dīn] bestowed these gifts, Shaykh Naṣīr ... al-Dīn was present and [Niẓām al-Dīn] gave nothing to him, so that those who were in attendance were astonished. For how could it be that [the Shaykh] bestowed favours on all, and yet gave nothing to Shaykh Naṣīr al-Dīn Maḥmūd. After prayer on Wednesday he sent for Shaykh Naṣīr al-Dīn Maḥmūd, and he bestowed all upon him, the cloak and the staff, the prayer-carpet (*muṣallā*), the rosary (*tasbīḥ*), the wooden begging bowl [and?] what he had received from Shaykh Farīd al-Dīn. He said: 'You must remain in Dehli; and you must endure the oppression and neglect of men.'

22 Qalandar, *Khayr al-majālis*, K.A. Nizami's English introduction, pp. 47–8.

23 Jamālī, *Siyar al-'ārifīn*, Dehli: Maṭba'-i Riẓvī, AH 1311/AD 1893, pp. 47–8.

> [The Shaykh] performed the afternoon prayer, and the sunset had not yet come when he departed to the precinct of God's mercy.

Jamālī's construction is ambiguous, but he seems to imply that all these *tabarrukāt* came down from Farīd al-Dīn. This is too stereotyped a death-bed scene not to arouse suspicion. In the *Siyar al-awliyā'*, Amīr Khwurd, who would personally have observed such a scene as a young man, is entirely silent about it; a number of remarks make it clear that the account of Jamālī is an entire fabrication. The mention by Jamālī of Shams al-Dīn Yaḥyā may have been prompted by the fact that Sayyid Jalāl al-Dīn Makhdūm-i Jahānīān, one of Jamālī's own spiritual predecessors had—as he observed *en passant*—received a 'garment of succession' (*jāma-yi khilāfat*) from this shaykh. The *Siyar al-awliyā'* reproduces the text of the *Khilāfat-nāma* granted to Shams al-Dīn Yaḥyā just under four months before Niẓām al-Dīn's death, written out by one of the Kirmānī Sayyids;[24] there is no mention of a gift of clothes. The other two Shaykhs mentioned by Jamālī stand for geographical areas of Chishtī influence; in the lengthy list of the *khalīfas* of Niẓām al-Dīn in the *Siyar al-awliyā'*, they are not singled out for especial honour.[25] The case of Burhān al-Dīn was more extreme than this. We have noted that he was in Dehli until after the death of Niẓām al-Dīn, not as Jamālī implies already in the Deccan. He was a disciple of advanced age and considerable note, and had *not* been granted Khilāfat by Niẓām al-Dīn. When the latter's final illness was far advanced, by a conspiracy of the higher khādims of the *khānqāh*, including Amīr Khwurd's Kirmānī relations, he was brought into the bedroom of the dying shaykh, whose personal servant unpacked a frock and cap which the shaykh had worn, and clothed Burhān al-Dīn in them. Niẓām al-Dīn

[24] Khwurd, *Siyar al-awliyā'*, pp. 228–31.
[25] Ibid., pp. 220–92.

did not speak and 'silence is the proof of satisfaction'.[26] As regards Shaykh Naṣīr al-Dīn Maḥmūd, four sections of the twenty-five in Amīr Khwurd's notice of the Khalīfas of Niẓām al-Dīn are devoted to him.[27] This is more than any other *khalīfa* received, and it is acknowledged at the outset of the notice that Shaykh Naṣīr al-Dīn Maḥmūd 'nowadays occupies the place of Shaykh Niẓām al-Dīn in the city of Dehli'.

The writer has heard his uncle, Sayyid Ḥusayn, remark: 'Nowadays the lofty position of Sulṭān al-Mashā'ikh [Niẓām al-Dīn] in the city of Dehli is occupied by Shaykh Naṣīr al-Dīn Maḥmūd; and inwardly and outwardly, to the best of his ability he does not pass beyond the practice of Shaykh Niẓām al-Dīn. Among the Khalīfas of Niẓām al-Dīn, in this work he had achieved complete distinction and arrived at the stage of perfection ...'.[28]

In this passage the suggestion that Naṣīr al-Dīn was the unique nominated heir of the shaykh's *baraka* is obviously lacking and implicitly denied.[29] Elsewhere, Amīr Khwurd describes the granting of *khilāfat* by Niẓām al-Dīn to Naṣīr al-Dīn Maḥmūd and Quṭb al-Dīn Munawwar, a *pīr* who enjoyed

[26] Ibid., pp. 281–2. This summary recognition of Burhān al-Dīn Gharīb's claims, the account of which bears the mark of plausibility, conflicts with that shaykh's own behaviour when, three years later, he was compelled by Muḥammad bin Tughluq to participate in the forced migration from Dehli to Dawlatabad. A staff, matching that which Naṣīr al-Dīn Maḥmūd claimed to have received as *tabarruk* from Niẓām al-Dīn was attached to the head of the palankeen in which Burhān al-Dīn travelled: Ḥammād Kāshānī, *Aḥsan al-aqwāl*, Urdu tr. M. 'Abd al-Majīd, Bombay: s.n., n.d., p. 33.

[27] Khwurd, *Siyar al-awliyā'*, pp. 236–47.

[28] Ibid., pp. 237–8.

[29] See also the account of the relations between Burhān al-Dīn Gharīb and Naṣīr al-Dīn Maḥmūd in Sayyid Muḥammad Akbar Ḥusaynī, *Jawāmi' al-kalim*, Hyderabad, Deccan: Taḥqīqātī Akāḍmī, Faṣlī 1356/AD 1946, pp. 239–40.

the esteem of Fērōz Shāh Tughluq.[30] The grants of *khilāfat* were accompanied by the injunction, 'You are brothers and must keep your minds free of ideas of precedence and subsequence.'[31]

Further evidence of the falsity of Jamālī's account of Niẓām al-Dīn's end are the parenthetical remarks of Amīr Khwurd about the *Khilāfat-nāmas* drawn up when it was realized that Niẓām al-Dīn's end was approaching, designed

[30] 'Afif provides detailed confirmation of Amīr Khwurd's statement as to the equality which existed between the two shaykhs, Quṭb al-Dīn Munawwar and Naṣīr al-Dīn Maḥmūd, as heirs of Niẓām al-Dīn's *baraka*. He too quoted the injunction that they should consider one another as equals; and he describes in detail the scrupulous observation of courtesies between them. The murīd of one, if he visited the *khānqāh* of the other, would be summoned to a close place beside the shaykh. When, after Sulṭān Muḥammad bin Tughluq's death at Ṭaṭṭha, Sulṭān Fērōz Shāh Tughluq returned to Dehli, Naṣīr al-Dīn Maḥmūd was in the entourage of the army. On the sulṭān's approaching Hansi, Naṣīr al-Dīn formally consigned him to the intercession of Quṭb al-Dīn Munawwar, through whose territorial *wilāyat* he was about to pass. After the sulṭān had met Quṭb al-Dīn Munawwar and received injunctions regarding his behaviour, Naṣīr al-Dīn Maḥmūd called at the *khānqāh*. The two shaykhs exchanged reminiscences of Niẓām al-Dīn and wept and then listened to *samā'*. At the time of prayer, both insisted that the other should act as imām; but Quṭb al-Dīn finally accepted the task when Naṣīr al-Dīn Maḥmūd urged that he had received his *khilāfat* earlier in the course of the same day. The two shaykhs bade farewell to one another knowing that it was to be their last meeting and that neither would be long in this world. Quṭb al-Dīn died later in the same year as Naṣīr al-Dīn Maḥmūd: 'Afif, *Ta'rīkh-i Fērōzshāhī*, Calcutta: Bibliotheca Indica, 1890, pp. 61, 79–84.

'Afif's account not only agrees with that of Amīr Khwurd, but also runs counter to the assumption that a greater share of *tabarrukāt* and authority were transferred to Naṣīr al-Dīn Maḥmūd. It shows that, in accordance with the general arguments of this paper, the actual influence wielded by Naṣīr al-Dīn Maḥmūd, then accompanying the Sulṭān's army on the march, reflected his proximity to the sulṭān's court.

[31] Khwurd, *Siyar al-awliyā'*, pp. 248–9.

to counter an opinion which was current, that they did not express the true intentions of the shaykh:

> ... And what some people say or write in their compositions regarding the *khilāfat-nāmas* to these *buzurgs*: that the blessed hand of the Shaykh was wholly paralysed; that he had no consciousness and they seized the hand of Shaykh Niẓām al-Dīn and drew his signature, this was not in fact the case. The loss of faculties (*ghalba-yi taḥayyur*) of the Shaykh was for not more than about forty days before his death; but the writing of the *Khilāfat-nāmas* of these *buzurgs*, and their being distinguished by bequests was three months and twenty-seven days before the death of Shaykh Niẓām al-Dīn.[32]

This corresponds exactly with the date of the *khilāfat-nāma* to Shams al-Dīn Yaḥyā and appears to indicate an attempt on the part of the higher khādims of the *khānqāh*, to put in order claims to succession when it was realized that Niẓām al-Dīn's health was failing.

The claims of Burhān al-Dīn, a popular and widely admired elderly disciple who had incurred the shaykh's displeasure, may have been satisfied at an even later date.

In these passages there is no reference to the disposition of the *tabarrukāt* which Niẓām al-Dīn had received from his own Shaykh Farīd al-Dīn. Niẓām al-Dīn appears to have been reluctant to grant Khilāfat to his closest and oldest disciples. He was unmarried, and after his death the *khānqāh* remained in the possession of its residents, led by those related to the shaykh or performing services in his devotions. One nephew of the shaykh, Rafī' al-Dīn, had been appointed mutawallī (administrator) in the shaykh's lifetime; descendants of another nephew, carrier of the shaykh's prayer-carpet, and his imām, remained among the leading khādim families at the beginning of [the twentieth] century.[33]

[32] Ibid., pp. 222–3.
[33] Khwurd, *Siyar al-awliyā'*, pp. 200–5.

In a different context the *Siyar al-awliyā'* states that two of the *tabarrukāt* which Niẓām al-Dīn had received from Farīd al-Dīn were interred with him. Amīr Khwurd's description occurs in a section on the bestowal of *khirqas*, after three statements attributed to Niẓām al-Dīn:

> [Niẓām al-Dīn] used to say that the garments which have been received from the company of a Shaykh cannot be bestowed upon another. If they are washed, this is not prohibited, though it is better that they should not be washed. He also said: 'If the presents (*tashrīfāt*) received from the companionship of a *pīr* are bequeathed [by the recipient] and not placed inside his grave, this is permissible: or if he makes a testament giving them to his offspring who are worthy (*ṣāliḥ*).'
>
> And he said: 'Once (*waqtē*) I received a cloak from the Shaykh of Shaykhs of the world, Farīd al-Dīn, a Chishtī cloak of wool (*gilīm khirqa-yi Chishtī*), and that is yet upon me.'
>
> The writer submits in this connection that when after his death they lowered Shaykh Niẓām al-Dīn into his grave, they stretched over his body the cloak (*khirqa*) which he had received from Shaykh Farīd al-Dīn; and they placed the prayer-carpet (*muṣallā*) of his Shaykh upon his blessed head.[34]

It is difficult to believe that the three sayings quoted before the description of the interment represent Niẓām al-Dīn's views regarding the transmission of authority. The first

[34] Ibid., pp. 342–3; quoted with omissions and slight verbal alterations by Abd al-Haqq in Dehlavī, *Akhbār al-Akhyār*, p. 59 (I am grateful to Professor Bruce Lawrence for drawing my attention to this passage). Either a failure to make any disposition with regard to the *tabarrukāt* or a decision to have them buried beside him would have been in accord with Niẓām al-Dīn's disposition and behaviour, described in this essay, as he approached death.

Some support for the idea that this was a conscious decision of the shaykh is given by Hamīd Qalandar's account of what occurred at the death of the next heritor, Naṣīr al-Dīn Maḥmūd. The account, examined below, is unlikely to be true in all particulars; but it might well have been modelled on the true course of events at the previous transmission.

is contrary to the example of the staff of Quṭb al-Dīn which he had inherited from Farīd, and the second is contrary to the moral of his story of the *pīr* at Ghaznīn (above). After two further anecdotes, one regarding a variety of *khirqas* inherited by the author, Amīr Khwurd records:

> Shaykh Niẓām al-Dīn also said: 'On the morrow of the Resurrection, some of this [Ṣūfī] band (*ṭā'ifa*) will be made to stand among the thieves, and they will say, "We have not stolen!" The answer will come, "You have put on the clothes of Men, and you have not acted [as such]!"
>
> 'In the end they also will attain salvation through the intercession of *pīrs*.'

The inclusion of this saying here may be an oblique reference to claims and counterclaims among the *khalīfas* of the shaykh at the time of writing. Amīr Khwurd's separate account of the shaykh's last days suggests that Niẓām al-Dīn had not made adequate arrangements for the undisputed transfer of his authority. In default of an injunction (*waṣīyat*), the decision to inter the *khirqa* and *muṣallā* may have been taken by the principal khādims. It is perhaps significant that in this passage Amīr Khwurd does not mention the *'aṣā*, which by Niẓām al-Dīn's own testimony descended from the *pīr* of his *pīr*. According to surviving evidence, two major *khalīfas*, Naṣīr al-Dīn Maḥmūd and Burhān al-Dīn Gharīb, each claimed to possess the staff of Niẓām al-Dīn.

By contrast with our lack of a coherent account of Niẓām al-Dīn's dying wishes, we have a circumstantial account of the death of Shaykh Naṣīr al-Dīn Maḥmūd, which claims to be immediately contemporary. This also claims that he had no worthy successor, and that the *tabarrukāt* which he had received from his *pīr*, or were his personal symbols of authority, were buried with him in his grave:[35]

[35] Qalandar, *Khayr al-majālis*, p. 287.

On the eve of Friday, the eighteenth of the month of Ramaẓān he wished to release the bird of his spirit from the cage of his body. Mawlānā Zayn al-Dīn ʻAlī [his nephew] submitted: ʻLord, most of your disciples are the possessors of ecstasy and the folk of perfection. Among all these, indicate one who may sit in your place, so that the *silsila* [ʻchain', Ṣūfī lineage] may not be totally broken.'

ʻGo!' he said. ʻBring me [a list of] those Darvishes of whom you have a good opinion, so that I may examine it.'

The Mawlānā had a list in three rolls, best, middling and worst. When the Mawlānā had placed the list in front of him and after he had studied it, he said: ʻShaykh Zayn al-Dīn, tell them to worry over their own faith; What capacity have they to bear the burdens of others?'

After that he pronounced his testament (*waṣīyat*): ʻAt the time of my burial lay over my breast the cloak which I received from Haẓrat ... Niẓām al-Dīn, and bind the staff of my *pīr* upon me in the gravecloth. Twist the rosary around my forefinger, and place the wooden bowl beneath my head like a brick, and also place my wooden sandals by my side.'

Those who were present at the time put into effect the wish of the Shaykh. Sayyid Muḥammad Gēsūdarāz washed the corpse, and took up the woven threads of the cot on which the water had been poured over his blessed body. He said: ʻThis is enough of a cloak for me!'

In the end the acceptance which that Sayyid obtained, was from the *barakat* [blessed influence] of it.

The author, Ḥamīd Qalandar, claims a few paragraphs later, at the conclusion, to have composed this account in the year of Naṣīr al-Dīn's death. Yet the reference which he makes to the acceptance (*qabūliyatī*) which Sayyid Muḥammad Gēsūdarāz had obtained as heir to Naṣīr al-Dīn's authority can hardly date from that year. This may be a later comment of the author, or even an interpolation by another hand; but the structure of the anecdote suggests the alternative conclusion that this anecdote achieved its present form a number of years, perhaps decades, afterwards, when the claims of Sayyid Muḥammad Gēsūdarāz were achieving widespread recognition.

The scene at the death bed of Shaykh Naṣīr al-Dīn Maḥmūd has parallels with those at the demise of his two predecessors in the lineage. Like Niẓām al-Dīn, he may have been unwilling to devise his spiritual authority to a single heir, and have desired that his *tabarrukāt* should be buried with him. He would certainly have received a cloak from Niẓām al-Dīn at the occasion of the issue of his *khilāfat-nāma*, which was probably not that passed on to Niẓām al-Dīn. The staff could have been that which Niẓām al-Dīn received from Farīd al-Dīn, though the evidence of the *Siyar al-awliyā'* does not favour this assumption. If 'Abd al-Ḥaqq's evidence regarding Niẓām al-Dīn's burial is accepted, the impulse may have been strong upon Naṣīr al-Dīn Maḥmūd not to pass on *tabarrukāt* to a chosen successor. On the other hand, his position resembled that of Farīd al-Dīn, in that his own kin within his lifetime had assumed control of the management of the shrine, and could limit access to the person of the shaykh. They would be likely to oppose any impulse of the shaykh to will his authority elsewhere. The parallel to the position described in the *Siyar al-awliyā'*, when Farīd al-Dīn lay dying with his sons anxious that no one else should get access to him, is obvious. Short of managing to persuade their uncle to appoint one of themselves to succeed him, the best thing which could happen for the nephews of Shaykh Naṣīr al-Dīn Maḥmūd was that his *tabarrukāt* should be buried on the premises.

It is not surprising that the account of Shaykh Naṣīr al-Dīn Maḥmūd's wishes, which has come down to us from the partisans of Sayyid Muḥammad Gēsūdarāz, contradicts the relation by Ḥamīd Qalandar which we have noted above in the most important particulars. In his conversations recorded in the *Jawāmi' al-kalim*, Gēsūdarāz once refers to himself as the inheritor of the authority and *tabarrukāt* of Shaykh Naṣīr al-Dīn Maḥmūd. After mentioning that Sulṭān Muḥammad b. Tughluq was ashamed of his behaviour towards Naṣīr al-Dīn Maḥmūd and therefore bestowed on him the distinction of a drum and standard, Gēsūdarāz related:

He has a very high rank among the saints of God. After the Shaykh that *wilāyat* [territorial spiritual authority] was divided among four people. The first was a Sūfī. The second was a box-maker (*ṣundūq-tarāsh*). The third was a potter, and the fourth was a woman. As each one of these died, more [of the *wilāyat*] returned to that same Ṣūfī: until, after him, God knows best to whom it will come.[36]

There can be little doubt that in this passage the Ṣūfī referred to was Gēsūdarāz himself, as such modest periphrasis is common in Ṣūfī literature. In the *Jawāmi' al-kalim*, which records ten months of Gēsūdarāz's conversations, there is no more detailed account of his succession to Naṣīr al-Dīn Maḥmūd, although there are some disparaging references to Ḥamīd Qalandar (author of the preceding account) and to Naṣīr al-Dīn's kin. Of the early *tadhkīras* of the life of Gēsūdarāz, the *Siyar-i Muḥammadī* has an extended notice of events at the time of Naṣīr al-Dīn Maḥmūd's death. The *Siyar-i Muḥammadī* was composed six years after the death of Gēsūdarāz. Thus, it should be regarded as a rather better authority for his life than the *Siyar al-awliyā'* is for that of Niẓām al-Dīn. It states that Sayyid Muḥammad Gēsūdarāz had been severely ill, coughing and spitting blood, and he attributed his recovery to his *pīr* Naṣīr al-Dīn Maḥmūd's intercession. When he had recovered, he called upon Naṣīr al-Dīn Maḥmūd; and he was told to wait in private after the other disciples had departed. Then Gēsūdarāz related to his shaykh a curious dream which he had dreamt (a precursor to the dreams and visions which he recorded in his old age). In this dream he was putting on and drawing

[36] Ḥusaynī, *Jawāmi' al-kalim*, p. 240.

off various garments, passing through *wilāyat*, *nubuwwat*, and *risālat* to end in *hu'yat* (identification with God). Naṣīr al-Dīn Maḥmūd's face shone with joy as Sayyid Muḥammad related this. Sayyid Muḥammad then added:

'I saw all different things with forms distinct from one another resolved into One Truth.'

The Shaykh was very joyful, and he brought both his hands down over his face, and said: 'Praise be to God, Lord of the Worlds.'

He then added some words to the effect that his life appeared to be drawing to its close. Next he took the rug (*galīm*) from in front of him and gave it into both hands of Sayyid Muḥammad ...; and he grasped firmly his hand and said: 'Afterwards, anyone who sees difficulty sees it for a motive [i.e. critics of Sayyid Muḥammad's spiritual inheritance must be so from self interest].'

Then he said: 'Sayyid Muḥammad, accept this act from me!' That is to say, 'Give me your hand in *bay'at*'.

Sayyid Muḥammad bent his head low and was silent.

'Have you accepted it?' the Shaykh then said.

'I have accepted it,' he replied.

Then the Shaykh made two testamentary admonitions, the first that he should not abandon his external recitations, and the second that he should cherish those who were attached to him.

Then the Mawlānā Zayn al-Dīn came.

'Go away, Zayn al-Dīn,' the Shaykh said. 'Make the arrangements for the ordering of the sweets for the *kandūrī* feast!'[37]

When Mawlānā Zayn al-Dīn had gone away, he threw a *nihālcha* [thin stuffed quilt used as a mattress] to him, and said: 'Sayyid, draw off the cover of this quilt,[38] and put it in your sleeve and go back!'[39]

[37] A feast held in honour of the Prophet's daughter, Fāṭima, attended by women (Steingass).

[38] The word used is *nihālcha*, meaning a stuffed quilt used as a bed-covering or mattress, with a detachable cover. If, as in the case of most modern *raẓā'īs*, this was patterned, it would be particularly apt for service as a prayer carpet.

[39] Muḥammad 'Alī Sāmānī, *Siyar-i Muḥammadī*, Allahabad: Yūnānī Davalkhānah, AH 1347/AD 1928, pp. 17–19.

> On the night of Tuesday, 15 Ramaẓān, Shaykh Naṣīr al-Dīn Maḥmūd fell ill. In the course of his illness several of his disciples represented to him that each *buzurg* at the time of his own passing away had appointed some people in his place and for his own part (*bi jihat-i khwud*) had especially distinguished one of them. Several of the shaykh's disciples had reached lofty spiritual stations and had become the recipients of revelations and illuminations. If he would give licence to several of them (i.e. *khilāfat-nāmas*), and single out one of them, it would not be in disaccord with the practice of the khwājas (of Chisht, the Chishtī *silsila*).

'Write out their names and bring them,' Shaykh Naṣīr al-Dīn Maḥmūd said.

They made out a list and Mawlānā Zayn al-Dīn brought that list to the Shaykh. The name of Sayyid Muḥammad was not on the list. When the Shaykh had scanned the list, he said, 'What a sack [?] of stones and clods you have brought. Tell them to worry about their own faith!' And he threw away the list.

Mawlānā Zayn al-Dīn again made a short list, and brought it back with some names omitted. He took it to the Shaykh who said: 'Read it out.'

He read it out and the Shaykh said: 'You have not written the name of Sayyid Muḥammad.'

Zayn al-Dīn grew afraid and began to tremble. Immediately he wrote the name of Sayyid Muḥammad. The Shaykh took the list, and with his pen made a *ṣād* [for *ṣaḥīḥ*, beside the name of Sayyid Muḥammad is implied].

On the eve of Friday, 18th of Ramaẓān Haẓrat Shaykh Naṣīr al-Dīn departed from this perishable world and took his abode into the world everlasting. He was seventy-two years old. The gifts [*ni'matē*, i.e. the *tabarrukāt*] came to four people. One of these was Sayyid Muḥammad Gēsūdarāz; and when the other three died, all these gifts came to him. After his third visit to the grave of Shaykh Naṣīr al-Dīn Maḥmūd, Sayyid Muḥammad sat upon the carpet of spiritual authority (*sajjāda-yi wilāyat*) and gave his hand in *bay'at* [acceptance of murīds]; and instructed and guided seekers after God.

Of the two *tabarrukāt* mentioned in this passage, the *galīm* was a rug, probably without pile, which could be worn by a *faqīr* as a blanket or shawl around the shoulders. It counted therefore as a *khirqa*, indicating that the recipient was a *khalīfa* of the shaykh. Gēsūdarāz was at this time 35 or 36 years old, a youthful age for the bestowal of *khilāfat*, especially in view of the practice of Naṣīr al-Dīn's predecessor Niẓām al-Dīn, though justified by anecdotes related by both these shaykhs regarding the actions of Farīd al-Dīn and of Shihāb al-Dīn 'Umar Suhrawardī.[40] The *nihālcha* or quilt was something on which the shaykh reposed. If we may judge by later Indian examples (no textiles from the Dehli Sultanate having survived) it was almost certainly patterned. It was an adequate *sajjāda*, or carpet of authority, and its bestowal by the shaykh indicated the transfer of an important part of the shaykh's spiritual authority. It was probably to this gift that Gēsūdarāz himself, in the conversation recorded in the *Jawāmi' al-kalim*, and his biographer in the *Siyar-i Muḥammadī* were referring, as the single gift in the possession of Gēsūdarāz at the time of Naṣīr al-Dīn's death. To this were added the three others which had been entrusted to persons—a box-maker, a potter, and a woman—who from their status in life must be interpreted as hidden *abdāls* secretly promoting the well-being of the world.[41]

[40] Gēsūdarāz had professed his allegiance to Naṣīr al-Dīn Maḥmūd when he returned from the Deccan as a student, aged fifteen, about twenty years earlier; see Sāmānī, *Siyar-i Muḥammadī*, pp. 3, 6, 10–11.

[41] In the Ṣūfī literature of the period concealed Abdāls or Walīs play a considerable role, which is discussed in my paper, 'Qalandars and Related Groups', in *Islam in Asia*, vol. 1, ed. Y. Friedmann, Jerusalem: Hebrew University, 1984, pp. 60–108 [*L&WSD* III.7]; see also S. Digby,

We may find the story of this subsequent transmission of the further three *tabarrukāt*, which completed Gēsūdarāz's claim to the entire *wilāyat* or spiritual authority of Naṣīr al-Dīn, improbable; if it is an invention, it can only be that of Gēsūdarāz himself.

Ḥamīd Qalandar's account in the *Khair al-majālis* of the role of Gēsūdarāz at Naṣīr al-Dīn's death bears the marks of hagiographical invention to explain away an awkward fact that was a matter of common knowledge, viz., that Gēsūdarāz possessed a *sajjāda* given by Naṣīr al-Dīn, when the latter's family, represented by Zayn al-Dīn, had done their best to prevent the transfer of such a gift. It is therefore explained as the threads of the cot or charpoy which Gēsūdarāz bore away (without permission) when he had washed the shaykh's corpse. The *Siyar-i Muḥammadī* contains no mention of Gēsūdarāz performing the *ghusl* (washing) of the corpse, and as he was neither a relation of the shaykh nor a permanent inmate at the *khānqāh*, it is unlikely that he would have been allowed this intimate distinction by those in control of the obsequies; or that his own biographers, if he had undertaken the *ghusl*, would have remained silent about it.

Ḥamīd Qalandar, both from the information which he gives of himself in the *Khair al-majālis* and other contemporary evidence, was a man of somewhat precious character, a 'hanger-on' at both the *khānqāh* and the sultan's court.[42] Gēsūdarāz in conversation expressed his dislike for him, and the favour of Zayn al-Dīn and his brothers would have been important to him. We have noted above that his reference to the 'acceptance' which Gēsūdarāz had

---

'The Waterseller's Pilgrimage', *Lycidas*, vol. III, Oxford: Wolfson College, 1975, pp. 20–1.

[42] The character and activities of Ḥamīd Qalandar are examined in my 'Qalandars and Related Groups'. Ḥamīd Qalandar's testimony with regard to one incident is rejected as less accurate than that of Gēsūdarāz.

gained amid the populace conflicts with the very early date at which Ḥamīd Qalandar states that he completed the account of the shaykh's death. Opposition to the claims of Gēsūdarāz provides a specific motive for an otherwise not very meaningful falsification of the date of composition. The textual tradition of the *Khair al-majālis*, in which two of the three manuscripts on which the modern critical edition was based lack the appendix describing the shaykh's death, also suggests that the work was already in circulation in manuscript form before the appendix was composed. This evidence is significant rather than conclusive, as the hundredth and last *majlis* is followed by a colophon dated Wednesday, 4 Ṣafar, without mention of the year. As composition of the work was begun in AH 754, these conversations must have been recorded between then and the year of the shaykh's death, i.e. AH 757, in a year when 1 Muḥarram fell on Thursday. Of the years in question, assuming that there was no unusually early sighting of the new moon, and bearing in mind that the Muslim day begins at dusk, 1 Muḥarram AH 757 exactly corresponds with Wednesday night/Thursday, 9–10 January AD 1356, and no such close correspondence can be found in the previous three years. The *Khair al-majālis* (without the appendix) was therefore completed only a little more than seven months before the death of Naṣīr al-Dīn Maḥmūd. In this period or in the three and a half months from the shaykh's death to the end of the Muslim year, transcriptions could have been made, from which the two surviving manuscripts which do not contain the appendix descend. This is, however, an uncomfortably short period, if the appendix was added before the end of AH 757, a proposition which we are inclined to deny. As regards the veracity of the two conflicting accounts of Naṣīr al-Dīn's deathbed scenes, the story in the *Siyar al-Muḥammadī* of the *nihālcha* being smuggled out by Gēsūdarāz with the goodwill and complicity of the dying shaykh past the vigilance of his relations appears the more worthy of belief.

Some evidence of the bitterness of the quarrel regarding the succession between Gēsūdarāz and Zayn al-Dīn may be adduced from Gēsūdarāz's own remarks, in the course of reflections upon his own remarkable longevity:

> He then said: 'Mawlānā, I don't know why God gave me this long life. I never asked from God but once for a long life. This was when my master, Shaykh Naṣīr al-Dīn Maḥmūd ..., departed from this world to the next. He had given me *khilāfat* and he had kept it hidden from Mawlānā Zayn al-Dīn. After the death of the Shaykh they cast doubt upon my *khilāfat*.'
>
> 'Anyone who will be the *khalīfa* of Shaykh Naṣīr al-Dīn Maḥmūd,' said Mawlānā Zayn al-Dīn, 'will reach a fulfilled age (*'umr-i mukammal*) like the Shaykh; and he will teach and guide God's servants, and the *silsila* of the shaykhs will continue from him.'
>
> 'At the time it passed through my mind that it would be good if God gave me a long life, so that the genuineness of my *khilāfat* would be manifest to them.'[43]

The remark about *'umr-i mukammal* is a sneer at the comparative youth of Gēsūdarāz, and perhaps takes into consideration the fact that Gēsūdarāz had only recently recovered from a severe illness. Its circumstantiality gives the conversation the ring of truth.

Sayyid Muḥammad Gēsūdarāz stands in contrast to his predecessors in the Chishtī *silsila*, whose conversations were recorded, but who were themselves never impelled to commit their teachings to writing. Some of Gēsūdarāz's extensive literary oeuvre has been published in the original Persian or in Urdu translation. He made observations regarding succession within the Ṣūfī *silsilas*. With regard to the difficulties of the earnest seeker in choosing a *silsila*

[43] Sāmānī, *Siyar-i Muḥammadī*, p. 5.

to which to attach himself, he remarked that 'nowadays' these were much increased by the failure of certain shaykhs to appoint a true successor, either by testament (*waṣīyat*), or on their deathbed. One may see in this a reflection of Gēsūdarāz's own difficulties at the death of Naṣīr al-Dīn Maḥmūd. This led, he continued, to 'certain people' putting the son of the shaykh in his father's place three days after the death, and clothing the son in his father's *khirqa*. Relations of the shaykh, also, without the necessary permission from him, began themselves to take disciples, a sure path into error.[44] Elsewhere he complained of the sons of shaykhs who usurped their father's authority, and he added to this a denunciation of the luxury and ease which they permitted their disciples.[45]

Gēsūdarāz admitted to some flagging in his powers of concentration after he had attained the age of 90. He then found it easier to dictate an important work on dreams, visions and allegories than to concentrate on the exposition of works on the traditional Islamic sciences and earlier Ṣūfī classics.[46] He may have felt that he had suffered unduly from Naṣīr al-Dīn's inability fully and publicly to express his intentions with regard to the succession while on his deathbed. In his own case he provided for the contingency many years before the event. Before, as a septuagenarian, he decided to leave Dehli in anticipation of the disasters of Timur's invasion of 1398—in retrospect a move of political prescience unparalleled in this period—he drew up a *waṣīyat-nāma* in Arabic. In the next two decades of his life some of his disciples and kin predeceased him, and a number

[44] Gēsūdarāz, *Ruḥ-i taṣawwuf*, Urdu tr. of commentary by Gēsūdarāz on Suhrawardī's *Awārif al-ma'ārif*, Dehli: Zawia Publishers, n.d. (c. 1958), pp. 199–200.

[45] Ḥusaynī, *Jawāmi' al-kilm*, pp. 26–7.

[46] Gēsūdarāz, *Asmār al-asrār*, ed. 'Aṭā Allāh Ḥusaynī, Hyderabad, Deccan: Aẓam Steam Press, Faṣlī 1350/AD 1941, p. 3.

of alterations were made until his death, at the age of 105 Muslim years, in Gulbarga in the Deccan in AH 825/AD 1422.[47]

Although Gēsūdarāz had denounced the practice of seating unsuitable sons of Ṣūfī shaykhs in their father's place, he did not doubt the spiritual competence of his own sons. He may have had cause for this confidence, for he himself was clearly an excellent teacher and his elder son, Sayyid Muḥammad Akbar, was the author of a work on Ṣūfī terminology as well as the compiler of the most reputed collection of his father's *malfūẓat*, the *Jawāmi' al-kalim*. Sayyid Muḥammad Akbar predeceased his father, who after his death testified to his high spiritual rank and his abilities, and constructed a tomb around which he performed the *ziyārat* or pilgrimage appropriate to the grave of a Ṣūfī shaykh of consequence. After the death of Muḥammad Akbar, Gēsūdarāz altered his *waṣīyat-nāma* in favour of his surviving son, Muḥammad Asghar, and he eventually bequeathed to him his *khirqa*, *sajjāda*, and finger-ring.[48] The *khirqa* and *sajjāda* may have been identical with the *galīm* and *nihālcha*, which his biographer claims with plausibility that he had received from Naṣīr al-Dīn Maḥmūd. The finger-ring, nowhere else mentioned as one of the *tabarrukāt*, may have been a personal inheritance of Gēsūdarāz from his honourable patrilineal ancestors established (according to his own testimony) as Sayyids in the Dehli Sultanate from the period when this was founded; or, it could have been a personal signet which many Muslims in South Asia and probably most of the Islamic world are predisposed to wear, regardless of any Ṣūfī connection. There is no mention of the disposal of the three remaining *tabarrukāt* which Gēsūdarāz claimed to have

[47] Sāmānī, *Siyar-i Muḥammadī*, p. 111; 'Abd al-'Azīz bin Shēr Malik, *Ta'rīkh-i Ḥabībī*, Urdu tr. Nawwāb Ma'shūq Yār Jang, Hyderabad, Deccan: s.n., n.d. (c. 1920), p. 44; Ḥusaynī, *Jawāmi' al-kalim*, Urdu intro., pp. 15, 19.

[48] Sāmānī, *Siyar-i Muḥammadī*, p. 117; Shēr Malik, *Ta'rīkh-i Ḥabībī*, p. 49.

received through humble intermediaries from Naṣīr al-Dīn. Possibly these may have been assumed to have passed once more into the keeping of the abdāls, to be produced again when a need for spiritual leadership arose.

At the death of Gēsūdarāz a minor claim remained unsatisfied. Under Muslim law an orphaned grandson in the male line lacks any major and ascertained claims on his grandfather's estate. This was the case of Mīān Ṣafīr Allāh, son of Muḥammad Akbar. At the death of Gēsūdarāz the lack of generosity which is so conspicuous a feature in most of the incidents which we have surveyed again recurred. Only after the mediation of the sultan of the Deccan, Aḥmad Shāh Bahmanī, was he recognized as custodian and sajjāda-nashīn of his father's tomb. Ṣafīr Allāh died without issue, and the main line of the sajjāda-nashīns of Gēsūdarāz at Gulbarga are referred to as inheritors of the *Rawẓatain*, the two tombs of Gēsūdarāz and his elder son Muḥammad Akbar.

At the death of Sayyid Muḥammad Gēsūdarāz, the alternative means by which spiritual authority could be inherited among the Chishtī shaykhs, by the transmission of *tabarrukāt* and by consanguinity, were united. At the same time the sources for such a conflict in succession were removed by the destruction of the political authority of the Dehli Sultanate over a large area of the Indian subcontinent after the invasion of Timur in AD 1398. It may be argued that the conflict regarding succession became of less importance with the fragmentation of political authority in the provincial sultanates, though the prestige of the Chishtī lineage led to Gēsūdarāz, in his old age, playing a decisive part in supplanting Ḥasan, the son of the Bahmanī sultan of the Deccan, Fērōz Shāh, by Aḥmad, the sultan's brother. This Ṣūfī authority of the Chishtī shaykhs was so overwhelming that it led to a search for an alternative with similar prestige. Aḥmad Shāh Bahmanī, set on the throne with the approval of Sayyid Muḥammad Gēsūdarāz, quarrelled with the latter's grandson, and sought the support of one of the most notable shaykhs of the early fifteenth century in Iran, Shāh Niʿamat Allāh Walī of Māhān, who himself declined to come to the Deccan, but despatched his grandsons there. Khilāfat was conferred upon the sultan, and with this spiritual authority he and his successors were described on their coinage and in inscriptions as *al-walī*, implying spiritual as well as temporal dominion.

The anecdotes of conflicts regarding succession which we have examined in this chapter sufficiently demonstrate that possession of the shaykh's tomb was an important asset, representing inheritance of a portion of his spiritual authority. Yet, against this was balanced the claims to charisma by living shaykhs and, in popular estimation, a single living shaykh to whom the *tabarrukāt* had passed. But after the invasion of Timur in AD 1398, we have no record of any living Chishtī shaykh of note to whom such an inheritance might have passed, or by whom the prestige of his predecessors might have been maintained. The power of the Dehli Sultanate was in eclipse, and the ruined city was no rival to the glittering capitals of the provincial sultanates. Dehli was a place of hallowed memories, a city of the sanctified Muslim dead. The Lōdī sultans and many Afghan nobles erected their splendid mausolea there, at a time when Agra was the administrative capital. By the sixteenth century this strong consciousness of a hallowed past is expressed by such authors as ʿAbd al-Ḥaqq Muḥaddith and Rizq Allāh Mushtāqī.[49] Only in the late seventeenth century, with the

[49] ʿAbd al-Ḥaqq Dehlavī, *Tadhkira-yi Muṣannifīn-i Dehlī*, ed. Shams Allāh Qādirī, Hyderabad, Deccan: Historical Society of Hyderabad/ Tarikh Press, 1930, text, p. 6; Rizq Allāh Mushtāqī, *Waqiʿāt-i Mushtāqī*, p. 26. By this time the idea that Dehli was the true capital of India, possession of which or enthronement in which ensured the legitimacy of the sovereign, was so entrenched in popular belief that it was repeated by English travellers of the first decade of the seventeenth century; cf.

arrival of Shāh Kalīm Allāh Awrangābādī at Shahjahanabad, do living Chishtī shaykhs again exert a significant influence on the religious life of the revived capital.

The memory of the great Chishtī shaykhs of the Dehli Sultanate continued to command widespread allegiance among Muslims of the subcontinent, and led to a hagiographical tradition blossoming into more and more fantastic anecdotes attesting their miraculous powers. Mu'īn al-Dīn, a figure about whom there is the most meagre information in thirteenth- and fourteenth-century sources, was enshrouded in a mass of symbolic legend, the motivation of which is not difficult to perceive. First of the Chishtī *silsila* in India, his arrival was the counterpart of the great triumph of Muslim arms which established the Dehli Sultanate. The fortress city of Ajmer in which he was buried was a symbol of the fragility of this military triumph. In the fifteenth and sixteenth centuries it was lost to Rajput chieftains, retaken and lost again by provincial sultans, and finally brought under Mughal domination.

The end of the Chishtī tradition of bequeathing *tabarrukāt* to a chosen successor led not only to the hereditarization of sanctity at the Chishtī shrines, but also to transferring the centre of devotion from the person of a living *pīr* to the graves of the dead *pīrs*, accentuating a tendency which was at work with varying force among Ṣūfī orders throughout the Islamic world. As we have noted in our account of the succession at Chisht, in Khurasan and elsewhere, the cult of Ṣūfī graves was firmly established before the creation of the Dehli Sultanate. In Dehli itself Niẓām al-Dīn and Naṣīr al-Dīn Maḥmūd were in the habit of performing the *ziyārat* of the tomb of their predecessor Quṭb al-Dīn,[50] which the Arab

---

Hawkins and Finch in W. Foster, ed., *Early Travels in India, 1583–1619*, Oxford: Oxford University Press, 1921, pp. 100, 126.

[50] Qalandar, *Khayr al-majālis*, p. 57; Khwurd, *Siyar al-awliyā'*, pp. 50–1.

traveller Ibn Baṭṭūṭa also remembered as the principal *mazār* of the capital city.[51] The Suhrawardī shaykh Sayyid Jalāl al-Dīn 'Makhdūm-i Jahāniyān', visiting Dehli in AD 1381–2, paid his respects at the tomb of Niẓām al-Dīn.[52] Another late fourteenth-century shaykh, Sayyid Ashraf Jahāngīr, remarks on the pleasure which the saintly dead experience from the graves being visited. The process of the identification of the *baraka* with the tomb is exemplified by Ibn Baṭṭūṭa's account of his visit to Ajudhan, where the Arab traveller confused the incumbent sajjāda-nashīn, Shaykh 'Alā' al-Dīn 'Mawj-i Daryā' with the latter's grandfather, Farīd al-Dīn himself.[53]

Neither Farīd al-Dīn nor Niẓām al-Dīn nor Naṣīr al-Dīn Maḥmūd had felt it incumbent on them to undertake the possibly dangerous journey to perform the *ziyārat* of the grave of the founder of the Order in India, Mu'īn al-Dīn, at Ajmer. The scanty records which we possess suggest that all his sons had settled elsewhere, and the grave was possibly untended at this time. Sayyid Muḥammad Gēsūdarāz, in a conversation of AD 1399–1400, notes a recommendation given to him by an unnamed *darvīsh* that a follower should have been told to perform the *ziyārat* of the five previous Chishtī *pīrs*, but evidently did not consider this advice binding.[54] On the other hand, when Shaykh Zayn al-Dīn, *khalīfa* of Shaykh Burhān al-Dīn Gharīb whose settlement in the Deccan we have mentioned earlier, came to northern India, he visited the five graves at Ajmer, Dehli, and Pakpattan.[55] Sultan

[51] Ibn Battuta, *Riḥla*, tr. C. Defremery and B.R. Sanguinetti, Paris: Societé Asiatique, 1853–7, vol. III, p. 156.

[52] Sayyid Abū 'Abdi'llāh, *Khulāṣat al-alfāẓ*, Digby MS. 11, f. 426 [now in the Bodleian Library, University of Oxford, MS. S. Digby Or. 8 ~DL]; see Ḥusaynī, *Jawāmi' al-kalim*, p. 143, for the continuance of *ziyārat* to the tombs of Quṭb al-Dīn and Niẓām al-Dīn after the ruin of Dehli caused by the forced migration to Dawlatabad, when many other graves fell into neglect.

[53] Battuta, *Riḥla*, vol. III, p. 135.

[54] Ḥusaynī, *Jawāmi' al-kalim*, p. 183.

Muḥammad bin Tughluq, while campaigning in Rajasthan around AD 1332, visited the tomb of Mu'īn al-Dīn,[56] as did Zafar Khan of Gujarat in the course of his march upon Dehli at the close of the century.[57]

The subsequent history of the *dargāhs* ('royal courts')—i.e. *khānqāhs*—around the graves of the six Chishtī shaykhs of this chapter shows remarkable variation in their fortunes and in the pattern of development in their individual geographical settings. A full account would be far beyond the scope of this chapter, beyond indeed the limits of my own researches. I can only indicate some salient features of their history. We may turn first to the three *dargāhs* away from Dehli, at Ajmer, Ajudhan (Pakpattan), and Gulbarga.

There is no evidence of a major *khānqāh* establishment at Ajmer before the conquest of that city by Sulṭān Maḥmūd Shāh of Malwa in AD 1455. There were, however, some attendants at the grave when he visited it.[58] In the reign of his successor Sulṭān Ghiyāth al-Dīn a mausoleum was built over the grave, and a shaykh previously resident at Mandu was installed as custodian.[59] It is probably also to these sultans that the great gate now known as the 'Alā'i Darwāza should be attributed. The custodian or his descendants claimed to be of the lineage of Mu'īn al-Dīn himself, and they are the ancestors of the present line of dīvānjīs or sajjāda-nashīns.[60]

[55] Ghulām 'Alī Āzād Bilgrāmī, *Rawẓat al-awliyā'*, Urdu tr., Aurangabad: Matba Kareemi, Faṣlī 1345, pp. 100–2.

[56] 'Iṣāmī, *Futūḥ al-salāṭīn*, ed. A.S. Usha, Madras: University of Madras, 1948, p. 466.

[57] Sikandar b. Muḥammad, *Mir'āt-i Sikandarī*, ed. S.C. Misra and M.L. Rahman, Baroda: Maharaja Sayajirao University, 1961, p. 18.

[58] Firishta, *Ta'rīkh-i Firishta*, vol. II, ed. Briggs, Bombay: Government College Press, 1832, p. 490.

[59] Dehlavī, *Akhbār al-akhyār*, p. 48.

[60] Abū'l-Faẓl, *Akbar-nāma*, vol. II, tr. H. Beveridge, Calcutta: Asiatic Society, 1902–39, p. 511; Badāyūnī, *Muntakhab al-tawārīkh*, vol. III, tr. Wolseley Haig, Calcutta: Bibliotheca Indica, 1884, pp. 136–7; Ilāh

Some of the families of khādims also claim descent from Mu'īn al-Dīn. Both claims were held in doubt in the sixteenth century, and are contested to the present day. Nevertheless, the shrine became increasingly important as a place of pilgrimage from the late fifteenth century onwards, while the corpus of legends about Mu'īn al-Dīn, the first great Ṣūfī in the heartland of India, grew apace. The almost annual pilgrimages of the emperor Akbar in the 1570s and 1580s assured its uncontested pre-eminence as the major Muslim pilgrimage centre of the subcontinent.[61] Later Mughal emperors also made substantial grants of *madad-i ma'āsh* to its inhabitants, after which the donations of Muslims of all ranks from the Nizam of Hyderabad downwards have contributed to the upkeep and embellishment of the shrine. In 1975 there were said to be 300,000 visitors to the 'Urs or festival of the death anniversary of Mu'īn al-Dīn.[62]

The *dargāh* of Farīd al-Dīn at Ajudhan (called Pakpattan in his honour from the sixteenth century onwards) was in fact the first *khānqāh* establishment founded by a Chishtī shaykh in India. Ajudhan was a staging-post along a main route from Dehli to Multan and even during the lifetime of Farīd al-Dīn, the *khānqāh* attended to the needs of travellers in the *qāfilas* that passed along this route, including the stabling of their mounts.[63] Like the Suhrawardī establishment at

---

Diyā Chishtī, *Siyar al-aqṭāb*, Lucknow: Naval Kishor, 1913, p. 137; P.M. Currie, *The Shrine and Cult of Mu'īn al-Dīn at Ajmer*, Oxford: Oxford University Press, 1989.

61 Faẓl, *Akbar-nāma*, tr. Beveridge, vol. II, pp. 243, 477, 496, 511, 516, 530, 539; vol. III, pp. 63, 111, 223, 259, 303, 363, 405; Badāyūnī, *Muntakhab al-tawārīkh*, vol. III, tr. Lowe, pp. 45, 108, 174, 188, 262, 280, 285; Currie, *Cult of Mu'īn al-Dīn*, p. 172.

62 Currie, in *Cult of Mu'īn al-Dīn*, discussed the annual numbers of pilgrims, according to census figures and newspaper reports.

63 Simon Digby, 'Sufis and Travellers in the Early Dehli Sultanate', in *Socio-Cultural Impact of Islam on India*, ed. Attar Singh, Chandigarh:

Multan, the *khānqāh* was at almost the highest point of an ancient tell which had been transformed into a fortified medieval town. Strategic as well as pious considerations may have influenced the massive patronage of the shrine by Muḥammad bin Tughluq and Fērōz Shāh Tughluq, who assigned the cultivable land of the adjacent riverain territory to the incumbents at the shrine, a grant which was repeated in Mughal times. Richard M. Eaton has cogently argued that in consequence the shrine played a decisive role on the agricultural settlement and Islamicization of the pastoral transhumant Jat and Rajput tribes of the area.[64]

Succession to the *sajjāda* or *gaddī* devolved through the third son of Farīd al-Dīn, installed (as at Chisht) by a consensus of the relatives. The descendants of Farīd al-Dīn, either resident in the vicinity or emigrating to other parts of India, multiplied so greatly that in the sixteenth century he was known as *Ādam-i thānī*, 'the second Adam'.[65] Unlike many other Ṣūfī lineages, they developed a characteristically north Indian social system of taking brides from tribes which were clients of the shrine. Their ascendancy over the local tribes parallels that of the Ṣafavid shaykhs of Ardabil over the Turkmans in the late fifteenth century. When a power vacuum occurred in the Panjab in the late eighteenth century, it is not surprising that the then sajjāda-nashīn or dīvān made a bid for independent power, which was ultimately crushed by Ranjit Singh. In the late nineteenth century, the Chishtīs settled around Pakpattan could appear to a British administrator as 'a semi-religious Mussalman

University of the Punjab, 1976, pp. 172–4 [*L&WSD* III.4]; A.M. Stow, 'The Road between Delhi and Multan', *Journal of the Punjab Historical Society*, vol. III, no. 1, 1914–15, pp. 26–37.

64 Eaton, 'The Shrine of Baba Farīd', pp. 10–21.

65 C.A. Storey, *Persian Literature: A Bio-Bibliographical Survey*, vol. II, London: Royal Asiatic Society, 1977, p. 986.

tribe', who owned land but did not cultivate it themselves.[66] A few years ago the *dargāh* maintained a characteristic variety of permanent or temporary inmates, but was under the charge of a *mutawallī* or custodian appointed by the Awqaf Department of the Pakistan Government.

We have earlier noted the kingmaking role of Gēsūdarāz in the Bahmanī Sultanate in his old age, and the fact that the Bahmanī sultans, following their quarrel with a grandson of Gēsūdarāz, relied on an alternative source of Ṣūfī legitimation until the downfall of the dynasty a century later. However, the prestige of the *dargāh* or *deoṛhī* (another term for 'court') of the tomb of Sayyid Muḥammad Gēsūdarāz at Gulbarga survived this disfavour. Later, there were marital alliances between his offspring and the families of the 'Ādilshāhs of Bijapur and the Quṭbshāhs of Golkonda, despite the professed Shī'ism of these ruling houses; and even more recently with the house of the Nizams of Hyderabad. The shrine attained greater splendour and possessions than any other in the Deccan. Colonel Meadows Taylor, in a novel published in 1875, described the lavish celebration of the *'urs* by the 'Prince of Goolburga', though his description was probably based on his observations of about twenty years earlier. He called the incumbent 'the Geesoodaraaz', a similar identification to that made by the fourteenth-century traveller Ibn Baṭṭūṭa regarding the incumbent of the shrine of Ajudhan.[67] In 1963 I attended the *'urs* at Gulbarga. Most of the devotees came from a more localized catchment area than was the case in the pan-Indian festivals of Niẓām al-Dīn and Mu'īn al-Dīn, and this had the advantage that modernizing influences were less apparent. Nevertheless, a

[66] Fagan, *Assessment Report for Pakpattan Tahsil*, 1896, p. 50; quoted by Eaton, in 'The Shrine of Baba Farīd', p. 18.

[67] Col. H. Meadows Taylor, *A Noble Queen*, 2nd edn., London: C. Kegan Paul & Co., 1880, pp. 301–9; cf. above and n. 53.

crowd of many tens of thousands of pilgrims were present. The fervour of the pilgrims was intense. A cordon of men linked arm-in-arm had to be formed around the person of the sajjāda-nashīn when he went in procession, to prevent his physical injury by those pressing to touch the hem of his garments; and I was privileged to participate in this.

The cults of the three Chishtī graves in Dehli fared unequally, and the courses of their development were different from those of the Ajmer, Ajudhan, and Gulbarga shrines. Quṭb al-Dīn had maintained no *khānqāh* in his lifetime, but had chosen his burial place with care, and purchased it. According to Niẓām al-Dīn, he had remarked: 'From this place comes the smell of hearts!' It is situated at Mehrawli, close to the outskirts of the first Muslim settlement at Dehli, *Dehli-yi kuhna*, the 'old Dehli' of that day. As Ibn Baṭṭūṭa testifies, his grave was the principal *mazār* among all the townships of Dehli in the fourteenth century. There appears to be no evidence for the continuous occupation of the shrine after Timur's invasion in AD 1398, but a factor in favour of the cult of the grave was its proximity to the great Quwwat al-Islām (or more correctly Qubbat al-Islām) mosque, the outstanding architectural monument of the establishment of the Dehli Sultanate. A fortuitous coincidence of name led to the Quṭb Minār being considered in popular folklore as '*Quṭb Ṣāḥib kī lāṭh*', 'the staff of Quṭb Ṣāḥib'.[68] This proximity evidently led the Emperor Bābur to visit the tomb when he went sight-seeing in Dehli in AD 1526; he had visited the tomb of Niẓām al-Dīn the evening before, but makes no note of a visit to that of Naṣīr al-Dīn Maḥmūd.[69] The paucity

[68] In the later fifteenth century Sulṭān Buhlūl Lōdī of Dehli is said to have seen Quṭb al-Dīn Bakhtyār Kākī in a dream, encouraging him in his war with Sulṭān Ḥusayn Shāh Sharqī of Jawnpur; al-Makkī, *Ẓafar al-wālih*, vol. I, ed. S. Denison Ross, London: J. Murray, 1910, vol. I, p. 135.
[69] Ẓahīr al-Dīn Bābur, *Bābur-nāma*, tr. A.S. Beveridge, London: Luzac, 1921, p. 475.

of sixteenth- and seventeenth-century structures at the *dargāh* seems to indicate that the shrine did not attract great patronage at this period; but in the late eighteenth century a Chishtī shaykh of note, Fakhr al-Dīn, took up residence there. When, in the twilight of the Mughal Empire, emperors living under British 'protection', Akbar Shāh II and Bahādur Shāh Ẓafar, sought an alternative, less oppressive part-time residence in Mehrawli during spells of absence from the Red Fort, the *dargāh* benefitted from the move. An elegant open pavilion was erected over the grave and a large entrance-gate added, which is a fine example of Mughal architecture in its latest period. An *'urs* is celebrated on a modest local scale—not to be compared to the major festival of Niẓām al-Dīn and at Ajmer and Gulbarga. The main officiant is a member of the leading khādim family of the *dargāh*. Among the Ṣūfī shaykhs of India today, or should I say twenty years ago, he does not appear to rank as a major sajjāda-nashīn, and doubt is cast on the claims of this family to be descendants of Quṭb al-Dīn himself.

The *dargāh* of Naṣīr al-Dīn Maḥmūd appears to have fared even worse. The ascendancy of the shaykh's eldest nephew, Mawlānā Zayn al-Dīn, and of the latter's brothers was established at the shaykh's death. The tomb itself, the entrance-gate, and the massive and defensible walls date from this period and indicate the patronage of Sulṭan Fērōz Shāh Tughluq. It was clearly a major *khānqāh* before Timur's invasion in AD 1398. Whether during the urban disturbances before this event or shortly after, the family of the shaykh appear to have abandoned the *khānqāh*. Among their descendants were a noted sixteenth-century Ṣūfī of Gujarat, Shaykh Ḥasan Muḥammad 'Miyānjīv'; his son, Shaykh Muḥammad, author of a Ṣūfī manual *Ādāb al-ṭālibīn*,[70]

[70] 'Alī Muḥammad Khān, *Mir'āt-i Aḥmadī*, supplement, ed. S.N. Ali, Baroda: Oriental Institute, 1930, pp. 75–6; ibid., tr. C.N. Seddon, Baroda:

which was lithographed in the nineteenth century; and the early eighteenth-century poet and lexicographer Sirāj al-Dīn 'Alī Khān Ārzū.[71] Though Ārzū lived in Dehli in the early eighteenth century, the poetical *tadhkīras* which record his life make no reference to his taking an interest in the *dargāh* of his ancestor. In the *dargāh* itself the only post-fourteenth-century structure of note is a minor rectangular tomb of the Lodī period, which was said in the nineteenth century to be the grave of Ṣultān Buhlūl Lodī. I have argued elsewhere that this is incorrect. In spite of the pressure of population in Dehli after Independence, the *dargāh* was very scantily populated in the 1950s and 1960s. I was then informed by one of the inhabitants that the descendants of Shaykh Naṣīr al-Dīn Maḥmūd in Gujarat still continued to make provision for the celebration of the *'urs* at the *dargāh* on a small scale.

Unlike the graves of Quṭb al-Dīn and Naṣīr al-Dīn, the grave of Niẓām al-Dīn at Dehli appears to possess a khādim population which has been continuously resident from the time of the shaykh's death. The celebration of the *'urs* is on a comparable scale to those at Ajmer, Gulbarga, and Pakpattan, though it differs from them in its more popular and less well-regulated character. The *dargāh* also differs from these shrines inasmuch as there is no clearly established tradition of *sajjādagī*. Historically, the reason for the failure of such a tradition to emerge must be seen to spring from the circumstances of Niẓām al-Dīn's death which we have surveyed earlier in this chapter.[72] At the time of the shaykh's death, his *khānqāh* was under the

Education Department, 1923, pp. 65–6 (inaccurate, with omissions); Shaykh Muḥammad, *Ādāb al-ṭālibīn*, Dehli: Matba'-i Mujtaba'i, AH 1311/AD 1893–4, p. 1.

[71] Ghulām 'Alī Āzād Bilgrāmī, *Sarv-i Āzād*, Hyderabad, Deccan: Kutub'khānah-i Āṣafīyah, 1913, p. 227.

[72] See also below.

administration of the khādims who were either intimate personal servants or distinguished residents who were not blood-relations. This may be contrasted with the situations at the *khānqāhs* of Farīd al-Dīn and Naṣīr al-Dīn Maḥmūd. Some of the figures of importance in the *khānqāh* at the death of Niẓām al-Dīn and later in the fourteenth century, notably the Kirmānī Sayyids, appear to have left no extant lineage at the *dargāh*, but the four main groups of the khādim population of the twentieth century are from lineages which appear authentic.

The apparently continuous preservation of the *dargāh*, in contrast with the periods of neglect of the other two Chishtī *dargāhs* in Dehli, suggests an element of choice among the local Muslim population in determining which was to be the single great Ṣūfī shrine of the area. The claims of Niẓām al-Dīn were clearly stronger than those of Quṭb al-Dīn, except on the grounds of antiquity. About the role of Quṭb al-Dīn in the capital city we have no contemporary record; by contrast we have the contemporary testimony of the historian Baranī as to the enormous influence wielded by Niẓām al-Dīn, as well as the easily comprehensible account of Niẓām al-Dīn's conversations in the *Fawā'id al-fu'ād*. The attachment of the most celebrated poet of the Dehli Sultanate, Amīr Khusrau, who lies buried at the feet of Niẓām al-Dīn, would doubtless also contribute to his posthumous esteem. The *Khair al-majālis*, which records the conversations of Naṣīr al-Dīn Maḥmūd, is a work of literary merit almost equal to that of the *Fawā'id al-fu'ād*; but it never enjoyed an equally wide circulation and popularity. Moreover, Niẓām al-Dīn's life spanned the apogee of the Dehli Sultanate, while that of Naṣīr al-Dīn Maḥmūd ended when the sultanate was entering into decline. Historic memories put forth the strongest claims for the shrine of

Niẓām al-Dīn. A final factor in its favour was the continuous habitation which we have suggested above.[73]

In the early sixteenth century the *dargāh* of Niẓām al-Dīn remained one of the centres of the religious life of Dehli. The historian Rizq Allāh Mushtāqī recalled his brother's manner of life in the reign of Sikandar Lōdī (d. AD 1517). He was a man of great piety, who used to spend eight months of the year at Dehli and four at Agra. When he was at Dehli, he would spend six days of the week in assemblies of 'ālims, men of accomplishment, Ṣūfī shaykhs, and qawwāls (singers)—Mondays at the Hawẓ-i Shamsī, Wednesdays at the *khānqāh* of Niẓām al-Dīn, Thursdays at Qadam Sharīf (the shrine of the Prophet's footprint), Fridays at Fērōzābād (Fērōz Shāh Koṭlā), and Saturdays at the Mālcha Maḥall, with some shikār to vary the routine.[74]

In the early twentieth century the khādims who divided the offices and offerings of Niẓām al-Dīn's shrine were divided into four families:

1. *Nabīragān* ('grandsons'), so called because they were the descendants of Khwāja Sayyid Muḥammad, a grandson of Farīd al-Dīn who acted as Imām of the *khānqāh* during Niẓām al-Dīn's lifetime;

[73] In the *dargāh*, inscribed dated structures or tombs are lacking in the period from 1379 to the reign of the Mughal emperor Bābur (1526–30); see M. Zafar Hasan, 'A Guide to Nizam ud-Din', *Memoirs of the Archaeological Survey of India*, no. 10, 1922, pp. 9–10, 23–4. Structures erected from the reign of the emperor Akbar in the later sixteenth century down to the present day are numerous. Nevertheless, the quotation from Mushtāqī, immediately below, indicated that the *dargāh* was frequented during the period from which there are no monuments.

[74] Rizq Allāh Mushtāqī, *Waqi'āt-i Mushtāqī*, British Library, Ms. Add. 11, 6333, f. 31a; Ms. Or. 1929, f. 31.

2. *Hārūnī* (more correctly *Hārvanī*), descendants of Khwāja 'Uthmān of Hārvan, *pīr* of Mu'īn al-Dīn, and of Khwāja Rafī' al-Dīn Hārvanī, whose mother was a sister of Niẓām al-Dīn. In 1919 the family became extinct in the male line, but two women from it were still alive;
3. *Hindōstānī*, the descendants of Khwāja Abū Bakr, the muṣalla-bardār (bearer of the prayer-carpet) of Niẓām al-Dīn;
4. *Qāẓī-zādagān*, descendants of Qāẓī Muḥiy al-Dīn Kāshānī, a *khalīfa* of Niẓām al-Dīn, who was also in some way related to him.[75]

Though the position of the great Chishtī shaykhs in their lifetimes depended on the military power of the sultanate and the great nucleus of population in the capital city, they never ceased to emphasize that the pursuit of the spiritual life was hindered by lack of solitude and the worldly concerns which pressed on them when they were in the proximity of the capital. Farīd al-Dīn as well as Mu'īn al-Dīn, if one is to believe the testimony of the *Siyar al-awliyā'*, believed that it was not a suitable place for a Ṣūfī shaykh to reside. One may feel today that such proximity does not aid the preservation of Ṣūfī traditions at the Niẓām al-Dīn *dargāh*.

The *'urs* of Niẓām al-Dīn continues to draw very large crowds and is one of the highlights of the year among the local urban population, both Muslim and non-Muslim; it also draws visitors of all classes from distant parts of the subcontinent. Yet it is celebrated in a fashion which is in some contrast to the ritual of the *'urs* at Ajmer and in even greater contrast to the ritual at Gulbarga, which is the Chishtī shrine least open to modernistic influences. In all

[75] Bashīr al-Dīn Aḥmad, *Waqi'āt-i dār al-ḥukūmat-i Dehlī*, vol. III, Dehli: Shamsi Machine Press, 1919, pp. 821–3; Zafar Hasan, 'Guide to Nizam-ud Din', p. 6, writes, 'The attendants of the shrine who reside in the village of Nizam-ud Din and are styled *Pīrzādas* are descendants of his sister.'

these shrines *samā‘* (listening to music) is a very prominent part of the ceremonies, but at the two more distant shrines this does not completely overshadow the rites of pilgrimage, and the washing of the tomb and the renewal of the shroud. Moreover, at both these shrines there is an attempt to observe propriety in the singing and the choice of singers, and in the admission of proper people to listen to the qawwālī conducted in the presence of the sajjāda-nashīn. Though some more or less traditional qawwāls are among the performers at the *‘urs* of Niẓām al-Dīn, the general content of the singing is more of a disorderly entertainment than a purgative spiritual experience, and most of the audience appear to regard it in this light. The latest fashions in the music of the Bombay film-industry make their appearance. Equally, the commercial modern style of qawwālī which fills the seats of theatres in Bombay owes much to the manner of certain mid-twentieth-century qawwāls attached to the *dargāh* of Niẓām al-Dīn.

4

Sufis and Travellers in the Early Delhi Sultanate

The Evidence of the *Fawā'id al-fu'ād*

As the narrative of Ibn Baṭṭūṭa reminds us, in the lands of Islam in the thirteenth and fourteenth centuries, travellers could cross vast distances in comparative ease and safety, and every class of wanderer, educated or uneducated, impelled by religious or other motives, abounded. In the pattern of travel, Sufi *khānqāhs* in Muslim India as in other areas of the Islamic world rendered almost indispensable service to the Muslim traveller; the independently founded *khanqāhs* of prominent Sufi sheikhs fed and lodged travellers, making it unnecessary for the government of the sultan to maintain *sarāys* for their needs.[1] Among these *khānqāhs*, that of Sheikh Farīd al-Dīn at Ajodhan (Pakpattan) was one of the most prominent. It was settled by a sheikh of great sanctity and it stood upon one of the main routes of the period, that which ran between

* Originally published in Attar Singh, ed., *Socio-cultural Impact of Islam on India*, Chandigarh: Panjab University, 1976, pp. 171–7.

[1] In some other cases the sultans of Delhi established *sarāys* organized as *khānqāhs* and placed them in the charge of individual Sufi sheikhs. See Afīf, *Ta'rīkh-i Fērōzshāhī*, Calcutta: Bibliotheca Indica, 1891, p. 331; Sirhindī, *Ta'rīkh-i Mubārakshāhī*, Calcutta: Bibliotheca Indica, 1931, p. 99.

Multan and Delhi.[2] It will figure many times in the anecdotes cited in this chapter.

A traveller, when he arrived at a settlement, would expect to stay at the *khānqāh*, where arrangements would be made for his accommodation for a limited number of days in a manner befitting his rank.[3] The distinction between such public hospitality and the private hospitality of the pious, especially in the capital city of Delhi, is somewhat blurred. The youthful Niẓām al-Dīn, when he left Badā'on and came to Delhi for the first time, lodged with other travellers of his party in the precincts of the house of Sheikh Najib al-Dīn Mutawakkil, with whom he had no previous acquaintance.[4] In the greater *khānqāhs*, particularly those in receipt of extensive *futūhāt* (offerings) or of some kind of maintenance from the government, facilities for the entertainment of travellers were well developed. The *langar-khāna* or communal kitchen had to feed not only the impoverished residents (*mujāwiran*) of the precincts but also such travellers as arrived at the *khānqāh*, whose numbers on a particular day might be a matter for calculation.[5] One anecdote of the *Fawā'id al-fu'ād* refers to

[2] See A.M. Stow, 'The Road between Delhi and Multan', *Journal of the Punjab Historical Society*, vol. III, no. 1, 1914–15, pp. 26–37.

[3] According to Afīf, *Ta'rīkh-i Fērōzshāhī*, in the reign of Fērōz Shāh Tughluq there were 120 *khānqāhs* in the capital city of Delhi, at each of which a traveller might spend three nights, thus being able to reside there for a whole (Muslim) year. For the splendid reception of Sheikh Sadr al-Dīn of Multan at the *khānqāh* of Sheikh Niẓām al-Dīn in Delhi, which included the presentation of 100 gold coins, see Amīr Khwurd, *Siyar al-awliyā'*, Delhi: Muhibb-i Hind Press, AH 1302/AD 1884, p. 139.

[4] Amīr Hasan Sijzī, *Fawā'id al-fu'ād*, p. 254. References are to the recent lithographed edition (ed. Muḥammad Latīf Malik, Lahore: Malik Sirāj al-Dīn and Sons, AH 1386/AD 1966). This edition, although it does not draw upon independent manuscripts, is superior to earlier lithographic printings, possessing indices and apparatus criticus.

[5] Cf. the story of Kamāl Jogī's cat, which used by mewing a number

the stables of the *khānqāh* at Ajodhan, where the mounts or pack animals of the travellers were lodged.[6]

Variety was given to the life and conversation of the inhabitants of *khānqāhs* by the arrival of travellers bringing news of distant places and a wider world; it was partly by their tales that the reputation of individual sheikhs and *khānqāhs* was spread abroad. The original impulse which directed the spiritual life of Baba Farīd's greatest disciple, Sheikh Niẓām al-Dīn Awliyā', the decision to become his disciple, originated in the conversation of a wanderer, a *qawwāl* (singer) who was also a carpenter. This man arrived in Badā'on when Niẓām al-Dīn was 12 years old, and he called upon the latter's teacher. The *qawwāl* had sung before Sheikh Bahā' al-Dīn Zakariyā' in Multan, and his conversation was full of descriptions of rites as they were performed there. From Multan he had passed through Ajodhan, visiting the *khānqāh* of Sheikh Farīd. His descriptions filled the heart of the 12-year-old boy with a desire to become this sheikh's disciple.[7]

Among travellers who stopped at the *khānqāhs*, the arrival of bands of *faqīrs* from the less-orthodox orders (*javaliqīs*, *Haydarīs*, *qalandars*) gave rise to anxiety. Their behaviour towards the inmates of the *khānqāhs* and, worse still, towards the sheikh might be quarrelsome, self-assertive, or even openly violent.[8] Nevertheless, the mystique of the poverty

---

of times to indicate the number of prospective visitors, according to an anecdote in Niẓām Yamanī, *Latā'if-i Ashrafī*, quoted in S. Digby, 'Encounters with Jogis in Indian Sufi Hagiography', seminar on aspects of religion in South Asia, SOAS University of London, 1970 [*L&WSD* II].

[6] Sijzī, *Fawā'id al-fu'ād*, p. 344.

[7] Ibid., pp. 252–3.

[8] Ibid., pp. 80–1; cf. also the anecdotes of murderous intention on p. 200. For *qalandars* causing disturbances at Sheikh Farīd al-Dīn's *khānqāh* at Ajodhan, see also Hamīd Qalandar, *Khair al-majālis*, ed. K.A. Nizami, Aligarh: Aligarh Muslim University, 1958, pp. 130–2; Jamālī, *Siyar al-'ārifīn*, Delhi: Maṭba'-i Riẓvī, AH 1311/AD 1893, pp. 35, 42.

of the *darwesh* and the belief that among these groups there must be concealed people of great spiritual powers led to their being not entirely unwelcome.[9]

Many anecdotes in the *Fawā'id al-fu'ād* concern the perils and adventures of travel, whether close or far afield. Considerable journeys were sometimes suddenly undertaken. A sheikh is described as setting out to visit another sheikh at a distance of three months' journeying in consequence of a dream; but this anecdote is of an earlier period and may be considered legendary.[10] A hanger-on at the *khānqāh* at Ajodhan, who had grown restless, meets down in the *khānqāh* stables a party of pilgrims bound for the holy places of Arabia, and decides to join them upon their journey.[11] Several anecdotes in this work concern the performance of *Hajj*[12] or visits to centres of Islam in the Middle East and Central Asia.[13] One visitor to the *khānqāh* of Niẓām al-Dīn at Delhi speaks of his own travels in a distant land (evidently the Hadramawt) where the Prophet Hūd is buried in 'a very high and long grave'. The party with which he had travelled had arrived there after starving for several days. They had no common language with the local people, who nevertheless fed them with cakes of *juwār* (millet) and milk. Niẓām al-Dīn comments on the generosity of this remote people.[14]

Cf. also the murderous attack made upon Sheikh Nasīr al-Dīn Chirāgh-i Dehlī described in *Khair al-majālis*, pp. 184–5; Muhammad Akbar Husaynī, *Jawāmi al-kalim*, Hyderabad: Taḥqīqātī Akāḍmī, Faṣlī 1356/ AD 1937, pp. 90–2.

[9] Sijzī, *Fawā'id al-fu'ād*, pp. 6–7.

[10] Ibid., pp. 222–3.

[11] Ibid., p. 334.

[12] Ibid., pp. 9, 62, 175.

[13] Ibid., pp. 269, 397–8, 400.

[14] Ibid., pp. 188–9. There are conflicting traditions with regard to the burial place of Hūd. Ibn Baṭṭūṭa, whose travels are not long subsequent to the composition of the *Fawā'id al-fu'ād*, visited the alleged grave of

In the *Fawā'id al-fu'ād* there are numerous anecdotes of travel in the territories of the Delhi Sultanate and in adjacent lands. These shed occasional light upon the state of communications and conditions of trade. Once, a *darwesh* from Bihar is mentioned, travelling from there to Ghaznīn in order to obtain a better price for the slaves in whom he traded; it is possible that this anecdote refers to a time early in the thirteenth century.[15] Elsewhere there is a story of a journey in Gujarat before that area was brought under the rule of the Delhi Sultanate.[16] Another anecdote mentions (apparently Muslim) traders from Lahore who used to go to Gujarat (where we are told the people were astonished at their manner of bargaining!) at a time before the sack of Lahore by the Mongols.[17]

Anecdotes of journeys performed through the north Indian countryside for the purpose of visiting sheikhs, friends, or relations are numerous, and mostly mention journeys from Multan to Ajodhan, Ajodhan to Delhi or Badā'on to Delhi. Sometimes the travellers on such journeys were in parties large enough to be considered *qāfilas* (caravans). On one occasion the *qāfila* was delayed for three days in Ajodhan before it set out.[18] Another anecdote provides us with rather important evidence regarding methods of transport during the thirteenth century in north India. It leaves us in no doubt

---

Hūd in the great mosque of Damascus: Ibn Baṭṭūṭa, *Riḥla*, vol. I, ed. C. Defremery and B.R. Sanguinetti, Paris: Societé Asiatique, 1853–7, p. 205; vol. II, p. 203. Another tradition that Hūd was buried near the *kā'ba* provides an even less suitable venue for this anecdote, which must refer to the Qabr Hūd at Bi'r Barahūt in Hadramawt; see *Encyclopedia of Islam*, 1st edn., Leiden: Brill, 1913–38, s.v. '*Hūd*'. The anecdote indicates that the travellers could not understand the dialectical Arabic of the area.

[15] Sijzī, *Fawā'id al-fu'ād*, pp. 316–17.

[16] Ibid., pp. 127–8.

[17] Ibid., pp. 201–2.

[18] Ibid., pp. 265–6.

that there were wheeled carriages bearing passengers along stages of the route between Delhi and Ajodhan, presumably plying for hire. A man was going from Delhi to Ajodhan in a *qāfila* with the intention of professing, in the presence of Sheikh Farīd al-Dīn, repentance for his sins. There was also among the travellers a female musician. 'As that man had a sincere purpose', we are told, 'he did not incline at all towards the adulteress, until at one stage of the journey it so befell that the man and the musician were both seated in a single cart (*gardūn*). The musician came and sat near the man in such a way that there was no veil or obstacle between them. In these circumstances the heart of the man inclined a little to say something or stretch out a hand towards her.' This, however, was prevented by the miraculous intervention of Sheikh Farīd al-Dīn.[19]

In these anecdotes of journeys from one north Indian town to another, Sufi sheikhs or their disciples set out through the countryside, sometimes mounted or (in the previous anecdote) upon a conveyance but more commonly on foot,[20] alone or with one or two companions. Sheikh 'Alī Makkī, who had continually prayed for a solitary death, died upon the road between Bajlāna and Badā'on.[21]

Wild beasts and dacoits were dangers upon the road, especially to solitary travellers and small parties. When Sheikh Niẓām al-Dīn set out upon his first journey to Delhi, an older member of the party of travellers, whenever there was 'fear of lions or fear of thieves', cried out to his *pīr*, who happened to be Sheikh Farīd al-Dīn;[22] thus reinforcing the impression which the conversation of the *qawwāl* had

[19] Ibid., pp. 371–2.

[20] Ibid., p. 99. Niẓām al-Dīn states: 'Although I was mounted, I felt thirsty.'

[21] Ibid., p. 266.

[22] Ibid., p. 253.

created in the mind of the 12-year-old boy.[23] When Sheikh Farīd al-Dīn himself took up residence at Ajodhan, he sent his younger brother to bring his mother there possibly from Multan. 'Upon the journey they sat down under a tree to rest. While they were there some water was required; and Sheikh Najib al-Dīn went off in search of it. When he returned he did not find his mother.' The presumption was that she had been carried off by a wild beast.[24]

The anecdotes referring to dacoits show how imperfect was the control exercised by the Delhi Sultanate over the north Indian countryside, even when it lay close to major trade routes. On one occasion Niẓām al-Dīn described how he was going from Ajodhan to Delhi, 'alone but for a single companion, until we reached a place where there was reason to be afraid of brigands. It began to rain and I and my companion stood beneath a tree. Then several Hindus appeared in the manner in which I had feared and came opposite us.' However, instead of attacking the two travellers, they dispersed peacefully, and Niẓām al-Dīn reached his destination in safety.[25] Another anecdote concerns the journey of a certain Abd Allāh from Ajodhan to Multan. On the way he was told that the *dhāṛs* (dacoits) had made preparations and were coming close.[26] But these brigands apparently lost their way and Abd Allāh reached Multan safely. An anecdote concerning a journey to Gujarat shows a similar insecurity prevailing beyond the frontiers of Muslim rule in India. According to the narrative of a *naqīb* (constable?) retold verbatim by Niẓām al-Dīn: 'Once I was travelling in Gujarat. In those days the Hindus held that

[23] See above.

[24] Sijzī, *Fawā'id al-fu'ād*, pp. 210–11.

[25] Ibid., pp. 319–20.

[26] Ibid., pp. 235–6: for the term *dhāṛ*, see J.T. Platts, *A Dictionary of Urdu, classical Hindi, and English*, London: W.H. Allen & Co., 1884, s.v., 'a band or gang of robbers, banditti'.

country. I travelled upon a road with one or two people accompanying me. We were unarmed, and suddenly we saw a Hindu appear with a naked sword in his hand.' But unexpectedly, and in a manner attributed to the miraculous protection of a distant *pīr*, the Hindu suddenly asked for peace and threw down his sword. 'Then we gave him his sword; and he went on his way and we on ours.'[27]

[27] Sijzī, *Fawā'id al-fu'ād*, pp. 127–8.

5

Early Pilgrimages to the Graves of Mu'īn al-Dīn Sijzī and Other Indian Chishtī Shaykhs

Ajmer, the burial place of Mu'īn al-Dīn Sijzī, was a frontier fortress of Muslim power after the establishment of the Dehlī Sultanate at the close of the twelfth century AD. Its initial strategic importance, like that of the yet more distant stronghold of Nāgawr, was to check the incursion of unsubjugated Rajput tribes with a powerful dynastic leadership into the Doab, heartland of the sultanate, and the capital city of Dehlī itself. The possession of Ajmer held in check the powerful Cauhāns (Cahamānas), who had controlled Dehlī before the defeat of Prithvirāja in AD 1192. Unlike Ajodhan/Pākpaṭṭan, where the *khānqāh* and grave of Farīd al-Dīn was situated upon the main caravan route between Multān and Dehlī, the pilgrimage to Ajmer involved an arduous and perhaps more than usually dangerous journey along a route upon which great trading *qāfilas* would not normally proceed at this period, though there must have been smaller armed bands travelling to carry the military supplies and provisions from the capital city of this frontier outpost.[1]

* Originally published in Milton Israel and N.K. Wagle, ed., *Islamic Society and Culture: Essays in Honour of Professor Aziz Ahmad*, New Delhi: Manohar, 1983, pp. 95–100.

[1] For the hazards of armed robbery even along the main route from Dehlī through Ajodhan to Multān, see Simon Digby, 'Sufis and Travellers in

In Khurāsān and elsewhere in the Islamic world the cult of Ṣūfī graves was firmly established before the creation of the Dehlī Sultanate. From the evidence of the *Fawā'id al-fu'ād* and the *Siyar al-awliyā'*, the performance of the *ziyārat* (visiting with due ceremony and circumambulation) of Ṣūfī tombs in the vicinity of Dehlī was common in the previous century. Farīd al-Dīn's tomb at Ajodhan/Pākpaṭṭan must also have been visited as easily, by passing travellers or those journeying with the specific purpose of acquiring *barakat*, as the shaykh himself was during his lifetime.

As the Chishtī *silsila* attained supremacy over rival orders in the capital city, the emphasis on its historical chain of transmission probably became greater. In Dehlī itself the major Chishtī shaykhs of the fourteenth century, Niẓām al-Dīn Awliyā' and Naṣīr al-Dīn 'Chirāgh-i Dehlī' paid visits to the tomb of their predecessor Quṭb al-Dīn Bakhtyār Kākī.[2] The Arab traveller Ibn Baṭṭūṭa, present in Dehlī in the 1330s, remembered the tomb of Quṭb al-Dīn as the principal *mazār* of the capital city.[3] Shaykhs of other *silsilas* also performed the *ziyārat* of the Chishtī graves. Thus, Jalāl al-Dīn 'Makhdūm-i jahāniān' (a Suhrawardī and *jāmi' al-salāsil*), present in Dehlī in AD 1381–2, paid his respects at the tomb of Niẓām al-Dīn.[4] Another important late fourteenth-century shaykh, Sayyid Ashraf Jahāngīr (a

---

the Early Delhi Sultanate: the Evidence of the *Fawā'id al-fu'ād*', in *Socio-cultural Impact of Islam on India*, ed. Attar Singh, Chandigarh: University of the Punjab, 1976, pp. 171–80 [*L&WSD* III.4].

2 Amir Khwurd, *Siyar al-awliya'*, ed. Chiranjī Lāl, Dehli: Muhibb-i Hindi Press, 1885, pp. 50–1; Hamīd Qalandar, *Khair al-majālis*, ed. K.A. Nizami, Aligarh: Aligarh Muslim University, 1958, p. 57.

3 Ibn Battuta, *Riḥla*, ed. C. Defremery and B.R. Sanguinetti, Paris: Societé Asiatique, 1853–7, vol. III, p. 156.

4 *Khulāṣat al-alfāẓ*, Digby MS 11, f. 42b [now in the Bodleian Library, University of Oxford, MS S. Digby Or. 8 ~DL]. Sultan Fērōz Shāh Tughluq visited the tomb of Niẓām al-Dīn, probably on numerous occasions, of which the historian 'Afīf was himself an eyewitness. It must have

Chishtī and *jāmi' al-salāsil*), remarks on the pleasure which the saintly dead experience from the visiting of their graves.[5] Other places associated with the lives of the great Chishtī shaykhs also became centres of pilgrimage, such as the 'holy spot' (*maqām-i mutabarrika*) at Uchch where Farīd al-Dīn hung upside-down in a well during his *chilla-i ma'kūs*.[6] The questionable practice of professing *bay'at* at the grave of a dead *pīr* instead of becoming the *murīd* of a living one occasionally occurred during this period.[7]

We have no record of pilgrimages to the grave of Mu'īn al-Dīn at Ajmer during the thirteenth century,[8] but with the

---

been late in the reign. His description of the reverent actions of the Sultan provides evidence of the rites of *ziyārat* at this period; see 'Afīf, *Ta'rīkh-i Fērōzshāhī*, Calcutta: Bibliotheca Indica, 1890, pp. 195–6. The peculiar sanctity of the tomb gave force to oaths sworn by high officials undertaking new charges during this reign; such an oath was sworn there by Shams Dāmghānī on his appointment as Nā'ib Muqta' (Deputy Governor) of Gujarat around AD 1375; see 'Afīf, *Ta'rīkh-i Fērōzshāhī*, p. 500. The date of this event is discussed in S.C. Misra, *The Rise of Muslim Power in Gujarat*, London: Asia Publishing House, 1962, p. 130.

5 *Latā'if-i Ashrafī*, John Rylands Library MS, f. 318b.

6 Khwurd, *Siyar al-awliyā'*, p. 70.

7 Amīr Hasan 'Alā' Sijzī, *Fawā'id al-fu'ād*, ed. M.L. Malik, Lahore: Malik Sirāj al-Dīn and Sons, 1966, p. 132. A denunciation of the practice by Gēsūdarāz is reproduced by Iqbāl al-Dīn Aḥmad, *Tadhkira-i Khwāja Gēsūdarāz*, Karachi: Iqbal Publishers, 1966, pp. 73–4. This work is a thoroughly unreliable, at times mendacious, modern compilation, but the *malfūẓ* or conversation appears plausible and cites a rebuke made by Farīd al-Dīn to one of his sons who made a *bay'at* at the grave of his own *pīr*, Quṭb al-Dīn. In the fifteenth century, in the Ṣābirī branch of the Chishtī *silsila*, such a *bay'at* was made at the grave of Shaykh Aḥmad 'Abd al-Ḥaqq by 'Abd al-Quddūs: see Rukn al-Din Quddusi, *Lata'if-i Quddusi*, Delhi: Mujtaba'i Press, AD 1894, p. 10: S. Digby, "Abd al-Quddūs Gangohi (1456–1537 A.D.): The Personality and Attitudes of a Medieval Indian Sufi', *Medieval India: A Miscellany*, vol. III, 1975, pp. 6–7 [*L&WSD* III.10; this volume, pp. 315–16].

8 The conversations of Niẓām al-Dīn, recorded between AD 1308 and 1317, contain only two references to Ajmer, neither concerned with

strongly developed consciousness of the historical role of the great Chishtī shaykhs which existed in the fourteenth century, the incentive to undertake the arduous journey to Ajmer must have grown. There are several references to the *ziyārat* of Mu'īn al-Dīn's grave during [the twentieth] century.

The poet 'Iṣāmī, whose historical *mathnavī Futūḥ al-salāṭin* was completed in AD 1350, referred to the *ziyārat* of Mu'īn al-Dīn's tomb by the reigning Sultan of Dehlī, Muḥammad bin Tughluq:

> Mu'īn al-Dīn, that Sijzī who was a refuge of the faith
> That Guide of the Road who is asleep at Ajmer,
> When the Sultan had performed *ziyārat* to him
> He took the road thence to his capital [Dehlī].[9]

The exact chronology of Muḥammad bin Tughluq's reign is a subject of controversy, but, according to the sequence of 'Iṣāmī's narrative, the visit took place after the Mongol invasion of Tarmashīrīn and before the disastrous Qarāchal expedition. It may therefore be placed between AD 1329 and 1335. Some evidence suggests that the visit may have been in the late summer or autumn of 1332. The opportunity to make a detour to visit Ajmer was offered to the sultan by a campaign, recorded by 'Iṣāmī alone, to suppress the Kacchwāha Rajputs.[10]

---

performance of pilgrimage to the tomb of Mu'īn al-Dīn: see 'Alā' Sijzī, *Fawā'id al-fu'ād*, pp. 76–7, 290. However, the references demonstrate that contact was maintained between Ṣūfī circles in Dehlī and Ajmer (presumably the *'Arhā'ī din kā jhoṅprā'*). Another anecdote refers to a different grandson of Mu'īn al-Dīn coming to Ajodhan, presumably from Ajmer, to become a *murīd* of Farīd al-Dīn: 'Alā' Sijzī, *Fawā'id al-fu'ād*, p. 405.

9 *Futūḥ al-salātīn*, ed. Usha, p. 466; ed. M. Husayn, p. 447.

10 Ibid. A date of late in AD 1332 is suggested by evidence of the sultan's presence in Nāgawr at this time. M.A. Chughtai plausibly corrects the

The *Rawżat al-awliyā'* of Ghulām 'Alī Āzād Bilgrāmī records the visit of the important Chishtī shaykh Zain al-Dīn (*khalīfa* of Burhān al-Dīn 'Gharīb', himself a *khalīfa* of Niẓām al-Dīn) from Khuldābād in the western Deccan to Ajmer and Pākpaṭṭan to perform *ziyārat* of his predecessors in the *silsila*. This pilgrimage is stated to have taken place in the first year of Fērōz Shāh Tughluq's reign, i.e. AD 1351–2.[11]

A further reference to regular pilgrimage to Ajmer in the latter half of the fourteenth century occurs in the

---

reading of the date on the great gateway there from AH 632 to AH 732 (*A Forgotten Kingdom*, Poona: Deccan College, 1941). This is supported by a clear statement in the fourteenth-century *Surūr al-ṣudūr* that this gateway was erected by Muḥammad bin Tughluq. It narrates an anecdote in which the sultan, present at Nāgawr, on waking observed a scrap of paper with apposite verses, which led him to build the gateway and enclosure (*ḥaẓīra*) of the *khānqāh* of Ḥamīd al-Dīn, though he failed to erect a central domed tomb or pavilion (*qubba*). At the same time he ordered the endorsement of a *farmān* assigning revenues of Nāgawr to the *khānqāh*. The text of this *farmān* is reproduced in the *Surūr al-ṣudūr* and it is dated 26 Dhū'l-Ḥijja 732/October 1332. No MS of the *Surūr al-ṣudūr* is available to me, but at this point the original Persian text is reproduced *in extensor* by Aḥsān al-Ḥaqq Fārūqī, *Sultān al-tārikīn*, Karachi: Dā'ira Mu'īn al-ma'ārif, 1962, pp. 62–4. As Nāgawr lies to the north-west of Ajmer and the area of Kacchwāha control to the north-east, in each case not more than 60 mi. away, it is likely that Muḥammad bin Tughluq's visit to Ajmer was between campaigns against the Bhaṭṭī and Kacchwāha Rajputs, though which campaign preceded the other is in doubt.

11 *Rawżat al-awliyā'*, Urdu tr. by 'Abd al-Majīd, Hyderabad: Matba Kareemi, 1345 Faṣlī, pp. 101–2. Zain al-Dīn went to Ajodhan from Dehlī and passed through Ajmer on his return to Dawlatābād in the Deccan. He stayed for a month with the *sajjāda-nashīn* at Ajodhan and spent three days and nights within the tomb of Farīd al-Dīn. At Ajmer he spent a week inside the tomb of Mu'īn al-Dīn, but there is no mention of a longer residence there or of any incumbent *sajjāda-nashīn* or *khādim* community. Although Āzād Bilgrāmī, well known for his biographical *tadhkiras* of Mughal officers and of Persian poets, wrote in the middle of the eighteenth century, he drew on fourteenth-century compilations at Khuldābād or Dawlatābād which are inaccessible (see *Rawżat al-awliyā'*, pp. 8–9) and there is no reason to doubt the historicity of this account.

conversations of Sayyid Muḥammad Gēsūdarāz, recorded in AD 1399–1400. Gēsūdarāz was talking about his refusal to impart further instruction to one Ḥusām al-Dīn, who had previously received Ṣūfī teaching from other shaykhs. An unnamed *darvesh* reproached Gēsūdarāz and gave him a resumé of what he might have imparted to him. This included an injunction to perform the *ziyārat* of the *panj pīr* ('five *pīrs*'), who, as explained in the anecdote, are the five great Chishtī shaykhs who preceded Gēsūdarāz, viz., Naṣīr al-Dīn, Niẓām al-Dīn, Farīd al-Dīn, Quṭb al-Dīn, and Mu'īn al-Dīn.[12]

Another visit to the grave of Mu'īn al-Dīn is reported from the last year of the greater Dehlī Sultanate, in the period between the death of Fērōz Shāh Tughluq (1388) and the invasion of Tīmūr (1398). In this decade the central administration in the capital city had collapsed into civil war, and the provincial *muqṭa's* (governors) were laying the foundations of the independent provincial sultanates of the following century. Ẓafar Khān, progenitor of the sultans of Gujarat, went from Manḍalgaṛh to Ajmer in AH 799/AD 1397. According to the sources this was with the express purpose of performing the *ziyārat* of Mu'īn al-Dīn, but it was probably also an attempt to extend his military power northwards into Rajasthan, with an eye to his chances of possessing Dehlī itself. Near Ajmer, at a distance of 3 *kos* (7–8 mi.) away, he dismounted and went on foot to the grave, clad in pilgrim garb (*iḥrām-i ziyārat*), after which he performed the appropriate ceremonies at the tomb.[13]

[12] Gēsūdarāz, *Jawāmi' al-kalim*, Kanpur: Intizāmī Press, AH 1352, p. 183.
[13] Sikander, *Mir'āt-i Sikandarī*, ed. S.C. Misra and M.L. Rahman, Baroda: Maharaja Sayajirao University, 1961, p. 18. All the MSS of the *Mir'āt* read Manḍū, in place of Manḍalgaṛh which is found in *Tabaqāt-i Akbarī* and Firishta. All three accounts must derive from an earlier chronicle of Gujarat (possibly the *Ma'āthir-i Maḥmūdshāhī*, Storey no. 979). As Sir E.C. Bayley pointed out, Manḍalgaṛh, a dependency of the Rāṇā of Citawr, is more likely to be correct, see *The Local Muhammadan Dynasties: Gujarat*, London: W.H. Allen and Co., 1886, p. 77; Misra, *The Rise of Muslim Power in Gujarat*, p. 149.

6

To Ride a Tiger or a Wall?

Strategies of Prestige in Indian Sufi Legends

The largely American-inspired impulse towards the sociological investigation of Indian religious and cultural traditions has made us all too familiar with the Great Tradition and the Little Tradition. The terminology may reflect the moral bias of the theorists in favour of centralism and the big battalions, and its application has been largely confined to a main topic of interest to the theorists, the depth and intensity of the penetration of brahmanical Hinduism in Indian society. Nevertheless, this crude conceptual formulation embodies the idea of a polarization and conflict of interest between the idea of a universal community of belief and an enduring loyalty to local interests.

This polarization of devotion between universal and local is also found in the Indian Muslim population as it evolved through the centuries. On the one hand was the proud concept of the spiritual power of Islam unbounded by frontiers, and on the other the emotional needs of distant groups of Muslims for a sanctification of their local earth and landscape by the identification of sources of spiritual power within them.

* Originally published in Winand M. Callewaert and Rupert Snell, ed., *According to Tradition: Hagiographical Writing in India*, Wiesbaden: Harrassowitz Verlag, 1994, pp. 99–129. For Simon Digby's substantial further exploration of Sufi-related anecdotes, see volume II in this series (*Encounters with Jogīs in Indian Sūfī Hagiography*), a book-length expansion of his previously unpublished 1970 paper of the same name. ~DL

Popular imagination saw the maintenance of the wellbeing of Islam and of Muslims as the result of the attention, the spiritual and intercessory power and the benevolent activities of Sufi shaykhs, who were a worldwide hierarchy. However, in the perception of the roles of these shaykhs a division was inevitable corresponding to the perceptions of the worldwide power of Islam and of the local power-places and vehicles of its grace. In this ideology some shaykhs were 'ceaseless' travellers, bearers of a universal message with power derived from the founts of Islam, the Middle Eastern lands of Islam's origin and growth. Other shaykhs, who excited particular devotion and allegiance on account of their familiar local connection, sat in their places in the Indian countryside, and were seen to exercise a spiritual governance over the locality and an intercessory role on behalf of the local inhabitants.

Indian Sufi hagiography is largely a product of local and individual devotion towards stationary and settled shaykhs who, possibly after a period of travel in which they received their spiritual authority, 'sat in their places' on their *sajjādas* or even *gaddīs* in their *khānqāhs* and *dargāhs* or amid less ostentatious surroundings, revered by their followers in their lifetimes and by successive generations after their deaths.

Challenges to Authority

In Indian Sufi hagiography challenges to the authority of the incumbent shaykh fall into distinct categories which provoke disparate anecdotal patterns:

1. Anecdotes of the establishment of *khānqāhs* are often set in virgin territories for Islamic penetration where the holders of material and spiritual power are *kāfirs*, non-Muslims. This is the only class of these anecdotes in which the winning shaykh is a wandering challenger, not stationary and already incumbent. Opponents include

an idol and his priests, a king or a local wonder-worker and spiritual powerholder, sometimes singly, sometimes combined. Triumphs are assured by idols speaking, falling, or shattering; by armies of human or sentient beings stopped in their course by the shaykh's prohibition; and by the vanquishing of non-Muslim wonder-workers in displays of levitation and divination;

2. Anecdotes of the hostility or disrespect of Muslim rulers or other people of worldly influence. These are countered by the simple operation of fate, which usually leads to their unexpected, sudden, and often painful or exemplary deaths;
3. Anecdotes of the arrival of wild bands of Muslim religious vagrants, usually organized as Qalandars, at the *khānqāh* of the resident shaykh. These are often treated with surprising gentleness, the alternative being a vision of the shaykh's *jalāl* or wrathful aspect; and they are accommodated or subdued by the shaykh's charisma without conspicuous miraculous activity;[1]
4. Anecdotes of the arrival of non-Muslim men of religion at the *khānqāh* of the shaykh. In the Indian environment these are usually *jogīs* (yogis), and they are often represented as not so much challenging the shaykh's authority but rather as anxious for the legitimation of their own by the recognition of the shaykh. They are often vanquished in a levitatory or less frequently in a divinatory contest. Offers of miraculous gifts on their part are countered by displays of their superfluity to the shaykh's need, e.g. the shaykh shows that he possesses the power to transmute to gold though he does not normally use it;[2]

[1] S. Digby, 'Qalandars and Related Groups', in *Islam in Asia I: South Asia*, ed. Y. Friedmann, Jerusalem: Hebrew University, 1984, pp. 76–8, 87–91 [*L&WSD* III.7; this volume, pp. 208–11, 223–8].

[2] For a demonstration of unused power of Sufis to produce gold, see the passage from *Manāqib al-aṣfiyyā'* quoted below, note 47. For contests

5. Anecdotes of the arrival of another shaykh from a different lineage but possessing formidable charisma, whose implied intention is to humble or dispossess the incumbent. At the sober level of remembered historical encounters, the visits of such shaykhs included ceremonious welcome and the exchange of gifts, participation in formal religious discussion, and sometimes a symbolic indication that the traveller should move on from the recognized area of the shaykh's *wilāyat* or spiritual territory.[3] If what, in fact, occurred was the settlement of a new, possibly more prestigious Sufi lineage in an area where an older line of shaykhs was established, the subsequent hagiography will be likely to represent this as a welcoming of an expected arrival.[4] But in symbolic anecdotes, the function of which is not to explain any real historical accommodation, but merely to exalt the status of the local shaykh by

---

with yogis, see my preliminary study, 'Encounters with Jogīs in Indian Sufi Hagiography', Seminar on Aspects of Religion in South Asia, London, School of Oriental and African Studies, 17 January 1970, cyclostyle, pp. 11–35. A more extended analysis is in preparation [for the latter, see *L&WSD* II ~DL].

[3] S. Digby, 'The Sufi Shaykh as a Source of Authority in Medieval India', *Puruṣārtha*, vol. 9, 1986, pp. 63–4 [*L&WSD* III.1; this volume, pp. 17–19].

[4] S. Digby, 'Hawk and Dove in Sufi Combat', in C. Melville (ed.), *Pembroke Papers 1: Festschrift for P. W. Avery*, ed. C. Melville, Cambridge: Pembroke College, 1990, p. 14; Muḥammad Sulṭān, *Armughān-i sulṭānī*, Agra: Maṭba'-i Mufīd-i 'Ām, 1902, p. 51; S. Digby, 'The Naqshbandīs in the Deccan in the Late Seventeenth and Early Eighteenth Century', in *Naqshbandis: cheminements et situation actuelle d'un ordre mystique musulman*, ed. M. Gaborieau, İstanbul/Paris: Isis, 1990, p. 179 [*L&WSD* VII, introduction]; Bābā Shāh Maḥmūd, *Malfuẓāt-i Naqshbandiyya*, Hyderabad, Deccan: Nizamat-i umru Sarkar-i 'ali, AH 1358/AD 1939, pp. 23–4 [since the original publication of this essay, Simon Digby published his translation of Maḥmūd's text (New Delhi: Oxford University Press, 2001), reissued in this series as volume VII, along with his previously unpublished companion volume to the translation in volume VIII ~DL].

comparison with hypothetical outside challengers, a miraculous contest is called for, comparable to the contests with visiting *jogīs* (Class 4 above). However, a levitatory display, or its countering (beating down the *jogī* with the shaykh's slipper or staff, etc.) would be quite out of place here. The symbolism of the anecdote requires the power of the shaykh to be linked with his sedentary, immovable position. It is therefore inappropriate for either the shaykh or his slipper to fly up in the air. By contrast, his challenger must come from the far horizon; he should be swift in his movements and awesome in appearance.

The anecdote of the Rider on the Tiger (Lion) and the Rider on the Wall serves this hagiographical purpose, and one might say that it is repeated by almost any narrator who feels that it will exalt the reputation of a local shaykh to whom he feels allegiance. Sometimes the narrator strives for a stronger semblance of historicity by giving the shaykh's opponent the name of a famous contemporary travelling shaykh who visited or might, with some plausibility, have visited the area of his subject's activities. The anecdote is found in Sufi hagiography far afield from the Indian subcontinent, from which it may have spread, in areas of strong ethnic Muslim cult loyalties, in Anatolia and among the Kurds.[5] We may, however, assume that it is invariably told by devotees of the local shaykh and his cult, and not by those of the wandering shaykh, if a name be given to him in the anecdote.[6]

[5] M. van Bruinessen, 'Haji Bektash, Sultan Sahak, Shah Mina Sahib and Avatars of the Running Wall', *Turcica: revue d'études Turques*, vol. 21, no. 3, 1991, 'Mélange offert à Irène Mélikoff', pp. 55–69. Dr van Bruinessen kindly furnished me with the final pre-publication typescript, of which use has been made in this paper.

[6] Among the anecdotes that we survey below, the Rider on the Tiger is a nameless *darwesh* in the anecdote of Khwāja Gurg, and he is also

The conflict is between a peripatetic challenger and a sedentary holy man who, alive or dead, is likely to remain the centre of a local cult. One is the irresistible force and the other the immovable object. The challenger arrives, usually in a way which displays his paranormal powers, riding on a lion or tiger. The local incumbent remains firmly seated. In the common elaborated form the incumbent rides out, still seated on the wall, to confront the intruder. The dichotomy of sources of power which has led to the construction of these anecdotes ensures a conclusion in which, while suitable acknowledgement may be paid to the charisma of the peripatetic challenger, the incumbent is left undisturbed in the exercise of his territorially limited authority.

The Two Riders seem first to come together in Sufi anecdotal tradition. The earliest literary record of it yet noted is in a hagiographical work of the Delhi Sultanate quoted below, that was composed in AH 771/AD 1370.[7] A late fifteenth-century Turkish source testifies that the anecdote was already current among the Bektashi in Anatolia in this form.[8] However, stories of the Rider on the Tiger and of the Rider on the Wall seem to have been independently current, in India and in Islamic lands, before their felicitous encounter in the anecdote of confrontation.

Stories of the Rider on the Tiger, with snake-whip, occur in the biographies of *siddhas* of the Vajrayāna Buddhist

---

unnamed (though probably identified in other sources or oral tradition) in the anecdote of the great-grandson of Gēsūdarāz. In the Gaṛhwālī folk-tale version the names are probably fantastic. In the final Hinduized anecdote from Bihar neither contestant is given a name.

7 For this date, not previously established, see S. Digby, 'Anecdotes of a Provincial Sufi of the Delhi Sultanate, Khwāja Gurg of Kara', *Iran*, vol. 32, 1994, pp. 99–109 [*L&WSD* III.9].

8 Van Bruinessen cites the *Vilayet-name*, a late fifteenth-century Turkish hagiography of Haji Bektash.

tradition, particularly regarding the *siddha* Dombi-pa. All of the anecdotes are preserved in the Tibetan hagiographical tradition. One source, Abhayadatta's *Description of the Eighty-four Siddhas* is a translation of a Sanskrit original which has been thought to date from the twelfth century but may be somewhat later.

The riding on the Moving Wall is associated with the *siddhas* in the Sikh *janam-sākhī* tradition and therefore must have been current among Nāth Yogīs in the period of the composition of the *janam-sākhīs* around the end of the sixteenth century. This does not preclude a quite recent borrowing from Sufi sources, particularly as it has not yet been noted in this simple form in the Tibetan Buddhist tradition. However, one anecdote in a Tibetan source, examined below, of a rider on a stone lion, seems to represent an evolved variant combining the two riders.

In Muslim sources, the Rider on the Lion/Tiger and the Rider on the Wall are found independently of one another before we have record of the encounter of the Two Riders. Similar Greek Christian legends may be imports from the East. At a later date there are recurrent legends at minor Indian Sufi sites of a Rider on a Tiger who has arrived and settled without local opposition.

The Antecedents of the Sufi Anecdote of the Two Riders

The Rider on the Tiger: The Siddha/Vajrayāna Tradition

Iconology demands that the sacred figure depicted should be identified by his attributes. On Tibetan *thang-kas*, the *siddha* Dombi-pa, in theory one out of eighty-four of such

Perfected Adepts, 'is usually portrayed holding a snake and riding on the back of a tiger'.[9]

In the legend of the Dombi-pa as told by Abhayadatta, the *siddha* was a king in Magadha who abandoned his throne after taking as his consort a low-caste girl. Later his subjects invited him back, and 'the king and his consort came riding out of the forest on a young tigress, using a poisonous snake as a whip'.[10]

Tāranātha gives a slightly variant account: 'The *Ācārya* arrived together with his consort, riding on a tiger and a milking yak respectively and holding venomous snakes in their hands.'[11] Dombi-pa made a second appearance to frighten a king of Rāḍha (south Bengal) who 'was harming the Buddha's doctrine ...'. Dombi-pa 'wore snakes whose touch was poisonous, as ornaments; he wore snakes whose look was poisonous, as a whip; and the seven snakes whose

[9] Abhayadatta, *Buddha's Lions: The Lives of the Eighty-four Siddhas*, tr. J.B. Robinson, Berkeley: Dharma Publishing, 1979, p. 267; for such depictions of Dombi-pa, see ibid., p. 33; Abhayadatta, *Masters of Mahamudra: Songs and Histories of the Eighty-four Buddhist Siddhas*, tr. K. Dowman, Albany: State University of New York, 1985, p. 55; Abhayadatta, *Masters of Enchantment: The Lives and Legends of the Mahasiddhas*, Harmondsworth: Arkana, 1988, p. 40, a colourful depiction in 'Tibetan' style by Robert Beer. A similar depiction is also found, labelled 'Nāgārjuna' in a set of postcards of the *siddhas* in Tibetan style, acquired by the present writer in Kathmandu in 1990. No literary justification for this label has yet been found in the corpus of legends regarding Nāgārjuna.

[10] Abhayadatta, *Buddha's Lions*, tr. Robinson p. 35; Abhayadatta, *Masters of Mahamudra*, tr. Dowman, p. 54; Abhayadatta, *Masters of Enchantment*, tr. Dowman, p. 42.

[11] Jo Nang Tāranātha, *The Seven Instruction Lineages*, tr. D. Templeman, Dharmsala: Library of Tibetan Works & Archives, 1990, p. 20. Tāranātha gives an account differing from Abhayadatta's of the origins of Dombi-pa: 'It is well-known in Tibet that [he] was a leather-worker [and] it is also said by my Guru that he was a king of the eastern land of Tripura'; ibid., p. 19.

breath is venomous, he wore on his head.' We are told that the king was terrified out of his wits.[12]

The priority in time of the first of these tales of the *siddhas* over the assumption of similar attributes in narratives of Muslim *pīrs* is clearly a matter of interest. The Sanskrit original of Abhayadatta's *Caturaśītisiddhapravṛtti* is assumed to have been written before the Muslim conquest of the Gangetic plain and Bengal in the late eleventh or early twelfth century. The Tibetan version is included in the *bs-Tan-'gyur* which ought to set a *terminus ante quem* of the middle of the fourteenth century.[13]

One Tibetan version of the story of Dombi-pa riding the tiger appears to associate the incident with a Muslim environment. This is a life of Guru Padmasambhava, allegedly by a disciple but 'discovered' (i.e. composed) in the later fourteenth century:

Five years later the Brahmin (who instructed Padmasambhava in the Khasarpāṇi temple) died. A great pandit named Dhombhi Heruka immediately appeared to claim the body. Many wolves came to attack the pandit, but, exercising yogic powers, he drove them away by looking at them; and, placing the body on his lap, mounted a tiger. He used serpents for the bridle, girth and crupper of the tiger, wore on his body ornaments of human bone, and,

[12] Ibid., p. 20.

[13] Abhayadatta, *Buddha's Lions*, tr. Robinson, pp. 2, 392; cf. David L. Snellgrove and Hugh Richardson, *A Cultural History of Tibet*, Boston: Praeger, 1986, p. 170; P. Kvaerne, *An Anthology of Tantric Buddhist Songs*, repr., Bangkok: White Orchid Press, 1986, intro., pp. 2–3. In view of the relative poverty of the hagiographical tradition which Abhayadatta's work embodies about figures whose namesakes were certainly active in the eleventh century (when contrasted with the richness and generally more authentic quality of information found in the works of Tāranātha) the present writer would favour as late a date of composition as is consonant with inclusion in the printings of the translation in editions of the *bs-Tan'gyur*.

carrying a three-pronged staff, went to the Muslim city of Dedan (Bde-ldan). Then he rode round announcing that he would make a gift of the body to anyone who could come and take it. A passer-by remarked, 'look at this yogi who is talking nonsense. He would not be riding the tiger had he not given it honey, nor making use of the serpents had he not given them musk.'[14]

The Defender Rides a Stone Lion

Candrakīrti, 'Abbot' of Nalanda, to whom an early seventh-century floruit is given, is said to have ridden out on a stone lion against invading Turuṣkas (sc. Turks, Muslims): 'Without being obstructed by pillars and ramparts of stone and riding a stone lion, he repulsed the Turuska army.'[15] This story, whatever its date, appears a conflation of the two sides and the contrasting mounts of attacker and defender. Such a conflation may have been prompted by the iconography of lions guarding the entrances of Buddhist religious buildings.[16]

[14] W.Y. Evans-Wentz, tr., *The Tibetan Book of the Great Liberation*, London: Oxford University Press, 1965, pp. 161–2. Sangye-lingpa, the 'discoverer' of the biography flourished from AD 1340 to 1396; information communicated by Michael Aris. According to the colophon, the block print of the biography from which Evans-Wentz's translation was made dates from the early seventeenth century, the reign of the Zhabs-Drung or first Dharmarāja of Bhutan; see M. Aris, *Bhutan: The Early History of a Himalayan Kingdom*, Warminster: Aris & Phillips, 1979, p. 203ff. The Muslim contest of Bde-ldan ('City of Bliss'), as found in Evans-Wentz's summarized translation, requires further elucidation; M. Aris in a personal communication. For a form of Padmasambhava riding a Tigress (but without snake-whip), see Aris, *Bhutan*, p. 142 and illustration on p. 145.

[15] Sumpa, *Pag-sum-jon-zang*, ed. S.C. Das, pp. 94–9, cited in Sukumar Dutt, *Buddhist Monks and Monasteries of India*, London: G. Allen and Unwin, 1962; repr., Delhi: Motilal Banarsidass, 1988, p. 346. Dutt notes the chronological discrepancy: 'The Turaṣkas [sic] were in their homes outside India ... when Candrakīrti was at Nalanda.'

[16] Such lions guarding the gateways of Buddhist monuments at the cardinal points can be traced back at least to the fifth century AD.

The great Buddhist establishment at Nalanda was sacked and virtually destroyed by the Muslim military adventurers who established the Sultanate of Bengal at the beginning of the thirteenth century. They may be identified with the Turuṣkas of the anecdote. The anecdote would therefore be of a later date than this.

The Moving Wall Alone: The Siddhas *in Sikh Tradition*

Among the compositions of Gurū Nānak (AD 1469–1539) included in the canonical collection of the *Ādi granth* is the *Siddh goṣṭ* ('Discourse with the *Siddhas*'). W.H. McLeod's conclusions regarding the historicity of a confrontation are that at least one encounter 'may perhaps be authentic if for Siddhas we read Kānphaṭ or Nāth yogis'; and that 'the location is not named in any of [Nānak's] compositions, but it seems evident from such a work as the *Siddh Goṣṭ* that he engaged them in formal debate.'[17]

In the *janam-sākhī* biographical tradition, which began to take shape before the end of the sixteenth century, 'inevitably the ... *Siddh Goṣṭ* ... was set in the context of a discourse with Siddhas (or Nāths)': 'Following a recital of Nānak's lengthy composition the Siddhas demonstrate their power by making deerskins fly, stones move, and walls walk. Nānak replies by reciting ... a brief work which proclaims

---

They have been noted at Butkara in Swat and at Bijbihara/Vijabror in Kashmir. As I have had occasion to observe around the temples of Nepal, free-standing sculptures of animals prompt small boys to ride them like rocking-horses. Such a practice would suggest the anecdote; cf. note 37 below.

[17] W.H. McLeod, *Gurū Nānak and the Sikh Religion*, Oxford: Clarendon Press, 1968, pp. 140–1. For the text of the *Siddh Goṣṭ*, see editions of *Ādi granth*, *Rāg Rāmkali*, e.g. vol. III, ed. Manmohan Sahgal, Lucknow: Bhuvan Vāṇī Trust, 1988, pp. 558–81.

the futility of both magic and extreme asceticism.'[18] In the *Purātan Janam-sākhī* the confrontation and magical display took place in Gorakh-haṭaṛī (Gor-khatrī in Peshawar). In the *B40 Janam-sākhī* the magical display takes place after a different recitation by Nānak at Achal (Batala): 'The Siddhs (Bhāgarnāth and his fellow yogis) begin by performing a series of miracles, including the magical propulsion of a wall and flight on a deerskin. In response Nānak challenges them to a game of hide-and-seek.'[19]

The descriptions are imprecise, but it is possible that the narrators intended to show that the *siddhas* rode on the wall, as on the deerskins, the normal vehicle for the aerial flight of *jogīs*. This is supported by another (later?) *janam-sākhī* quoted by Trumpp. In this case the opponents are female sorcerers performing similar acts: 'One came mounted on a tree, another on the moon, another on a wall, another brought with her a tiger, another beating a drum.'[20] J.C. Oman, Professor of Natural Science in Lahore and an early commentator on popular Indian religious practices, in his characteristic style reproduces, from an unspecified *janam-sākhī* current at the beginning of [the twentieth] century, an account of a contest between Gurū Nānak and the *siddhas*: 'One boastful *Siddha* would ride on flames of fire, and another on a bit of stone wall as if it was a horse.'[21] The *janam-sākhī* tradition shows many signs of Sufi hagiographical influence. While the deerskin (*mṛgachāl*) is the preferred aerial mount of tales of the

[18] W.H. McLeod, *Early Sikh Tradition: A Study of the Janam-sākhīs*, Oxford: Clarendon Press, 1980, p. 149.
[19] McLeod, *Early Sikh Tradition*, p. 152.
[20] E. Trumpp, *The Adi Granth*, London: W.H. Allen & Co., 1877, intro., p. xix.
[21] J.C. Oman, *The Mystics, Saints and Ascetics of India*, London: T. Fisher Unwin, 1905, pp. 32, 33 n. 1.

Jogīs, the Moving Wall may derive either from Sufi or as yet unnoted non-Muslim Indian antecedents.

The Rider on the Lion and Rider on the Wall in Muslim and Western Sources

The Rider on the Lion

HAẒRAT 'ALĪ AS LION

'Haẓrat 'Alī', i.e. 'Alī b. Abī Tālib, son-in-law of the Prophet, is often represented by the symbol of a lion, e.g. in small Shi'ī shrines in the Deccan. In pictures illustrating romantic accounts of his wars, he is normally depicted with his face veiled riding a horse or a camel. The topic of his possible connection with the Rider on the Lion remains to be investigated.

KHIẒR AS LION-RIDER: A LATE FOURTEENTH-CENTURY SUFI TESTIMONY

A late fourteenth-century Indian Sufi source tells of the ever-living prophet Khiẓr arriving mounted upon a lion. Sayyid Jalāl al-Dīn Bukhārī 'Makhdūm-i Jahāniyān' is recorded as relating:

> He had been told by a *darwesh* whom he had met in Damascus to go and sit with him in a certain place. Seated there, he saw a man approaching, mounted upon a lion (*sher*) and wearing green garments [which are a sign of Khiẓr]. The rider dismounted beside the *darwesh* and they began to recite the *Qur'ān* together. After the reading was completed the man again mounted the lion's back and rode away. When Jalāl al-Dīn inquired from the *darwesh* he was told that this was Khwāja Khiẓr.[22]

[22] Aḥmad Baranī, *Sirāj al-Hidāya*, ed. Q. Sajjād Husayn, Delhi: Idarah-i-Adabiyat i-Delli, 1983, pp. 340–1.

A CHRISTIAN LION-RIDER

The saint who rides a lion can be found in Christian legends of the eastern Mediterranean: 'St. Mamas of Morphou (in Cyprus) was beloved because he refused to pay taxes, and when ordered to the royal palace in Nicosia to explain why, rode there on a lion with a lamb in his arms.'[23]

THE SUFI AS LION-RIDER

In a twelfth-century Khurāsānī source, the *Asrār al-tawḥīd*, we already find Bāyazīd Bistāmī described, by Shaykh Abū Sa'īd b. Abi'l-Khayr, as riding a lion with a snake whip.[24]

SOLITARY TIGER-RIDERS IN THE INDIAN-MUSLIM ENVIRONMENT

Amont the known Muslim graves in *Shaykhoṅ kā qabristān* at Chanderi is one of a Shaykh 'Abda', a descendant of Sulaymān of Mandu, described as *sher-sawār māre ba-dast.*[25] In Muhammad A'ẓam's *tadhkira* of the shaykhs buried in the vicinity of Thatta, two holy men are noted as having arrived on a lion or tiger. Sayyid Ya'qūb came from Mashhad in AH 901/AD 1495–6: 'They say that that Lion of the Thicket of Reality came riding a lion.'[26]

[23] J. Morris, *The Venetian Empire: A Sea Voyage*, London: Faber and Faber, 1988, p. 101. For a Greek Christian relation of the anecdote of the Two Riders, with one St. Charambolos riding the wall and the Prophet Muhammad, the lion, see F.W. Hasluck and M.M. Hasluck, *Christianity and Islam under the Sultans*, London: Clarendon Press, 1918, vol. I, p. 289n; cited by van Bruinessen, n. 20.
[24] Muḥammad b. Munawwar, *Asrār al-tawḥīd*, ed. Dhabīḥ Allāh Ṣafā, Tehran: Amīr-i Kabīr, Shamsī 1332/AD 1953, p. 266.
[25] Communication of Professor Muzaffar Alam.
[26] M. A'ẓam Tattawī, *Tuḥfat al-ṭāhirīn*, ed. B.A. Rabbānī, Hyderabad, Sindh: Sindī Adabī Board, 1956, p. 27.

In the early sixteenth century, in the reign of Jām Ferōz b. Jām Niẓām al-Dīn, Pīr Ṣalāḥ al-Dīn came from India (Hind) to Sind, also riding a lion or tiger (*sher-sawār*):

> Jām Ferōz paid no attention to him, remarking that: 'Men also teach bears and monkeys, and make elephants and wild asses obedient to themselves. It is not improbable if someone subjugates a lion and makes it obey him.'
>
> That Holy Man was affected when he heard these words, and said: 'It will not be long before the house of his prosperity will be ruined and the hall of his rule will fall down!'[27]

This pronouncement was followed by the invasion of Sind by Mīrzā Shāh Beg Arghūn and the downfall of Jām Ferōz and his native dynasty.

THE IMAGE OF THE LION-RIDER IN INDO-PERSIAN POETRY

The distance between hagiographical anecdote and poetic fancy is at times diminished, and so we may note an example of the lion-rider in an imaginative *mathnavī* filled with the imagery of distant travel. The description occurs in one of the five narrative poems (*mathnavīs*) that 'Fānī', a seventeenth-century Persian poet of Kashmir, like other more famous Persian poets, wrote in imitation of the similar five (*Khamsa*) of Niẓāmī of Ganja. Fānī composed his *Haft Akhtar* ('Seven Stars') on the pattern of Niẓāmī's *Haft Paykar* ('Seven Countenances'), in the Hijrī year 1068/AD 1657–8.

The connecting thread of the fairly silly plot of Fānī's *Haft Akhtar* is the description of the travels of Hilāl ('Crescent'), a young courtier and emissary of an unnamed Shāh of Iran. Hilāl is sent to China bearing a portrait of his extraordinarily

[27] Ibid., p. 114. For Sufi prophecies of the downfall of hostile rulers, see S. Digby, 'The Sufi Shaykh and the Sultan: A conflict of Claims to Authority in Medieval India', *Iran*, vol. 38, 1990, pp. 71–8 [*L&WSD* III.2; this volume, pp. 42–76].

beautiful monarch to display to a Chinese princess on whom he has set his heart. The embassy proceeds on its travels all mounted on lions, which also serve as beasts of burden. While the riders carouse quaffing red wine with the local rulers through whose territories the cortège passes, the lions are hospitably regaled with huge heaps of bloody flesh, lovingly described.[28]

The Moving Wall Alone

AN EARLY KHURASANI SUFI VERSION

The anecdote occurs in its simple form, without the lion-rider, in a conversation of Shaykh Niẓām al-Dīn of Delhi recorded in the year AH 707/AD 1308. Though this great Chishtī shaykh was born in northern India and was talking in Delhi, much of the legendary lore of the Sufis which fills his conversations is of anecdotes of famous shaykhs of Khurasan (modern eastern Iran and Afghanistan) who lived one or two centuries earlier. This reflects the historical antecedents of the sultanate, established from Ghūr and Ghaznī.

It is said of Shaykh Luqmān of Sarakhs that he failed to perform the Friday prayer and other external observances of the *Shar'*. *A'imma* (pious leaders) came out from the city to censure him. He was told that the *A'imma* of the city were coming to dispute with him. Shaykh Luqmān asked: 'Do they come riding or on foot?'

He was told that they were coming riding. At that time the Shaykh was seated on a wall. He said: 'By the command of God, may he be honoured and glorified, start moving!' The wall immediately started to move.[29]

[28] *Mathnawiyyāt-i Fānī Kashmīrī*, ed. S.A.H. Abidi, Srinagar: Jammu and Kashmir Academy of Arts, Culture and Languages, 1964, English introduction, p. 10; pp. 414–15.

[29] Amīr Hasan 'Alā' Sijzī, *Fawā'id al-fu'ād*, Bk. I, 7th *Majlis*, 19 Shawwāl, ed. M.L. Malik, Lahore: Malik Sirāj al-Dīn and Sons, 1966, p. 13; tr.

In the cumulative tradition of Sufi hagiography, the anecdote in this form may represent the stage before the lion/tiger has been introduced into the story. The anecdotal tradition was probably brought to Delhi from Khurasan in the early thirteenth century, and Shaykh Luqmān himself is a figure of the tenth Christian century (fourth century of the *hijra*), the period of more narrowly localized centres of *barakat* in Khurasan before the 'institutionalization' and wide geographical range of the post-twelfth-century Sufi orders. The group of 'imāms (*a'imma*) must refer to members of the large groups of pious high-status inhabitants of the Khurasani urban settlements (e.g. Nayshāpūr). Luqmān Sarakhsī appears in a number of anecdotes of the *Asrār al-tawḥīd* as an inspired madman who leads the youthful Abū Sa'īd to take the Sufi Path. The anecdote of the moving wall is not to be found in the *Asrār al-tawḥīd*, but is in character with Luqmān's levitatory activities.[30]

Indian Sufi Anecdotes of the Two Riders

The Shaykhs to Whose Names the Story is Attached

Among the pairs of contestants about whom the anecdote of the Rider on the Tiger and the Rider on the Wall is told are Shaykh Aḥmad-i Jām as challenger against Khwāja Mawdūd of Chisht, in Khurasan/western Afghanistan in the eleventh century; Khwāja Gurg and an unnamed *darvesh* in the north

Bruce Lawrence, *Morals for the Heart*, New York: The Paulist Press, 1992, p. 89. For the early currency of legends of Luqmān's levitatory activities, see Munawwar, *Asrār al-tawḥīd*, p. 28; cf. remarks on *Luqmān-i paranda*, 'Luqmān the flyer' in Hamīd Qalandar, *Khayr al-majālis*, ed. K.A. Nizami, Aligarh: Aligarh Muslim University, 1958, p. 160.

[30] Munawwar, *Asrār al-tawḥīd*, ed. Safa, p. 266.

Indian town of Kara in the late thirteenth century; Shāh Bū 'Alī Qalandar of Panipat and Shāhbāz Qalandar of Sehvan in the late thirteenth century; the fourteenth-century Chishtī shaykh Quṭb al-Dīn Munawwar of Hansī in the Punjab and Sayyid Tāj al-Dīn Sher-sawār, who is buried at Narnaul; and another later fourteenth-century Chishtī Shaykh, Shāh Mīnā of Lucknow and Badī' al-Dīn Madār of Makanpur.

A more ornate version of the anecdote is found at the *khānqāh* of Sayyid Muhammad Gēsūdarāz at Gulbarga with the device of 'distancing' the shaykh from the performance of the miracle. A fierce but unnamed *shersawār* (rider on a lion or tiger), with scorpion reins and snake whip, comes to the *dargāh* where he is confronted and repelled by the 7-year-old great-grandson of Gēsūdarāz. Apart from the case of Khwāja Gurg, a *majdhūb* with Suhrawardī connections, in all these Indian narratives the shaykh on the wall is Chishtī. Probably this merely reflects the better survival of Chishtī hagiographical sources. In examples noted in the Middle East the winning local shaykh belongs to such diverse sects as the Bektashī and the Ahl-i Haqq.

In the concluding section of the paper three further repetitions of the anecdote are examined, in which the Sufi form of the anecdote appears to have passed back into non-Muslim Indian traditions.

Our examination of the morphology of the anecdote can best proceed from simpler to more elaborate examples, rather than in a chronological sequence, of either the alleged date or period of the confrontation or the probable date of the literary record, the latter of course being dependant on the hazards of survival and discovery by the researcher. However, the first narrative to be considered below (that of Khwāja Gurg), which is the simplest in its morphology, also happens to be the earliest source yet noted for the anecdote of the Two Riders.

A Provincial Encounter in the Delhi Sultanate

The simple Sufi form of the anecdote is exemplified in a *tadhkira* exalting a *majdhūb* (divinely crazed madman) in a provincial town of the Delhi Sultanate in the later thirteenth century:[31]

It is related that one day Khwāja Gurg was seated, when a man came and said: 'A *darvesh* is coming riding a lion [/tiger] with a live snake in his hand!'

The *Khwāja* said: 'Where is he?'

The man said that he was close. The *Khwāja* then mounted a wall and said: 'By the Lady's head![32] Move!'

By God's will the wall moved. On the other side the *darvesh* rode up on a lion. On this side the *khwāja* mounted the wall. When the two came close together, the *darvesh* dismounted and fell like a slave at the *khwāja*'s feet, saying: 'What is your order for me?'

The *khwāja* said: 'Your place is not here!' And [the *darvesh*] laid hold of the lion and took the road.

The fourteenth-century *tadhkira* from which this anecdote is taken consistently lays stress on the role of this outwardly disreputable and ragged shaykh as protector of a provincial Muslim settlement on the banks of the Ganges. Khwāja Gurg sees the lion-riding challenger off from his *wilāyat* in the same way that he drives off a wandering band of murderous Qalandars and turns troublesome *parīs* out of the bounds of the town.[33]

[31] Muḥammad Ismā'īl Lāhawrī, *Asrār al-majdhūbīn*, Anecdote 183, Digby MS 10, f. 74 a–b. For the character of a *majdhūb* and Khwāja Gurg's range of activities, see S. Digby in *Iran*, vol. 32, 1994, forthcoming [published as 'Anecdotes of a Provincial Sufi of the Dehli Sultanate, Khwāja Gurg of Kara', pp. 99–109; included in this volume, *L&WSD* III.9].

[32] *Ay bībī kā sīr*; this exclamation often appears in the conversation of Khwāja Gurg as reproduced in the *Asrār al-majdhūbīn*. No explanation is forthcoming.

[33] See Digby, 'Anecdotes of a Provincial Sufi'; Lāhawrī, *Asrār al-majdhūbīn*, Anecdotes 9 and 205, ff. 6, 86–7.

A Visual Representation of the Encounter

A modern Indian Muslim coloured print provides a detailed representation of the encounter between the Rider on the Tiger and the Rider on the Wall. The print lacks the name of artist, distributor, and place of publication. Though the impression of the print was purchased in Sind in Pakistan by a Dutch scholar about a decade ago, the blocks for it probably date from around 1950 and the probable place of publication was Bombay.[34]

It is an accomplished example of its style of popular art, and it is valuable for the visual allusions which it makes to the issues that are involved in popular perceptions of such encounters. There can be no doubt that the print was made for devotees of the shrine and cult of Shāh Mīnā in Lucknow and not for the adherents of the rival shaykh, Badī‘ al-Dīn Madār, whose tomb at Makanpur is centre of a cult of usually low-class adherents.[35]

In the upper centre, beneath the Profession of Faith, is an inset of the ‘Place of Rest (*ārāmgāh*, tomb) of Haẓrat Makhdūm Shāh Mīnā Ṣāhib’ of Lucknow, a very large cenotaph covered by the customary cloth, in an open pillared and domed pavilion. Beyond the pavilion are the large central arch/*aywān* and three onion domes of a mosque. Above, the tomb is flanked to the right (the side of greater

[34] This conjecture is based on a comparison with Indian Muslim religious prints in my own archive. The print of the Two Riders is in the collection of Dr van Bruinessen and has been published by him in ‘Haji Bektash, Sultan Sahak, Shah Mina Sahib and Avatars of the Running Wall’. I am most grateful for the photograph of the print that he gave me.

[35] J.A. Subhan, *Sufism: its Saints and Shrines*, Lucknow: Lucknow Publishing House, 1960, pp. 316–17; M. Titus, *Islam in India and Pakistan*, Calcutta: Y.M.C.A. Publishing House, 1959, pp. 134, 143; Mūbad Shāh, *Dabistān-i madhāhib*, ed. R. Rāzazāde, vol. I, Tehran: Kitābkhānah-’i Ṭahūrī, 1362 Shamsī/AD 1983, pp. 190–1.

'honour') by a vision of the Ka'ba at Mecca and to the left by a similar inset of the tomb of the Prophet at Medina.

The foreground is filled by the representation of the two shaykhs and their attributes. The figures are dressed in contrasting styles, but they are both wearing luxurious clothes of the height of traditional elegance. Though *faqīr* may mean 'poor', the *faqīrs* are spiritual monarchs. In the imagination of the Indian poor the poverty of *faqīrs* was not equated with their own often desperate indigence. The Sufi *dargāh* was, as its name implies, a royal court, glittering in the imagination if not always in the reality. Hence, a conflict of intentions existed in the mind of the artist of this print, in which symbols of the humble way of life of '*faqīrs*', the wall, the waterpot, the unwalled tomb open to the air and the thatched hut, are invested with the solidity, ornateness or elegance that, from another point of view, was only to be expected in such a spiritually resplendent place.

From the left 'Hazrat Shāh Madār' has entered upon his mount. The *sher* (Persian, 'lion') of the label is, as usually in the popular Indian imagination, a male tiger. In Shāh Madār's right hand is a snake to be used as whip (Hindi, *koṛā* in the label). He is dressed in 'exotic' traditional Muslim costume considered to be of non-Indian origin, a long cloak (*qabā, 'abā*), a domed felt cap (*kullāh*), and *salīmshāhī* slippers with curled-up toe.

To the right, the more 'honourable' position, Shāh Mīnā sits on his wall. From two patches where the plaster has peeled off the brickwork, we are to understand that this is an old ruined wall, a detail that is mentioned in many versions of the anecdote (cf. *dīwār-i kuhna* in the anecdote of Khwāja Gurg reproduced above). But the wall is strangely reminiscent of an elegant late Mughal or Nawābī period marble or *chūnam* (hard white lime-plaster) bench, a style of outdoor furnishing appropriate to noblemen's *havelīs* and substantial Sufi *dargāhs*. Even the patches that show the brickwork recall the cusped arches of the bracket legs of such a bench. Beside the shaykh on the platform are his *būriyā*, rush-mat, and his ablution pot (*badhnā*, the Indian Muslim spouted *loṭā*);[36] but the artist has given the *badhnā* horizontal registers of decoration, and a fashionable handle and outline deriving from the Sino-European teapot rather than from any variety of *āftāba* or ewer.

Shāh Mīnā's clothes are of local Muslim cut, a *kurāt* and *pāyjāma* of fine white muslin, the former embroidered in the *chikandoz* manner for which Lucknow is famous.

The physiognomies of the two shaykhs are also deliberately contrasted. The aquiline feature of Shāh Mīnā and his oiled and carefully tended black locks and beard are those of a *sharīf* north Indian Muslim. Shāh Madār's darker complexion, more rounded face, long white locks and glittering eyes appropriately suggest another familiar, but perhaps wilder, less mild and domesticated type of Indo-Muslim piety.

The middle landscape, by the symbols that are laid out in it, alludes to the contrasting sources of prestige of the two shaykhs. In the distance across the water is the Holy Land of Arabia. Towards the left (the direction from which Shāh Madār is riding) is a lofty mosque with white walls and domes set amid date-palms. From this stretch out the sands of the desert with barren hills on the far horizon. Across the picture the placid surface of a band of water runs. This represents not what it more closely resembles in appearance, one of the great rivers of the north Indian plains, the Ganges or the Gomati, but the sea that Shāh Madār has had to cross on his way to Hind. Nineteenth-century north Indian *qiṣṣas*

[36] For the nomenclature of Indian Muslim metal vessels, see G.A. Grierson, *Bihar Peasant Life*, 1885; repr., Delhi: Cosmo Publications, 1975, p. 133, para. 711.

or 'folk-romances' have a similar notion of the 'Seven Seas', across which the hero's bowshot could strike a target on the other side.[37]

By contrast with the Arabian sands, Shāh Mīnā's wall stands in the green, watered, luxuriant Indian landscape. Behind him is the thatched hut in which he appropriately resides. Once again, the ambivalence of the artist's intentions is visible. A thatched hut of the north Indian countryside it may be, but it is an unusually large and substantial one.

Between the two shaykhs is a brief explanatory text in Urdu describing the incident, of which I have not found a description in accounts of Shāh Mīnā in *tadhkiras*.[38] It states that Shāh Mīnā ordered the wall to go forward for Shāh Madār's 'reception' (*peshwā'ī*). But this is a double-edged term. It is used for the reception of a guest, but it can also mean 'leadership, ... guidance, ... supremacy'.[39] There is no doubt who has the upper hand in the confrontation.

[37] Cf. *Madhumālatī ko kathā*, Chapter Three: 'Then the brothers began to discuss how they could cross these seven seas ... The youngest brother Madhukar ... loosed an arrow at a tree on the far side ...'. [Readers may wish to consult Simon's translation of this tale in his *Wonder-Tales of South Asia*, Jersey: Orient Monographs, 2000/New Delhi: Oxford University Press, 2006, as well as his previously unpublished essay in this series, 'The North Indian *Kissa* Tradition and the Nepali *Madhumalati*', *L&WSD* IV.5 ~DL]

[38] 'Abd al-Haqq Dihlavī in his brief notice of Shāh Mīnā mentions his habit of staying awake all night seated on a wall; 'Abd al-Haqq Dihlavī, *Akhbār al-akhyār* (Storey No. 1298 [1]), Delhi: Mujtabā'ī Press, AH 1309/AD 1892, p. 153; Ghulām Sarwar, *Khazīnat al-aṣfiyyā'* (Storey No. 1391 [1]), vol. I, Lucknow: Naval Kishor, AH 1332/AD 1914, p. 398. The association with a wall in the *dargāh* would have prompted the telling of the anecdote of the Two Riders about him.

[39] J.T. Platts, *A Dictionary of Urdu, Classical Hindi, and English*, London: W.H. Allen & Co., 1884, s.v.

An Ornate Confrontation in Khurāsān

The strategies of prestige in the pictorial representation that we have just considered are equally well represented in a long and ornate anecdote of confrontation in a seventeenth-century *tadhkira* regarding the shaykhs of the Chishtī lineage who are, both historically and in popular consciousness, so closely associated with the Muslim presence in India. The anecdote concerns one of the predecessors of the lineage in India who flourished in the eleventh century, Khwāja Mawdūd Chishtī. Chisht, from which the lineage takes its name, lies in modern Afghanistan, north of Herat. Shaykh Aḥmad of Jām (Torbat-e Jām towards Mashhad) was a powerful shaykh who was Khwāja Mawdūd's contemporary. There are other traditions of a conflict and accommodation between these two figures in the same geographical setting, which indicate that this was indeed a historical confrontation.[40]

The device of the Rider on the Lion/Tiger and the Rider on the Wall is employed in a summary way which makes

[40] Ilāh-diya Chishtī, *Siyar al-aqṭāb* (Storey No. 1325), pp. 81–4. For a different view of the confrontation between Shaykh Aḥmad and Khwāja Mawdūd, see Sadīd al-Dīn Muḥammad Ghaznavī, *Maqāmāt-i Zhinda-pīl*, ed. H. Mu'ayyad, Tehran: Intishārāt-i Bungāh-i Tarjumah va Nashr-i Kitāb, Shamsī 1340/AD 1962, pp. 70–5; 'Abd al-Rahmān Jāmī, *Nafaḥāt al-uns* (Storey No. 1274), ed. M. Tawhīdīpūr, Tehran, Shamsī 1336, pp. 326–9. Both these verbally almost identical accounts emphasize the vanquishing and humble submission of Khwāja Mawdūd, the *Khwāja*'s youth and inexperience, and the murderous intentions of his very numerous followers. Aḥmad of Jām tells his followers to close their eyes and transports them across the swollen river without many of them wetting their shoes. The motif of the Two Riders does not occur. The textual relation between these two accounts from opposing points of view will repay further study in the context of the surviving hagiographical tradition regarding the *Khwājas* of Chisht, predecessors of the more influential lineage of the Indian Chishtī shaykhs.

evident that any hearer or reader would, by its occurrence, recognize the nature of the confrontation. The grandiosity of the narrator's vision limits the effectiveness of the device. Khwāja Mawdūd is accompanied by thousands of adherents, and he goes out scores of miles to confront the challengers. The wall is made to travel over this distance with the speed of the wind.

The narrative and the recurrence of the key word *wilāyat* in the sense of the spiritual jurisdiction of a Sufi shaykh over a defined territory indicate the motivation of the anecdote more clearly than some of the variants with other actors that we quote in this chapter. The anecdote is not purely factitious, but probably represents the memory of a real historical rivalry of two powerful shaykhs with adjacent spheres of influence. Consequently, another respect in which this anecdote differs from most of its cogeners is that the challenger is not from the far horizon but from a contiguous *wilāyat* or area of authority. The anecdote establishes a precise frontier, of a type recognized by Chishtī shaykhs elsewhere, at the river Tūnak (?). This detail, like the murderous intentions of some of the shaykh's followers and the *samā'* or musical party held after the meeting, probably reflects a genuine historical memory.[41]

A device of 'distancing' should be noted in the employment of *munāfiqīn*, a Qur'ānic term of abuse here used to mean 'ill-disposed people' to define cruder elements and possibilities of action in the confrontation. Frank expression of these possibilities would not be in character with the lofty persona

[41] These details are common to the accounts from the other side, cited immediately above, which are equally explicit in maintaining that this was a conflict about territorial *wilāyat*, though they include a mocking observation by Shaykh Aḥmad Jām that *wilāyat* belongs to the ruling Sultan Sanjar, not to Sufis. For the recognition of exact territorial frontiers to the *wilāyat* of Sufi shaykhs, see Digby, 'The Sufi Shaykh as a Source of Authority', p. 63 [this volume, pp. 15–16].

of a Sufi shaykh. These nasty people, the *munāfiqīn*, serve their purpose and are then chastised. The peacemaking of the two shaykhs and the exaltation of their authority over their followers is celebrated by a bout of *samā'* (listening to sung poetry) on neutral territory. There may be some historical basis for this detail also, as among Chishtī shaykhs of the Delhi Sultanate a *ghazal* attributed to Shaykh Aḥmad of Jām was familiar and subsequently attained great emotional significance in the lineage.[42]

[42] The second of the Chishtī shaykhs in Hindostan, Quṭb al-Dīn Bakhtyār Kāki (d. 633/1236) is said to have died in ecstasy after hearing the prolonged chanting of a *bayt* (couplet) attributed to Aḥmad-i Jām:

> *kushtagān-i khanjar-i taslīm-rā*
> *har zamān az ghayb jān-i dīgar ast*
>
> For those slain by dagger of Submission [faith in Islam]
> every time there is new life from the Unseen.

The historical memory of this death has continued to charge the couplet with high emotional significance in Indian Sufi circles, resulting in deaths in ecstasy at its recitation in the [twentieth] century. The earlier record of the incident is by Amīr Khwurd in the latter half of the fourteenth century: Amīr Khwurd, *Siyar al-awliyā'* (Storey No. 1259), ed. Chiranjī Lāl, Delhi: Muhibb-i Hind Press, 1302/1885, p. 55. However, the *bayt* is not there attributed to Aḥmad-i Jām. It is found in the *Dīwān* of Aḥmad-i Jām (*takhallus* Aḥmad) and the attribution is made in most subsequent narratives. However, the *Dīwān* has been rejected as almost wholly spurious by the modern Iranian editor of Ghaznavī, *Maqāmāt-i Zhinda Pīl*, intro., pp. 24–37. Eastern Indian manuscript tradition attributes this *Dīwān* to the Firdawsī Aḥmad Chiramposh ('leather-clad'), otherwise Aḥmad Bihārī, who was put to death in Delhi by Sultan Fērōz Shāh Tughluq; see Digby, 'The Sufi Shaykh as a Source of Authority', p. 67 [this volume, p. 25]. This attribution is just chronologically possible (the main difficulty being verses taken from Hāfiz and Ni'mat Allāh Kirmānī) and it is consonant with some doctrinally risqué contents. The inclusion of this already well-known couplet in a *ghazal* by Aḥmad Chiramposh would then be an example of the device of *tazmīn* (deft quotation, 'inserting the verses of another in one's own poem'—Steingass). If this

The narrative reproduced below is characteristic of the early seventeenth-century author, Shaykh Ilāhdiyā, whose *tadhkira Siyar al-aqṭāb* ('Conduct of the Poles') usually provides the most ornate and picturesque of the variant accounts of the lives and deeds of the Chishtī shaykhs who were his predecessors.

When the revered father of Khwāja Mawdūd joined the Mercy of God and the *Khwāja* sat on the *sajjāda* [prayer-carpet of authority], he was yet young, being twenty-four years of age. The news reached Hazrat Shaykh Jām 'Zhinda Fīl' ['Strong Elephant']. The latter pronounced: 'Khwāja Mawdūd is from a great house and he is as yet young. I must go there to educate him. With my own hand I will set him on the carpet and that *wilāyat* [spiritual jurisdiction] will also be from me. If I do not do this, I worry that something may happen that will be reason for casting scorn on his lofty lineage.'

So the *Shaykh al-Islām* Aḥmad of Jām set out from Jām for Chisht. When he approached Herat ill-disposed persons (*munāfiqīn*) conspired together and went before Khwāja Mawdūd and said: 'Hazrat Shaykh Aḥmad of Jām "Zhinda Fīl" has heard that your

---

has occurred it would create a subsequent attribution of the couplet to Aḥmad-i Jām as presumed author of the whole collection.

No reference is made to Aḥmad-i Jām in Niẓām al-Dīn's conversations recorded in the *Fawā'id al-fu'ād*; see above and note 27 for Khurāsānī anecdotes in this work. *Siyar al-awliyā'* does not mention an encounter of Khwāja Mawdūd with Aḥmad-i Jām, though the compiler does not belittle the spiritual state of Khwāja Mawdūd in his brief notice. Mawdūd bestowed the *wilāyat* of Naishāpūr on one of his followers. When Mawdūd wished to behold the Ka'ba, angels brought it to circumambulate him: Khwurd, *Siyar al-awliyā'*, p. 42. The seventeenth-century account of the confrontation with Aḥmad-i Jām that we have reproduced from *Siyar al-aqtāb* would seem to have been provoked, at a late date, by the contrary account included in the *Nafaḥāt al-uns*. This was a widely circulated Transoxanian *tadhkira* by the famous poet Jāmī, who, as his *nisba* suggests, was a devotee of Aḥmad-i Jām: Jāmī, *Nafaḥāt al-uns*, introduction by Tawhīdīpūr, p. 155.

revered father has passed away and you are yet young. So he intends to intrude on your *wilāyat* and make it part of his own.'

Haẓrat Khwāja Mawdūd passed into meditation for a moment and in a flash raised his head and said: 'What you have said is entirely wrong and to be rejected. Haẓrat Shaykh Aḥmad of Jām is coming out of love and devotion to strengthen me.'

At this time someone brought news that Shaykh Aḥmad was coming closer. Khwāja Mawdūd made preparations for his reception. Ill-disposed persons said: 'Your Honour should go with all caution. Whether or not he is bent on coming here, you should go with many men and with equipage.'

Khwāja Mawdūd did not pay attention to their words, [but] he took the road with the disciples and Sufis who attended on him, in all about four thousand men. As he drew near and the friends of Shaykh Aḥmad saw this host of people, they informed the *Shaykh*, who said: 'It is no cause for concern. Khwāja Mawdūd Chishtī is coming to receive me. The throng that you see are his Sufis and *murīds* [disciples].'

Now at that time Khwāja Mawdūd had twelve thousand *murīds* and *khalīfas* [deputies], from the Pure Land of Chisht as far as to Herat. They set out beside the Stirrup of Felicity from every town that the *khwāja* passed. So it happened that there were great numbers attending on him. So it happened that the two holy men came close by the river Tūnak [?] between Mārān and Sāfilān. Shaykh Aḥmad of Jām, who had come riding on a lion stopped on the further side of the river. Haẓrat Khwāja Mawdūd came to the near side of the river. He had been riding out from Chisht on a wall, and the wall was faster than the wind as it went.

Then the *Shaykh*'s friends on the farther side called out: 'Friends, will you now cross the water, or shall we come over there?'

Haẓrat Khwāja Mawdūd said: 'Out of your concern you have come a long way. Now it is better that I should come to serve you.'

Khwāja Mawdūd said this and recited, 'In the Name of God, the Merciful and the Compassionate!'

Then he mounted the wall and passed over the river like a flash of lightning. The two shaykhs met and Shaykh Aḥmad of Jām said to his friends: 'What we had imagined is not the case.

He is one of the Perfected of the Age. By God, I am honoured by the sight of him!'

They then sat down and conversed and adduced stories for a long while. Then Khwāja Mawdūd said: 'You are our guest. It would be fitting if you deign to visit my humble abode, and attain the pilgrimage to my *khwājas* [i.e. the *khwājas* of Chisht, Khwāja Mawdūd's ancestors].'

Shaykh Aḥmad Jām replied: 'My purpose in coming was to meet with yourself. That has been granted in the best possible manner, and here [i.e. by meeting you] the pilgrimage to the *khwājas* is attained; for the dominion of the spirits of the saints (*awliyā'*) and the effect of their *wilāyat* is in all places! Wherever need occurs I turn to them and they pay attention!'

Then Shaykh Aḥmad of Jām turned his face towards Chisht and kissed the ground. He recited *fātiḥa* and turned away. Shaykh Aḥmad Jām then lodged in the house of Khwāja 'Alī Hakīm, who was a devotee of his, and Khwāja Mawdūd also went with him. These two Holy Men, Possessors of Secrets, stayed there for three days, and they held an assemblage of song (*samā'*) and grew ecstatic.

Before this the servitor of Shaykh Aḥmad of Jām had come to Khwāja Mawdūd and submitted: 'I will lay your bedding wherever you indicate.'

The *Khwāja* said: 'There is business before us!'

Night fell and the two Holy Men were at the singing. The ill-disposed persons, embarrassed that their previous suggestions had not been heeded however much they had urged on Khwāja Mawdūd this despicable act, now saw their opportunity. They came to the party armed, and wanted by sword and dagger to put an end to Shaykh Aḥmad of Jām. But when they looked at him, trembling overcame their limbs. Then Khwāja Mawdūd glanced at them and they lost their senses and fell down. All the time that the two renowned Holy Men were in *samā'* they lay there. Afterwards, when the session came to an end, Haẓrat Shaykh Aḥmad of Jām observed them, and he turned to Khwāja Mawdūd and said: 'Khwāja Mawdūd, what is this that I see?'

Khwāja Mawdūd knew what had happened and told him about their affair from beginning to end. *Shaykh al-Islām* Aḥmad of Jām said: 'My *bābā*! They have received punishment for what they did. Now one should pardon them, passing over their faults!'

After further mutually deferential conversation the two Holy Men both agreed to pardon them. The plotters were restored to their senses and fell at their feet. Then Shaykh Aḥmad of Jām recited *fātiḥa* and went back to Jām, his own *wilāyat*. Khwāja Mawdūd set off for Chisht. At the time of parting Shaykh Aḥmad of Jām advised Khwāja Mawdūd to acquire learning, saying: 'A *darvesh* without knowledge is nothing! …'

Khwāja Mawdūd accepted his advice and went back to the Pure Land of Chisht. Next year he set off for Balkh [to acquire learning].[43]

Shāh Abū 'Alī Qalandar and Shāhbāz Qalandar

Two brief references in a standard English work to the riding of a wall by Abū 'Alī Qalandar (d. 1324) of Pānipat and Karnāl in the east Panjab do not mention a challenger. 'It is said that he used to ride about on a wall' … 'There is a shrine erected over the place where he used to ride the wall.'[44] One might, however, anticipate that the anecdote when told in a prominent Indian Sufi *dargāh* would not lack a challenger. In a *tadhkira* compiled by a descendant of the shaykh, probably in the seventeenth century, the challenger is Shāhbāz Qalandar of Sehvan in upper Sind.

When the fame of the miracles and powers of the Lover of God [Bū 'Alī Qalandar] had become known through the whole world, Shāhbāz Qalandar, who was a perfect *walī* of his Age, came from the *wilāyat* of Sehvan to visit Haẓrat, riding on a lion with a snake in his hand, accompanied by a gathering of *faqīrs*, of whom one group was manifest and the other concealed.

[43] Chishtī, *Siyar al-aqṭāb*, pp. 81–4.
[44] W. Crooke, *The Popular Religion and Folklore of Northern India*, London: Archibald Constable & Co., 1896, pp. 218–19; cited by van Bruinessen, 'Haji Bektash', note 40.

Stage by stage they traversed the road, till they arrived at Bū 'Alī's place near Karnal. He knew all about their coming before they arrived. As Shāhbāz Qalandar was riding along accompanied by the contingent mentioned above, the Lover of God sat down to ride on a wall of unbaked brick. Angels were standing politely in his presence and he ordered them to meet and receive honourably Shāhbāz Qalandar and his party. The wall also started to move like an Iraqi horse.

That Pair of God's Chosen Ones met. Bū 'Alī brought his guests to his own place and feasted them. He made a sign towards a space of water or a well, from which they should eat and take away any kind of food and drink that was required. The *qalandars*, Possessors of Powers, with a lavish expenditure of their interior attraction, tried hard to take it [all] away, but because of the internal strength of Bū 'Alī they had no success. Shāhbāz Qalandar became a devotee of him and after much praise left for his own homeland.[45]

Several details vary from the common pattern. Both the contestants are prominent leaders of the *qalandars*, though in this *tadhkira* the conduct and lifestyle of Bū 'Alī is not close to the common *qalandar* stereotype. The anecdote, like other accounts of Bū 'Alī's miracles, is attached to a local site at some distance from his main shrine. This probably indicates that there was a round of pilgrimage for devotees to travel in the course of several days of the annual *'urs* or commemoration of the date of death.

The two equal groups of followers, visible and invisible, in the cortège of Shāhbāz Qalandar seem to reflect Panjabi beliefs. In one popular account of Gorakh Nāth setting out from Ṭilla with his Jogīs flying on their deerskins, his followers are '5,200 invisible and 5,200 accompanying'.[46]

[45] Hamīd al-Dīn b. Shāh Būdh, *Sharaf al-manāqib*, Urdu tr. Munshī Jagannāth, Delhi: Afzal al-matābi', *c.*1885, p. 19.

[46] R.C. Temple, *The Legends of the Panjāb*, vol. II, Bombay: Education Society's Press, 1885, p. 375:

The details of the angels standing in attendance of Bū 'Alī as he mounted the '*cutchah*' wall, and of the wall itself leaping forward like a fine Iraqi war-horse match the florid piety of the style and are not found in any other narration of the anecdote. The circumlocutions make it difficult to be certain what happened at the feeding from the well. In north Indian phrasing such feedings of large bands of travelling men of religion are often called 'looting' of a 'treasury' (*bhaṇḍār lūṭnā*). The probable meaning is that the *qalandars* strove to eat their way through the food produced by the Well of Plenty, but were not successful.

A Shaykh and his Murīd as Contenders

Among the pairs of Indian shaykhs who figure as the contenders are the Chishtī shaykh Quṭb al-Dīn Munawwar of Hansi (later fourteenth-century) and Sayyid Tāj al-Dīn Sher-sawār (challenger), who is buried at Narnaul. A modern Indian anthology of anecdotes of 'Muslim miracle workers' tells the story in vivacious English:

The Saint who Rode a Lion with a Serpent as a Whip in his Hand

> Sayyad Taj-uddin Shersawar was a disciple of Shaikh Qutb-uddin Mannawar [*sic*] Hansoi and performed his austerities in the hills of Narnaul. When Shaikh Shersawar used to go to meet his Master at Hansi, he passed through a jungle where he caught a lion and rode on it and used a live serpent to whip the lion. He discarded both when he reached the town and thereafter marched on foot to the hut of his Master.
>
> Once when he was riding the lion, he found his Master sitting on a wall, and [his Master? omitted] said to him, 'The animal you are riding is a living one. If you order [one orders?] even a wall to walk, it will.'

Ṭilloṅ Gorakh chaṛhia, chaṛhia nādh bājāe
Bāwan sai chele guptiā, bāwan sai chele nāl.

Just then the wall on which the Master was sitting began to walk and so the master said to the wall: 'I was only giving you an example and I never told you to walk.' So the wall stopped walking.[47]

Like other anecdotes of this anthology it is a fairly literal translation with occasional interpolated explanations. The unspecified source is identifiable as 'Abd al-Haqq Dihlavī's well-known sixteenth-century *tadhkira*, *Akhbār al-akhyār*. A literal translation will enable us to identify some modern turns in the hagiographical process:

Sayyid Tāj al-Dīn Sher-sawār ... was a disciple of Shaykh Quṭb al-Dīn Munawwar Hansawī. He performed severe austerities in the hills of Narnaul.... It is related that one day Shaykh Quṭb al-Dīn Munawwar was sitting on a wall. Sayyid Tāj al-Dīn was in a[n ecstatic] state and in this world of unconsciousness of self he came before the Shaykh riding on the back of a lion. When the gaze of Shaykh Quṭb al-Dīn fell upon him, he said: 'Sayyid! This animal is a living creature. Men of God order a wall, which is inanimate, and it will come into motion.'

They say that the Wall on which the *Shaykh* was sitting began to move.

The *Shaykh* said: 'O Wall! I was saying something by way of example. Stay in your own place!'[48]

The statement in the English retelling that the shaykh had caught the lion in the jungle is a rationalizing modern interpolation. Older listeners and readers in this tradition did not question from where or how the lion might have come beneath the girth of the shaykh. The confusion of persons regarding the speaker in the first statement reflect the customary lack of indications in the Persian original. 'Abd

[47] Jagat S. Bright, *Muslim Miracle Workers*, Bombay: Jaico Publishing House, 1984, p. 86.

[48] Dihlavī, *Akhbār al-akhyār* (Storey No. 1298, 1), p. 146; copied almost verbatim in Sarwar, *Khazīnat al-aṣfiyyā'* (Storey No. 1391, 1), vol. I, pp. 398–9.

al-Haqq was a great scholar of his time, and probably wrote with intentional irony: 'They say that the Wall ... began to move.' The modern re-teller is less sophisticated.

This differs from any other example of the anecdote that we have collected in that the actors are a shaykh and his disciple. The motive for the anecdote is therefore didactic and the element of conflict has been reduced to simple correction. The narrative merely emphasizes that the Master is superior and supernatural powers should not be displayed.

Also reductive is the example of the 'distancing' device of 'I was only giving an example!' The implication is that Sufis possess powers that they do not deign to use. One may compare the use of this device to indicate possession of the power to transmute to gold:

'How do you recognize a *siddha*?' the *Jogī* asked the *shaykh* [Sharaf al-Dīn Aḥmad Manerī].

'If he tells the jungle to turn to gold,' the *Shaykh* replied, 'it turns to gold.'

The jungle immediately turned to gold. The *Shaykh* made a sign to the jungle and said: 'Stay as you were! I was only telling a story!'[49]

The Tiger-rider Ridden off by a Child

A version of the anecdote of the Two Riders is found at the *khānqāh* of Sayyid Muḥammad Gēsūdarāz at Gulbarga with a device of 'distancing' the shaykh from the performance of the miracle.

A fierce but unnamed *Shersawār* [Rider on a Lion or Tiger], with scorpion reins and snake whip, came to the *dargāh* to meet Gēsūdarāz. His seven-year-old great-grandson Nadīm Allāh was playing outside the western gate. Seeing the rider, the boy

[49] Shāh Shu'ayb, *Manāqib al-aṣfiyyā'*, Calcutta: Nūr al-āfāq Press, 1895, p. 139.

mounted an old wall and told it to advance. The fierce rider learnt from other boys at play who the wonder-working child was and was suitably impressed. 'If the child has such wondrous powers, how much greater must be those of his illustrious forefather!'

The lion-rider then left in the direction of Kalyani. But when Gēsūdarāz heard of this display, he turned his eye on the boy, who fell ill with fever and died on 21 Sha'bān 817/[Friday, 4] November 1414.

There is no dome over the boy's tomb, but a new tent is placed over it every year, to which women tie votive cords: and wonders continue to flow from it.[50]

What inspires this variant is clearly the existence of the cult of the child's grave in the shrine of Gēsūdarāz at Gulbarga. The cause of the disfavour of Gēsūdarāz that led to the death of the boy is disapproval of the display of miracles, a sentiment often expressed by Sufi shaykhs. It is linked with a more general sentiment, illustrated in many anecdotes, that the revelation of a concealed miracle will result in the death of the talker. The mention of the town of Kalyani suggests that in other narrations of the anecdote at Gulbarga the name of a shaykh with a tomb and cult at Kalyani may have been attached to it.

Non-Muslim Derivatives from the Sufi Anecdote of the Two Riders

We have seen above that the anecdote as found in Indian Sufi hagiography was probably preceded by anecdotes of Indian *siddhas* riding on tigers and possibly on walls. Of the following three anecdotes told by non-Muslims, the first is

[50] Sulṭān, *Armughān-i Sultānī*, pp. 109–10. The author gives as sources for this story common knowledge (*'amm qawl*) and the *Ta'rīkh-i Khwurshed-Jāhī*.

probably a calque of a Muslim original, repeated regarding the Marathi *bhakta* Jñāneśvar, with a Nāth Jogī as challenger. The second is an adaptation of the Sufi anecdotal pattern into a folktale intended to amuse rather than edify. Told by Hindus in an 'exotic' Muslim and Sufi mode, it concerns two Sufi shaykhs and is set not in the locality of the narrator, but in a distant and romantic place, the Mughal capital of Delhi as seen by the villagers of the Garhwal hills. The third is evidently a legend attached to a local landmark and sacred site, remembered and Hinduized after a recent depopulation of the Muslim occupants of the site.

The Stock Anecdote in Maharashtra: Jñāneśvar Repels the Jogī Cāṅgadeva

The anthropologist Ghurye gives a version of the anecdote with his own comments, but does not specify his source:

> Nāthapanthīs had spread their network in Maharashtra with the help of mystic powers and were consequently dreaded. Jñāneśvara's chief contestant was the Nāthapanthā Jogī Cāṅgadeva, who might have been the Mahanta of a Jogī monastery not far away from Paithana, where Jñāneśvara first made his mark. And Cāṅgadeva is traditionally represented as commonly riding a tiger and a live cobra to whip it, thus demonstrating his control over nature.[51]

The missing element in Ghurye's summary is provided by an allusion in the life of Eknāth in the *Bhaktilīlāmṛta*. Brahmans, when they see a miracle of Eknāth, recall those of Jñāneśvar: 'And when Cāṅgadeva, the *Siddha*, came to visit him, he made the lifeless wall move forward.'[52]

[51] G.S. Ghurye, *Indian Sadhus*, 2nd edn., Bombay: Popular Prakashan, 1964, p. 133.
[52] *Bhaktilīlāmṛta*, tr. J.E. Abbott, *The Life of Eknāth*, repr., Delhi: Motilal Banarsidass, 1983, p. 134.

A Himalayan Version from Garhwal

In South Asia there are abundant examples of the esteem in which Muslim *faqīrs* were held by the non-Muslim masses of the population, as holy men and as wonder-workers. From the remote Himalayan region of Garhwal, in which Muslims were an insignificant portion of the population, the Rev. E.S. Oakley collected a charming variant of the standard anecdote regarding two Muslim riders:

It was during the reign of a certain Mohammadan ruler that a common Mohammadan dervish by name Alam Shah used to live in one of the suburbs of Delhi. He used to beg cooked food from door to door, and live in a hut thatched with leaves and grass.[53] He had nothing but a cow, which he used to tether and drink her milk in the same way as her own calf did. He was said to be very fond of the boys to whom he was wont to teach Persian and Arabic....[54]

Another Mohammadan dervish by name Shutarbeg ... started from Arabia with a view to have some communion with Alam Shah about God and divine things.... He mounted and rode on a lion, with a bridle made of two living cobras.... The nearer he approached Delhi the more widely the alarm spread and struck the people of the city with wonder and terror.... When the news came to Alam Shah that Shutarbeg was only at 2 miles distance, he was teaching boys on one of the walls of a house in ruins.... The citizens of the city and suburb earnestly requested Alam Shah not to go to receive him on foot, but to ride either on an elephant, a pony, or a chariot of theirs. On this Alam Shah said that he wanted nothing of the sort for his vehicle, but directed the wall on which he and the boys sat to take him to the foreign ascetic....

They met, one showing the other the merit of his own devotion. The former brought the latter to his own hut, tying his lion with

[53] Cf. Shāh Mīnā's hut in the coloured print discussed above.

[54] For Hindu stereotypes of Muslim traits, cf. Rupert Snell, 'Raskhān the Neophyte: Hindu Perspectives on a Muslim Vaishnava', in *Urdu and Muslim South Asia: Studies in Honour of Ralph Russell*, ed. C. Shackle, London: SOAS, 1989, pp. 29–37, especially p. 34.

his own cow. They remained together for many weeks. At last when the foreign ascetic was ready to depart he found his lion had disappeared, and asked the Delhi faqir for it. In reply to his query he said that it was consigned by him to the care of his cow, so he should ask the cow for it. The other faqir accordingly asked the cow for his lion, which she vomited up, to the amazement of the Arabian faqir.[55]

The structure of the anecdote as usual leads to the victory of the resident contender, who can ride his own wall and engages the loyalties of the local population. In this Garhwali version the names of the contenders are stereotypic. 'Alam Shāh' reflects a tendency for monarchs ruling in Delhi to be called 'King of the World' (Shāh 'Ālam/'Ālam Shāh).[56] 'Shutur Beg' is equally suitable for the rider from the far horizon. 'Beg' suggests Central Asian and military stock, while 'shutur', 'camel', conjures up the Muslim Holy Land of Arabia. The local *faqīr* appears particularly well integrated with a Hindu environment, for his sole possession was an admirable cow which proved itself superior to the lion from foreign parts.

A Hinduization from Bihar

The previous anecdote from Garhwal, collected early in the twentieth century, was a tale of Muslim holy men in far-off

[55] 'A faqir alone can judge the merit of another faqir', in Rev. E.S. Oakley and Tara Dutt Gairola, *Himalayan Folklore*, Allahabad: Superintendent, printing and stationery, 1935, pp. 198–200.

[56] However, a Sufi called Shāh 'Ālam is said to be buried in the central tomb in the small fourteenth-century mosque complex by the Jamuna at Wazirabad in north Delhi near Timarpur; see Y.D. Sharma, *Delhi and its Neighbourhood*, New Delhi: Archaeological Survey of India, 1964, p. 114, 'a saint of Fīrūz Tughluq's time'. He is more correctly identified as Sayyid Shāh 'Ālam, a descendant of Makhdūm-i 'Ālam Husayni Ilāhābādī, who took up residence in these buildings in Awrangzeb's reign and died in AH 1134/AD 1721–2; Muḥammad 'Ālam Shāh Farīdī, *Mazārāt-i awliyā Dihlī*, Delhi: Kutub Khānah-yi Naẕīriyyah, AH 1346/AD 1928, p. 145.

Delhi told as entertainment by non-Muslims. This anecdote was improved, in a humorous but Hinduizing fashion, by the role of the cow that the sedentary holy man kept, which was more powerful than the foreigner's lion. By contrast, a variant of the Moving Wall anecdote that has appeared in a collection of folktales from Bihar published in 1991 is told with more serious purpose and appears to represent a recent Hinduizing of a version of the anecdote of the Two Riders that was current locally.

The site, marked by a shady neem tree, is called Pīr Pahāṛī, near Monghyr. Monghyr until recent times had a powerful Sufi presence, but according to recent information has been largely deserted by its former Muslim population. According to the version collected:

It is said that when the town of Monghyr came into the hands of the Muslims the Hindus were forbidden to enter the fort area nearby. But one day a Hindu magician arrived who ventured to disregard the ban. On the hill nearby lived a Muslim saint (*pīr*) giving the hill its name. He did not like the Hindu intruder....[57]

The next move is a contest anecdote involving discovery and transformation of a hidden object. The *pīr* sent the 'magician' (here one lacks the more revealing term of the vernacular narrative) 'a packet of cooked meat' in conflict with the challenger's dietary observances. The packet was returned to the *pīr* and when opened 'to everyone's surprise it contained sweetmeats'. The confrontation followed:

The *pīr* was eager to meet the Hindu magician. The *pīr* rode a tiger and arrived at the door of the magician. The magician was seated on a wall of the house, brushing his teeth with a twig of *neem*. In order to greet the saintly visitor in a proper manner he

[57] Mira Pakrasi, *Folk Tales of Bihar*, New Delhi: Sterling Publishers, 1991, pp. 17–18.

stuck the *neem* twig in the ground and ordered the wall to move. The wall started moving and the magician riding on it came face to face with the *pīr*.

The *pīr* acknowledged the supremacy of the Hindu magician. That twig became the present famous *neem* tree. Since then there has been no ban and the Hindus and Muslims have lived happily together.

The sectarian allegiances of the narrator are adequately demonstrated by the previous contest anecdote, in which the *pīr* tried to trick a Hindu holy man into dietary defilement and naturally was not successful. Equally inevitably, from the point of view of the current narrator, the *pīr* 'acknowledged the supremacy of the Hindu magician'. But, with a corpus of other anecdotes of the Moving Wall before us, it does not require great perspicacity to perceive that this retelling reflects the recent takeover by 'Hindus' of a current 'Muslim' local legend.

Another feature from the legend as recorded, that appears to be taken over from an earlier Muslim version and reversed, is the statement that Hindus were forbidden to enter the fort area nearby. Such prohibitions on entry into Hindu settlements as well as temples are characteristic of Indo-Muslim foundation legends, in which a solitary Muslim Sufi or Ghāzī brings an Islamic presence and sanctification to a territory before or independently of the arrival of conquering armies.[58]

The preservation and adaptation of the legend is ensured by its 'explanation' of a local sanctified landmark, the *neem* tree. The original winner of the contest must have been, as in the other Moving Wall anecdotes, the local incumbent,

[58] Cf. the legend of Mu'īn al-Dīn encamping outside Ajmer, Chishtī, *Siyar al-aqṭāb*, p. 124; tr. in P.M. Currie, *The Shrine and Cult of Mu'īn al-Dīn Chishtī of Ajmer*, Delhi: Oxford University Press, 1989, pp. 72–3.

the nameless *pīr* after whom the hill itself is still named. His challenger from afar, whether he was another Sufi or a non-Muslim wonder-worker, would have ridden the tiger and the *pīr* himself would have triumphed by riding the wall. We have here an interesting example of local legend, somewhat awkwardly adapted, surviving a dispossession and takeover of a sacred site.

7

Qalandars and Related Groups

Elements of Social Deviance in the Religious Life of the Dehlī Sultanate of the Thirteenth and Fourteenth Centuries

This chapter attempts to survey the activities of Qalandars and other related groups of Muslim religious mendicants as depicted in the Persian literature of the Dehlī Sultanate. The hagiographical literature of the sultanate, with its strong tradition of *malfūẓāt*, the recorded conversations of Ṣūfī shaykhs, is rich in anecdotal narratives of actual behaviour in comparison with that produced in Iran or elsewhere in the Islamic world at this time. Even a reading of Yazıcı's article 'Ḳalandar' in the *Encyclopedia of Islam* or his edition of the verse *Manāqib* of Jamāl al-Dīn of Sāva[1] will show many parallels to the material here presented, but regrettably I am unable to extend the survey to the activities of the Qalandars and related groups who spread through the Arab Middle East at the same time as they made their appearance in South Asia. We are not here concerned with the validity of the religious experience of the Qalandars, nor with any moral assessment of the utility of their behaviour in promoting

* Originally published in Yohanan Friedmann, ed., *Islam in Asia, Volume 1: South Asia*, Jerusalem: The Hebrew University, 1984, pp. 60–108.

[1] Khaṭīb-i Fārisī, *Manāḳib-i Jamāl al-Dīn-i Sāvī*, ed. T. Yazıcı, Ankara: Anjuman-i Tārīkh-i Turk, 1972.

the general welfare of society. We avoid any attempt, like that of the late Professor R.C. Zaehner, to judge the validity of early Ṣūfī mystical experience from a moral or ethical criterion which could not be other than highly personal. We must accept that the Qalandars, like other more orthodox or reputable Ṣūfīs, enjoyed moods of exaltation, in their particular case sometimes aided by drugs as well as induced by meditative or auto-hypnotic techniques of ecstasy. Our concern is with the relations between the Qalandars and those in our sources who describe them, and with the social causes, transactions and interactions, and consequences of a particular tradition of religious behaviour. Later in the study we shall attempt a typology of the anecdotes regarding Qalandars in our Ṣūfī sources, not so much out of a concern for their truthfulness or historicity, but rather to determine what were the lessons their narrators intended to transmit. A number of terms are in use in the literature of the Dehlī Sultanate applied to groups of *darwīshes* of the variety known in modern times as *bē-shar'*,[2] though this is not a wholly satisfactory term. Such *darwīshes* could be distinguished from more orthodox or reputable Ṣūfīs by peculiarities of appearance, costume, and insignia; by their frequent failure to perform in public the prescribed Muslim religious duties (*farā'iḍ*) or supererogatory pious acts (*tarāwīḥ*, *nawāfil*); and sometimes by violent, scandalous, or immoral conduct. The groups mentioned in the sources of the Dehlī Sultanate are denominated *qalandars*, *ḥaydarīs*, *juwāliqs*, and *muwallihs*. We are less well informed about the *muwallihs*. Modern writers on the religious life of the Dehlī Sultanate have generally failed to identify them, although they provided a figure of importance in its political life.

[2] E.g. Murray B. Titus, *Islam in India and Pakistan*, Calcutta: YMCA Publishing House, 1959, p. 135.

The term Qalandar may be taken as older than the institutionalization of a Qalandar *ṭarīqa*. If one can accept the authenticity of any of the dialectical *du-baytī* verses of Bābā Ṭāhir 'Uryān', that in which he describes himself as a Qalandar has strong claims:

Mu ān rindum ki nāmum be qalandar
Na khūn dērum na mūn dērum na langar
Chu rūz āya bagardum gard-i gītī
Chu shav garda ba-khishtī wā nihum sar[3]

I am that wanderer whose name is Qalandar;
I have neither home nor goods nor kitchen.
When day comes I wander round the world;
When night falls I lay my head on a brick.

It would appear that in eleventh-century Khurasan the term Qalandar was used for a very poor, ill-clad, wandering religious mendicant, probably weak in learning and the performance of prescribed Muslim religious observances, but with a popular appeal and charisma deriving from the intensity of his poverty, which was often closer to the ideal of *faqr* than the actual behaviour of settled Ṣūfī shaykhs established in hospices.

The growth and diffusion of groups of wandering Qalandars is attested by an anecdote in 'Aṭṭār's celebrated poem, the *Manṭiq al-ṭayr*, which was composed not later than AH 573/AD 1177. An Arab, coming to 'Ajam (Iran and adjacent Persian-speaking areas), was amazed by the unfamiliar customs of the land. On his road he fell in with a band of shaven Qalandars, a people he had never seen before. He joined them, shaved his hair, and participated in various

[3] Wajāhat Ḥusayn ('Andalīb Shādānī), ed., *Rubā'iyyāt-i Bābā Ṭāhir*, Lahore: Alamgir Electric Press, n.d., p. 22.

obscurely described but probably orgiastic experiences with them; but was maltreated, assaulted, and robbed by them before he returned to his own land.[4] The anecdote appears to indicate that groups of wandering Qalandars were a spectacle in Khurasan in the third quarter of the twelfth century; but had not then reached the Arab Middle East. They were also by that time characterized by wild and antinomian behaviour similar to that found in the thirteenth-century anecdotes discussed in this chapter, and had adopted the practice of shaving their eyebrows and all facial hair.

References to Qalandars, Ḥaydarīs, and Juwāliqs made by the writers of the Dehlī Sultanate, as well as what we know about their activities outside India during the thirteenth century, make it clear that all these groups (denominated indifferently *ṭā'ifa*, *ṭarīqa*, *silsila*, or *mashrab*) were closely related and with a recently developed lineage. Their institutionalization evidently took place not long after that of the more regular *ṭarīqas* or *silsilas* in Khurasan at the close of the twelfth century. Early in the following century the groups appear to have been led by two notable shaykhs, Muḥammad ibn Yūnus Jamāl al-Dīn of Sāva and his disciple Quṭb al-Dīn Ḥaydar. The former is considered to be the great shaykh of the Qalandars, while the latter is the eponymous founder of the Ḥaydarīs. Though the presence of Qalandars in Syria is attested during the previous decade,[5] a great impetus was given to the diffusion of Qalandars and Ḥaydarīs throughout the Islamic world by the Mongol conquest and devastation of Khurasan in 1220–1. Jamāl al-Dīn of Sāva fled and settled in Damascus, where he died in 1232. Ḥaydar advised his disciples to flee before the Mongols and

[4] Farīd al-Dīn 'Aṭṭār, *Manṭiq al-ṭayr*, ed. S. Gawharīn, Tehran: Amir Kabir, 1348 Shamsī, pp. 191–2. I am indebted to Dr R.J. Baldick for drawing this passage to my attention.

[5] Maqrīzī, *Khiṭaṭ*, vol. II, Būlāq: Dār al-Ṭibā'ah al-Miṣrīyah, AH 1270/AD 1853, p. 433.

was himself never seen again.[6] In India a Qalandar of note, Shāh Khiżr Rūmī, was resident in Dehlī for a while before 1235,[7] while according to the historian Baranī, a Qalandar enjoyed the especial esteem of the rebel governor of Bengal, Ṭughril, before 1279.[8] In the reign of Balban (AH 664–86) the Darwīsh Sīdī Muwallih came to Dehlī and founded a *khānqāh* outside one of the city gates, which had become a considerable establishment before his death in the reign of Jalāl al-Dīn Fērōz Khaljī (AH 689–95).[9] At the same time a Ḥaydarī *khānqāh* had been established at Dehlī by Shaykh Abū Bakr Ṭūsī.[10] In the following reign, of 'Alā' al-Dīn Khaljī (AH 695–715), one of the notable *langars* (free kitchens) of the capital was run by a certain Ramażān Qalandar.[11]

In the references found in the literature of the Dehlī Sultanate, the terms *qalandar*, Ḥaydarī, and Juwāliq are not quite interchangeable. One may express the relationship by saying that all Ḥaydarīs and all Juwāliqs could be called Qalandars, but not every Qalandar could be called a Ḥaydarī, i.e. a follower of Quṭb al-Dīn Ḥaydar, or a Juwāliq (i.e. a wearer of a *duwāl, juwāl, juwāliq, jaulakh,* or *dilap*).[12] However, when we find such collocations as *qalandarān u*

[6] Amīr Hasan 'Alā' Sijzī, *Fawā'id al-fu'ād*, Lahore: Malik Sirāj al-Dīn and Sons, 1966, p. 30.

[7] 'Abd al-Ḥaqq Dehlavī, *Akhbār al-akhyār*, Dehlī: Mujtabā'ī Press, AH 1309/AD 1892, p. 50.

[8] Ziya' al-Dīn Baranī, *Ta'rīkh-i Fērōzshāhī*, Calcutta: Bibliotheca Indica, 1862, p. 91.

[9] Ibid., pp. 209–12.

[10] Dehlavī, *Akhbār al-akhyār*, p. 73; Baranī, *Ta'rīkh-i Fērōzshāhī*, p. 211.

[11] Ḥamīd Qalandar, *Khayr al-majālis*, Aligarh: Aligarh Muslim University, 1960, p. 185.

[12] The garment itself is called a *juwāliq* in the *Manāqib-i Jamāl al-Dīn-i Sāvī*, ed. Yazıcı, p. 58. The same passage makes it clear that to the fourteenth-century author, writing outside India, *juwāliq* and *palās* were one and the same garment, and strongly suggests that it was of a red colour, 'the colour of those who slay themselves'.

ḥaydariyān, or *qalandarān u juwāliqān*, the two nouns are often being used as synonyms. Other near-synonyms for the groups are *āhan-pōshān* and *chiram-pōshān*, 'wearers of iron' and 'wearers of leather'.

The basic distinction of the appearance of the Qalandar lay in the shaving of all facial and bodily hair, including the scalp and eyebrows, following the practice of Shaykh Jamāl al-Dīn. One may speculate whether there was not a sound medical reason for the adoption of this practice as well as scarification of the body; these must have contributed to the elimination of bodily parasites among groups of men who were ill-clad, travelling in conditions of hardship, and dependent upon charity. The *Khayr al-majālis* describes a group of Qalandars as wearing neither clothes nor *khirqa* (Ṣūfī cloak), in fact nothing but their irons, fragments of blanket, and loin-cloths.[13] Baranī refers on several occasions to the *palās*, a coarse garment, worn by Qalandars, apparently the reddish-ochre-hued garments (*gerwā bhes*) characteristic of Indian ascetic orders.[14] The wearing of leather and iron appears to have been optional. Possibly the garment which gave the Juwāliqs their name may have been of leather and, as we have noted above, *chiram-pōsh*, 'a wearer of leather', denotes a Qalandar. Among the possessions of a Qalandar might be *ustara*, a razor, and *juwāl-dōz*, a large needle for sewing the *juwāl*. Both of these could be used as weapons, as in the case of the assault of a Ḥaydarī on Sīdī Muwallih, discussed below;[15] and so could the Qalandar's *kachkūl*,

[13] Qalandar, *Khayr al-majālis*, p. 131.

[14] This identification is made in the late Professor M. Ḥabib's translation of Baranī, *Ta'rīkh-i Fērōzshāhī*, in the course of editing for publication. The connection between Persian *palās* and its Hindi homophone (= *āk*, *ṭesū*, 'flame of the forest'), though it has not entered Persian lexicography, is established in Yazıcı, ed., *Manāqib-i Jamāl al-Dīn-i Sāvī*, p. 58, see nn. 1, 12 above.

[15] Baranī, *Ta'rīkh-i Fērōzshāhī*, p. 212.

begging bowl, as in the anecdote of a Qalandar raising his *kachkūl* to strike Shaykh Badr al-Dīn Isḥāq.[16] In India by the late fourteenth century, if not earlier, groups of Qalandars travelled with the insignia of a banner and drum and they had developed a special vocabulary or patois of their own.[17]

Some lines of division between the groups are referred to by Ḥamīd Qalandar, in the description of the classes within the estate of his *pīr* (*dawlat-i pīr-i man*), the great Chishtī shaykh Niẓām al-Dīn of Dehlī. For personal reasons, discussed elsewhere, he places Qalandars above Ṣūfīs, and he does not mention Ḥaydarīs as a separate group. He refers to shaving of facial hair of the Qalandars and the scarification of their bodies; the 'correct' turban, short garments, and ceremonial cleanliness of the Ṣūfīs; the lamentations of the Muwallihs; and the rings worn through the ears by the Juwāliqs.[18]

Of the related groups it would appear that the Ḥaydarīs were the most strongly associated with the wearing of iron. An anecdote by Shaykh Niẓām al-Dīn to the effect that Quṭb al-Dīn Ḥaydar in former times took up red-hot iron bars with his bare hands and bent them into rings, suggests that they practised the actual working of iron as smiths.[19] They could, therefore, have had an alternative source of

[16] Qalandar, *Khayr al-majālis*, pp. 130–31.

[17] 'Abd al-'Azīz b. Shēr Malik, *Ta'rīkh-i Ḥabībī*, Urdu tr., Haydarabad, Deccan: s.n., n.d. [c. 1920], pp. 108–9. This important text, composed in AH 849, twenty-four years after the death of the shaykh, by an associate of his immediate family at the *khānqāh* of Gulbarga (see tr. p. 4), is unfortunately only accessible to me in this apparently very literal translation by Nawwāb Ma'shūq Yār Jang. A seventeenth-century hagiography depicts Abū 'Alī of Panipat stating that 'the kettledrum (*naqqāra*) of Qalandarī has sounded in the whole world and sky'; see Ḥamīd al-Dīn, *Sharaf al-manāqib*, Urdu tr. Munshi Jagannāth, Dehlī: Afẓal al-Maṭābi', n.d. [c. 1885], p. 35.

[18] Qalandar, *Khayr al-majālis*, p. 6.

[19] 'Alā' Sijzī, *Fawā'id al-fu'ād*, Lahore, 1966, p. 30; Naval Kishor, 1894, pp. 19–20.

livelihood to charity as itinerant smiths, but this is a point on which the hagiographical literature is unlikely to give any clue. We may draw a parallel with the metalworking of Romanys, whose wanderings extended over an even wider area to medieval Europe, though the groups were organized on a different social and religious basis. The Romanys were a Hinduized low-caste north-Indian people, closely connected with the Ḍoms from whom their name derives, with elements of Śaivite rituals and beliefs, and organized on a basis of travelling households. The Ḥaydarīs professed Islam, and were at any rate predominantly celibate groups perpetuated by recruitment.

If the conjecture that the Ḥaydarīs had a subsidiary source of livelihood in metalworking is correct, a parallel may be drawn with what we know has happened in more modern times as to the manner in which other fringe groups of religious vagrants have been accommodated or encapsulated in South Asian society. Bands of Rifāʿī *darwīshes* in the Deccan, apart from offerings made on account of their self-flagellation and 'displays' (*maẓāhir*), sell whips and potions made from reptiles.[20] By the early twentieth century, the Qalandar in northern India was either a very poor religious mendicant or an entertainer with a performing bear or monkey.[21]

Two other practices recorded by the fourteenth-century Arab traveller Ibn Baṭṭūṭa, among a group of Ḥaydarīs he met at Amroha in northern India, require comment.[22] In the first place he describes the Ḥaydarīs as walking upon red-hot coals. Fire-walking is a form of religious display

[20] Observed by the present writer in India in the 1950s and 1960s. A command performance of *maẓāhir*, with knives stuck into flesh and eyeballs protruding beyond eyelids, was given before the *sajjāda-nashīn* of Gulbarga in 1963, at which the writer was present.

[21] Titus, *Islam in India and Pakistan*, p. 135.

[22] Ibn Baṭṭūṭa, *Riḥla*, ed. Defrémery, vol. III, Paris: Societé Asiatique, 1853–7, pp. 79–80; tr. Gibb, vol. III, p. 583.

which occurs sporadically and apparently spontaneously in widely different societies.[23] In the case of the Ḥaydarīs, it could easily have developed from their skill in the handling of red-hot metal. The practice links the Ḥaydarīs with the rival group of the Muwallihs, regarding whom this practice is also recorded.[24]

Ibn Baṭṭūṭa also observed a Ḥaydarī *faqīr*, who, apart from the irons which adorned other parts of his person, displayed an iron ring passed through his penis; the occasional currency of this practice among the Ḥaydarīs is confirmed in a passage of some obscurity by the sixteenth-century *tadhkira*-writer Jamālī.[25] The social function of such an act and display is obvious; the visual evidence of the abandonment of the means to gratify male sexual lust presents a claim to sanctity and support by offerings. One may compare the actual evidence of emasculation sometimes demanded from Hijṛas, apart from their donning of women's clothes, before they can receive alms or dance at weddings or childbirth ceremonies.[26]

The passing of an iron ring through the penis has also been recorded among non-Muslim Indian ascetics by the tenth-century Arab merchant Sulaymān and by European seventeenth-century travellers.[27] We should consider this as possible evidence of 'Indianization'. The Ḥaydarīs had been

[23] This practice among the Tamils of Ceylon has been the subject of investigation by Professor Richard Gombrich. Now popular, it appears to have originated there only after the second World War.

[24] See p. 195.

[25] Jamālī, *Siyar al-'arifīn*, Dehlī: Maṭba'-i Riẓvī, 1891, p. 67; Ibn Baṭṭūṭa, *Riḥla*.

[26] See H.R. Lynton and M. Rajan, *The Days of the Beloved*, Berkeley: University of California Press, 1974, pp. 195–6.

[27] Careri in S. Sen, ed., *Indian Travels of Thevenot and Careri*, New Delhi: National Archives of India, 1949, p. 258. The ascetics there mentioned are Hindu.

in India for a century when Ibn Baṭṭūṭa observed them there, and much of the recruitment must have been from the low strata of the local population. On the other hand, there is the possibility of a residual influence of varieties of Indian asceticism in the formation of the behaviour of *darwīsh* groups in Central Asia at an earlier period. Elwell-Sutton, in his survey of the role of the *darwīsh* in Persian folklore, notes the *darwīsh*'s generally frightening and amoral character and suggests that it derives from the behaviour of Śaivite *yogins* present in Khurasan before Islamization.[28] There are further parallels with the practice of Indian ascetic orders in the shaving and depilation of the Qalandars and related groups and celibacy or the rejection of the life of a householder, but our evidence suggests that if there was any influence of Indian ascetic traditions, it took place in Central Asia or Khurasan before the arrival of these groups in India itself.[29]

Regarding the Muwallihs (MWLLHĀN) in the Dehlī Sultanate, less is known than is the case with other *bē-shar'* groups. One *darwīsh*, Sīdī Muwallih (SYDY MWLH), played an important role in the political life of the city of Dehlī in the late thirteenth century.[30] The order was evidently known in the Middle East since the *Nafaḥāt al-uns* has a brief reference to Sulaymān Turkmān Muwallih, who died in

[28] L.M. Elwell-Sutton in *Proceedings of the Twenty-sixth International Congress of Orientalists, New Delhi, 1964*, vol. II, Poona: Bhandarkar Oriental Research Institute, 1968, pp. 200–3.

[29] On the symbolic significance of depilation and celibacy, and its specific inversion in Sikhism, cf. J. Singh Uberoi, 'On being Unshorn', in *Sikhism and Indian Society*, Simla: Indian Institute of Advanced Study, 1967, pp. 89–100.

[30] In modern historical works his name is generally given, with some disregard for orthography, as 'Sidi Mawla'. A. Mahdi Husayn proposed Sayyidi Mawlā to fit the metrical pattern of 'Isāmī's *mutaqārib mathnavī*. Usha in his edition of *Futūḥ al-salāṭīn* correctly vocalizes PYR MWLLH, p. 217, two lines from bottom.

Damascus in AH 714.[31] In Dehlī in the late fourteenth century, the Suhrawardī shaykh Jalāl al-Dīn 'Makhdūm-i Jahāniyān' explained that their name referred to their practice of lamentation (*walwalah*).[32] This seems to be confirmed by Ḥamīd Qalandar's remark in his exordium of Shaykh Niẓām al-Dīn that 'the hair of the Muwallihs has stood on end from his lamentation'.[33]

A reference to the Muwallihs walking upon fire occurs in the conversations of Sayyid Muḥammad Gēsūdarāz. In the time of his father (Sayyid Rājū Qattāl) there was one day in Dehlī a *samā'*, at which Muwallih *faqīrs* were present. They rubbed preparations on the soles of their feet and danced upon fire.[34] This aids the interpretation of an incident in the story of the downfall and death of Sīdī Muwallih given by the historian Baranī. These references imply that the Muwallihs were not common in India in the later fourteenth century, and there is no reference to their presence in India before the reign of Sultan Balban (AH 664–86).

The story of Sīdī Muwallih at Dehlī, based on two fourteenth-century sources,[35] is to be found in modern historical works.[36] It may be given only in summary outline here.

[31] 'Abd al-Rahmān Jāmī, *Nafāhāt al-uns*, ed. M. Tawhīdīpūr, Tehran: Kitabfurushi-i Saadi, 1336 Shamsī/AD 1958, p. 519.

[32] *Malfūẓ al-makhdūm*, f. 24a [Digby's original reference is as given. It may refer to a manuscript then in his collection: Jalāluddīn Makhdūm-i Jahāniyān Jahān Gasht, *Khulāṣat al-alfāẓ-i Jāmi' al-'ulūm*, Bodleian Library, University of Oxford, MS S. Digby Or. 8 ~DL].

[33] Qalandar, *Khayr al-majālis*, p. 6.

[34] Shēr Malik, *Ta'rīkh-i Ḥabībī*, Urdu tr., p. 81.

[35] Baranī, *Ta'rīkh-i Fērōzshāhī*, pp. 209–12; 'Isāmī, *Futūḥ al-salāṭīn*, ed. Usha, Madras: University of Madras, 1948, pp. 215–17.

[36] *Inter alia* see S.H. Hodivala, *Studies in Indo-Muslim History*, vol. I, Bombay: Popular Book Depot, 1939, pp. 267–8; K.A. Nizami, *Some Aspects of Politics and Religion in India during the Thirteenth Century*, Aligarh: Aligarh Muslim University, 1961, pp. 288–91.

Sīdī Muwallih was a *darwīsh* who, according to Baranī, came from upper Asia (*mulk-i bālā*)[37] in the reign of Balban. Though he observed the rules of prayer, he did not do so in congregation, nor visit the mosque on Fridays. He was known for his austerities, his simple clothing and food, celibacy and abstention from material lusts; but what most gained him his reputation was an apparently miraculous ability to produce large sums of gold or silver money for expenditure on lavish feasts or to give away to supplicants, without on his own part accepting either offerings or permanent grants of endowment. This ability frequently took the form of directing supplicants to find treasure concealed beneath a brick or stone or in a niche.

According to an informant of Baranī, he had been warned by the Chishtī shaykh Farīd al-Dīn of Ajodhan to avoid associating with *maliks*, *amīrs*, and high officers of government when he set up in Dehlī; but from the days of Balban's successor Mu'izz al-Dīn Kayqubād, and even more under the new dynasty of Jalāl al-Dīn Fērōz Khaljī, he ignored this advice, and established close relations not only with the eldest son of the sultan, but also with other politically influential figures, including *mawlāzādas*, descendants of the royal Turkish slaves of the previous dynasty. He was accused of being party to a plot by which the sultan was to be assassinated, the Muwallih himself to be proclaimed caliph and married to a daughter of the ancient Sultan Nāṣir al-Dīn, and the offices of state distributed among those dispossessed by the new Khaljī dynasty.

On information being laid, initial proceedings against this plot were taken by the sultan's son, Arkalī Khān, while the sultan was away from Dehlī on a military campaign. After the sultan's return he decided to make a public spectacle

[37] For the use of this phrase, see S. Digby, *War-Horse and Elephant in the Dehli Sultanate*, Oxford: Orient Monographs, 1971, p. 34 [*L&WSD* V.1].

of the plotters and ordered a great fire to be lit in an open space outside the city, with a royal pavilion set up in front of it and a great crowd of spectators from the city. He, in fact, intended an ordeal of the conspirators by fire, but when he sought the approval of the *'ulamā'* in a *fatwa*, it was refused. The reference to the fire-walking activities of the Muwallihs by Sayyid Muḥammad Gēsūdarāz, cited above, suggests that the ordeal was intended as a blow to the reputation of Sīdī Muwallih. In the event, Sīdī Muwallih was brought bound before the pavilion of the sultan, who incited groups of *darwīshes* present to revenge the wrong done to him. The attack upon Sīdī Muwallih by a Ḥaydarī *darwīsh* then took place. Then Arkalī Khān, the son of the sultan, gave a sign to an elephant driver to trample Sīdī Muwallih to death.

A black wind arose on the day of the death of Sīdī Muwallih and both Baranī and 'Iṣāmī attribute the subsequent drought and famine of Dehlī and neighbouring areas to his death; Baranī also ascribes the subsequent troubles of the realm of the Khaljī dynasty to the misfortune of his death.[38]

Recruitment to the Qalandars and Other *Bē-shar'* Orders

Not unlike some of the Hindu devotional and ascetic orders, the Qalandars were maintained in their wandering and antinomian existence by a combination of attitudes shown in society towards them: superstitious awe, tolerance, and a willingness to send trouble-makers onwards to a further destination. Recruitment to the Qalandar bands was from those who found their lifestyle more attractive than what society had currently to offer them and from those who merely sought to escape from punishment or

[38] Baranī, *Ta'rīkh-i Fērōzshāhī*, p. 212; 'Isāmī, *Futūḥ al-salāṭīn*, pp. 218–9.

oppression. Many recruits were evidently runaway children or adolescents, but older men might also abandon their professions and join the Qalandars. Thus, a falconer, who had flown a hawk against the express prohibition of his employer, the military governor of Ajodhan, and had lost it, said to himself, 'There is no alternative but to sell my horse and become a Qalandar'.[39] The appearance of the Qalandars may also have served as an effective disguise for a wanted man.

A Qalandar, asked by Gēsūdarāz why he joined the order, replied that as a boy he was angry with his parents and ran away from home. A group of older Qalandars encouraged him to join them and he went off with them. Gēsūdarāz accused the Qalandars of enticing boys to join them and he forbade his grandchildren and other young members of his family to have any contact with them, including listening to their conversation.[40]

The thirteenth-century poet Fakhr al-Dīn 'Irāqī, if one may trust the rather fanciful biography which prefaces his *Dīwān*, grew up in Hamadān in south-west Persia, a model of adolescent piety, industry, and learning. At the age of 17, when a group of Qalandars passed through Hamadān, his eye fell upon a beautiful boy among them. After they had set out again from Hamadān, he threw away all his books on the Islamic sciences and religious disciplines and caught up with the Qalandars. He later accompanied them when they decided to go to India. They went to Multān and on to Dehlī and they are then said to have decided to go to Somnath, which would at this period have been under Hindu rule. 'Irāqī was separated from the band by a storm in the Rajasthan desert, returned to Dehlī and after parting

[39] Qalandar, *Khayr al-majālis*, p. 148.
[40] Shēr Malik, *Ta'rīkh-i Ḥabībī*, Urdu tr., p. 107.

from his friend, decided to return to Multān to settle in the *khānqāh* of Bahā' al-Dīn Zakariyā'.[41]

Both those who entered a more orthodox Ṣūfī *ṭarīqa* as a wholetime way of life and those who joined the Qalandars and related groups were, to varying degrees, 'opting out' from the demands made on them by high medieval Muslim society and their choice probably reflects the social, economic, and psychological circumstances of the individual. Many, perhaps most, of the great Ṣūfī shaykhs were born into the Islamic religious classes or received instruction from them as children of a locally established Muslim nobility. With their lineage and education they could have obtained employment under a Muslim ruler as *'ulamā'* and *faqīhs* serving the state in the maintenance of social order and the attempt to establish an ideal Muslim society as mapped out by al-Māwardī and other jurists. A similar process of social selection may be observed in recruitment of the full-time or long-term inmates of a large Ṣūfī *khānqāh*. Leadership among the *mujāwirīn* tends to be vested in members of *ashrāf* lineages, like the Kirmānī Sayyids at the *khānqāh* of Niẓām al-Dīn in the later fourteenth century. On the other hand, in the selection of *khalīfas* by the great shaykhs, an attempt to satisfy the spiritual needs and preferences of the different social classes of their adherents may be discerned; placed right at the end of the lists there will often be one or two *darwīshes* of more dubious orthodoxy or social standing.

These will often be Qalandars. They are the origin of the later affiliation of the Qalandars to the four great high Ṣūfī orders found in the Indian subcontinent, for instance, the

[41] 'Irāqī, *Kulliyāt*, ed. S. Nafīsī, Tehran: Kitābkhānah-i Sanā'ī, 1958, pp. 49–51. Cf. a more ornate version of the same tale in a seventeenth-century Indian source, which represents the poet as a man of mature years: Ḥamīd al-Dīn, *Sharaf al-manāqib*, Urdu tr., pp. 4–5.

Chishtiyya Qalandariyya, whom the writers of the *tadhkiras* of the Mughal period trace back through Shaykh Najm al-Dīn and Shāh Khiżr Rūmī to Quṭb al-Dīn Bakhtyār Kākī. Similarly, although we lack early Suhrawardī sources, and notwithstanding the disapproval which Shaykh Bahā' al-Dīn Zakariyā' of Multān displayed towards Qalandars, we may accept as not improbable his bestowal of *khilāfat* on Shaykh 'Uthmān Marandī, the 'Shāhbāz Qalandar' of Sehvān. This suggests that the division between the Qalandars and related groups, on the one hand, and more orthodox Ṣūfīs on the other, was social and psychological. In modern times the two groups have been called *bā-shar'* and *bē-shar'*, reflecting their observance or non-observance of the *sharī'at*, though these are not entirely satisfactory terms. Yet we may distinguish as 'orthodox' the major shaykhs of the established orders, who sought to minimize their divergences from Islamic law as expounded by the *'ulamā'* and often demonstrably sprang from the same social class as the *'ulamā'*. The social division is not complete. The Qalandars were given effective organization as a recognizable order by Shaykh Jamāl al-Dīn of Sāva, a *muftī* described by one of our sources as 'a walking library'.[42] A youth or man of respectable antecedents might for personal and psychological reasons decide to join the Qalandars, as we have seen in our evidence upon recruitment to the groups. The reputation of the charisma of a particular Qalandar might ensure offerings which would enable them to establish a hospice. As noted earlier, in the capital city of Dehlī we have mention of that of Shaykh Abū Bakr Ṭūsī Ḥaydarī at the end of the thirteenth century,[43] and of one of the major *langars* (free kitchens) of the city in the early fourteenth century run by one Ramażan Qalandar.[44]

[42] Qalandar, *Khayr al-majālis*, p. 131.
[43] Baranī, *Ta'rīkh-i Fērōzshāhī*, p. 198.
[44] Qalandar, *Khayr al-majālis*, p. 185.

Ṣūfī allegiance and an interest, however superficial, in mystical doctrine was widely prevalent among the literate classes of Dehlī and among the courtiers of the sultans. Similarly, the garb and personal appearance of a Qalandar might be adopted by an educated man as a matter of choice, one might almost say affectation. Of those who are said to have led astray Sultan Muḥammad Tughluq in his disastrous preference for philosophic rationalism (*ma'qūlāt*) against received truth (*manqūlāt*) one was Malik Sa'd al-Dīn Manṭiqī—'the logician'. Baranī records that Jalāl al-Dīn Fērōz Khaljī raised him 'from the *palās* garments of a Qalandar' to the offices of *nā'ib* and *qarā beg* with a retinue, ceremonial honours, and a land-assignment (*iqṭā'*).[45] A solitary Qalandar who arrived at the *khānqāh* of Shaykh Naṣīr al-Dīn Maḥmūd in Dehlī is described as a learned traveller and was treated to courteous discourse by the shaykh.[46] In the almost contemporary testimony of Baranī, the founder of the Qalandar shrine at Sehvān, Shaykh 'Uthmān Marandī, known as La'l Shāhbāz ('the Red Hawk'), appears as a great shaykh whose presence at Multān and attendance at *samā'* was courted by Sultan Balban's son, the 'martyred prince' Muḥammad Khān, together with the great Suhrawardī shaykh Bahā' al-Dīn Zakariyā'.[47] Another anecdote of this historian regarding princely patronage of a Qalandar furnishes less evidence of his reputability in a 'high' Ṣūfī tradition. On the suppression of the revolt of the governor Ṭughril in AD 1279, Sultan Balban gibbeted his followers,

[45] Baranī, *Ta'rīkh-i Fērōzshāhī*, p. 198: *az jāma-yi palās-i qalandarī bīrūn āvurda.*

[46] Qalandar, *Khayr al-majālis*, p. 250.

[47] Baranī, *Ta'rīkh-i Fērōzshāhī*, p. 67; the significance of the reference has escaped attention, from the fact that the printed text (as well as the uncirculated edition by S.A. Rashid, vol. II, Aligarh: Aligarh Muslim University, c. 1960, p. 79) reads MRYDY in place of MRNDY. Marand lies on the road between Erzerum and Tabriz.

including even a Qalandar known as Sultan Darwīsh whom Ṭughril held in high esteem and to whom he had given three *mans* of gold to be used to replace the irons which he and his companions wore.[48]

Ḥamīd Qalandar was not only the compiler of the conversations of the great Chishtī shaykh Naṣīr al-Dīn Maḥmūd, but also a court-poet, author of *qaṣīdas* in praise of Sultan Fērōz Shāh Tughluq, or commemorating the latter's victories.[49] When asked by Shaykh Naṣīr al-Dīn Maḥmūd whether he should call him 'Ṣūfī' or 'Qalandar', and why he should call him 'Qalandar' when he was an educated man (*mard-i muta'allimī*), Ḥamīd explained the rather fanciful circumstances of his allegiance to the Qalandars. As a boy he had been present at the *ifṭār* of the Chishtī shaykh Niẓām al-Dīn. The shaykh had broken a round of bread and placed one half before himself, giving the other to the boy, who placed it in his sleeve. When he went out, a group of Qalandars approached him and asked for alms. 'Shaykhzāda, give us something!' The boy said that he had nothing on him, but the Qalandars revealed the bread which he was hiding in his sleeve, telling him to give them the half-loaf which he had received from the shaykh. The small boy was astonished at their knowledge and felt obliged to give them the bread. The Qalandars then sat down in the antechamber to the great mosque of

[48] Baranī, *Ta'rīkh-i Fērōzshāhī*, p. 91. For the weight of the *man* or 'maund' in the Dehlī Sultanate, considerably lighter than in Mughal or British times, see W. Hinz, *Islamische Mässe und Gewichte*, Leiden: Brill, 1955, pp. 22–3.

[49] Though Ḥamīd Qalandar's poetical works were thought by his editor, K.A. Nizami, to have been lost, several *qaṣīdas* are copied in a fifteenth-century anthology compiled in Jawnpur: British Library, MS Or. 4110. One *qaṣīda* celebrates the return to Dehlī of Sultan Fērōz Shāh Tughluq with the elephants captured on his Bengal/Jājnagar expedition of AD 1359–60 (ff. 101–2).

Kilokhrī (the suburb of Dehlī where the shaykh's *khānqāh* and some royal palaces were situated) and broke and shared the bread. Then the father of the boy came down from the shaykh's audience and demanded what he had done with the bread. The boy said that he had given it to the Qalandars. The father lamented this, saying that it was a blessing from the shaykh, and returned to the shaykh in a state of distress. When Niẓām al-Dīn was informed, he reassured the father and said: 'Your son will be a Qalandar'. As Niẓām al-Dīn, his *pīr*, had called Ḥamīd a Qalandar, Naṣīr al-Dīn Maḥmūd should do so, too. Ḥamīd evidently valued his Qalandar allegiance sufficiently highly to name them before Ṣūfīs in general in his exordium.[50]

Both the Ṣūfīs of the *khānqāhs*, headed by the great shaykhs, and the bands of Qalandars and the wandering *darwīshes*, were groups which had 'opted out' of the community in their rejection of gainful employment (*shughl-i dunyā*). Like similar groups in later times, the need to remain alive involved them in transactional relationships with the society which they claimed to have rejected. Even if, in extreme cases of rejection, an ascetic attempted to live off the fruits of the jungle (like Shaykh Farīd al-Dīn in early life or the brahmaṇas of the period of the Upānishads) or from the cultivation of barren land (*iḥyā-yi zamīn*, as Shaykh Ḥamīd al-Dīn Suwālī Nāgawrī), uninterrupted pursuit of this way of life depended on the absence of a rival claim to this surplus, in essence political even if it took the form of defence of freedom by partisans of a superior charisma. These were extreme choices of ways of life and in practice the material support of these dissident groups was mainly out of the surplus of those either gainfully employed or of those, by their position in the structure of power, entitled to a share in the distribution of income.

[50] Qalandar, *Khayr al-majālis*, p. 6.

The Ṣūfīs received maintenance in return for services, real or imaginary, or—and here it is difficult to draw a close line of division—as a peace offering designed to buy the favour of an element in society which had real political and widely believed charismatic or spiritual influence. Thus, with the establishment of *khānqāhs* under shaykhs of *ashrāf* lineage, who followed the Muslim conquests in India, we find that those Ṣūfīs who claimed to have withdrawn from society were, in fact, serving the needs of Indo-Muslim society in a number of ways, and for these services received material support from the current surplus product available for distribution. The debate between the Chishtī and Suhrawardī shaykhs regarding the acceptance of land grants or permanent endowments assumes an academic ethical character, with undertones of political *savoir-faire*. In a society as unstable as the Dehlī Sultanate, and in its western hinterland subject to periodic dominance by the Chaghatayid Mongol government, the consequences to men of religion dependent upon or apparently dependent upon unsuccessful contenders for power might be disastrous, as in the case of the Qalandar with rings of gold favoured by Ṭughril in Bihar or in that of Sīdī Muwallih at Dehlī. Nevertheless, the acceptance of substantial *futūḥāt* (offerings) for distribution in the near future, necessary to maintain a large *khānqāh* and its temporary and permanent residents, demanded a considerable accommodation with the wealthy and power-holding classes. The numerous anecdotes in the Chishtī hagiography, which is our principal source for the Muslim religious pathology of the Dehlī Sultanate, regarding the refusal of shaykhs to meet sultans and the unwisdom of consorting too closely with *maliks* and *amīrs*, as well as the refusal to accept permanent assignments of income, need to be considered as political decisions as well as a demonstration of superior moral excellence. Nevertheless, it was from the sultan, his great officers, or from the excessively wealthy classes in society that the offerings came to maintain the *khānqāhs* which provided *baraka*, good fortune, and self-assurance to those concerned with pious exercises as a full-time occupation, as well as to Muslim travellers, to those who were unemployable or did not wish to be employed, and to the great variety of *khuddām* and *mujāwirīn*, like those who may be seen, possibly in slightly more decayed circumstances, around South Asian *dargāhs* today.

Similarly, the relations which existed between the high Ṣūfī shaykhs and the *'ulamā'* in the service of the state express a high degree of mutual accommodation. Though at intervals arguments might break out between them, notably over the legality of the practice of *samā'* (listening to music) which was a strong element of Chishtī practice, and though the shaykhs might condemn the *'ulamā'-yi ẓāhir* ('external *'ulamā'*') or *'ulamā'-yi sū'* ('wicked *'ulamā'*'), there was a large area of common assumptions between the two parties regarding the principles on which an Islamic society should be run, the differences that arose being of an interpretative character. Both parties negotiated from positions of high esteem within the Muslim community; both were maintained in their extensive establishments from the surplus produce of society, and in both the leadership was mainly provided by educated men of *ashrāf* Muslim descent.

By contrast, the way of life and recorded behaviour of the Qalandars and associated orders are those of militant protest groups of an extremist nature, not only rejecting current Indo-Muslim assumptions of what constituted a good life, but also acting in public in a manner intended to provoke opposition. Their garb was a deliberately bizarre and outrageous uniform. Their *samā'*, or musical gatherings, from the time of their organizer Jamāl al-Dīn of Sāva (if we may credit his *manāqib*), placed strong insistence on the practice of *naẓar ilā 'l-murd*, gazing at good-looking boys; and Gēsūdarāz accuses them of 'bringing the children of

Musalmans into evil courses'.[51] They not only resorted to drugs of the *ḥashīsh* family, but could be seen to do so in the most provocative circumstances, scattering the waste over the *sajjāda* (prayer-carpet) of a great shaykh.[52] In many of the instances recording the arrival of Qalandar bands or of individual Qalandars at Ṣūfī *khānqāhs*, their behaviour is of a calculated impropriety, designed to question the atmosphere of reverence which surrounded the presiding Ṣūfī shaykh. 'What, have you made yourself into an idol (*chi tu khwud-rā butī sākhta-ī*)?', a Juwāliq demands of Shaykh Farīd al-Dīn.[53] Demands for accommodation and alms were made in an aggressive and threatening manner, with resorts to violence if their demands were not met. There are also a number of recorded instances of murderous attacks on Ṣūfī shaykhs and other charismatic figures. Though we have already noted the occasional presence of educated or gentle Qalandars, there can be little doubt that the strength and attraction of the movement lay in its extreme antinomianism or repudiation of the received values of society.

Yazıcı, in his Turkish introduction to the *Manāqib-i Jamāl al-Dīn-i Sāvajī*, has drawn a parallel between the lifestyle of the Qalandars and that of a recognizable group of wanderers who are seen in Eastern countries today, the 'Hippies'. There is, indeed, a curious superficial parallel in the distinguishing uniform, the garb of leather, metal studs, and crude jewellery adopted by a large portion of the youth of the USA and the UK as a symbol of mutual solidarity in the rejection of the bourgeois values from which they sprang.

[51] Shēr Malik, *Ta'rīkh-i Ḥabībī*, Urdu tr., p. 107. Cf. also the remark regarding Bū 'Alī of Panipat, reported as derived from an earlier source, that young boys used to live in his *khānqāh*, but were driven out when their beards began to grow, in Ḥamīd al-Dīn, *Sharaf al-manāqib*, p. 8.

[52] Qalandar, *Khayr al-majālis*, p. 130.

[53] 'Alā' Sijzī, *Fawā'id al-fu'ād*, Naval Kishor, 1894, p. 48; Lahore, 1966, p. 81.

At a less superficial level, like the Qalandars, the hard core of the Hippie movement, influenced by the writings of Watts, Kerouac, Ginsburg, and Burroughs in the 1960s, seem committed to a permanently footloose and ecstatic way of life, sustained by drugs and hallucinogens, with marked freedom or license in sexual conduct and the assumption that almost all the principles of order within stable society, as well as the value of the rewards offered by it, are open to debate. However, degrees of similar antinomian thought and conduct among wandering fraternities have occurred sporadically through the centuries in the civilizations of the Eurasian landmass, and attained the prominence which made local historians take note of them in periods of massive political displacement or accelerating changes in the structure of society. Dissimilarities between the medieval antinomian mendicant fraternities and the Hippies of today are related to widely different environments: one a theologically oriented society in which poverty was endemic and a belief in the supernatural powers and function of holy men was equally widespread; the other to a society where religion has a much diminished influence on civic values and the economic surplus, notwithstanding its fluctuating level and areas of deprivation, is greater than ever before. The travelling Hippie is seldom a total mendicant, wholly dependent, as the Qalandar was, on the support of the settled population through whom he passed. The Hippie has almost no claim to charisma or magical powers, though one may see the widespread interest among the community in Indian ascetic practices, Tantra, Zen Buddhism, and other exotic cults, as a yearning in that direction. Though he may provoke the anger of the local population and himself be provoked to it, and though he may leave a trail of social disorder in his wake, by his lesser degree of dependence the Hippie is not driven to the passionately assertive, aggressive, or didactic behaviour which is characteristic of the Qalandars. His 'opting-out' or 'doing his own thing' is akin to more gentle Ṣūfī attitudes.

The transactions between high Ṣūfī shaykhs and the Qalandars and related groups, as recorded in the *malfūẓāt* and *tadhkira* literature, with its natural bias in favour of the shaykhs, reveal a variety of considerations. Unlike anecdotes of encounters of Ṣūfīs with Hindu *jogīs*, which I have analysed elsewhere,[54] there was no simple need to demonstrate a superiority of charisma matching false supernatural powers (*istidrāj*) by those which derived from Allāh (*karāmāt*). The anecdotes, therefore, have a less factitious and overtly miraculous quality. The lifestyle of the Qalandars possessed some qualities which made them formidable competitors with more orthodox Ṣūfīs. They were Muslims and lived in a style of *faqr* (poverty) in which they at least equalled the Ṣūfīs of the *khānqāhs*. They laid claim to charisma and could on occasions display *karāmāt*, which were as credible both to the Ṣūfīs themselves and their adherents as those which the great shaykhs, or the anecdotal tradition regarding their predecessors, displayed. Yet the Qalandars, or at any rate a large portion of them, were living outside the pale of orthodox social respectability in which the shaykhs and their followers were included; and upon this behaviour they were staking their claim to charisma, prestige, and maintenance by society. The Qalandars were for the most part aggressive, and in the Chishtī tradition of which we have the best record, the shaykhs were conciliatory and accommodating, even if their followers were less so. By the end of the fourteenth century the more hostile remarks of Sayyid Muḥammad Gēsūdarāz appear to be a reaction against this. The policy of conciliation and mutual accommodation had its success

[54] [See Simon Digby, 'Encounters with *Jogīs* in Indian Sūfī Hagiography', paper presented at SOAS University of London, 1970, and the expanded version in this series, *L&WSD* II. ~DL]

in producing yet another class of devotees, of those entitled to support by the Muslim faithful or the Muslim-dominated state as part of the *lashkar-i du'ā'* ('the army of prayer'), in such mixed orders as the Chishtiyya Qalandariyya. In 1976 the Qalandars still enjoyed a part in the ceremonial of the *'urs* (commemoration of the decease) of the founding figure of the Chishtī *silsila* in India, Mu'īn al-Dīn Chishtī.[55]

One anecdote of the first half of the fourteenth century shows the degree of accommodation which had been reached between the *khānqāhs* of the great Chishtī shaykhs and visiting groups of Qalandars.[56] It shows the Qalandars settling down to a course of wanderings which is characteristic of their annual peregrinations in later times, in which they perform the *ziyārat* (pilgrimage) to a notable shaykh's tomb at the time of the *'urs* or anniversary of his death; and participate in the ceremonies and the singing, as in the Ajmer case being offered a definite though subordinate place in the ritual.[57]

Shaykh Shams al-Dīn Yaḥyā, a Muḥaddith and *khalīfa* of Shaykh Niẓām al-Dīn Awliyā', was visiting the latter's *khānqāh* at Dehlī a few years after Niẓām al-Dīn's death in AD 1324. With other *khalīfas* he was listening to *samā'* in the tomb (*gumbad*, possibly the roofed structure erected over the tomb by Sultan Muḥammad Tughluq about this date).

Travellers, Ḥaydarīs, and Qalandars were listening to the *samā'* and performing *raqṣ* in the great arch (probably

[55] Observed by my pupil Dr P.M. Currie.

[56] Amir Khwurd, *Siyar al-awliyā'*, ed. Chiranjī Lāl, Dehli: Muhibb-i Hindi Press, 1885, pp. 227–8.

[57] See Katherine Ewing, '*Malangs* of the Punjab: Intoxication or *Adab* as a Path to God', paper presented at the Seminar of the Center for South Asian Studies, University of California, Berkeley, June 1979, pp. 13–18 [since published in Barbara Daly Metcalf, ed., *Moral Conduct and Authority: The Place of* Adab *in South Asian Islam*, Berkeley: University of California Press, 1984, pp. 357–71 ~DL].

the principal arch of the mosque now called *jamā'at-khāna*, erected by sons of Sultan 'Alā' al-Dīn Khaljī early in the century). *Qawwāls* and *darwīshes* were beating drums and singing a *qaṣīda* of the Persian poet Sa'dī. Shams al-Dīn went forth from the great dome, and joined them as they performed a *samā'* and beat the drums. He was overcome by the ecstasy of *samā'* in the company of these *darwīshes.* He rubbed his hand on his heart and rocked, to the extent that when the *samā'* ended, he was so overwhelmed by its pleasure that he made an impassioned dance. His friends and acquaintances in the assembly saw the situation. He did not return (to sobriety?) till he joined God's mercy (died, shortly afterwards).

A spectrum of attitudes is visible among the Ṣūfī shaykhs, ranging from sentimental tolerance and forbearance to strongly expressed condemnation. Shaykh Naṣīr al-Dīn Maḥmūd in the 1350s, when a solitary Qalandar arrived at his *khānqāh*, lamented the days when they used to arrive in bands of twenty and thirty.[58] He, together with his immediate predecessors in the Chishtī order, Farīd al-Dīn and Niẓām al-Dīn, are shown as acting with gentleness in the face of aggression, and expressing belief in the power of the charisma of Qalandars. Among the Suhrawardīs, we are told that Bahā' al-Dīn disliked the Juwāliqs.[59] Yet we should probably accept as historical the arrival at his *khānqāh* in Multān in a Qalandar band of the poet 'Irāqī, to whom he later gave his daughter in marriage;[60] and also his and his son Ṣadr al-Dīn's association with Shaykh 'Uthmān

[58] Qalandar, *Khayr al-majālis*, p. 185.

[59] 'Alā' Sijzī, *Fawā'id al-fu'ād*, Naval Kishor, 1894, p. 48; Lahore, 1966, p. 81. From the anecdotes a suspicion arises that *Juwāliq* was the most pejorative term used for members of the groups; however, Ḥamīd Qalandar includes Juwāliqs among those in the *dawlat* of his *pīr*, see above, Qalandar, *Khayr al-majālis*, p. 5.

[60] Biographical preface to 'Irāqī, *Kulliyāt*, and later *tadhkiras*.

Marandī (La'l Shāhbāz Qalandar) of Sehvān is attested both by Baranī and by later *tadhkiras* written in Sind.[61] A later Suhrawardī shaykh in Dehlī around 1380, Jalāl al-Dīn 'Makhdūm-i Jahāniyān', accepted the repentance of a Qalandar, who was commended for abandoning the leather garments and admitted as a Murīd.[62] In the Firdawsiyya *silsila*, strongly established in Bihār, there is a straightforward anecdote, described in detail below, in which the shaykh demonstrates his superior charisma.[63] However, the same source enumerates among the disciples of the shaykh in question, Sharaf al-Dīn Aḥmad b. Yaḥyā of Maner, a *chiram-pōsh* named Aḥmad. Aḥmad Chiram-pōsh is to be identified with the Aḥmad Bihārī mentioned in the *Futūḥāt-i Fērōzshāhī*, put to death by the sultan in Dehlī for a claim to Godhead; Shaykh Sharaf al-Dīn and his followers attributed the downfall of the Dehlī Sultanate at the end of the fourteenth century to the wickedness of the martyrdom of Aḥmad and another of his disciples.[64]

The strongest, though not unequivocal, condemnation of the Qalandars is that of Sayyid Muḥammad Gēsūdarāz, which is in keeping with the greater severity of his attitudes by

[61] ['Abd al-Ghafūr bin Haidar Sīvistānī,] *Tadhkira-yi mashā'ikh-i Sīvistān*, ed. S.H. Rashdi, in *Mehrān*, vol. 23, no. 3–4, 1974, p. 205 [this edition of the *Tadhkira* was prepared by Rashdi and published in *Mehrān*, the literary magazine of the Sindhi Adabi Board, 'the manuscript of which is available in the Royal Asiatic Society, London, the photostat of which was provided to me by my friend Simon Digby'. A digitized version, lacking original pagination, is available at http://sindhiadabiboard.org/Catalogue/mehran/Book64/Book_page19.html ~DL]; Baranī, *Ta'rīkh-i Fērōzshāhī*, p. 68.

[62] *Khulāṣat al-alfāẓ*, Digby MS, f. 244 [now in the Bodleian Library, University of Oxford, MS S. Digby Or. 8 ~DL].

[63] Shāh Shu'ayb Firdawsī, *Manāqib al-aṣfiyā'*, Calcutta: Anwār al-āfāq Press, AH 1313, p. 140.

[64] *Futūḥāt-i Fērōzshāhī*, ed. S.A. Rashid, Aligarh: Aligarh Muslim University, 1954, p. 6–7; Firdawsī, *Manāqib al-aṣfiyā'*, pp. 129–30.

contrast with those of the earlier great shaykhs of the Chishtī order. It is also in accord with his views on the primacy of *sharī'at* over *ṭarīqat* and *ḥaqīqat*, and his advancement of his fourfold claim to pre-eminence as a Sayyid, a Ṣūfī, a Sunnī, and an *'ālim*. In a biography of Gēsūdarāz shortly after his death, the Qalandars are listed as eighth in a number of causes of the shaykh's displeasure.[65] We may quote here the opening of this passage:

8th [cause of the Shaykh's displeasure]. The times when he saw Qalandars or heard their names and tales about them and their acts he used to be displeased and say, 'These are the people who bring the children of Musalmans into evil courses and lead people astray.' Once, when there was some mention of Qalandars, he said, 'On one occasion a Qalandar came before me and I asked him, "Why did you join this group?"

'He said, "I was angry with my parents and ran away from home. I met these old men who enticed me and took me away with them."'

He used to warn his grandchildren and young relations, 'I don't want any child of my house to allow a Qalandar to stay in his presence and talk to him; or for him to listen to the talk of Qalandars.'

Gēsūdarāz is represented as being in the habit of casting doubt on the proposition embodied in anecdotes of our Class 3, below, that there are men of powerful charisma concealed among the Qalandars:

He used to say, 'Why did Shaykh Shihāb al-Dīn ['Umar Suhrawardī of Baghdād] say that in the order of the Qalandars there was also such a man who stood out—that is to say a *walī* [saint]? That mystics, gnostics and perfect men are to be found among them?' Well, it is possible that some *walī*, to conceal himself, may join this order and remain hidden; but what connection has this with

[65] Shēr Malik, *Ta'rīkh-i Ḥabībī*, pp. 107–9; cf. ibid., p. 36, for Gēsūdarāz's statement of the four causes of his pre-eminence.

the statement that out of this order appears such a person, a man who is a *walī* and *'ārif* and *kāmil* and shaykh and *murshid*? These people are of evil stock and faith and among them there is no good record of religious observance.

Two anecdotes regarding Gēsūdarāz's own transactions with Qalandars follow, which will be noted in detail below. The first belongs to Class 3 of our typology, and does not show consistency with the views expressed above. He entertained a body of Qalandars and 'endured their *samā'*' because he had divined that there was a Man of God (*mard-i khudā*) concealed among them. In the following anecdote he rejected the claim of a Qalandar to charisma, but bade him sit down and gave him some money on his departure. Though Gēsūdarāz was their opponent, the Qalandars were entitled to a measure of dialogue and of alms. In these remarks of Gēsūdarāz the main line of argument to justify an accommodation between the high Ṣūfī shaykhs and the Qalandars has already made an appearance. Notwithstanding their way of life, individual Qalandars appeared to possess an undeniable and formidable charisma. Hence, such a possessor of charisma might have deliberately adopted this way of life as a disguise. We may elaborate upon the theoretical basis for this concept.

The theory of a supernatural hierarchy, set forth by Hujwīrī in *Kashf al-maḥjūb*, found widespread acceptance in the Dehlī Sultanate and endures in the popular consciousness of South Asian Muslims to this day.[66] In the beliefs advanced by Hujwīrī, the *abdāls* (or *walīs*) were the lowest rank of a hidden hierarchy, maintained by constant recruitment to the vacant posts, who ascended through *awtād* ('tent-pegs')

[66] For an account of the powers and services of a concealed Walī, recorded in Haydarabad, Deccan, in 1963, see S. Digby, 'The Waterseller's Pilgrimage', in *Lycidas*, vol. III, Oxford: Wolfson College, 1974–5, pp. 20–1.

to a supreme *quṭb* ('polestar' or 'apex'). This hierarchy, by the exercise of their concealed supernatural powers, guided the temporal affairs of the world along the paths of righteousness. It was a condition of the existence of the *abdāl* that he should remain concealed from common view, his good works unknown. Hence, the garb and behaviour of a Qalandar could provide an effective disguise for an *abdāl*. The association between *abdāls* and Qalandars is often made, and the author of the *Khayr al-majālis*, relating the customarily difficult and arrogant behaviour of a Qalandar at the *khānqāh* of Naṣīr al-Dīn Maḥmūd in Dehlī, at the outset described him as *abdāl-ṣifat*, 'with the qualities of an *abdāl*'.[67]

The association of Qalandar and *abdāl* found expression even in the non-Muslim literature of northern India. In the sixteenth-century Sikh scripture, the *Gurū Granth Sāhib*, a hymn ascribed to Nāmdev and, therefore, probably of some antiquity at the time of record, contains the lines:

> Come God, the Qalandar
> Wearing the dress of an Abdālī.[68]

The activities of an *abdāl* were essentially beneficent. It is, however, in accordance with the antinomian behaviour of the Qalandars that the recorded instances of their display of supernatural powers are generally of an angry character, reflecting to a greater degree than was common among Ṣūfī

[67] Qalandar, *Khayr al-majālis*, p. 129.

[68] M.A. Macauliffe, *The Sikh Religion: its Gurus, Sacred Writings, and Authors*, 6 vols., Oxford: Clarendon Press, 1909, vol. 6, p. 69. There follows a brief description of costume and insignia. It is likely that the poet himself was slightly muddled and should have said 'an Abdāl in the dress of a Qalandar'. One cannot accept the Panjābī/Western Hindī verses ascribed to Namdev in the *Gurū Granth Sāhib* as the compositions of the thirteenth-century Maharashtrian poet Nāmadeva, but the ascription probably indicates a sixteenth-century date.

shaykhs the attribute of *jalāl* ('awe', 'wrath') which was the complement of *jamāl* ('beauty', 'beneficence').[69]

In the Indian Ṣūfī literature of the thirteenth and fourteenth centuries the anecdotes regarding Qalandars may be classified under the following headings:

1. Descriptions of their physical appearance. These often follow a note of their arrival at a *khānqāh* and lead on to anecdotes of classes 2, 3, 4, or 6. Occasionally the descriptions occur within anecdotes of all other classes;
2. Anecdotes of two founders of groups, viz., Jamāl al-Dīn of Sāva, his disciple Quṭb al-Dīn Ḥaydar, and Shaykh Khiżr Rūmī; related to class 3;
3. Anecdotes of men of powerful charisma or *abdāls* concealed among the Qalandars;
4. Anecdotes of conflict between Ṣūfī shaykhs and Qalandars, in general leading to a degree of accommodation. They may display the supernatural force of the Qalandars' wrath but demonstrate either the superior charisma of the shaykh or his extreme gentleness and humility in the face of insults or violence;
5. Anecdotes of murderous attacks upon Ṣūfī shaykhs; related to class 4;
6. Mention of individual Qalandars of peaceful and respectful behaviour or with learned attainments; related to classes 1 and 3.

[69] The degree to which the benevolence of the great Chishtī shaykhs of Dehlī could be modified by hostility or anger has not been emphasized in the writings of K.A. Nizami. At a lower social level, many of the anecdotes regarding the fourteenth-century *majdhūb* Khwāja Gurg, one of which is examined in this chapter, show him extracting exemplary vengeance for slights. The behaviour of the fifteenth-century Chishtī shaykh Aḥmad 'Abd al-Ḥaqq, which displays a general lack of benevolence, is examined by S. Digby in *Medieval India: A Miscellany*, vol. III, Aligarh: Aligarh Muslim University, 1975, pp. 1–66 [*L&WSD* III.10].

Almost all the descriptions of physical appearance, garb, and accoutrements of our class 1 have been utilized earlier in this chapter. The most extended description is to be found in the *Khayr al-majālis*,[70] and additional references supplying details in the same work, the *Fawā'id al-fu'ād*[71] (reproduced in *Siyar al-awliyā'*[72] and, possibly deriving from an earlier source, in the *Siyar al-'ārifīn*).[73] References of class 6 are brief and have been noted above. Perhaps the most significant depicts a mid-fourteenth-century wandering scholar in this garb.[74]

Class 1: Descriptions of Physical Appearance

See the descriptions above and below, pp. 190–1, 216–18, 230.

Class 2: Anecdotes of the Founders

In the *Khayr al-majālis*, Shaykh Naṣīr al-Dīn Maḥmūd mentions Shaykh Jamāl al-Dīn of Sāva, following a favourite Chishtī anecdote of class 3 below. He referred to Jamāl al-Dīn as a Muftī and added that he was called 'a walking library'. He then related an anecdote of Jamāl al-Dīn's encounter with an unnamed shaykh, in which Jamāl al-Dīn demonstrated his superior charisma.

A group of Qalandars, including Jamāl al-Dīn, called upon this shaykh, wearing neither clothes nor *khirqa* (Ṣūfī cloak), in fact nothing but their irons, fragments of blanket, and loin-cloths. When questioned by what authority they thus attired themselves, Jamāl al-Dīn passed into an ecstatic trance. After shaving his beard and donning his coarse cloth (*palās*), he was seen to retire into a grave, with his mouth open and

[70] Qalandar, *Khayr al-majālis*, p. 131.

[71] 'Alā' Sijzī, *Fawā'id al-fu'ād*, Naval Kishor, 1894, pp. 19–20; Lahore, 1966, p. 30.

[72] Khwurd, *Siyar al-awliyā'*, p. 575.

[73] Jamālī, *Siyar al-'ārifīn*, Delhi: Maṭba'-i Riẓvī, AH 1311/AD 1893, p. 67.

[74] Qalandar, *Khayr al-majālis*, p. 250.

his eyes raised to heaven. The shaykh ordered poison to be melted and poured down his throat, which Jamāl al-Dīn swallowed like cold water. When Jamāl al-Dīn had returned a little to his senses, he was told that the shaving of his beard was against the *shar'*. He asked those present if they wanted a beard, hid his head inside his cloak and reappeared with a long white beard stretching down his chest, after which the Qalandars at that place were left in peace.[75]

Niẓām al-Dīn in his conversation depicted Quṭb al-Dīn Ḥaydar as a *darwīsh* possessed of formidable charisma, undoubtedly a member of the unseen hierarchy which controls the affairs of the world, but worsted by an unnamed *darwīsh* of even greater powers, who was responsible for the Mongol conquests. The account may be quoted in literal translation:

Mention occurred of Ḥaydar of Zāva[76]—Allāh's Mercy upon him. Shaykh Niẓām al-Dīn said with his blessed tongue:

[75] Qalandar, *Khayr al-majālis*, p. 131. The anecdote appears in a closely similar form, as regards his shaved state and appearance with a beard, heard by the fifteenth-century Arab traveller Ibn Baṭṭūṭa in Egypt, see Ibn Baṭṭūṭa, *Riḥla*, ed. Defrémery, vol. I, p. 64.

[76] The editor of the 1966 edition does not note any variants for *Ḥaydar-i zāviya*, 'Haydar of the hospice', which might indeed have served as a place-name. Khwurd, *Siyar al-awliyā'*, p. 575, which reproduces the passage verbatim, also reads *zāviya*. The reading *Ḥaydar-zāda* is found in the Dehlī lithograph of AH 1272, but escaped the 1966 editor's attention. This is close to the correct reading *Zāva*, which is provided by Ibn Baṭṭūṭa's and Ḥamd Allāh Muṣṭawfī's accounts of the burial-place of the shaykh: see Ibn Baṭṭūṭa, *Riḥla*, ed. Defrémery, vol. III, pp. 79–80, and tr. Gibb, vol. III, p. 583; Guy le Strange, tr., *The Geographical Part of the Nuzhat al-qulūb*, Leiden: Brill/London: Luzac, 1919, p. 152. Zāva was a fortified town in Khurasan south of Mashhad; from the presence of the shaykh's tomb there it later became known as Turbat-i Ḥaydar.

Both Ibn Baṭṭūṭa and Muṣṭawfī call the founder of the Ḥaydarīs Quṭb al-Dīn Ḥaydar. Richard Gramlich, *Die schiitischen Derwischorden Persiens*, vol. I, Wiesbaden: Franz Steiner, 1965, pp. 70–81, has Jalāl al-Dīn Ḥaydar, without however mentioning his authority.

He was of Turkish stock[77] and a Darwīsh, *ṣāḥib-i ḥāl*.[78] When the onslaught of Chingiz Khān occurred, the infidels turned towards Hindūstān [*sic*, read Khurāsān]. One day in those times he turned towards his companions and said:

'Flee from the Mongols who will be the conquerors!'

'Why?' they asked.

'They are bringing a *darwīsh* along with them,' Ḥaydar said, 'and they themselves are coming under the protection of that *darwīsh*. In secret I have wrestled with the *darwīsh* and he threw me to the ground. Now the truth is that they will conquer. You should flee!'

Then he himself went into a cave and became invisible.[79] The outcome was as he had said.

After the telling of this story the writer [Amīr Ḥasan Sijzī] asked:

'This group who wear a collar and bangles of iron on their necks and wrists, are they followers of his?'

'Yes', the Shaykh replied, 'but he attained such a state of mystical exaltation that in it he would seize the red-hot iron and with his hands fashion collars or bangles. The group who are alive now put on the collar and bangles all right, but where is that mystical exaltation?'[80]

Niẓām al-Dīn referred elsewhere briefly to Haydar of Zāva's disappearance from mortal view. He was alive when

[77] *Turk-bachcha* in Malik's edition and in the Dehlī and Naval Kishor lithographs. Khwurd, *Siyar al-awliyā'*, reads *SRKBYJH*, probably a corrupted transcription.

[78] *Ṣāḥib-i hāl*. No single English translation will convey the range of attributes implied by the Persian phrase. *Ṣāḥib* is a 'lord', 'possessor' of *ḥāl*, the state of mystical illumination and ecstasy, closeness to God and with supernatural perceptions.

[79] The notion that Ḥaydar disappeared into a cave at the time of the Mongol onslaught is consonant with Trimingham's unreferenced statement, in *The Sufi Orders in Islam*, Oxford: Oxford University Press, 1971, p. 199n., that Quṭb al-Dīn Ḥaydar died in 618/1221.

[80] 'Alā' Sijzī, *Fawā'id al-fu'ād*, Naval Kishor, 1894, pp. 19–20; Lahore, 1966, p. 30; Khwurd, *Siyar al-awliyā'*, p. 575; Qalandar, *Khayr al-majālis*, p. 176.

the door of his place of retreat was opened one hundred years later. Possibly we should understand that he was waiting for a sign to reappear (*ummīdwār-i sukhanīst*), though Niẓām al-Dīn's remark is ambiguous.[81] The conversation was recorded just about a century after the Mughal conquest of Khurāsān, and so had this incident occurred at this time it would, in fact, have been very recent news in Dehlī.

The last anecdote which we include in this section has close links with class 4—of conflict and accommodation between Ṣūfī shaykhs and Qalandars. It is reproduced, probably deriving from an unrecognized earlier source, from the *Akhbār al-akhyār* of 'Abd al-Ḥaqq Muḥaddith Dehlavī, a late sixteenth-century compendium of brief lives of Indian Ṣūfīs. The subject, Shāh Khiżr Rūmī, appears to have been a younger contemporary of Jamāl al-Dīn and Quṭb al-Dīn Ḥaydar, and therefore may have claimed equal status with them instead of enrolling in their lineages. On the other hand, the fact that he was from such a distant area as Rūm (Anatolia) suggests that he was a later recruit. Nevertheless, if the chronological setting—i.e. within the lifetime of Quṭb al-Dīn Bakhtyār Kākī—is credible, this is the earliest date for which we have a reference to the presence of Qalandars in India. 'Abd al-Ḥaqq reports as follows:

> He followed the Qalandariyya way (*mashrab*). He was originally from Anatolia (*Rūm*). Through him many miracles and breaks in the natural order came to pass, even though he never observed the custom of repentance and profession of discipleship (*bay'at*).[82] When he came to Hindūstān, Shaykh al-Islām Quṭb al-Dīn Bakhtyār Ūshī was yet alive. He urged this kind of repentance upon him, also sending a cap (*kullāh*, of discipleship) and a robe (*khirqa*, of succession) to his place of residence and made him depart. After this it befell that Shāh Khiżr set out for Jawnpūr.

[81] 'Alā' Sijzī, *Fawā'id al-fu'ād*, Naval Kishor, 1894, p. 250.

[82] This is the standard practice of the acceptance of disciples by a shaykh.

When he reached the Sarāy of Haripur, Shāh Quṭb [Shāh Quṭb al-Dīn] became his disciple (*murid*). After bestowing *khilāfat* [succession in the order] upon Shāh Quṭb, he set out for Rūm. To this day this *silsila* [order] survives in Hindūstān; this is the Qalandariyya Chishtiyya.[83]

This anecdote may have been transmitted to or by 'Abd al-Ḥaqq in a garbled form, but the two nineteenth-century lithographs show no significant textual variants. The information that Quṭb al-Dīn in turn became Khiżr's *murīd* and Khiżr bestowed a reciprocal *khilāfat* on Quṭb al-Dīn clearly troubled two seventeenth-century Chishtī hagiographers, who acknowledged the *Akhbār al-akhyār* as their source but omitted this detail.[84] As it stands, the anecdote embodies transactions of mutual legitimation and a definition of spheres of influence between two shaykhs with independent sources of charisma, with Quṭb al-Dīn negotiating from a position of established power threatened by an intruder, and both parties prepared to reach an advantageous settlement. It was Quṭb al-Dīn who called on Khiżr, gave him insignia and evidently indicated that Khiżr should set out again on his travels. Senior members of the Chishtī *khānqāhs* were treated in a similar manner when they might have contested the succession, the bestowal of *khilāfat* and insignia being accompanied by an injunction to set up a *khānqāh* elsewhere. Khiżr was not in a strong enough position to remain in Dehlī; and his bestowal, when at safe distance from the metropolis, of *khilāfat* on Quṭb al-Dīn, might appear a retaliatory gesture, followed as it was by a reversal in the direction of his wanderings—from his destination of Jawnpūr in the east back towards

[83] Dehlavī, *Akhbār al-akhyār*, Mirath, 1861–2, pp. 47–8; Dehlī, 1891–2, pp. 49–50.

[84] Muhammad Bulāq, *Maṭlūb al-ṭālibīn*, India Office MS Ethé 653, f. 143b; Barasavī, *Savāṭi' al anwār*, India Office MS Ethé 654, f. 116a.

Anatolia.[85] Yet ʻAbd al-Ḥaqq's account states that Quṭb al-Dīn in turn became Khiżr's *murīd* (incidentally implying that Haripur was at no great distance from the capital). This implies that the transaction had advantages for both the Chishtī and the Qalandar, with conflict averted and charisma replenished from another fount. One of the seventeenth-century hagiographies adds to ʻAbd al-Ḥaqq's account the detail that Shaykh Najm al-Dīn enrolled as a disciple of Shāh Khiżr, evidently before his final departure towards Anatolia and implying that it was through Najm al-Dīn and as a result of Quṭb al-Dīn's farsightedness (*az sabab-i Shāh Quṭb-i bīnā dil*) that the Qalandariyya Chishtiyya order became established in various places in India. In this work the Qalandariyya Chishtiyya is treated as one of fourteen subsidiary branches (*furūʻ*) of the Chishtī order.[86]

Class 3: Abdāls Concealed among the Qalandars

The most often repeated anecdote of this class makes its first literary appearance very early in the conversations of Niẓām al-Dīn recorded in the *Fawāʼid al-fuʼād.*[87] The context is that of the arrival of a Juwāliq at Shaykh Niẓām al-Dīn's *khānqāh.* The shaykh remarks that few had access to Bahāʼ al-Dīn at Multān, but every kind of *darwīsh* could reach (his own *pīr*) Farīd al-Dīn. Elsewhere he comments on Bahāʼ al-Dīn's hostility to Juwāliqs,[88] and there is an implication

85 A reference to Jawnpūr at a date early in the thirteenth century appears unacceptable; but it probably indicates a desire to travel eastwards in the lands of recent conquest by the Muslims.
86 Barasavī, *Savāṭiʻ al anwār*, ff. 116a–b.
87 ʻAlāʼ Sijzī, *Fawāʼid al-fuʼād*, Fakhr al-maṭābiʻ, 1872, p. 6; Naval Kishor, 1894, pp. 4–5; Lahore, 1966, p. 6.
88 ʻAlāʼ Sijzī, *Fawāʼid al-fuʼād*, Naval Kishor, 1894, p. 48; Lahore, 1966, p. 81.

of the superiority of Chishtī over Suhrawardī practice. The anecdote is related with more circumstantial detail by his successor Naṣīr al-Dīn Maḥmūd,[89] and later finds its way into the repertory of the biographical *tadhkiras*.

As related by Naṣīr al-Dīn Maḥmūd, when Bahā' al-Dīn Zakariyā' was returning from Baghdad (i.e. after receiving his *khilāfat* there from Shihāb al-Dīn 'Umar Suhrawardī), he descended at a stage of the journey where there was no *sarāy* and he lodged in a mosque. Qalandars also arrived and took up lodging in a part of the mosque. During the night, while the shaykh was awake at his devotions, he saw a Qalandar whose head was bathed in light from on high (*az sar-i u tā 'ulūww nūr girifta*). The shaykh approached the Qalandar and said:

'O Man of God, what are you doing in the midst of these?'

'In order, Zakariyā', that you may know', the Qalandar replied, 'that in the midst of every common gathering (*'āmmī*) there is an especial person (*khāṣṣī*), on whose account the commonality may be forgiven.'

Naṣīr al-Dīn Maḥmūd then added that the *darwīsh* in question was Muftī Jamāl al-Dīn of Sāva (the founder of the Qalandariyya order).

On several points the narration of Naṣīr al-Dīn Maḥmūd varies from that of Niẓām al-Dīn. The group are called Juwāliqs by Niẓām al-Dīn, Qalandars by Naṣīr al-Dīn Maḥmūd. This supports our contention that no firm distinction can be drawn between such groups. The setting is described with more circumstantial detail, and the occasion as well as the identity of the 'Man of God' are given only in the later source. Bahā' al-Dīn Zakariyā' received his *khilāfat* comparatively young, at a date early in the thirteenth century before Jamāl al-Dīn's death at Damascus in 1232.

[89] Qalandar, *Khayr al-majālis*, pp. 130–1.

A possible venue would be in Iraq or southern Persia. One may still doubt the correctness of the identification, even if the anecdote has a basis in an actual encounter. There is a likely connection between this anecdote and the views which Sayyid Muḥammad Gēsūdarāz attributed to Bahā' al-Dīn's *pīr* Shihāb al-Dīn 'Umar, noticed above.[90]

Class 4: Anecdotes of Encounter or Conflict between Ṣūfī Shaykhs and Qalandars

Some of the anecdotes previously surveyed in Class 2 might also be assigned to this class. The majority of the examples are illustrative of the aggressive behaviour of the Qalandars, leading in general to their accommodation but sometimes to their subjugation by argument or superior charisma.

1. Niẓām al-Dīn related the arrival of some Juwāliqs before Bahā' al-Dīn Zakariyā' (at Multān), while remarking on his great dislike of such groups (*u-rā ba-īn qawm bad-i 'aẓīm būd*). When the group came in, they demanded alms, which the shaykh did not give. They retired, growing so angry that they picked up bricks. The shaykh ordered the door of the *khānqāh* to be closed and they began to hurl the bricks at it. Some time elapsed. The shaykh said, 'I have been set here by Shaykh Shihāb al-Dīn ['Umar Suhrawardī]. I do not sit here of my own accord. I have been set here by a Man [of God].' Then he ordered the door of the *khānqāh* to be opened. When it was opened, the Juwāliqs bent their heads to the ground and departed.[91]

The Juwāliqs therefore appear to have gained nothing but proper respect for Shaykh Bahā' al-Dīn's charisma. We have seen in the anecdote of Class 3 above that respect for

[90] See above, pp. 212–13.

[91] 'Alā' Sijzī, *Fawā'id al-fu'ād*, Naval Kishor, 1894, p. 48; Lahore, 1966, p. 81.

possible charisma among the Qalandars was inculcated upon Shaykh Bahā' al-Dīn himself.[92]

This anecdote, like others already surveyed, concerns the aggressive behaviour of a Juwāliq or Qalandar at a *khānqāh.* A Juwāliq arrived as Niẓām al-Dīn was telling a story and spoke unsuitable words, unbecoming in the presence of the shaykh. Niẓām al-Dīn did not say anything but satisfied his demands. He then turned to those present, observing that many such people come, and one had to pay attention to them and give them something. They also had to come and speak whatever they had to say without restraint. The one set of acts was recompensed by the other. (The sense of the Shaykh's rather elliptical remarks is far from clear.)

2. Niẓām al-Dīn then relates the case of another of these speakers of wild words (*parēshān-gōyān*), who had said many unsuitable things, to which the shaykh had not replied, and had concluded: 'As long as the world endures, the crime (*jurm*) will be ours and yours the endurance of it (*iḥtimāl*)'.

3. Niẓām al-Dīn then relates the story of one of them coming before Farīd al-Dīn and starting to say, 'What! Have you made yourself into an idol?'

Farīd al-Dīn said, 'I have not made [*sākhta*, 'created', *sc.* 'set myself in this position']. God—may He be exalted—has made [set me there].'

'Haven't you made yourself?' the questioner repeated.

'No', replied the Shaykh, 'I have not made myself, God has made [me].'

When the questioner heard this answer, he grew ashamed.[93]

The most extended notice of the Qalandars in the *Khayr al-majālis,* which takes up the entire 38th *majlis,* or conversation, begins with a similar incident.[94]

[92] See above, p. 222.

[93] 'Alā' Sijzī, *Fawā'id al-fu'ād,* Naval Kishor, 1894, p. 48; Lahore, 1966, p. 81.

[94] Qalandar, *Khayr al-majālis,* pp. 129–32.

4. The author (Ḥamīd Qalandar) was about to partake of *iftār* with Shaykh Naṣīr al-Dīn Maḥmūd. A Qalandar who is described as 'with the characteristics of an *abdāl*' (*abdāl-ṣifat*) was present, who suddenly rose up when the servants were about to wash the hands of the guests, and left the gathering. The shaykh sent servants to bring him back, but on his return he insisted on sitting in a different place, above the author, like a madman with one knee raised up.

5. The shaykh then told a story of a Qalandar who had come to the *khānqāh* of Shaykh Farīd al-Dīn. Farīd was occupied in his cell, and on such occasions the door was closed and none had the right of entry. The *galīm*, which served as a *sajjāda* (prayer-carpet), of the shaykh was spread in front of the door, on which the Qalandar proceeded to sit. The khādim on duty was Shaykh Badr al-Dīn Isḥāq, a senior disciple, who out of politeness said nothing and brought some food before the Qalandar. The Qalandar said that he wished to see the shaykh before he ate the food. The khādim said that the shaykh was occupied inside his cell, which no one had permission to enter, and told him to eat the food, after which he would take him to the shaykh. The Qalandar stretched his hand to the food and ate. After this he drew from his person the grass (*giyāh—sc. ḥashīsh*) which the Qalandars eat and began to knead it in his *kachkūl* (begging bowl), so that droppings of it fell upon the prayer-carpet of the shaykh. Badr al-Dīn Isḥāq came forward and told him that that was enough. The Qalandar exploded and grasped the *kachkūl* to strike Badr al-Dīn with it. Shaykh Farīd ran out from inside the cell, came to the Qalandar and took his hand, asking him to forgive the khādim for his sake. The Qalandar said that *darwīshes* did not raise their hands in anger, but when they did so, they did not bring them down. The shaykh told him to strike the nearby wall. The Qalandar struck the wall with his *kachkūl* and the wall fell down. Naṣīr al-Dīn Maḥmūd then remarked that among every common

gathering there was some especial person (*miyān-i har ʻāmmī khāṣṣī hast*), and told the anecdote noted in class 3 above, followed by another regarding Jamāl al-Dīn of Sāva, also noted above. At its close, Naṣīr al-Dīn Maḥmūd persuaded the Qalandar present at his *khānqāh* to partake of the *ifṭār*. The recorder Ḥamīd remarks that he did not recognize the Qalandar, whom he had never seen before.

Two encounters between Qalandars and Sayyid Muḥammad Gēsūdarāz described in the *Ta'rīkh-i Ḥabībī* probably relate to the period after his migration from Dehlī to Gulbarga in the Deccan at the end of the fourteenth century. This shaykh's less sympathetic attitude to Qalandars has been discussed above and the anecdotes also show the Qalandars themselves behaving in a less aggressive fashion and more anxious to reach an accommodation with the shaykh.[95]

6. Informants relate that once a group of Qalandars came to the door of the Shaykh's *khānqāh*, making a loud noise and commotion and bearing a flagpole. From his occult power the shaykh knew that in the group there was also a Man of God. Therefore, he called them before him and they held *samāʻ* in their own manner. Although the shaykh did not like meeting this sect, or having his hand kissed, or conversation with them, out of consideration for the Man of God who had decided to conceal himself among them, he called them before him and endured their *samāʻ*.

7. One day a Qalandar called Manṣūr came to the door of the *khānqāh*, with the accoutrements of Qalandars—standard, lance, polo stick, and earthen drums—making useless noise and commotion. The shaykh was informed that Manṣūr Qalandar had come. He smiled and said: 'What a noise he has been making.' He kept them waiting for a while but finally had to summon him. He was brought to the shaykh after leaving outside the banner and drum which

[95] Shēr Malik, *Ta'rīkh-i Ḥabībī*, Urdu tr., pp. 108–9.

he had with him. On coming into the shaykh's presence, the Qalandar began to talk in their own special vocabulary. After kissing the feet, he sat down before the shaykh and stated that he had come because he had been sent by *pīrs*. He cited the names of various lineages and shaykhs from earlier times. The shaykh turned his eyes somewhat towards his heart and straightaway replied, 'No, no one has sent you. Come and sit down.'[96]

Then he gave an order to Qāżī Sirāj al-Dīn, who was his servant, 'Mullā, bring something to eat and give it to him.'

Finally, he gave the Qalandar some cash and sent him away.

Two further anecdotes of Qalandars with shaykhs are to be found in non-Chishtī sources. They have been briefly referred to above, but may be given in greater detail here.

1. In Delhī in the ninth decade of the fourteenth century, a Qalandar appeared in the assembly of the Suhrawardī shaykh Jalāl al-Dīn 'Makhdūm-i Jahāniyān'. He stated that he had been clad in the leather garments of the group for fifteen years and now repented. He wished to be a Ṣūfī and asked for the clothes of a Ṣūfī. The shaykh commended this and made him a *murīd* (disciple), and told him to take off his leather so that he might appear in garments which some of the friends of the Messenger of Allah had worn.[97]

2. A Qalandar wearing iron came into the assembly of Shaykh Sharaf al-Dīn Aḥmad b. Yaḥyā of Manēr. The shaykh said: 'O Darwīsh, why do you not take off your irons?'

'Is there anyone who takes them off?', he replied. The shaykh bent his head forward in *murāqaba* (meditation), and every piece of iron fell off the Qalandar's body and broke into little pieces.[98]

[96] Cf. the rejection by Gēsūdarāz of the *jogi* claiming to be a Bārgundāī (= Jālandharī, Jālandhara Nāth) discussed by S. Digby in 'Encounters with *Jogīs* in Indian Ṣūfī Hagiography' [L&WSD II, chapter 6].

[97] *Khulāṣat al-alfāẓ*, Digby MS, f. 244.

[98] Firdawsī, *Manāqib al-aṣfiyā'*, p. 140.

As in the story of the confrontation of the Majdhūb Khwāja Gurg with the Qalandar who attacked him, noticed in class 5 below, the purpose of the narrator is merely to convey the superior charisma or *baraka* of his subject. These two anecdotes, like those related in the *Ta'rīkh-i Ḥabībī* regarding Sayyid Muḥammad Gēsūdarāz, appear to indicate that at the end of the fourteenth and beginning of the fifteenth century the Qalandars had lost something of their initial force and charisma.

Class 5: Anecdotes of Murderous Attacks

A series of anecdotes of murderous attacks by Qalandars or Ḥaydarīs upon Ṣūfī shaykhs, either intended or actually carried out, show either the intense hostility of these two groups towards the great shaykhs or the condition of psychological disturbance of individuals identified as belonging to these groups.

1. One non-hagiographical source records an attack by a Ḥaydarī *faqīr* on a rival man of religion, to which we have referred above. Incited by Sultan Jalāl al-Dīn Fērōz Khaljī, a Ḥaydarī *darwīsh* called Baḥrī from among the followers of Shaykh Abū Bakr (Qalandarī Ḥaydarī Ṭūsī) attacked Sīdī Muwallih (whose execution had been noted above), wounding him with his razor and his *juwal-dōz* (sacking-needle).[99]

From the description of this incident given by Baranī we can presume the existence of an inclination to murderous acts among the Qalandar groups, which is of value in assessing the evidence when the hagiographical sources are not wholly clear as to whether the assailant was a Qalandar. Political

[99] Baranī, *Ta'rīkh-i Fērōzshāhī*, p. 211; cf. an anecdote of Qalandars threatening to attack with their needles Shaykh Zāhid Gīlānī in Shirvān at the close of the thirteenth century, *Ṣafwat al-ṣafā'*, Bombay: Maṭba'-i Muẓaffarī, AH 1329/AD 1911, p. 31. The Qalandars are punished, cf. pp. 236–7 below. I am indebted to Mr A.H. Morton for the reference.

assassination was not unknown in the Dehlī Sultanate and the memory, at any rate, of the assassinations of the Nizārī Ismā'īlīs of Alamut survived.[100] The context of the anecdote of an intended attack on the Chishtī shaykh Farīd al-Dīn also demonstrates this point. It was told by Niẓām al-Dīn on an occasion in the year AH 716 when a man had been found in his own *khānqāh* harbouring a knife, about whom the recorder, Amīr Ḥasan remarked, 'And Allāh knows best who he was!' The story of the intended attack on Farīd al-Dīn was followed by an anecdote of a *mudhakkir* (preacher) at Ghaznī, who was killed by a man with a knife when he descended from the *minbar*.[101] This clearly refers to a period before the rise of the Qalandar groups.

2. An intended attack upon Shaykh Farīd al-Dīn: the account of Niẓām al-Dīn.

One day Shaykh al-Islām Farīd al-Dīn had offered the dawn prayers and was occupied [with interior devotions]. He placed his head upon the ground and was overwhelmed with his occupation. Since it was winter and the air was cold, a fur-coat (*pōstīn*) had been brought and thrown over the body of the shaykh. There was no servitor there but myself [Niẓām al-Dīn]. Then someone came in and said *salām* in a loud voice, so much so that it distracted the shaykh. Notwithstanding the fact that his head was on the ground and the fur coat on him, he said, 'Who is there?'

[Niẓām al-Dīn] said, 'I spoke and said "I am"'.

The Shaykh then asked, 'Is the man who has come a Turk of medium height and yellow complexion?'

[100] According to one early source the conqueror Mu'izz al-Dīn Muḥammad b. Sām was murdered by an Ismā'īlī fanatic in AH 602/AD 1206, though his death at the hands of Gakkar tribesmen appears more likely. In the mid-fourteenth century Baranī refers to *fidā'īyān*, probably in this specific sense, and 'Isāmī to 'Alamūtīs' (Alamūtīyān)—'Isāmī, *Futūḥ al-salāṭīn*, p. 301, lines 1–2.

[101] 'Alā' Sijzī, *Fawā'id al-fu'ād*, Naval Kishor, 1894, p. 153–4; Lahore, 1966, p. 261.

I [Niẓām al-Dīn] looked at the man and he was as described. I replied, 'He is so'.

Then the Shaykh asked, 'Has he a chain around his waist?'

I looked at him and he had—I said, 'Yes'.

Then he asked, 'Has he something in his ears?'

I looked at him. He had, and I replied, 'Yes, he has rings'.

As I was looking at him, I gave my answer and he was disturbed. Then I said, 'Yes, he has rings in his ears'. The Shaykh said, 'Tell him to go before he is disgraced'.

When this time I turned towards him I saw that he himself had departed.[102]

This is an incident of the mid-thirteenth century, described by its only eyewitness and recorded about half a century later. It is not explicitly stated that the aggressive visitor was a Qalandar, or that he intended a murderous attack upon the Chishtī shaykh. The physical description of the man was that he was a Turk, of yellowish complexion, wearing a chain around his waist and rings in his ears. Jamālī, writing at the beginning of the sixteenth century, concerned to provide a coherent *tadhkira* of the lives of the major Chishtī and Suhrawardī shaykhs, is unlikely to have had any alternative source, and his additional details are therefore purely inferential. He states that the man was a Qalandar, had a knife (*kārd*) hidden upon his person and was urged to this attempted attack by the qāżī of Ajodhan.[103]

Regarding the inferences made by Jamālī, we may say that: (1) It is likely that the visitor contemplated a murderous attack, from the context in which the anecdote was originally recorded; (2) A Turk wearing a chain and rings in the ears

[102] 'Alā' Sijzī, *Fawā'id al-fu'ād*, Naval Kishor, 1894, p. 153; Lahore, 1966, p. 260.

[103] Jamālī, *Siyar al-'ārifīn*, pp. 34–5. See also K.A. Nizami, *The Life and Times of Shaykh Farid-ud-din Ganj-i Shakar*, Aligarh: Aligarh Muslim University, 1955, pp. 37–8, who does not rigorously examine the extent of dependence of the latter source.

is likely to have been a Ḥaydarī or Qalandar;[104] (3) It need not necessarily have been a knife which he had concealed, in view of the other anecdotes of attacks by Ḥaydarīs and Qalandars in which a razor or needle was used as the instrument of attack; (4) The detail that the man was urged to attack the shaykh by the qāżī of Ajodhan appears to have been inferred by Jamālī from another anecdote of the impotent hostility of the qāżī towards the shaykh.[105] This appears groundless, although in the incident of Sīdī Muwallih's death the Ḥaydarī attacked a member of a rival order at the behest of the Sultan.

Regarding a subsequent more effective assault on a great Chisitī shaykh, Naṣīr al-Dīn Maḥmūd, we are fortunate in possessing two long circumstantial accounts by those who, if they were not themselves eyewitnesses, were certainly closely connected with the Shaykh's *khānqāh* when the incident took place. The testimonies differ considerably in detail, as is often the case with evidence of witnesses of sudden violent acts, which is presented in the law courts of today. From one of the accounts it would not have been apparent that the attacker was a Qalandar.

3a. The attack upon Shaykh Naṣīr al-Dīn Maḥmūd: Ḥamīd Qalandar's account.

One day after performing the noonday prayer the Shaykh went from the *jamā'at-khāna* to his private chamber (*ḥujra-yi khāṣṣ*). He had no doorman; his special servant was Shaykh Zayn al-Dīn 'Alī, his sister's son. He also used to attend him in his private quarters, but sometimes he was not there. While the Shaykh was occupied [in meditation] a reckless unclean Qalandar came into his private room. He had a knife at his waist and began to stab

[104] The founder of the Ḥaydarīs is described as of Turkish stock, cf. 'Alā' Sijzī, *Fawā'id al-fu'ād*, Naval Kishor, 1894, p. 19; Lahore, 1966, p. 30; quoted above.

[105] 'Alā' Sijzī, *Fawā'id al-fu'ād*, Naval Kishor, 1894, p. 96; Lahore, 1966, p. 166; *Siyar al-ārifīn*, p. 43.

the Shaykh with it. He stabbed the Shaykh's pure body eleven times. The Shaykh was totally absorbed (*dar istighrāq*) and did not interfere. There was a conduit in that room and his blessed blood came out through that conduit. Some disciples who saw this went inside and they saw this reckless Qalandar stab the Shaykh while the Shaykh said nothing. The disciples wanted to punish the wretch severely, but the Shaykh did not allow anyone to harm him in any way. He made 'Abd al-Muqtadir Thānēsarī, who was one of his special disciples, and Shaykh Ṣadr al-Dīn the physician, swear in his presence that no one should be concerned to injure the Qalandar. He also gave 20 silver *tankas* (*tanka-yi safēd*)[106] to the Qalandar on the grounds that perhaps when he was stabbing with the knife his own hand had been injured.... After this incident the Shaykh lived three more years.[107]

3b. The murderous attack on Shaykh Naṣīr al-Dīn Maḥmūd: the account of Sayyid Muḥammad Gēsūdarāz.

The conversation turned to the orders of Shaykh al-Islām Niẓām al-Dīn. [Gēsūdarāz] said:

There was a madman called Tūrābī who used to go in private with the shaykh and once he was as usual alone with the shaykh. He rose and took a pencutter's knife and began to stab the shaykh. The story which the shaykh used to tell himself is a long one. Its point is that he stabbed the shaykh five times with the knife. While he was striking the shaykh he kept on saying, 'Tūrābī, what has happened to you? And what has occurred to the hand in front of you?'

[106] The reference is to the pure silver *tanka* of c. 170 grains, very rare in this reign, as opposed to the debased billion *tanka* of c. 140 grains. Cf. H. Nelson Wright, *The Coinage and Metrology of the Sultans of Dehlī*, Delhi: Manager of Publications, 1936, p. 218; Digby, *War-Horse and Elephant in the Dehli Sultanate*, p. 39; ibid., chapter on the currency of the Indian Sultanates in *The Cambridge Economic History of India* (forthcoming) [since published; also *L&WSD* V.4].

[107] Qalandar, *Khayr al-majālis*, pp. 286–7. From the last sentence it is apparent that the incident must have taken place around AH 754/AD 1353.

He put his hand in front of Tūrābī and Tūrābī stabbed until all the fingers of the shaykh had been cut, to the extent that when he wrote he used to keep his fingers unbent and in the ritual of prayer his fingers remained straight. At last the blood passed from the room of the shaykh over the courtyard which was ten *gaz*[108] broad and flowed out through a conduit to a place near the kitchen where Mawlānā Zayn al-Dīn and other *khādims* were sitting. When they saw the streak of blood they ran up. Mawlānā Zayn al-Dīn came first. Tūrābī pursued Mawlānā Zayn al-Dīn, ran and hit him with the knife. The latter put out his hand to parry it and he too was somewhat wounded in the hand: the skin was cut. Finally, Khwāja Bashīr caught him and took the knife from his hand.

Shaykh Niẓām al-Dīn used to say, 'It was the grace of God that at that moment I had not lost consciousness, for I said that anyone who said anything about this would incur my displeasure. If I had not said this, people of the house would have cut him to pieces.'

In the city an uproar broke out that the shaykh had been stabbed. Some said that he was dead, others the contrary. People who heard this story in the bazaars or at home bared their heads and began to weep. The pencutter's knife was small and its work ineffectual. Only one wound under the ribs (*nazdīk-i tuhīgāh*) was serious. Physicians, people, the Qāżī Ṣadr-i Jahān and the Khāṣṣ Ḥājib Malik Nathū all came to visit the shaykh. Malik Nathū said:

'I am the King's official. Hand over Tūrābī to me'.

The shaykh did so and said to Ṣadr-i Jahān:

'Qāżī Ṣadr-i Jahān, I am the injured party. They are the next-of-kin: I have forgone my right [to blood-money]. The next-of-kin are my brothers' and sisters' children. They are present and they have also forgone it'.

The Qāżī asked: 'You also forgo it?'

[108] I have no evidence for the length of the *gaz* in fourteenth-century Dehlī. It is fairly well defined in H. Yule and A.C. Burnell, *Hobson-Jobson*, London: J. Murray, 1903 [1886], s.v. 'gudge': 'A Persian yard-measure of thereabouts; but in India applied to measures of varying lengths, from the *hath* or natural cubit, to the English yard'.

They replied: 'We have also forgone it. Legally there is no charge against him'.

Ṣadr-i Jahān said: 'I will go to the *wālī* [local governor] and tell him. We shall do as he orders'.

In those days Malik Kabīr was the governor [of Dehlī] in the sultan's absence (*nā'ib-i ghaybat*). Ṣadr-i Jahān went and stated the case to him:

'He does not incur any legal blood-money',[109] he replied.

Tūrābī was in the house of Malik Nathū, and on the day when he was released, the people (*khalq*) were standing with stones ready in their hands in the streets and bazaars, saying, 'When he comes out, now, let us stone him!' The shaykh sent for Malik Nathū and said: 'The populace will kill him. Send fifty footguards (*pā'ik*) with him; and he is also hungry.' The shaykh ordered two *tankas* to be given to him. 'Take him and release him outside the city and come back'.

They took him out with the populace wanting to stone him, but when they saw the footguards to the left and right of him and not allowing anyone to get near him, the populace made no move. After a year or two Malik Kabīr happened to meet the shaykh. He said:

'The sultan has written asking what I have done to the assassin of Shaykh Maḥmūd: what am I to write?'

The shaykh replied: 'If things come to a head, I will arrange it with the sultan myself'.[110]

Of the two accounts, the first is found in the biographical supplement to the *Khayr al-majālis* which Ḥamīd Qalandar claimed to have completed in AH 756, the year of Niẓām al-Dīn's death,[111] whereas that of Gēsūdarāz, claiming to be based on Naṣīr al-Dīn Maḥmūd's own account of the incident, was recorded in his conversations of around AD 1400. Yet

[109] Or, possible, we should amend *zi rūyi shar'*, for the lithograph's reading *zarī-yi shar'*, 'He is not guilty according to the law'.

[110] *Jawāmī' al-kalim*, Haydarabad, Deccan: Intizami Press, AH 1356, pp. 90–2.

[111] Qalandar, *Khayr al-majālis*, p. 289.

Gēsūdarāz's account appears the more circumstantial and we cannot be certain that AH 756 was the true date of composition of the supplement of the *Khayr al-majālis.*[112] Significant details in which the two accounts differ may be noted. Gēsūdarāz calls the would-be assassin Tūrābī and states that he was a madman. Ḥamīd calls him 'a reckless unclean Qalandar' (*qalandar-i bē-bāk-i nā-pāk*) and repeats the word Qalandar three more times. As Ḥamīd himself was a Qalandar we may accept his testimony on the point.[113] Ḥamīd describes the shaykh as totally absorbed at the time of the assault, while Gēsūdarāz shows him gently reasoning with the assailant. Gēsūdarāz has him stab the shaykh five times, mainly on the fingers, with a serious wound under the ribs, and mentions that it was only a pencutter's knife that was used. Ḥamīd states that he was stabbed eleven times. Gēsūdarāz provides a much more circumstantial account of the assailant's release, which Naṣīr al-Dīn Maḥmūd was obliged to negotiate with the civil authority. Ḥamīd makes Naṣīr al-Dīn Maḥmūd give the assailant 20 'silver' *tankas*, but according to Gēsūdarāz it was the more reasonable sum of 2 *tankas*, to satisfy his hunger, probably of the devalued billon variety current early in Fērōz Shāh Tughluq's reign.[114]

[112] The supplement is lacking in one of the two complete manuscripts; and, as I show elsewhere, Ḥamīd Qalandar appears to be propagating a misleading account of some details of the shaykh's death, to which the alleged date of composition would lend a spurious authority.

[113] The statement by Gēsūdarāz that the man used to visit Naṣīr al-Dīn Maḥmūd in private seems to indicate that this was an attack motivated more by individual psychological disturbance than by coherent ideological hostility.

[114] See Wright, *The Coinage and Metrology*, pp. 163–4, 174, 218; see also above, n. 106. Following his eastern expedition, Fērōz Shāh Tughluq distributed bags of silver to mosques and Ṣūfī establishments in Dehlī in August 1354 (Baranī, *Ta'rīkh-i Fērōzshāhī*, p. 597); but Ḥamīd appears to be mentioning silver *tankas* at a time some months or a year before the supply of this coin in Dehlī was replenished.

A further anecdote mentions a murderous attack by a Qalandar directed not against a Ṣūfī shaykh of the great *silsilas* but against a *majdhūb*. The *majdhūbs*, literally those irresistibly drawn away and, therefore, not accountable for their actions, were individuals distinguished by a divine frenzy or madness. Unlike the Qalandars, who usually travelled in bands, they were generally solitaries and established figures in particular urban settlements. This anecdote comes from *Asrār al-majdhūbīn* ('Secrets of the drawn-away'), composed in the later fourteenth century about a figure living in the important settlement of Karra, near modern Allahabad, some seventy years earlier. It is a crude contest-anecdote, the purpose of which is to exalt the charisma of the subject of the hagiography over possible rival objects of devotion. As with many other anecdotes in this hagiography of Khwāja Gurg, it is a fanciful tale which can have little basis in reality.

The anecdote concerns a Qalandar with his companions who attempted to kill Khwāja Gurg in his sleep and were mauled by lions. Having received their deserts, they were driven from the settlement of Karra by the *muḥtasib* on the following day.

4. An attack by Qalandars on Khwāja Gurg of Karra, late thirteenth century.

It is related that one day Khwāja Gurg was asleep.[115] An unlucky Qalandar was an enemy of Khwāja Gurg and with several persons tried to kill him. Each of them wished to harm the Khwāja but they saw that from all four quarters lions appeared.[116] They seized

[115] In modern times this Ṣūfī figure is known as Khwāja Kaṛak (Hindi, 'thunderclap') but it is clear from this work that the name must be read as Gurg (Persian, 'wolf'), cf. the reference to himself in this passage as 'a wolflike sheep'.

[116] *Shērān*: the writer is probably using the word loosely for beasts of prey.

the Qalandar who was Khwāja Gurg's enemy and brought him to the ground. They blinded the eyes of each of them and crushed their hands. When the Khwāja awoke from his sleep, he saw the Qalandars lying there and said:

'By the lady's head![117] This was what you were hunting!'

They said, 'O Khwāja, we have repented and we have learnt the truth of your spiritual jurisdiction (*wilāyat*): Now forgive us, for we have committed a great sin.'

'How is this?' the Khwāja said.

'We have sought to kill the Khwāja', they replied. 'When we came here we wanted to injure you. We saw lions appear on all four sides, which struck us to the ground and wounded our hands and feet and eyes.'

'By the truth of God who has created your desire and that of the eighteen thousand worlds, I have no knowledge of this. I have not seen man or wolf near me, but rather have made myself a wolflike sheep (*gusfand-i gurgīn*). I have enmity towards none. If you desire to kill me be quick and kill me, in the name of Allāh the Merciful, the Compassionate; for I have no hatred or resentment at all.'

As he was speaking the Qalandars grew ashamed, and then fell at the feet of the Khwāja like slaves and wept. The Khwāja said:

'Your weeping is of no profit now. What was ordained has come to pass'.

The next day the whole being of the Qalandars was pulverized and the *muḥtasib* drove them out of the city.[118]

Available references of our class 6 have been utilized above.[119]

[117] *Ay bībī kā sīr* [*sic*]. This Hindī exclamation frequently occurs in Khwāja Gurg's conversation reproduced in the work.

[118] Muḥammad Ismā'īl, *Asrār al-majdhūbīn*, Digby MS 10, ff. 6a–b; for a lithographed ed., title mistranscribed, Fathpur, 1893, see C.A. Storey, *Persian Literature: a Bio-Bibliographical Survey*, London: Royal Asiatic Society, 1977, p. 141, no. 38.

[119] See above, pp. 199–202, 214.

We have now squeezed dry the evidence on the activities of the Qalandars and related groups in the Dehlī Sultanate, reproducing all possibly significant details and advancing upon the sum of it some speculative hypotheses for which confirmation is lacking. A number of examples of the *malfūẓ* and *tadhkira* literature of the period have not been accessible to us, through lack of time or industry or because they exist in remote or inaccessible collections. It is to be expected that these will provide further items of evidence.

In the fifteenth century a curtain of darkness descends on the activities of the Ḥaydarīs and Qalandars in South Asia. This is a period when the Ṣūfī hagiographical sources decline in quality, becoming much less rich in circumstantial and anecdotal detail. The name Qalandar survives as a description of a recognizable group down to the present day; and two graves of thirteenth-century Qalandars have remained the centres of Ṣūfī cults of importance, that of Bū ʻAlī at Panipat and that of ʻUthmān Marandī (Laʻl Shāhbāz) at Sehvān in Sind. The name Ḥaydarī disappears in India, while in Iran the followers of Ḥaydar of Zāva became a Shīʻa *darwīsh* order. It is possible that many similar devotees became absorbed into low-class Muslim religious groups bearing other names, the Madārīs in northern India or the Rifāʻīs in the Deccan.[120]

[120] K. Ewing's recent field research in Lahore indicates that Madārīs and Qalandars are to some extent synonymous in the Panjab, as are Malangs. The preoccupation with the use of drugs of the *ḥashīsh* family is still strong, as it was among both Qalandars and Madārīs in earlier centuries. The depilation or shaving of all facial and bodily hair, with leather garments, survived in the Panjab in the late nineteenth century, as in Sir D. Ibbetson's ethnographic description (quoted by Ewing, '*Malangs* of the Punjab', p. 50, n. 56 [published version, p. 358]), but this has apparently now vanished, and the Qalandars have become confluent with such peculiarly Indian *bē-sharʻ* groups as the Sadā Suhāgins ('perpetual brides') who dress in women's clothes and ornaments. Celibacy is maintained, as well as an open-air life wandering on a round of *'urs* festivals, except

When sources again become more copious in the sixteenth and seventeenth centuries, the wandering Qalandar groups do not attain the same prominence in South Asia which they possessed during the thirteenth and fourteenth centuries, nor are there records of their provocative acts against more orthodox branches of the Ṣūfī establishment.

Appendix

Bū 'Alī of Panipat, Fakhr al-Dīn 'Irāqī, and the Chishtī Shaykhs: The Embellishment of a Legend

In the northern half of the Indian subcontinent two Qalandar shrines became established among the grave-cults of early Ṣūfī shaykhs, that of 'Uthmān Marandī (La'l Shāhbāz) at Sehvān and that of Bū 'Alī Qalandar at Panipat. 'Uthmān Marandī is established as a figure of importance in his own lifetime by the historian Baranī's allusion to him, noticed in this paper.[121] The case of Bū 'Alī is less well attested. He does not find mention in the *Fawā'id al-fu'ād* or the *Siyar al-awliyā'*. A late seventeenth-century *tadhkira*, the *Sharaf al-manāqib* of Shaykh Ḥamīd b. Shāh Budh, claims to draw upon earlier written sources as well as upon the oral tradition at the shrine. The date of Bū 'Alī's death is given as 9 Ramażān 724/30 August 1324, at an alleged age of 122 lunar years. Given the importance of the date of death at *'urs* festivals, we may accept this date as possibly genuine. Bū 'Alī would therefore be a Qalandar of the late thirteenth century, when the order had considerable power and prestige in north

in the case of professed Qalandars who also have a claim to be *sajjāda nashīn* of a Ṣūfī *khānqāh* or tomb, on whom it is thought to be incumbent to marry and continue the lineage.

121 See pp. 210–11 and n. 61, above.

India, who had established himself as a charismatic figure at Panipat, an ancient town and early stage on the road from Dehlī to the north.

An element in the traditions regarding him which appears to be early is the narrative of his attraction to young boys and his relations with them. Like a crazed *'āshiq* he is said often to have been stoned by them in the streets, at which he would remark that he was in the seventh heaven, where angels were honouring him and blowing trumpets. Boys would come to live in his *khānqāh*, but he would turn them out when their beards began to grow.[122] He did not marry, and the inheritance of the shrine appears to have been transmitted through his brother's children. The author of the *Sharaf al-manāqib* claimed descent from this brother, Shaykh Niẓām al-Dīn 'Irāqī.

From the *Sharaf al-manāqib* it is clear that Bū 'Alī was not a member of a wandering Qalandar band. He was born at Panipat, where he established his *khānqāh*, and his wanderings do not appear to have taken him further afield than the neighbouring capital city of Dehlī. Attempts had evidently been made to identify his spiritual authority with a Suhrawardī or a Chishtī lineage. It had been stated that he had professed allegiance (*bay'at*) to Quṭb al-Dīn Bakhtyār Kākī, or to an obscure Suhrawardī whose tomb is also stated to have been at Dehlī, Shaykh Shihāb al-Dīn, *khalīfa* of Imām al-Dīn Abdāl (the *abdāl* association may be noted). The author of the *Sharaf al-manāqib* rejects both these founts of authority, stating that Bū 'Alī had received instruction from the pure spirit of Ḥażrat 'Alī, son-in-law of the Prophet. He states that 'Abd al-Ḥaqq had written in the *Akhbār al-akhyār* that there is no mention of his allegiance being to either of these *buzurgs*, but Bū 'Alī was in the habit of attending the assemblies of Quṭb al-Dīn. There is, however, no notice of

[122] Ḥamīd al-Dīn, *Sharaf al-manāqib*, p. 8.

Bū 'Alī in the AH 1209 edition of the *Akhbār al-akhyār*,[123] and Quṭb al-Dīn Bakhtyār Kākī predeceased Bū 'Alī by ninety-one lunar years. The connection therefore appears to be a much later hagiographical invention. The same is probably true of the accounts of his relations with his contemporary at Dehlī, Shaykh Niẓām al-Dīn Awliyā', as these find no mention in the fourteenth-century Chishtī sources. A more interesting connection is made in the account of his parentage. His father is stated to have been Shaykh Fakhr al-Dīn Sālār 'Irāqī; his mother's name is given as Bībī Ḥāfiẓa bint Jamāl.

The identification of Bū 'Alī's father with the famous Fakhr al-Dīn 'Irāqī is made in a variant of the anecdote which has been cited in the text of this paper, regarding 'Irāqī joining a Qalandar band and his reception as a *murīd* by Shaykh Bahā' al-Dīn Zakariyā'. The name of the mother may indicate a claim of descent from the poet and Chishtī *khalīfa* Shaykh Jamāl al-Dīn Hansavī, but this is not made explicit by the *Sharaf al-manāqib*. Chronologically neither of these claims regarding Bū 'Alī's parentage appears well founded.[124]

Nevertheless, if the claim that Bū 'Alī was the son of the poet 'Irāqī was an ancient one, possibly made by him or during his lifetime, it helps to explain his identification as a Qalandar. Many of the *manāqib* recorded of him, his lack of attachment to a band, and his sedentary life in a particular locality would make him fit better into the category of a *majdhūb*. A characteristic anecdote appearing more in that

[123] See n. 7, above.

[124] The poets Fakhr al-Dīn 'Irāqī and Jamāl al-Dīn Hasnavī were contemporaries, the latter being acquainted with some of the *ghazals* of 'Irāqī and writing *jawābs* ('replies') in the same metre, which in fact provide evidence dating these *ghazals* to the earlier portion of his life spent in the *khānqāh* of Bahā' al-Dīn Zakariyā' in Multān. Hānsī, where Jamāl al-Dīn resided, like Ajodhan, lay on a main route between Multān and Dehlī. I am indebted to Dr R.J. Baldick, currently working on the life and poetry of 'Irāqī, for drawing my attention to the connection.

tradition records why he did not observe the ritual duties of Islam:

In his passion for God he experienced seventy orgasms in a night. Thus for several nights he performed ablutions seventy times. From washing with cold water his body was split—'and in such a place'—and the Unseen Voice (*hātif-i ghayb*) told him that by God and by the Prophet he was exempted (*ma'dhūr*) and excused (*mu'āf*) from the performance of a prayer.[125]

Bū 'Alī's founding of the *khānqāh* at Panipat established claims to a local territorial *wilāyat* similar to that exercised by more orthodox Ṣūfī shaykhs during their lifetimes and after their deaths. An anecdote in the *Sharaf al-manāqib* depicts Bū 'Alī engaged in a levitatory contest of a type I have examined elsewhere, in which he vanquished a *jogī* and established his control over a subsidiary site in the vicinity of Panipat. 'To this day the grave of the Jogī and the seat of Abū 'Alī are to be found on that hill and are a pilgrimage-place for rich and poor.'[126]

The Qalandar identification ensured that in later times the graves of Bū 'Alī at Panipat and of Shaykh 'Uthmān Marandī at Sehvan became major pilgrimage centres for Qalandars and other confluent groups in their annual round of travels.

[125] Ḥamīd al-Dīn, *Sharaf al-manāqib*, p. 7.

[126] Ibid., p. 36; see the revised version of my paper mentioned above, n. 96 [in this series, *L&WSD* II, § 'Class 3, ii, 6: Abū 'Alī Qalandar's Contest with the *Jogī* on the Hill'].

8

The *Tuḥfa i naṣā'iḥ* of Yūsuf Gadā

An Ethical Treatise in Verse from the Late-Fourteenth-Century Dehlī Sultanate

This chapter is concerned with the work called *Tuḥfa i naṣā'iḥ* or *Tuḥfa an-naṣā'iḥ* (A present of counsels), which, for reasons detailed below, may be ascribed with confidence to the last decade of the fourteenth century of the Christian Era and to a milieu connected with the great Indo-Muslim capital city of Dehlī. The number of surviving manuscripts and of recorded lithographed editions shows that it enjoyed popularity as a work of edification and instruction among Indian Muslims throughout the Mughal period and until the beginning of the twentieth century.

The popularity of the *Tuḥfa i naṣā'iḥ* sets it apart from other ethical works produced in the Dehlī Sultanate. Its transmission is in striking contrast to that of the two great 'Mirrors for Princes' of the Dehlī Sultanate, works of a far higher literary quality. Two manuscripts of the *Ādāb al-harb wa ash-shajā'a*[1] of Fakhr i Mudabbir and but one of the *Fatāwā*

* Originally published in Barbara Daly Metcalf, ed., *Moral Conduct and Authority: The Place of Adab in South Asian Islam*, Berkeley: University of California Press, 1984, pp. 91–123.

[1] Fakhr i Mudabbir, *Ādāb al-harb wa ash-shajā'a*, ed. E.S. Khwansari, Tehran: Iqbāl, Shamsi 1346/AD 1967; Ziya' al-Dīn Baranī, *Fatāwā i jahāndārī*, ed. A. Salim Khan, Lahore: Idārah-i Tahqīqāt-i Pākistān, Dānishgāh-i Panjāb, 1972.

i jahāndārī of Ḍiyā' ad-Dīn Baranī have survived the ravages of time. Although, as we shall see below, the popularity of the *Tuḥfa i naṣā'iḥ* owes something to its author's Chishtī connections and to erroneous ascriptions to Chishtī shaikhs of importance, the number of manuscript copies recorded exceeds that of any Ṣūfī devotional work of the sultanate period; and the number of recorded lithographed editions greatly exceeds even those of Amīr Ḥasan's *Fawā'id al-fu'ād.*[2]

As in the case of other Indo-Muslim works, errors in the description of the *Tuḥfa i naṣā'iḥ* have travelled from catalogue to catalogue, and it is therefore necessary to establish:

1. That this Persian poem is an Indo-Muslim work of the period of the Dehlī Sultanate;
2. The correct date of composition;
3. What reliable information exists regarding the author.

The *Tuḥfa i naṣā'iḥ* is a verse treatise in an unusual, perhaps unparalleled literary form. The author describes his poem as a *mathnawī*, but it does not follow the universally accepted verse form of a Persian *mathnawī*, of mutually independent *baits* or couplets, the hemistich of each of which rhyme with one another. Metrically, it can best be classed as an extended *qaṣīda*, but with subject matter and arrangement uncharacteristic of this verse form. The *baits* are in the metre *rajaz muthamman* (eight 'feet' of the measure *mustaf'ilun*) with the *rawī rā'*. For the benefit of those more familiar with European prosodic notation, one may explain that each couplet is a quantitative octameter, each foot

[2] Amīr Ḥasan Sijzī, *Fawā'id al-fu'ād*, ed. M.L. Malik, Lahore: Malik Sirāj al-Dīn and Sons, 1966. Despite the popularity of this collection in fourteenth-century Dehlī (see Ziya' al-Dīn Baranī, *Ta'rīkh-i Fērōzshāhī*, Calcutta: Bibliotheca Indica, 1862, p. 346), manuscripts are scarce in public collections. This relatively critical modern edition is based on three nineteenth-century lithographed editions and three Urdu lithographed translations.

being – – ˘ –, with a caesura between the two hemistichs and the terminal rhyme *–ar*. The number of *baits* in the *Tuḥfa i naṣā'iḥ* is variously estimated by differing colophons or unusually industrious cataloguers between 771 and 785. The numbers most often mentioned seem to be 775 and 776, and the range of variation is remarkably small. We may accept, therefore, that the textual transmission has been subject to few interpolations (some possibly of the author himself) and few losses due to the carelessness of scribes.

The versification, by the standards of courtly Persian poetry, verges on doggerel, partly as a result of the intractable and monotonous rhyme scheme that the author has chosen, but there are also many false quantities that cannot be righted by any textual emendation, a tendency to add or omit short vowels in consonantal groups in accordance with the lax standards of popular Indo-Muslim pronunciation, and equally in accord with this tradition, a tendency to ignore the genitive *iḍāfa*.

The syntax agrees with that of Indo-Persian writers of the fourteenth century, showing the influence of Modern Indo-Aryan causative verbal constructions and a general lack of conformity to the self-consciously correct Persian norms that were characteristic of later Mughal authors. In the poem we find references to non-Iranian habits—e.g. the eating of *tambul* (*pān*)—and also common north Indian words constantly employed by fourteenth-century Indo-Persian authors (Baranī, Amīr Ḥasan, Amīr Khusrau, 'Afīf)—e.g. *karoh*, 'kos' (a measure of distance), *lak*, 'a lac' (100,000), *pag*, a turban. The linguistic evidence strongly indicates that the *Tuḥfa i naṣā'iḥ* is an Indian work, most probably written in the fourteenth or fifteenth century of the Christian era.

This evidence is strongly supported by that of the distribution of manuscripts. Subject to the vagaries or errors of cataloguers, in the published catalogues to which I have had access or reference there are seventeen recorded manuscripts in collections in South Asia and eleven in collections in the Western world (including St. Petersburg [Leningrad] and Philadelphia); many of the latter are of demonstrable South Asian provenance. There appears to be no corresponding distribution of manuscripts in Iran or Central Asia, though copies of the late-nineteenth-century lithographic printings must have reached Iran and Central Asia in consignments from Indian booksellers.[3]

Having established the likelihood of the composition of this work in South Asia, we may turn to the internal evidence provided by the text itself regarding authorship and date of composition. The author calls himself Yūsuf Gadā (Yūsuf the Beggar). The third poem of the work, the *madḥ* or eulogium in praise of a Muslim holy man, is addressed according to the common rubric to *Shaikh al-'ālamain Maḥmūd Naṣīr ad-Dīn*; a variant rubric more specifically states *Bandagī Shaikh Maḥmūd Naṣīr ad-Dīn Chirāgh i Dihlawī*. Even given that the less specific rubric *Shaikh al-'ālamain* is commonly found in Ṣūfī sources of the Dehlī Sultanate referring to the great shaikhs of the Indian Chishtī tradition and that the *laqab* Naṣīr ad-Dīn with the *ism* Maḥmūd may be expected in conjunction with each other,[4] the identification with the great Chishtī shaikh of mid-fourteenth-century Dehlī may be regarded as extremely plausible. This section clearly refers to the death of the shaikh in question: 'The travellers (of the Ṣūfī path) became blind when that Lord of vision departed.'[5] We are therefore limited to a date of composition after the reliably recorded death of Shaikh Naṣīr al-Dīn Maḥmūd in AH 757/AD 1356.

[3] In the search for catalogue entries regarding manuscripts of the *Tuḥfa i naṣā'iḥ*, I must acknowledge the assistance afforded by the late Professor C.A. Storey's unpublished notes and index cards in the library of the Royal Asiatic Society of Great Britain and Ireland, London.

[4] The conjunction derives from Qur'ān, 17: 81–2.

[5] MS A, f. 2a; lithograph, p. 4; MS B, f. 3b. For the three texts used in preparing this paper, see note 12 below.

The conclusion of the work records the date of completion. In order to get all the information into a single couplet, the final couplet is in a rather crabbed style, *metri gratia* omitting *iḍāfas*:

Hifṣad nawwad (u) panj dīgar hijra muḥammad mustafā 'Ashir rabī'i ākhirīn waqt i ḍuḥā' roz i qamar

In the year of the Hijrat of Muhammad Mustafa, seven hundred ninety and five
The tenth of the latter Rabi', a midday, Monday.[6]

This corresponds to the Christian date 24 May 1393. There is about it the measure of confusion that we would expect in scribal traditions of older Indo-Muslim texts in the transcription of this date as found in some manuscripts. In one of the India Office Library copies, *nawwad* has been corrupted by the transposition of a single dot to *būd* (was), yielding a date of AH 705. According to Dorn, the date in the St. Petersburg manuscript reads AH 752, which Ethé, while cataloguing the India Office Library manuscripts, thought, in view of the reference to Maḥmūd Naṣīr al-Dīn, had 'decidedly the better chance'. Dorn's reading and Ethé's opinion are duly quoted by other cataloguers, but Sarfarāz, dealing with the manuscript in the Bombay University library and reading with attention the couplet which I have cited above, drily remarked: 'I am afraid that 752 has no chance at all.' Sarfarāz has given the best published description of the contents of this poem.[7] His only error I have been able to detect is a miscalculation of the equivalent Christian date by about three months. One may safely say that a majority of the

[6] Litho., p. 87; MS B, f. 95b.
[7] Shaykh 'Abd al-Qādir-i Sarfarāz, *A Descriptive Catalogue of the Arabic, Persian, and Urdu Manuscripts in the Library of the University of Bombay*, Bombay: University of Bombay, 1935, pp. 129–32.

manuscripts and lithographic transcriptions give the date as 795, and that this date is historically possible. For a volume concerned with a much broader topic, as is this collection of essays, I perhaps should not have devoted so much space to establishing this small but significant detail, yet it relates to a general point that I wish to make, that in almost every aspect of older Indo-Muslim history it is unwise to accept the descriptions or received opinions of earlier scholars as a safe basis for the erection of more theoretical structures.

As mentioned above, at least twenty-eight copies of the *Tuḥfa i naṣā'iḥ* are recorded in catalogues of manuscripts. Of these, six are in the Asafiyyah Library, Hyderabad, Deccan, but unfortunately this catalogue does not distinguish between manuscripts and lithographic printings. Twelve manuscripts bear dates in their colophons. The earliest is Ethé, India Office Library 2559, dated AH 1097/AD 1685–6. Six are of the twelfth century Hijrī and five of the thirteenth. The latest of these, which is in the Lewis Collection at Philadelphia, is dated AH 1261/AD 1845. No fewer than twenty-three separate lithographic printings have been noted, of which eighteen are to be found in the India Office Library, four (one duplicate of an edition in the IOL) in the British National Library, and two in the writer's own collection. The earliest recorded printing is of AH 1282/AD 1866–7, and the latest of AD 1928. Editions of 1914 and 1924 carry an interlinear Pashto translation and one of 1920 an interlinear Urdu verse translation; all of these were printed at Lahore. Recorded places of printing of these lithographs are Bombay (two: 1283/1866–7, BNL; 1289/1872–3, SD), Delhi (two), Lahore (eight, including those with interlinear translations), and Hyderabad (one, SD). Many printings have interlinear glosses and commentaries and super-commentaries on the margins, the latest additions to which are sometimes those of the scribe for the lithograph, who may also be the manager of the press. Although the commentaries are of value in identifying *ḥadīth* on which Yūsuf Gadā's opinions were based, they are often misleading in their interpretations of verses whose meaning would be obscure to a nineteenth-century reader.

The India Office Library's heavy holding of Lahore printings probably reflects more zealous remittances from that place to the library's official collection in London. The late date of the printings with interlinear vernacular translations reflects the reason for this work eventually passing out of currency in the present century, viz., the decline of Persian as a vehicle for elementary instruction among the Muslims of South Asia, particularly in the teaching of children in their home household or under the instruction of a local *maulawī*. No printing after AD 1928 has been recorded.[8]

The *Tuḥfa i naṣā'iḥ* is therefore a work completed in the last decade of the fourteenth century, about five years before the catastrophe of Amīr Tīmūr's invasion of Dehlī,

[8] For the India Office Library holdings, see A.J. Arberry, *Catalogue of the Library of the India Office*, London: Secretary of State for India, 1937, vol. II, part VI, p. 542. Arberry does not note the places of printing of a number of editions, but the IOL does not appear to have received copies from Bombay or Hyderabad, Deccan. The place of printing affords only approximate evidence of the market for which the edition was intended. Thus, many lithographs printed in Bombay were intended mainly for the market in Hyderabad state, in some cases being actually commissioned from there, whereas the Lahore printings with Pashto translation must have mainly circulated in the North-West Frontier Province and Afghanistan.

Modern Iranian bibliographers, following Khān Bābā Mushar, *Fihrist i kitābhā i chāpī-i fārsī*, 2nd edn., Tehran: Chāpkhānah-i Arzhang, 1972, p. 812, do not indicate to what extent their list derives from Arberry's catalogue or is based on copies held in Iranian libraries. No manuscripts from Iran appear to be recorded. In the later nineteenth century, lithographic editions of specifically Indo-Muslim texts reached the Persian booksellers from India, and introduced such works for the first time to an Iranian readership.

not predominantly Ṣūfī in content but by an author with metropolitan Chishtī affiliation. Although Yūsuf Gadā expressed the hope that it would attain a worldwide reputation, it was written for his young son, called in the text Abū al-Fatḥ Rukn i Dīn (*Rukn ad-Dīn*). The son is called 'my pretty-faced boy' (*an walad i khwush laqā*), 'new moon' (*māh i nau*), and even 'soul of his father' (*jān i pidar*); he is not yet pubertal (*bāligh*). Given that Yūsuf Gadā was a disciple of Naṣīr al-Dīn Maḥmūd (d. AH 757) and that the poem was written thirty-eight Muslim years later, this suggests that he became father of this son at a moderate age. Yūsuf Gadā was unlikely to have been accepted as a *murīd* of the shaikh before he was 12 or 13 years old. If his son was 14 years old or younger in AH 795, he must have been born in AH 781 or later. At the nearest perimeter, Yūsuf Gadā would have been thirty-seven Muslim years old at the time when this son was born to him, which is well within the bounds of probability. If we take into account Yūsuf Gadā's extremely unfavourable sentiments towards women, which are examined below, it is not unlikely that these reflect a late marriage or a previous marital experience.

The date of composition and the age of the author are important in enabling us to reject two false ascriptions of the *Tuḥfa i naṣā'iḥ*, which may have played a role in its subsequent popularity among Indian Muslims, particularly in the Deccan. Yūsuf Gadā would have been acquainted with other disciples of Shaikh Naṣīr al-Dīn Maḥmūd, and therefore with Sayyid Muḥammad Gēsūdarāz, who claimed to be the principal heir of the shaikh's *baraka* (spiritual authority). Gēsūdarāz left Dehlī shortly before Amīr Tīmūr's invasion on his progress to the Deccan capital of Gulbarga. Yūsuf Gadā's work would have been in circulation as a recent composition in the same Chishtī circles. It is probably that one or more manuscripts of the *Tuḥfa i naṣā'iḥ* accompanied the entourage of Gēsūdarāz on his southward migration and would have been placed in the *khānqāh* library at Gulbarga.

In one of the manuscripts in the Mulla Firuz Library at Bombay there is apparently an ascription to Sayyid Muḥammad Gēsūdarāz himself. This may be rejected on the following grounds:

1. Gēsūdarāz was the author of numerous Persian compositions, the highly literate style of which is in total contrast to that of the *Tuḥfa i naṣā'iḥ*;
2. In his elegant Persian *ghazals* he most frequently used the *takhalluṣ* Muḥammad; and there is no record of Yūsuf among his personal names.[9]

An attribution that is found beside all the notices in the Asafiyyah catalogue is to Sayyid Shāh Yūsuf, known as Rājā or Rājū Qattāl, the father of Sayyid Muḥammad Gēsūdarāz. This is repeated in the Peshawar catalogue. Against this ascription the following evidence appears decisive: according to Gēsūdarāz's own testimony, recorded in early-fifteenth-century sources, he was born in AH 721, and became a disciple of Shaikh Naṣīr al-Dīn on 16 Rajab AH 736, after the death of his father.[10] He would therefore have been 74

[9] In his *Dīwān* called *Anīs al-'ushshāq*, Gēsūdarāz often does not append any *takhalluṣ* to his *ghazals*. Apart from Muḥammad, he also refers to himself as Abū al-Fatḥ and Muḥammadī, if all the *ghazals* in this brief *Dīwān* are correctly ascribed to him; see *Anīs al-'ushshāq*, ed. M.H.S. 'Ata Husain, Haidarabad, Deccan: Barqī Press, Fasli 1360/AD 1941. The presence of the *kunya* Abū al-Fatḥ among the personal names of Gēsūdarāz, which is also that of the young son of the author mentioned in the *TN*, probably aided the identification, which we reject below, of Yūsuf Gadā with the father of Gēsūdarāz, particularly if, as we conjecture, a manuscript of the work was carried by the entourage of Gēsūdarāz to the Deccan and later formed a part of the *khānqāh* library at Gulbarga. The coincidence of *kunya* also suggests that, in the naming of his son, Yūsuf Gadā may have been influenced by the presence of Gēsūdarāz at Dehlī.

[10] Muḥammad 'Alī Samanī, *Siyar i muḥammadī*, Allahabad: Yūnānī Davalkhānah, AH 1347/AD 1928, pp. 3, 6, 10–11.

Muslim years of age at the date of the composition of the *Tuḥfa i naṣā'iḥ*—and his father already fifty years in his grave.

The popularity of the *Tuḥfa i naṣā'iḥ* in the Deccan is attested not only by the numerous copies in the Asafiyyah Library in Hyderabad, but also by its translation into Daknī verse by Quṭbī, one of the court poets of the seventeenth-century Sulṭān 'Abd Allāh Quṭbshāh of Golkonda. Apart from the false sanctity conferred by these ascriptions, an independent reason for the popularity of the *Tuḥfa i naṣā'iḥ* is that it provided for South Asian Muslims with a lower level of education, and especially for the children of such Muslims, a comprehensible guide to the good life in an easy mnemonic verse form. It can be classified with numerous other short verse treatises, mostly of later date and often bilingual vocabularies, under the heading *niṣāb aṣ-ṣibyān* (the capital stock of children). One may contrast the fate of the *Tuḥfa i naṣā'iḥ* with that of a longer prose work with a similar mélange of contents, written in the fourteenth-century Dehlī Sultanate, the *Miftāḥ al-jinān* (The Key of Paradise) by Muḥammad Mujīr, which appears to have survived in a single manuscript.[11]

A critical edition of the *Tuḥfa i naṣā'iḥ* is a desideratum; it would not be a work requiring great labour as it is a comparatively short poem. For the purposes of this chapter, I have collated readings from an old manuscript, unfortunately defective at the close and therefore lacking a colophon, but probably of sixteenth/seventeenth-century date, with the readings of a lithograph published by the Haydari Press of Bombay in AH 1289/AD 1872–3. From this brief collation, points of interest emerge. Some variant readings may be second thoughts of the author in copies which he circulated,

[11] British Library, MS Egerton 691; see the notice in Rieu, *Catalogue of the Persian Manuscripts in the British Museum*, London: British Museum, 1879, vol. I, pp. 40–1.

e.g. in the lithograph, he cites as his authority *'ulamā' i mu'tabar* (reliable *'ulamā'*); but in the two manuscripts he cites *Nu'mān i nāmwar* (the famous Nu'mān, i.e. the jurist ash-Shiblī). Second, a number of phrases and *baits*, which would have been immediately intelligible in the Dehlī Sultanate, were not equally so in later times; there is a tendency on the part of copyists to amend the phrases or drop the *bait*.[12]

[12] The first MS (Digby no. 59) [Bodleian MS S. Digby Or. 56] was acquired by A.H. Harley, Principal of the Anglo-Muhammadan Madrasah, Calcutta, in 1928, probably in eastern India. It measures 6¼ by 3⅝ inches and is written in a minute, rather archaic *nasta'līq* hand, twelve lines to the page, breaking off at the fortieth *bāb*, twenty-nine folios. The second manuscript (Digby no. 170) [Bodleian MS S. Digby Or. 152], which the writer acquired after the initial draft of this paper, bears a note saying that it was 'bought at the sale of Mr. Orme, May 1796'. Mr Orme may be the historian Robert Orme (1728–1801), though if this is the case the manuscript must have entered his possession after he finally returned to the United Kingdom. Below the colophon it bears an owner's note dated in the twentieth year of Shujā' ad-Daula, Nawwāb-Wazīr of Awadh (AD 1773–4). The manuscript was copied for a *sayyid* (name erased) who was resident at Kalpi, an old fortified Muslim settlement in southern Uttar Pradesh, which for a brief period in the early fifteenth century was the centre of an independent sultanate established in the aftermath of the downfall of the Dehlī Sultanate; the manuscript may therefore represent a local tradition of Muslim learning. The author is described as '*Makhdūm al-a'ẓam* ... Yūsuf Gadā', a curious example of exaggerated reverence for the written word. The manuscript measures 9⅝ by 6 inches, and is written in clear, broadly spaced *nasta'līq*, nine lines to the page, ninety-five folios and four blanks from an earlier rebinding. Spaces for the rubrics are blank, but the titles of the *bābs* (chapters) have been inscribed in various hands in the margins. The manuscript also contains the date-verse in the form quoted in the text of this chapter.

Collation of the three texts used in this chapter discloses one point that can be settled only when an edition of the *Tuḥfa i naṣā'iḥ* based on the wide range of manuscripts or lithographed printings, or both, is prepared. Some of the more striking *baits* (couplets), which, as I have argued, can best be set in a late-fourteenth-century context, are absent

Thus, in a passage discussed below, the manuscript (f. 16b) reads *poshad barāte chūn kase,* the lithograph (p. 38) *ānkas ki poshad 'āriya* (he who wears something borrowed). The

---

from one or more of the texts that I have consulted. The omitted couplets usually occur at the close of the *bābs* (sections). The explanation that I favour is that these additional couplets are not copyists' interpolations, but are afterthoughts of Yūsuf Gadā himself. Of the texts used, MS A represents the earliest stage of compilation, MS B an intermediary stage, and the Bombay lithograph a more complete version.

Against this theory it may be argued that the sequence corresponds to the recognizable age of the three texts. However, I do not think that such a random argument will commend itself to any scholar who has worked on Indo-Persian texts of all periods and is aware of the idiosyncrasies of place and time that distinguish them.

MS B and the lithograph agree in the final couplets as regards the date of composition with the majority of recorded manuscripts, and also as regards the number of sections (*bābs*), namely forty-five. B states that the work is of 781 verses (*baits*) and the lithograph 786. B is in a state of confusion after the forty-fourth *bāb,* called forty-third in this manuscript. The discrepancy in numbering, common to A and B, derives from the omission of *bāb* 21 on the obligation of children towards their parents. B, however, includes most of the *baits* of this section as well as the anecdote of the companion of the Prophet 'Alqama, which illustrates the moral of this *bāb,* in the concluding matter. Another characteristic of this late portion of the text in B is the reproduction of the first hemistichs of *baits* without the concluding hemistich, as on f. 90b. I find it impossible to account for the textual peculiarities of B at this point by any process of textual corruption or damage in an intermediary manuscript. I conclude that at this point B derives from an original author's manuscript which was here no more than a rough draft. Because MS A lacks its final folios, breaking off at the fortieth–forty-first *bāb,* one cannot say whether it represents an earlier finished recension of the author.

These problems of the textual recension of the *Tuḥfa i naṣā'iḥ* parallel, in a miniscule way, those of the transmission of a more important work of the Dehlī Sultanate, Baranī's *Ta'rīkh-i Fērōzshāhī;* see S. Digby, 'Muḥammad bin Tughluq'a Last Years in Kāthiāwār and His Invasions of Thattha', *Hamdard Islamicus,* vol. 2, no. 1, 1979, p. 83 [*L&WSD* VI.3].

section is discussing employment by the sultan, and *barāt*, also *barātī jāma*, were common Dehlī usage for 'a robe of office or uniform from the sultan', although this usage will not be found in the Persian lexicographical tradition of later times. Elsewhere the first manuscript (f. 6a) drops a *bait* which is preserved in the lithograph (p. 13) and appears to be original:

> When you see Maḥmūd, Aḥmad, and Tāj i Dīn as labourers on every side
> Shādī, Qabūl and Zīrak who have become *muqṭa's* and famous.[13]

This *bait*, which appears among the Signs of Doomsday, seems to reflect the bitter civil war that was taking place between the royal slaves and the free population of Dehlī in the decade in which Yūsuf Gadā was writing. Shādī and Qabūl were characteristic names of slaves, and slaves of both these names had attained high offices of state in the fourteenth century. *Muqṭa'* was the standard term for 'governor' of an important town or province during the Dehlī Sultanate, but would probably not have been intelligible in this sense to ordinary South Asian Muslims of the sixteenth and seventeenth centuries.

As Sarfarāz describes it, the *Tuḥfa i naṣā'iḥ* 'treats, in forty-five sections, of various religious observances and ethical subjects such as the Unity of God, the Articles of Faith, Ablutions, Prayers, Legal Alms, Fasting, Pilgrimage, Reading of the Qur'ān, Contentment, Marriage, Charity, Lawful and

[13] MS A, f. 6b, this *bait* omitted; litho., p. 13; MS B, f. 13b. An attractive alternative reading was suggested by the lithograph, *shādī qabūlān zīragān* (low-born Shadi-Qabuls), but Zīrak (skillful) is attested elsewhere as a name for a slave in this period; see Ḥasan, *Fawā'id al-fu'ād*, pp. 5–6. The sense is confirmed by MS B which reads *shādī qabūlā zīrakā*, which represents not the plural, but a slightly pejorative form of the singular name.

Forbidden Food, etc.'[14] It would be out of place here to provide a table of contents. Moreover, remarks relevant to some of the topics that we shall survey appear in widely separated sections; and Yūsuf Gadā frequently combines injunctions on a wide variety of subjects into single couplets, e.g.:

> All the time give thanks to God; buy a Qur'ān out of your own property;
> Buy a bow and a thumb-ring; serve your father and mother![15]

This is one of the courses of action that lead to wealth (section 42). The following section is on actions that lead to Paradise, where in one couplet we find a comparable conglomeration:

> Be generous to guests; make war with the *kāfirs* [unbelievers];
> If anyone tells you a secret, do not reveal it to men.[16]

The author is equally capable of expressing divergent or contradictory opinions within the same couplet, e.g.:

> If you reject *futūḥe* [Ṣūfī alms], you will be afflicted with hunger [in the future];
> Some notable shaikhs have rejected *futūḥe*.[17]

[14] Ḥasan, *Fawā'id al-fu'ād*, pp 129–30.
[15] *Bāb* 41, missing in MS A; litho., p. 75, reads *tāzī*, 'an Arab (horse)'; MS B, f. 79a, *yā zihe*, 'and/or an archer's thumb-ring', *lectio difficilior* and metrically better. Though Yūsuf Gadā elsewhere exhorts his son to learn to ride, an Arab thoroughbred war horse was probably beyond the means that Yūsuf Gadā thought that his son would possess; see S. Digby, *War-horse and Elephant in the Dehlī Sultanate*, Oxford: Orient Monographs, 1971, pp. 37–8 [*L&WSD* V.1].
[16] Litho., p. 77; MS B, f. 80b.
[17] Litho., p. 82; MS B, f. 90b.

Do not take a Qur'ān on a military expedition, or a woman who is legally free (*ḥurra*);
If a military expedition has strength, take both of them on it.[18]

There are also unresolved contradictions in the general advice that he gives his son. Poverty is praised, but there is also a section of advice on thirty (not very practical) means towards acquiring wealth; in yet another place he tenders much more practical advice regarding ways of earning a livelihood. Apart from the many promises of palaces of gold or of jewels in paradise following particular courses of action, he does not hesitate to promise lavish rewards in the present world. Thus, a section on forty causes of poverty and misfortune concludes:

If you avoid all these forty, writing them in your heart and soul,
You will never once become needy; you will receive a hundred jewels a day![19]

In a didactic work this naïveté may not be wholly artless; extravagant statements are more likely to attract the fancy of a child and the precepts are more likely to impress themselves on the youthful memory. A further contradiction is that Yūsuf gives instructions to his son as how to avoid the shame of beggary, while using the pen name Gadā (the Beggar). There is a comparable case from his period and probably from among his personal

[18] Ibid. In both this and the preceding couplet, MS B reproduces only the first hemistich, with variations. In note 12, above, a reason for the confusion of the manuscript at this point is suggested. This implies that these apothegmatic and sometimes self-contradictory *baits* are among the author's latest additions to the poem.
[19] Litho., p. 74; MS B, f. 78b.

acquaintances, as Ḥamīd Qalandar, co-disciple and biographer of Shaikh Naṣīr al-Dīn Maḥmūd, was also a panegyrist of Sulṭān Fērōz Shāh Tughluq and no ordinary illiterate and dirty Qalandar.[20]

We cannot dwell at length on Yūsuf Gadā's eschatology. At the outset of the poem he has a fine and graphic account of the dead in their graves after their first visit by the inquisitorial angels; the dead are alive there as are the living, conscious of whether a male or female sparrow is perching on the cenotaph. He has a spirited description of the final Day of Judgement and the contrasted fates of the righteous and the sinners, and concludes this extended section with the portents that the Day is at hand. These begin with the episodic elements which in Muslim tradition largely derive from the Apocalypse of St. John, Dajjāl the Anti-Christ, the reappearance of Jesus, and the rising of the sun in the west, and proceed to signs of the evil times. In one couplet, which we have quoted above, there is an unmistakable reflection of the conditions of the Dehlī Sultanate. Other couplets concern ills for which evidence is to be found in the period and environment in which he wrote; but they may also be considered endemic or epidemic in Islamic society on earth: a multitude of women, some riding horses; a craze for building palaces; and the erection of many mosques with but a few worshippers within them.[21]

[20] The situation and preoccupations of Ḥamīd Qalandar are discussed in my two forthcoming papers, 'Qalandars and Related Groups', International Conference on Islam (The Hebrew University of Jerusalem, 1977), in press [since published; see *L&WSD* III.7] and '*Tabarrukāt* and Succession among the Great Chishtī Shaikhs of the Dehlī Sultanate', presented to the Indian History Seminar-Workshop, Center for South Asian Studies, University of Wisconsin, Madison, October–November 1979 [since published; see *L&WSD* III.3]. Ḥamīd Qalandar's panegyrics on Fērōz Shāh Tughluq are included in the Jawnpur anthology, British Library MS Or. 4110.

[21] MS A, ff. 4a–6a; litho., pp. 7–13; MS B, ff. 7b–13b.

At the close of the work there are further descriptions of heaven and hell, with equally vivid detail: heaven with its four streams proceeding from the centre, one of them of *khimr*, the intoxicants forbidden on earth; hell with snakes as large as mountains and scorpions as large as camels, each with 400 fortresses-full of poison in its tail.[22] Yūsuf Gadā is inclined to promise *saqar* (hell) for a large variety of acts, partly, one suspects, because it fits into his rhyme scheme as conveniently as *zar* (gold) and *guhar* (jewels). Nevertheless, one of the more attractive features of his beliefs is that no Muslim (*mu'min*) will endure the pains of hell forever, but only for a period according to the measure of his sins; for unbelievers this is not the case.

Again, for the sake of brevity, we have no space for an extended notice of Yūsuf Gadā's opinions on Muslim religious observances. He describes these in considerable detail and also has notices of such Ṣūfī practices as *dhikr* and *samā'*. The total of religious observances inculcated is sufficient to occupy a considerable portion of an individual's life, and more of life would be consumed by his instructions regarding auspicious and inauspicious acts, hours, days, Muslim months, and zodiacal mansions and seasons. As the concept of *adab* embraces both moral authority and etiquette in the individual's ordinary daily behaviour, a sample of his advice on the latter aspect may be desirable, bearing in mind that his manual has probably exercised a significant influence on the manners of Muslims in South Asia in later centuries. I have selected his section on the *adab* of eating (section 14):

> When you eat food, eat it once in a day and night;
> That will be nourishment which suffices you, anything more causes illness and headache.

[22] Litho., pp. 76–80; MS B, ff. 80a–83b. B lacks the couplets regarding the snakes and scorpions of hell.

When you are hungry and eat, know that food has no ill-effect;
If you eat when you are sated, that food eats your heart and liver.
Eat food in your own place, don't stretch out your hand in front of others;
Take a small and moist mouthful and chew it well.
When you want to eat, first wash your hands;
When you have eaten wash them, for this comes in the Tradition [of the Prophet].
If a crumb falls on the ground, take it up bit by bit;
Put salt at the beginning and end; keep your eye on the mouthful.
Don't criticize anyone's food; eat whatever you are offered;
Don't say that it's bitter or tasteless or any such thing.
If you wish surely to become rich and find endless wealth,
Clean your teeth when you have eaten food, my son.[23]

There are further instructions on the *adab* of eating, as on those of drinking water, wearing clothes, embarking on journeys, visiting the sick and attending mourning, and many other contingencies of human life. Whatever traditions Yūsuf Gadā draws upon—and some of these we shall examine later—one has a strong impression from the *Tuḥfa i naṣā'iḥ* of an individual with idiosyncratic personal views who has left his imprint on subsequent Indo-Muslim culture. In this he resembles Baranī, the greatest historian of the Dehlī Sultanate, although within a shared intellectual environment Yūsuf Gadā's personal prejudices differ from those of Baranī. Both writers had strong Chishtī Ṣūfī allegiances; neither was largely concerned with Ṣūfī topics. Both had a grounding in the religious sciences of Islam. Both expressed themselves freely in the colloquial Persian of the Dehlī Sultanate. In the writings of both, an ascetic ideal evidently conflicted with a keen appreciation

[23] MS A, ff. 14a–b; litho., p. 32; MS B, ff. 34b–36a.

of the pleasures of the world. Yūsuf Gadā does not appear much less hostile than Baranī to the Hindu population of India, though the term Hindu does not occur at all in his poem. Nevertheless, his remarks upon *kāfirs* and his view of *jihād* as a current obligation, together with his remarks on military matters, seem to fit well with the environment of the Dehlī Sultanate.

Yūsuf Gadā sets the borders of old age at the fortieth year of life. From the evidence cited above, he had passed this when he wrote the *Tuḥfa i naṣā'iḥ*.[24] We have here a further parallel with the writings of the historian Baranī, whose major work, the *Ta'rīkh-i Fērōzshāhī*, attained its final form when he was bordering on senility.[25] Baranī described the evils of the times with acidity and gloom. A similar moroseness is reflected in Yūsuf Gadā's account of the signs of the approach of the Day of Resurrection:

> You should recognize a multitude of women as a sign of the Resurrection;
> When you see women riding horses, the Resurrection will come more swiftly.
> Another sign is that people will study branches of knowledge without acting;
> You will see few worshippers, but find more mosques.
> When you see people engaged, heart and soul, in building,
> Pray for death at that time, consider dying preferable.
> When in every direction you see Maḥmūd, Aḥmad, and Tāj-i Dīn as labourers,

[24] Yūsuf Gadā's age is discussed near the beginning of this chapter.

[25] For an examination of Baranī's failing memory of the sequence of recent historical events, see Digby, 'Muḥammad bin Tughluq's Last Years in Kathiavad and His Invasions of Thattha', in *Sind Through the Centuries*, ed. H. Khuhro, Karachi: Oxford University Press, 1981, pp. 130–8 [*L&WSD* VI.3].

Shādī, Qabūl, and Zīrak become Governors and famous men,[26]
Nomads, peasants, drovers, shepherds, and ploughmen,
With never a shoe on their feet, nor a turban (*pag*) on their heads.
You will know the Resurrection without doubt, when you see people in the cities,
Occupied each in building a splendid palace.[27]

Both Yūsuf Gadā and Baranī are elderly moralists, keen to point out the evil consequences of unlawful, licentious, and profligate acts. Yet, in the recollections by Baranī of his youthful participation in the courtly follies of the reign of Jalāl al-Dīn Fēroz Khaljī, there is an aura of regret for vanished and reprehensible pleasures that adorns his tale rather than points the moral which with much vigour he professed to expound.[28] A similar conflict is at times evident in Yūsuf Gadā's poem, between, on the one hand, remembered practices and desires and, on the other, the usually sombre and grave rules for the conduct of life that he sought to inculcate into his son. His remarks on the buying of concubines and on the pursuit of an independent livelihood, both quoted below, contrast with his view of the sanctity of poverty and with his ideas on sorrow, trouble, and illness. These are upheld as signs of God's special favour:

Know that affliction and calamity are a favour sent down upon [God's] friends;
His enemies do not receive this favour, only the faithful of good conduct.

[26] See note 12 above.
[27] MS A, f. 6a; litho., pp. 12–13; MS B, ff. 13a–b. B has the reading *būtān* (idols) for *binā'* (building), which breaks the continuity of sentiment with the previous *bait.*
[28] Baranī, *Ta'rīkh-i Fērōzshāhī*, p. 200.

When affliction strikes you, give alms [in thanksgiving] from your soul and heart;
The Sultan does not give poison except to a trustworthy and able man.

This illustration, though inept or inappropriate in justifying the ways of God to Man, is in keeping with Yūsuf Gadā's other views about the service of the sultan, examined below. His remarks on ill health continue:

A body which you see without diseases verily is without blessing (*baraka*);
God loves that body which day and night has pain and headache.
Affliction, O my soul, is a kingdom of which not everyone is worthy;
Job knew its worth and Georgius and the famous Jonah...
[God's] enemies have a hundred kinds of favour, sufficient in this world;
His friends are distressed and lack their bread...
When God cherishes a servant, wishing to make him one of his friends,
He is infirm of body, sorrowful of heart, and sees no prospect of wealth.[29]

In contrast to the afflictions of the ancient prophets, cited from the allusions in the Qur'ān and the later expository *Qiṣaṣ al-anbiyā'* literature, Yūsuf Gadā refers to the comforts in this world of the oppressor Pharaoh of Egypt (*Fir'aun*):

Pharaoh the dog was for four hundred years on his throne;
He was not ill a single time, nor even saw injury.[30]

[29] MS A, f. 28a; litho., pp. 67–8; MS B, ff. 70b–71a.
[30] MS A, f. 28b; litho., pp. 68; MS B, f. 71b.

When you hear that an acquaintance is injured or sick, you should straightaway go to visit him
Even if he is over a *karoh* [a *kos*, about an hour's walking distance] away.
If you visit a sick man, give him something;
Seek his prayers, my love, in any difficult matter ...
When you see someone ill, immediately give alms;
Do not give medicine to the sick man, only alms, my son![31]

Like most of the descriptions of the subject in medieval European and Eastern literature, Yūsuf Gadā gives a harrowing description of old age. In the literature of the Dehlī Sultanate, once more there is a parallel in Baranī's references to his own toothless decrepitude, contrasted with his erring youth:

When your age reaches forty years, sit not idle one instant;
Abandon erring and sin; increase obedience and worship.
If you do not do so, but act to the contrary,
Erring oft, obeying little, get ready for the fire of Hell.
Know that a man's ordinary span of life is sixty to seventy years:
You have spent one third in games, and one third heedless from intoxication;
Know that in the last third which remains there is misfortune and calamity;
Your hands and feet will swell, and your head will ache a hundred times a day.
You will not find health for a moment, but pain and misfortune all the time;
No sweet sleep will come at night, and you will cry out till the dawn ...[32]

[31] MS A, f. 28b; litho., pp. 68–9; MS B, ff. 71b–72a.
[32] MS A, f. 27a; litho., p. 65; MS B, ff. 67b–68a.

If [an old man] looks at beauty, he or she will immediately show distaste;
The lovely and the sugar-lipped will sit as far away as possible from him.
When your hair has gone white the beautiful flee,
For old age is as nothingness; otherwise why should they turn away from you?
If a king be fortunate, the whole of the world within his grasp,
When he is a weak old man he has neither appetite nor comfort ...
When the musk has turned to camphor, the scarlet judas-tree to saffron,
The arrow of your stance to a bow, your body become thin as a bowstring,
No one will look towards you and no friend will once ask about you;
No one will employ you and you will not receive a wage.[33]

However, the help of the helpless is at hand:

Come to Me that I may cherish you better than this;
I will give you a thousand houris in paradise and endless palaces of jewels;
I have mercy upon the old which is without bound or count;
Your hair is white from My light; I shall not burn it in hell.[34]

As the old are incapable of work, you should work while you are able-bodied and consider youth a blessing. When you see the old you should serve them with heart and soul, so that you become a good old man (*pīr*) and a powerful *shaikh*.[35]

[33] MS A, f. 27b; litho., p. 66; MS B, ff. 68b–69a.
[34] MS A, f. 27b; litho., pp. 66–7; MS B, ff. 69b.
[35] The allusion is a commonplace of Persian literature. *Pīr* means 'old', 'elder', and also a 'Ṣūfī teacher'. This is a slightly condensed version of *baits* which follow those quoted above.

At this point there is a significant variant between the readings of the texts that I have consulted. The manuscript reads *shaikhe dhū al-qadr* (scanned *qadar*, 'a powerful shaikh'); the alternative reading is *shakhṣe* ('a person'). On account of the linkage *pīr-shaikh* (*pīr*, 'old man, elder' and/or a Ṣūfī shaikh), the former reading is preferable. The *Tuḥfa i naṣā'iḥ* is largely a guide to practical ethics for a Muslim who is not going to pass his life as a Ṣūfī in a *khānqāh*, who is not going to pass his life living off *futūḥāt* (alms) or even more dubious income from land grants, or from the forms of communal labour or self-support which may have occasionally occurred in the *khānqāhs* of medieval India. Nevertheless, Yūsuf Gadā, like most of the authors of the Dehlī Sultanate, had Ṣūfī allegiances and participated in Ṣūfī observances. In his pen name he adopted a Ṣūfī garb. The advice given reveals a characteristic quirk in the thinking of Yūsuf Gadā, and shows how this functioned at several different levels of morality and practicality.

After his descriptions of the ills of old age and of God's mercy towards the old, he has in fact concluded with a reference to the one field of life in which old age gave a practical superiority. In pretentions to spiritual authority as a Ṣūfī shaikh, a venerable age was a clear asset (cf. the remarks of Sayyid Muḥammad Gēsūdarāz, who stated that he was in the habit of praying to God for an early death, until he realized that God had destined him to live to a very advanced age in order to demonstrate to those who doubted it his succession to the *baraka* of Shaikh Naṣīr al-Dīn Maḥmūd).[36]

After the exposition of Yūsuf Gadā's views on this aspect of the individual human predicament, and before we turn

[36] Samanī, *Siyar i muḥammadī*, p. 5; cf. Digby, '*Tabarrukāt* and Succession', cited in note 20.

to his advice on how to gain a livelihood or his attitudes towards the sultan and the state, we may examine his injunctions regarding family life.

Yūsuf Gadā had a view of women more unfavourable than that commonly prevailing among the literate classes in the medieval Islamic environment. We have noted their preponderance as a sign of the approach of Doomsday. His forty-fourth section on hell begins:

> Hell is for unbelievers, rebels, and heretics;
> There are more women (*'aurāt*) resident in it than men.
> Nine hundred and ninety-nine men out of every thousand are in paradise;
> Out of every thousand women nine hundred and ninety-nine are in hell.[37]

The advice he gives to his son on marriage (section 12) shows an ideal of almost total male dominance and female subservience, limited only by the Islamic prohibitions on extramarital sex; but it reveals that Yūsuf Gadā has little hope that his idea of the perfect wife for his son will be realized. In defence of his views on women, it may be said that they are not as cynical and facetious as those expressed by Sa'dī in the *Gulistān*, a literary classic which has been even more popular than the *Tuḥfa i naṣā'iḥ* as an ethical guide for the upbringing of Muslim children in South Asia.

> While you have strength refrain from marriage;
> My son, know that in marriage there is calamity, anxiety and grief.
> When you can contain yourself no longer, take a wife, beautiful and abstinent,
> Who will obey you, serve you and be your solace eve and morn,

[37] Litho., p. 78; MS B. f. 82a, first *miṣrā'* defective.

Who will not bring any anxiety before you, but will herself bear all the anxiety and grief:
If she does not possess this quality, divorce her as quickly as possible.
When you marry, [she should be] in four things lower than you:
In years, height, rank, and wealth;
But when you are about to ask for a wife, you should never ask for one who is not
Superior to you in good-nature, looks, manners (*adab*), and the fear of God.
Don't marry a short fat woman or a tall thin one:
You should never marry an older woman; she will bear a worse son.
You should never marry a woman who weeps, nor one with hairy legs;
Avoid a demanding one who is an ugly deceiver.
The woman who causes trouble, with prancing legs and feet,
Who speaks ill of you to your face and whom you always see with her head closed [to reason];
Who, when you speak softly, answers back and shrieks,
Who goes out without permission and wanders around from door to door;
Who, when people come to her, complains to them about you,
And says how exceedingly unhappy she is, though she is comfortable;
Who does not ever cover her head, nor wash her face, hands and feet,
Nor put antimony on her eyes nor comb her hair;
Who secretly talks about you and considers your guests enemies;
Who eats her food before you do; and eats more than a man:
He who has such a wife, consider him verily in hell.
If you have such a wife, straightaway put her out of the door.[38]
If you desire ease in this world, immediately go and buy a concubine
Like a moon of the fourteenth night, sweet-voiced and silver-bodied,

And if you find her good, abstinent, and content—and she serves you,
Get on with her and live happily; but if not, buy another.
Don't see lust in the face of another's woman: how could she be yours?
Also don't look in the face of a young boy: keep away from him.
If you commit sodomy or adultery, even kissing and touching,
The good deeds of all your life become as nothing.[39]

This section is followed by another on bringing the bride home and the rules for sexual intercourse. These are fairly detailed and show Yūsuf Gadā's characteristic mélange of Islamic law and a large body of auspicious and inauspicious acts, times, and settings, that will affect the character and capabilities of the child engendered.[40]

In writing the *Tuḥfa i naṣā'iḥ* for the instruction and edification of his son, Yūsuf Gadā demonstrates, by implication rather than overt expression, a high view of parental obligations towards male children. His sole reference to daughters is to the effect that on the birth of a girl one should sacrifice a sheep, but on the birth of a boy a brace of sheep. After an exhortation to his son toward unremitting hard work, a slightly obscure couplet seems to express the opinion that as a result of industry and endeavour one will be in a position to feed one's wife and family:

Become like the nether millstone; endure labour and bring benefit;
Otherwise you will wander from door to door seeking bread like a helpless fool.

[38] Litho., p. 29, line 2, has here an interlinear gloss explaining that Yūsuf Gadā meant 'divorce her!'
[39] MS A, ff. 12a–13a; litho., pp. 27–9; MS B, ff. 30a–32a.
[40] MS A, ff. 13a–14a; litho., pp. 29–31; MS B, ff. 32a–34b.

Lucky is that bird which falls in the snare of manliness;
Sell it and buy bread to give to your wife, daughter, and son.[41]

It is clear from his injunctions on employment that Yūsuf Gadā does not see it as part of the parental role to ensure that his son enjoy a prosperous rather than an honoured position in life. Contemplating his son's future, he recognizes that he may exist with wealth to spare or in want and poverty:

When you turn away an asker, or withhold a morsel from him,
You will receive for this sin a thousand years in hell ...
These precepts are for the rich, not for the poor and hungry;
If he himself is in need of bread, how can he give it to another?[42]

Yūsuf Gadā is not indifferent to the acquisition of wealth, but rather to its avaricious retention. One cannot oneself take it beyond the grave, nor is it right to hoard it for one's children, for whom the Lord will provide:

Consider the fellow who makes a profession of avarice the enemy of God;
A man is beloved of God who scatters gold and silver ...
Do not put treasure under the ground for a daughter or a son;
When the need befalls them, no one will give them the information.
Consign them to God's keeping: you die; He does not die:
Do not grieve about their affairs, put worry out of your heart.[43]

[41] MS A, f. 21a; litho., pp. 53–4; MS B, f. 55a.
[42] MS A, f. 21b, omits second *bait*; litho., p. 54; MS B, f. 55b, reads *badānī* for *barānī* in the first *bait*, manifestly incorrectly, and also omits the second *bait*, which, as in other cases quoted in this chapter, appears to be a late addition by the author.
[43] MS A, f. 20b; litho., p. 52; MS B, ff. 53a–b. B again omits the last couplet, which concludes the *bāb*.

One may here note that the practice of the burial of treasure (in a context other than that of grave-goods) has been common in South Asia at almost all periods.

Yūsuf Gadā's exposition of the rights of parents over their children (section 21) is short and simple:

Be generous to your parents, so that you may receive uncounted reward;
Know that their service is a duty according to the Qur'ān and the Traditions.
Do whatever they desire, and without doubt you will enter into Paradise,
As the Creator has told the Prophet. Remember, my famous one.
Serve all, and without doubt you will become one who is served;
He who performs service becomes a lord with a crown on his head.
Consider good him who gives honour to his parents;
Such a man has honour in the two worlds, and is respected among all men.[44]

Yūsuf Gadā exhorts his son to acquire *'ilm* (knowledge—section 4). From his remarks it is clear that he had in mind 'education' in the narrow sense of the scholastic sciences which down to the present day form almost the whole curriculum of Muslim *madrasas* and were also the main subjects in which individual teachers instructed their pupils. What we should nowadays call the humanities, as well as most useful arts and sciences and works on Ṣūfī practice and self-discipline, were extracurricular. Yūsuf Gadā

[44] Litho., pp. 40–1. This brief *bāb*, followed by an illustrative anecdote about one of the Prophet's companions, 'Alqama, and his behaviour toward his mother, is absent from both manuscripts at this point. However, MS B includes three out of the four *baits* with some variant phrases on ff. 83b–84a, after which the tale of 'Alqama follows.

himself possessed some grounding in *'ilm* of this kind. His extracurricular education was much slighter. He had some knowledge of *nujūm* (astrology—on the borderline of the medieval curriculum) and probable also with *fa'l* and *ta'bīr* (omens and interpretations of dreams). At one point he urges his son to acquire a smattering of astrology:

> Learn enough astrology for you to know the time
> For marriage, and the direction of prayer; and also when to go on a journey.[45]

I find no evidence in the *Tuḥfa i naṣā'iḥ* of Yūsuf Gadā's familiarity with Persian *akhlāq* literature. Of Persian poetry within the high literary canon (including Amīr Khusrau and other poets of note in the Dehlī Sultanate) there is a single echo of a very well-known couplet by Sa'dī:

> If you wish to dwell a while beside anyone,
> If he says that day is night, show him the Pleiades and the moon.[46]

By *'ilm*, therefore, Yūsuf Gadā means the scholastic sciences. They were to be acquired for their own sake, not for the limited number of prospects of employment that they would open to his son:

[45] Litho., p. 82, *bāb* 45. This is the last *bāb* of the work. MS A is defective after *bāb* 40/41; in MS B, *bāb* 45 is absent, replaced by couplets on a variety of topics, which have been incorporated under their appropriate headings in the text represented by the lithograph. Despite this, MS B concurs in the statement that the poem was to consist of 45 *bābs*; see note 11.

[46] MS A, f. 20b; litho., p. 52; MS B, f. 53b. Cf. Sa'dī, *Gulistān*, *bāb* 1, *ḥikāya* 32:

> If he himself says that day is night,
> One must say, 'Behold the moon and Pleiades!'

> If you learn *'ilm* for the sake of God, without doubt it will save you,
> Not to pronounce *fatāwā* [legal opinions] nor to act as a *qāḍī* [religious judge]; nor for bread in another employment.[47]

If a man acquired much *'ilm* and yet performed little worship (*'ibāda*), he was nevertheless closer to God than pious ascetics (*'abidīn*):

> The superior grace which a learned man [*'ālim—'ilm*] has over the pious and the ascetics
> Is like the superior grace which the Prophet had over the very least of mankind.[48]

'Ilm was not, in Yūsuf Gadā's opinion, a suitable means for gaining a livelihood. As we see below, he regarded with disfavour all forms of official employment under the sultan. His eleventh section is on 'professions, contentment, and beggary'. In it he displays a fairly coherent succession of thought regarding what was an honourable way for the individual to survive in society:

> Do not be ashamed or modest at pursuing a trade, my soul;
> Learn a trade and also *'ilm*, become a master of arts, possessor of more than one accomplishment,
> Learn *'ilm* and also a skill, so that you will not go round many doors [begging];

The couplet was so well known that it was quoted in the original Persian by the seventeenth-century French traveller François Bernier, who remarked, 'There is no Mogul who does not glory in repeating this proverb in Persian verse!' (F. Bernier, *Travels in the Mogul Empire*, tr. I. Brock, ed. A. Constable, London: Oxford University Press, 1981, p. 264).

[47] MS A, f. 6b; litho., p. 13; MS B, f. 14a.

[48] MS A, f. 6b; litho., p. 14; MS B, f. 15a.

The man who has a skill will not ask for bread from door to door.
Eat from your own labour, and from the toil of your hand;
Do not beg anything from anyone, and you will become like sugar and honey.
Work immediately, for laziness is like unbelief;
Consider a man who is idle like an ox or an ass.
If on your back you bring stones or firewood from the wilderness,
And you sell them and eat bread—this is better than your eating a hundred pieces of bread from your father.[49]
If you eat squeezed vegetables and drink bitter and salt water,
This is better than if you go to the Sultan and consume sherbet and other delicacies.
Do not linger at anyone's table, waiting for a chance to eat;
Whomever you see like this consider worse than a dog.
Follow a trade and eat your bread; profess patience and satisfaction;
If you do not beg from anyone you will without doubt find a palace of gold.
If you take from anyone, people call you a beggar [*gadā*],
But if you give to anyone, people call you a 'real king'.
I will give you an excellent piece of advice, lend ear and hear well;
Do not tell your condition to anyone; toil and eat your bread;
And in the Law [*sharī'a*] without doubt to beg is condemned.
If you have bread for the day, whether fresh or dry.
If you want possessions and gold for honour and prestige,
Truly know that such possessions will be burning in hell like a spark.
If you sow a field and it provides a living,
Cultivate and you will bear away plentiful fruit.

[49] Litho., p. 26, has an interlinear gloss remarking that this is an exaggeration!

The benefit of this toil is counted in the world,
Cultivation benefits a whole world, its profit is not limited.
At no time let your hand get out of practice with bow and arrow;
Learn to swim and ride a horse, also a camel.[50]

A further chapter (section 18) is concerned with buying and selling. It distinguishes between commodities in which trade is auspicious or commendable and those in which trade is reprehensible and unlucky:

Engage in trade, my dear; among means of livelihood consider this good;
Trade in sheep is most auspicious, also buy horses and cattle.
Do not buy grain with the intention of selling it dear; and do not trade in slaves either;
Refrain from these two and you will not become an accursed regrater (profiteer).
In trading in slaves or in grain you will never find blessing;
You will lack a grave-cloth, and someone else will eat the profit.
In whatsoever you see someone's injury, whether it be firewood or straw or lime-plaster,
And especially human foodstuffs [?], this is truly regrating.
If you have grain of your own growing, make stores of this,
You will not be a regrater, according to the famous Nu'mān.[51]

Yūsuf Gadā proceeds to give the practical advice that one should never swear oaths in business; if the oaths you swore

[50] MS A, ff. 11b–12a; litho., pp. 26–7; MS B, ff. 28a–29b.
[51] MS A, f. 16a; litho., p. 37; MS B, f. 40a. The lithograph and MS B agree in reading 'according to trustworthy *'ulamā*" in place of 'according to the famous Nu'mān'. Their reading apparently reflects the later choice of the author.

were true, your sustenance would be diminished. You should always weigh and measure what you buy before you bring it from the shop to your house, and you should never sell without weighing and measuring (elsewhere he recommends buying and selling grain by measure rather than weight). Two couplets follow concerning the purchase of concubines, and ascertaining their menstrual state before engaging in intercourse. The section concludes with an injunction against lending money at interest (*ribā'*), a sin which Yūsuf Gadā assesses as worse than having committed incest with one's mother seventy times![52]

As we know from Baranī and Ibn Baṭṭūṭa, measures against regrating and profiteering by grain dealers in times of scarcity occupied the attention of the Dehlī sultans, as they do that of the rulers of South Asia in modern times.[53] In the late fourteenth century the supply of skilled and able slaves probably did not fill the demand. Baranī lamented that slaves from Central Asia were almost unobtainable, and the Sulṭān Fērōz Shāh Tughluq made special arrangements in the tax farm of the province of Gujarat for an annual supply of high-quality slaves.[54] These circumstances may have had some bearing on Yūsuf Gadā's view of slave-dealing as an inauspicious trade.

We may proceed to Yūsuf Gadā's opinions about obligations towards the ruler and the state, and upon gaining a livelihood from such service. His attitudes, I suggest, reflect the conditions of the Dehlī Sultanate. He foresees, in passages quoted above, that his son will be likely to

[52] MS A, f. 16b; litho., pp. 37–8; MS B, f. 40b.

[53] Baranī, *Ta'rīkh-i Fērōzshāhī*, pp. 304–6; Ibn Baṭṭūṭa, *Riḥla*, tr. C. Defremery and B.R. Sanguinetti, Paris, 1853–7, vol. 3, pp. 148, 290.

[54] Baranī, *Ta'rīkh-i Fērōzshāhī*, p. 314; Sirhindi, *Tārīkh-i mubārakshāhī*, Calcutta, 1931, p. 132.

participate in military expeditions, and urges upon him the necessity of practice in military arts. Obedience to the sultan in time of emergency, when he is waging war on rebels to authority, is incumbent:

> Never come out against monarchs or draw the sword against them,
> Even if they do wrong, a hundred kinds of violence and oppression.
> Make war against rebels under the standard of the Sultan;
> When you see anyone who has become a rebel, kill him as quickly as possible.[55]

In his chapter on employment, Yūsuf Gadā briefly expressed his view on waiting upon the favour of the sultan:

> Eat squeezed vegetables and drink bitter and salt water:
> This thing is better than if you go to the Sultan and consume sherbet and other delicacies.[56]

In his discussion of the reasons why God has brought afflictions on his chosen servants, we have quoted the analogy that the sultan gives poison only to trustworthy advisers; and in his views about the desirability of the acquisition of *'ilm* (the theological sciences), that such knowledge was not to be employed in giving legal decisions or in acting like a *qāḍī* (judge). It is not surprising that Yūsuf Gadā, in his chapter on 'companionship' of the sultan, advised his son in forceful terms against undertaking any form of official employment (section 19):

[55] MS A, f. 5b; litho., p. 11; MS B, f. 12a.
[56] *Bāb* 18, extensively translated above; see note 51.

Be a *darwesh* and sit in solitude; do not ask for food from anyone;
Know that contentment is a kingdom, a mansion full of pearls and jewels.
Do not yourself go near the Sultan; know that the Sultan is such a one;
When you long for the Sultan, there will be fear and danger for you.
Never seek kindness and generosity from kings;
When you take a village or land, you will fall down in front of a door.[57]
Do not follow the King's employment; know that there is continuous misfortune in it;
You will see little ease, more discomfort and punishment.
Do not consider the employment of the Sultan unexceptionable—like an official robe;
When someone else wears an official robe, you should not consider him trustworthy …
Keep away from *mīrs* and *māliks*; know that proximity to them is a deadly poison;
When you sit by a *mālik*, every moment you will see a hundred dangers …
By contrast, you should sit with *darweshes* and not refuse them if they ask something from you.
If you do so through greed of money, two-thirds of your faith will depart.
When the Sultan is generous, never become proud about this;
You should regard the sugar which the Sultan gives as poison rather than sugar.
Consider the tenderness of *māliks* as a calamity, their favour as wrath and anger;
You will not obtain comfort from them, they do not show affection to anyone.

[57] There is an allusion here to *zamīn i uftāda*, land that was not currently in cultivation, a phrase common in official land grants.

When you go into the Sultan's assembly, you must guard your tongue:
Do not say anything in front of him, and when you come out be as one who is deaf.
Do not go to Kings uncalled; if they summon you, go instantly;
Obey their commands; know that this category is obligatory.
If anyone is obedient in a just act which the King performs,
Consider this better and more than sixty years of private worship.[58]

Yūsuf Gadā's views on employment and on the service of the sultan stand in sharp contrast to those of the main political theorist whose writings have survived from the Dehlī Sultanate, Baranī. Baranī spent most of his life as a *nadīm* (courtier) of the Dehlī sultans, although he apparently was never trusted with a post of political responsibility.[59] Yūsuf Gadā regarded such employment not only as dangerous—which it must often have been—but also as uncommendable, even odious. Yūsuf Gadā regarded humble and manual occupations as entirely honourable, whereas Baranī's political theory, as expressed even in the opening sentence of his great history, was permeated by belief in a divinely established division between noble and base, with inherited aptitudes for one's allotted position in society, a stratified society in which social mobility was an evil—a belief that has strong parallels with the traditional Hindu *varnāśramadharma*.[60] The nearest approach to this point of

[58] MS A, ff. 16b–17a; litho., pp. 38–9; MS B, ff. 40b–42a. The syntax of the last *bait* is obscure, but it would be difficult to interpret it in any other way.

[59] Baranī, *Fatāwā i jahāndārī*, intro., p. 25.

[60] Cf. Baranī's theory of the development of inborn aptitudes among the noble and the base, *Fatāwā i jahāndārī*, pp. 295–7. For a Persian rather than Indian source for Baranī's formulation, see Ibn al-Balkhī, *Fārsnāma*, ed. G. Le Strange and R.A. Nicholson, London: Luzac, 1921, pp. 30–1.

view in the whole of Yūsuf Gadā's work is in the two couplets cited above, which appear to reflect the conditions of the late fourteenth century, when the slave party was pitted against the free urban population and a number of people from tribal or other low indigenous origins were attaining positions of influence (e.g. the Meo chief Bahādur Nāhar).[61] By contrast, one may note that in Baranī's writing the status of a slave was no bar to the possession of inherited noble aptitudes; his *noblesse d'épée* consisted mainly of the 'great' Turkish slaves who rose to command the armies of the sultanate or ascend its throne.

The conflict between the attitudes of Baranī and Yūsuf Gadā is not explicable in terms of the general Islamic education or the Ṣūfī allegiances of the two writers. Baranī was probably better grounded in traditional *'ilm* than Yūsuf Gadā himself. Both writers were *murīds* (disciples) of the same line of Chishtī shaikhs. Yūsuf Gadā's thinking regarding the undesirability of associating with monarchs and taking their employment is in accord with many pronouncements of the Chishtī shaikhs; but he is clearly opposed to their practice of taking *futūḥāt* (alms)[62] and he has a conception of the duty of serving the sultan in certain political contingencies which is nowhere expressed in the remarks of the Chishtī shaikhs.

A manual that endeavours to explain the elementary duties of Islam must eventually contain some reference to *jihād*, the obligation of making war upon the *kāfirs* (unbelievers). Yet from the vigour with which Yūsuf Gadā expressed his views on this subject, as well as his injunctions elsewhere concerning conduct on a military expedition, maintaining a

[61] For the events of this decade, see Digby, *War-Horse and Elephant*, pp. 74–82.

[62] Cf. K.A. Nizami, *Some Aspects of Religion and Politics in India during the Thirteenth Century*, Bombay/Aligarh: Aligarh Muslim University, 1961, pp. 199, 227. Nizami minimizes the question of the acceptance of *futūḥāt* in the Chishtī *khānqāhs*.

proficiency in military arts and marching beneath the banner of one's sultan, it seems probable that he regarded making war upon unbelievers as a contingency that was unlikely to occur in the course of his son's life:

> Make war upon the *kāfirs*; know that this war is a duty
> At such time as you see that the *kāfirs* have been making a general disturbance.
> If you flee once from war, you become a coward fit for hell;
> This is one of the greatest of the major sins; avoid it totally.
> If there are ten believers and twenty-one of the enemy,
> Know that the time when they show their faces is a lawful one, my son.[63]

He devotes further attention to the occasions when it is lawful to slay *kāfirs*. Considering these remarks in the context of the Dehlī Sultanate, it seems probable that Yūsuf Gadā was thinking not only of the Hindus, but also of the Mongols, whose assaults had been a serious danger to the sultanate in the early fourteenth century. Only a few years after the composition of the *Tuḥfa i naṣā'iḥ* there occurred the catastrophe of the invasion of Amīr Tīmūr. On this occasion both sides saw the context as a *jihād* against the infidels. The historians of the Timurid court blithely described the massacre of 'Hindus' taking refuge in the great mosque of Dehlī, yet at Dehlī itself an *'īdgāh* that was one of the first buildings erected after the event bears an inscription referring to the invading host as 'accursed Mongols and devilish *kāfirs*'.[64]

This may lead to the vexed question of the possible influence of Hindu beliefs, practices, and social observances

[63] MS A, f. 9b; litho., p. 23; MS B, f. 25a. Both A and B lack the last *bait*, again at the close of the *bāb*.
[64] Zafar Hasan, *List of Muhammadan and Hindu Monuments, Delhi Province*, vol. III, Calcutta: Superintendent Government Printing, 1922, pp. 164–6.

upon Yūsuf Gadā's writing. A modern school of Indo-Muslim historians, somewhat influenced by their own political predicaments, has been inclined to emphasize the syncretistic nature of Indo-Muslim culture. One of the writers of this school, the late K.M. Ashraf, has made use of the *Tuḥfa i naṣā'iḥ*; his views on it may be quoted: 'Its particular interest lies in showing how far Hindu beliefs and practices and other common superstitions were being incorporated into the scheme of orthodox Muslim life in Hindustan.'[65] This appears to me grossly to overstate the case. One may think that one sees the influence of the Hindu environment in Yūsuf Gadā's preference for female hypergamy, but to establish this, one would have to demonstrate that it was not practised elsewhere in the medieval Muslim world. Some of Yūsuf Gadā's references to *kāfirs* we have examined above; he does not even once use the term Hindu, though at times he refers with deprecation to the Jews, of whose presence there is no evidence in medieval Dehlī. Similarly, injunctions that one should not go to heathen women for the interpretation of dreams, and that it is lawful to condole with *ahl i dhimmi* (non-Muslim protected peoples) in the case of death,[66] are ambiguous and probably derive from earlier Muslim tradition.

The sources of authority to which Yūsuf Gadā appeals are the Qur'ān, *ḥadīth*, works on *fiqh*, the opinion of individual classical Islamic jurists, and 'tales of the Prophets' (*Qiṣaṣ al-anbiyā'*). The considerable portion of the content of the *Tuḥfa i naṣā'iḥ* devoted to auspicious and inauspicious acts and situations reveals no overt Hindu influences. In

[65] K.M. Ashraf, *Life and Conditions of the People of Hindustan*, repr., Delhi: Jiwan Prakashan, 1959, intro., p. xxii.

[66] MS A, f. 29b; litho., p. 70; MS B, f. 73b. Yūsuf Gadā here refers to the *Hidāya* as his authority. A reference to an indubitably Indian custom at Muslim burials shortly follows this—the placing of *tambul* (*pān*) on the grave; MS A, f. 29b; litho., p. 71; MS B, f. 74a.

the medieval world these preoccupations extended well beyond the frontiers of India, and Yūsuf Gadā's sources must be sought in the body of Islamic literature on this subject, much of it ultimately derived from the culture of the Mediterranean world in late classical times. Yūsuf Gadā's auspicious and inauspicious days are either those of the Islamic months or those of the days of the week as governed by the planets. One may suspect a pervasive influence of the Indian environment, but the work itself does not provide the evidence in which K.M. Ashraf thought 'its particular interest' lay. The similarities to Hindu belief and practice are a part of the general tenor of life in the civilizations of the Eurasian landmass during the medieval period.

9

Anecdotes of a Provincial Sufi of the Dehlī Sultanate, Khwāja Gurg of Kara

The contemporary and near-contemporary literature of Sufis of the Dehlī Sultanate sheds welcome light on the religious and social life of north India in the thirteenth and fourteenth centuries, and upon the ideas and concepts which prevailed in Muslim and Sufi circles in this environment. But the chances of manuscript transmission have left us with but a selection out of all that was originally composed in this period, and this selection is heavily weighted in favour of the more highly literate sections of the diverse and divergent body of Sufi men of religion. Leaving aside the 'spurious *Malfūẓāt*' attributed to the early Chishtī shaykhs in India, first recognized and denounced in Professor Mohammed Habib's pioneering article,[1] we are still exceptionally well informed on the attitudes and activities of the later great Chishtī shaykhs from the clearly, often precisely dateable records of the conversations of Niẓām al-Dīn 'Awliyā'', Naṣīr al-Dīn 'Chirāgh-i Dehlī', Burhān al-Dīn 'Gharīb', and Sayyid Muḥammad Gēsūdarāz. In addition, there are two posthumous but valuable Chishtī biographical

* Originally published in *Iran*, vol. 32, 1994 pp. 99–109.

[1] M. Habib, 'Chisitī Mystic Records of the Sultanate Period', *Medieval India Quarterly*, vol. I, no. 3, 1950, pp. 1–42; repr. in K.A. Nizami, ed., *Politics and Society during the Early Medieval Period: Collected Works of Professor Mohammad Habib*, New Delhi: People's Publishing House, 1974, pp. 385–433.

tadhkiras of the fourteenth century, the *Surūr al-ṣudūr* and the *Siyar al-awliyā'*.[2] The literature of the Firdawsī shaykhs of eastern India has survived equally well, including letters and recorded conversations of Sharaf al-Dīn Manērī and a useful *tadhkira, Manāqib al-aṣfiyyā'*.[3] By contrast, unless more authentic manuscript sources are found, the Suhrawardī shaykhs of Multan have fared very badly.[4] From the late

[2] The *Surūr al-ṣudūr*, written by a grandson of Shaykh Ḥamīd al-Dīn Nāgawrī, remains unpublished. It is frequently cited by K.A. Nizami, from a manuscript in his personal possession; see K.A. Nizami, *On History and Historians of Medieval India*, New Delhi: Munshiram Manoharlal, 1983, pp. 183–7. Use has been made of another MS in the *dargāh* at *Nāgawr*, Rajasthan, in a modern Urdu hagiography of Shaykh Ḥamīd al-Dīn; see Pīrzāda Aḥsān al-Ḥaqq Fārūqī, *Sulṭān al-tārikīn*, Karachi: Dā'ira Mu'īn al-ma'ārif, 1963.

Amīr Khwurd, *Siyar al-awliyā'* (Storey, no. 1250), ed. Chiranjī Lāl, Dehlī: Muhibb-i Hind Press, AH 1302/AD 1885; photo-repr. from the last with variant page numbers: Lahore: Mu'assisa-i intishārāt-i Islāmī, AH 1398/AD 1978.

[3] Shaykh Shu'ayb Manērī, *Manāqib al-aṣfiyā'*, Calcutta: Nūr al-āfāq Press, AH 1313/AD 1895. For a summary notice of the extant literature of the early Firdawsī shaykhs of Bihar, see S.H. Askari, *Islam and Muslims in Medieval Bihar*, Patna: Khuda Bakhsh Oriental Public Library, 1989, pp. 30–6.

[4] Fażl Allāh Majawī's *Fatāwā al-ṣūfiyya*, written in Arabic around AD 1350 and extant in MS at Oxford (Bodleian, Uri 321), still awaits detailed analysis. It contains valuable information on the organization and regulation of the Suhrawardī *khānqāh* at Multan; see Julian Baldick, *Mystical Islam: An Introduction to Sufism*, London: I.B. Tauris, 1989, pp. 95–6. The *Khulāṣat al-'ārifīn* regarding Bahā' al-Dīn Zakariyyā' of Multan (= Storey, p. 1057, no. (33)?) clearly belongs to the class of bogus compilations. An edition has been published; Bānū Daktar Shamīm Maḥmūd Zaydī, *Aḥwāl u āthār-i Shaykh Bahā' al-Dīn Zakariyyā' Multānī u khulāṣat al-'ārifīn*, Rawalpindi: Markaz-i Taḥqīqāt-i Fārsī, 1974, pp. 123–91. For *Fatāwā ṣūfiyya* and *Majma' al-akhbār fī manāqib al-akhyār* (*sic*, *apud* M. Shafī'), a work regarding Shaykh Rukn al-Dīn and inaccessible, if any longer extant, see Nūr Aḥmad Khān Farīdī, *Tadhkira Shāh Rukn-i 'Ālam Multānī*, Lodhran (Zila Multan): Qasar al-Adab, AH 1381/AD 1961,

fourteenth century we have two collections of *malfūẓ* (discourses) of Shaykh Jalāl al-Dīn 'Makhdūm-i jahāniyān' of Ucch, both compiled in Dehlī, though one of these has been characterized as inauthentic by its editor.[5]

This, then, is almost the entire corpus of Sufi biographical literature from the Dehlī Sultanate up to and shortly after the disaster of Timur's invasion of AD 1398.[6] This chapter examines and describes another work that may be added with confidence to the corpus surviving from before AD 1400. It is of interest in that it describes a different and lower level of religious behaviour. We have, however, first to establish four basic items of information: the correct title of the work, the name of its author, the correct name of the holy man whose activities it describes, and the date of composition.

---

pp. 280–1; 'Abd al-Ḥaqq Dehlavī, *Akhbār al-akhyār* (= Storey, no. 1298 [1]), Dehlī: Mujtabā'ī Press, AH 1309/AD 1892, p. 62.

[5] Both of these substantial medieval Indo-Persian texts have fairly recently been published from Delhi: *Sirāj al-hidāya*, ed. Qazi Sajjad Husain, Delhi: Indian Council of Historical Research, 1983 [1984]; *Jāmi' al-'ulūm*, ed. Qazi Sajjad Husain Delhi: ICHR, 1987.

[6] For general surveys of this literature, see the following modern works: C.A. Storey, *Persian Literature: A Bio-Bibliographical Survey, N. Biography: (b) Saints, Mystics, etc.*, vol. I, part 2, London: Royal Asiatic Society, 1953, pp. 923–1066; Bruce B. Lawrence, *Notes from a Distant Flute: The Extant Literature of Pre-Mughal Indian Sufism*, Tehran: Imperial Iranian Academy of Philosophy, 1978; K.A. Nizami, *Supplement to Elliot and Dowson's History of India, Vol. III*, Delhi: Idarah-i Adabiyat-i Delli, 1981, pp. 92–112; K.A. Nizami, *On History and Historians of Medieval India*, New Delhi: Munshiram Manoharlal, 1983, pp. 163–97. For the *malfūẓ* literature of the Firdawsīs in Bihar, see S.H. Askari, *Maktub and Malfuz Literature as a Source of Socio-Political History*, Patna: Khuda Bakhsh Oriental Public Library, 1981, pp. 30–64, supplemented at some points by the same author's *Islam and Muslims in Medieval Bihar*, Patna: Khuda Bakhsh Oriental Public Library, 1989, *passim*. For another valuable early fifteenth-century regional *malfūẓ*, see Z.A. Desai, *Malfuz Literature as a Source of Political, Social and Cultural History of Gujarat and Rajasthan*, Patna: Khuda Bakhsh Oriental Public Library, 1991.

The work in question has not escaped the vigilant eye of the veteran historian of north Indian Sufism, Khaliq Ahmad Nizami, who provides a brief description: 'The *Asrar-u'l-Makhdumin* is the *malfuz* of Khwaja Karak and contains interesting anecdotes concerning the saint. It was compiled by Karim Yar. Nothing is known about the compiler or the date of compilation.'[7] The work has previously been known only from the rare lithographic printing of the Nasīm-i Hind Press, Fathpur Haswa, 1893. As was common in Urdu and Persian printings of this period, the name of the patron who commissioned and doubtless subsidized the edition appears prominently upon the title page. It was Karīm Yār, Ra'īs of Yuhan, who was alive a hundred years ago, and not an author of earlier centuries. The erroneous identification of this '*Ra'īs*' as the author first appears in Edward's *Catalogue of Persian Printed Books in the British Museum*; and it is repeated in C.A. Storey's *Persian Literature: A Bio-Bibliographical Survey* (no. 1411, Appendix, no. 38).[8] We may note that the work is loosely described as a *malfūẓ* (record of conversations) rather than a *tadhkira* (collection of biographical anecdotes) on the title page of the lithograph, and this mild inaccuracy has been passed down through Edwards and Storey. No manuscript of the work was known to Storey, nor to my knowledge has any notice of one appeared in any other published catalogue. This is of importance, because in the text of the lithographed edition there is no clear mention either of the name of the author and the date of composition is garbled. However, even without these a close perusal of the anecdotes would have revealed that the author was the grandson or great-grandson (*nabīsa-pisarē*, the phrase leaving room for either interpretation) of a contemporary of the

[7] Nizami, *On History and Historians of Medieval India*, pp. 117–78. Cf. Nizami, *Supplement to Elliot and Dowson's History of India, Vol. III*, pp. 102–3.

[8] Storey, *Persian Literature*, p. 1057.

shaykh, who came from a family which had removed from Lahore to the town of Kara on the Ganges (Anecdote no. 129). Given that the subject of the *tadhkira* died in AH 700/AD 1301, this would suggest a date of compilation not later than the third quarter of the fourteenth century.[9]

The matter would rest there, but for a manuscript which came to light in an old private collection in western Europe.[10] The text differs very little in its readings from the lithograph, though it is evidently not this manuscript from which the lithograph was copied. From a perusal of the opening it becomes evident that the second folio was missing from the manuscript from which the lithograph was transcribed, and the copyist, as in such instances is often the case, has not even noticed the break (in effect, he has copied straight on from the bottom of the original folio 1 verso to the top of the original folio 3a). It is upon the second folio that the present manuscript provides us with the name of the author, which we read as Muḥammad ʿAlī Ismāʿīl (son of?) Masʿūd ʿAlī, *ʿurf* ʿSajjanʾ Lāhawrī. It also describes in brief detail the circumstances of the compilation of the work and the date of its completion (*khutima bi-tawfīqiʾllāh*), the beginning (*ghurra*) of Rajab AH 771, corresponding to the end of January AD 1370.[11]

[9] For the date of Khwāja Gurg's death, 3 Rajab AH 700, see below; Muḥammad ʿAlī Ismāʿīl Lāhawrī, *Asrār al-majdhūbīn*, Manuscript, Private collection of Simon Digby, MS 10, n.d., Anecdote no. 210.

[10] Formerly in the collection of A.H. Harley, Principal of the Anglo-Arabic Madrasa, Calcutta, *c.*1920; now Digby MS 10.

[11] Though it is not made clear in the text, the date may be related to the death anniversary on 3 Rajab, see below. The portion of the text which has dropped out of the lithograph, p. 2, line 1, runs from f. 2a of the present MS, line 1, *wisāwis-i mukhālif* to folio 2b, line 11, *az shanīdan-i (īn) sukhan-i mubārak*. With this omission, it is not surprising that those who have previously examined the lithograph, among them possibly Storey and Nizami, have failed to recognize the date of composition given four lines later, in which the century 700/*wa sabʿmiʾa* is garbled to *MSTʿMAYTH*.

We may now turn to the title of the work. In the lithographed printing, this appears as *Asrār al-makhdūmīn* ('The Secrets of the Lords'). This has no obvious relevance to the personality and the activities of the holy man described in the work. In the manuscript, the title appears in the alternative form of *Asrār al-majdhūbīn* ('The Secrets of Those Drawn Away'). Those conversant with Arabic script will realize that this variation of the name represents a minor alteration in the placing of the dots and the thickening of one initial. The term *majdhūb* is used in Sufi literature in India and elsewhere (e.g. in a whole section of 'Abd al-Ḥaqq Dehlavī's *Akhbār al-akhyār*) for a class of 'madmen' who are so 'drawn away' by divine love that they appear to have abandoned the ordinary norms of behaviour of Muslim believers.[12] In this text, the subject is often described, both by others and from his own mouth, as *majdhūb* and *dīvāna* ('mad'). *Asrār al-majdhūbīn* is therefore to be preferred as a more apt title for the work.

The last ambiguity of which we can dispose concerns the name of the holy man. In modern times, in the nineteenth and twentieth centuries, he has been remembered as Shāh Karak (it may be noted that he is called Khwāja, not Shāh, throughout the text). *Kaṛak* with retroflex 'flapped' *ṛ* is an onomatopoeic north Indian word used much like its English homophone, *bijlī kī kaṛak*, 'a crack of thunder'. In Arabic script it is represented by the letters *kāf*, *rā'*, *kāf* (in older palæography, there is seldom a sign over the *rā'* to indicate the retroflex *ṛ*). In most pre-modern handwriting, the Persian *gāf* is not differentiated by a superscript stroke

[12] Dehlavī, *Akhbār al-akhyār*, *dhikr-i ba'żē majādhīb*, pp. 297–85. The *majdhūbs* who are described in Uzganī's fantasizing *History of the Uwaysīs*, translated by Julian Baldick, are not so segregated. Several are described as *majdhūb* from birth. Dr Baldick renders *majdhūb* as 'enraptured'; see his *Imaginary Muslims: The Uwaysī Sufis of Central Asia*, London: I.B. Tauris, 1993, pp. 57, 81, 132, 159, 189.

from *kāf*. *Kāf*, *rā'*, *kāf*, as students of the *Shāhnāma* will be aware, may equally well represent *karg*, a rhinoceros, and *gurg*, a wolf. Through this amphibology, in medieval illustrations to Firdawsī's poem, the wild beasts which Isfandiyār confronts are sometimes represented as wolves with a single horn growing from their foreheads.[13] In the text of the *Asrār al-majdhūbīn*, the subject is described by others and by himself in verses and in conversation as *KRK-i gūsfandīn* 'sheeplike KRK'; *KRK-i pāyband* 'KRK with chained feet'; and '*KRK-i pīr* 'old KRK'. These epithets make no sense if they are applied to 'a crack of thunder', but perfect sense when qualifying 'a wolf' in the phrases 'a sheeplike wolf', 'a chained wolf', and 'an old wolf'. The last phrase is used in the Persian poetry of this period, as in modern English, for a cunning and experienced veteran. One may add that *gurg-i pīr* 'old wolf' (applied to the Khwāja) occurs in a poem

[13] Cf. the enormous single horn on the head of the wolf slain by Bahrām in the 'Great Mongol' *Shāh-nāma* dispersed by Demotte; O. Grabar and Sheila Blair, *Epic Images and Contemporary History: The Illustrations of the Great Mongol Shahnama*, Chicago: University of Chicago Press, 1980, fig. 53 and colour plate facing p. 19. See also R. Ettinghausen, *Studies in Muslim Iconography: The Unicorn*, Washington: Smithsonian Institution, 1950, pp. 37–43, and plates 9 (another 'Great Mongol' *Shāh-nāma* page), 23, 25, and 26. For the distinction of *karg* and *gurg*, cf. the *qaṣīda* of the thirteenth-century Dehlī Sultanate Persian poet Shihāb al-Dīn of Badā'ūn, in which by way of artifice every couplet mentions four animals, *sher* ('lion', or, in the Indian context, often 'tiger'), *pīl* (elephant), *karg*, and *gurg*; see Iqbal Husain, *The Early Persian Poets of India (A.H. 421–670)*, Patna: Patna University, 1938, pp. 184–90. One may quote a typical couplet:

pīl bakhshā dar badā'ūn bāyad-am wīrana'ī
garchih jay-i gurg u karg u shēr bāshad īn diyār

'Elephant-bestower, I desire a desert place in Badā'ūn, even though these regions are the abodes of the wolf (*gurg*) and the rhinoceros (*karg*) and the lion.' (Husain, *The Early Persian Poets of India*, p. 189).

in the text in the *mutaqārib* metre which would not scan if one read *karak*.[14]

It may help us to understand the character of this strange hagiographical work if we next examine the information which the *Asrār al-majdhūbīn* provides concerning the author or compiler and his family. We should probably understand his name as Muḥammad Ismā'īl, *son of* Mas'ūd 'Alī. His *'urf* name, which is shared by earlier members of his family, in the manuscript is consistently written in *shikasta* script as *SJN*, which we should probably read as 'Sajjan'.[15] The lithographer reads Sanjar and Sanjarī.[16] The compiler's *nisba* is Lāhawrī, indicating that his family came from Lahore,

[14] This is not the sole instance from this period in northern India where ambiguities of Arabic script or of manuscript transmission have led to a corrupt form of a famous name prevailing in popular tradition. Another instance is that of the name of the pious sultan of Dehlī, Shams al-Dīn Iltutmish ('world-grasper', cf. *Jahāngīr*, which has the same sense), later remembered as Altamish or Altamsh. See S. Digby, 'Iltutmish or Iletmish? A Reconsideration of the Name of the Dehlī Sultan', *Iran*, vol. VIII, 1970, pp. 57–64 [*L&WSD* VI.1]. Cf. also the scribal corruption of the Sijzī to Sanjarī as *nisba* of Mu'īn al-Dīn Chishtī, a form long and firmly established in popular consciousness.

[15] Cf. such Indian names as Rāja, Rāwat, etc., borne by Muslims of the early Dehlī Sultanate. 'Sajjan' (usually m., 'good man' > 'friend' > 'lover') would have been a pen-name (cf. A.P. *takhalluṣ*). Variously derived from Skt. *sant-* + *jan-* or *sat-* + *jan-*, the word has been current in this form for two millennia from Pali texts to present-day spoken north Indian vernacular usage; see Ralph Turner, *Comparative Dictionary of Indo-Aryan Languages*, London: Oxford University Press, 1966, no. 13090, *sajjana*[2]; C. Shackle, *A Gurū Nānak Glossary*, London: School of Oriental and African Studies, 1981, pp. 31–2, 45; R.C. Varma, *Saṅkṣipt Hindī śabdsāgar*, Kāshī: Nāgarī Pracāriṇī Sabhā, 1933, s.v.

[16] Cf. note 14 above for Sanjarī in place of Sijzī in the *nisba* of Mu'īn al-Dīn Chishtī, also found in that of the poet Amīr Ḥasan Sijzī Dehlavī. The manuscript, written in generally unpointed *shikasta*, does not vary in the orthography of the name, with an upward curve at the close which is correctly used for *nūn* and not *yā'*. Mr Ziyauddin Desai, formerly Arabic

though, as we shall see below, they had been settled for some generations in Kara.

The compiler of the anecdotes states that when he was attending on Sayyid Jalāl al-Dīn Abū Sa'īd Bukhārī,[17] a *darvēsh* gave him stories and verses about the miracles, sayings, and spiritual authority (*wilāyat*) of Khwāja Gurg Abdāl. This *darvēsh* told him that he had been happily passing his days reading Sufi works when he saw Khwāja Gurg in a dream. Gurg commanded him to give the material about himself which was in his house to Muḥammad Ismā'īl Lāhawrī. The compiler gladly accepted the material from the *darvēsh*, but did not feel inclined to proceed with the composition until he also had a dream, in which Khwāja Gurg appeared and said: 'Young man, why have you not heeded the words of this madman? And why are you not putting them together?' The compiler began to tremble and woke with a start. After recitation of the Holy Qur'ān and the performance of the dawn prayer, Muḥammad Ismā'īl started to compose the work.

From the proem and from a number of anecdotes (nos. 59, 51, 104, 117, 129), it is possible to gain some picture of the family of the compiler and their connection with Khwāja Gurg. They bore the *nisba* Lāhawrī, but appear to have come from Lahore to Kara on the Ganges at least some decades

---

and Persian epigraphist to the Archaeological Survey of India, who read with attention and interest the photocopy of the MS that I brought to the New Delhi conference, initially suggested 'Shaykhan' (an Indianized nickname or pen-name), but later, in view of the consistency of the orthography which lacks a 'tooth' after initial *sīn*, agreed that 'Sajjan' was the more probable reading.

[17] Abū Sa'īd is not recorded as a name of Sayyid Jalāl al-Dīn Ḥusayn 'Makhdūm-i Jahāniyān' Bukhārī, though this great shaykh was a *khalīfa* of Rukn al-Dīn of Multan, and therefore in the same Sufi lineage as the compiler of the *Asrār al-majdhūbīn*. Such an identification therefore remains uncertain but not impossible.

before the end of the thirteenth century. There is no indication that they were *sharīf* Muslims of other than South Asian lineage, but it is claimed that the names of 'Alā' al-Dīn and Mas'ūd had been borne in alternation by men of the family for twelve generations (anecdote no. 117). They had links, not with the capital city of Dehlī, but with Lahore and Multan. Some other anecdotes suggest that this was true of other members of the Muslim population of Kara, an indication which may be of relevance when the settlement patterns of the Dehlī Sultanate are studied. Successive members of the family of the compiler appear to have used the *'urf* 'Sajjan'. They are nowhere claimed to be great shaykhs with *khilāfat*, but their Sufi allegiance is to the Suhrawardī shaykhs of Multan. Among the family, Gurg's older patron Mas'ūd 'Alī was a *murīd* of Bahā' al-Dīn Zakariyyā'. At Mas'ūd 'Alī's funeral at Kara, Khwāja Gurg claimed to have seen the three great Suhrawardī shaykhs of Multan, Bahā' al-Dīn, Ṣadr al-Dīn, and Rukn al-Dīn, invisibly and supernaturally present (anecdote no. 104). The family appear to have been wealthy citizens, and they maintained a building called the *Ṣūfi-khāna*, in which Qalandars and other *darvēshs* received lodging and maintenance. An element of loyalty and pride of family has entered into the compilation of *Asrār al-majdhūbīn*.

Biographical statements about Khwāja Gurg himself are rare in the work. It is likely that he was a locally born Muslim who never travelled far from his birthplace of Kara on the Ganges. His parents evidently died when he was still young; one anecdote has him weeping beside the grave of his father (anecdote no. 175). We may discount the numerous anecdotes, sometimes denied by him and sometimes tacitly acknowledged, of Gurg being seen by travellers from far away at the Ka'ba (nos. 144, 176), or at the Prophet's grave in Medina, or in Bukhara (no. 194).

One of the most attractive features of the work is the local feeling which Khwāja Gurg and the compiler show for the settlement of Kara and its surroundings on the Ganges. Both Gurg and the compiler contribute to the Muslim sanctification of the local landscape.[18] Outside Kara, Gurg had a vision of the Prophet passing by (no. 49). This was a sign of the death of a member of the compiler's house, a disciple of Bahā' al-Dīn Zakariyyā' of Multan. It was at his funeral that Gurg, seen conversing with invisible personages, claimed that the three great Suhrawardī shaykhs were present, though invisible to others (anecdote no. 104). In an anecdote which is historically possible, Khwāja Gurg was urged by Sultan 'Alā' al-Dīn Khaljī to come to Dehlī (Anecdote no. 57). He declined the invitation, and recited a favourite quatrain of his own composition:

qāni' shudam bi-khushk nānē u tara
mailam nabuvad bi-sūyi biryān u bara
dihlī u samarqand u bukhārā u 'irāq
har chār turā bād u marā bād kara

I am content with dry bread and vegetables;
My appetite is not for roast meat and lamb.[19]
Dehlī and Samarqand and Bukhara and 'Irāq,
You can take them all and leave me Kara!

A further instance of Khwāja Gurg's local feeling was when he visited a boys' school (no. 61). He remarked: 'The boys of

[18] On this emotional need among the growing domiciled medieval Muslim communities of northern India for a legendary Islamic sanctification of their homeland and the features of its familiar landscape, see S. Digby, 'The Sufi *Shaykh* as a Source of Authority in Medieval India', *Puruṣārtha*, vol. 9, 1986, pp. 58–9 [*L&WSD* III.1; this volume pp. 3–6].

[19] The contrast is a recurrent commonplace in Persian. Steingass notes: '*tara dar kūh biryān ast,* Proverb founded on a play of words between *tara* (*tarra*), "herb", and *bara* (*barra*), "lamb", to express that in case of need any food is welcome.' (F. Steingass, *A Comprehensive Persian–English Dictionary*, London: Routledge, 1892, s.v. *tara*).

Kara have a good temperament. Whatever they write, they write well! There is no place like Kara (*hamchū maqām-i kara jā'ī nēst*)!' Gurg then observed to the boys that 'this madman' (*īn dīwāna*) had written a quatrain out of regard for them and they should memorize it. We may quote it as another typical and favourable example of his style of verses:

'ishq-i azalī tā bi-abad khwāhad būd
jūyanda-i 'ishq bē-'adad khwāhad būd
fardā chu qiyāmat āshkārā gardad
ay harki na 'āshiq ast rad khwāhad būd

Eternal love will endure till the end of time;
The seekers of love will be without number;
On the day when God's judgement is made manifest,
Yea, any man who is not a lover will be cast forth.

Once, when in a happy mood, we are told, Khwāja Gurg described his entry into religious life, and what he considered to be his particular vocation (anecdote no. 102). He was an active youth of some 16 or 18 years, and he was accompanying a local armed band encamped not far from Kara at a place called Bhambharolī.[20] In the middle of the night he awoke, but he saw no one around, and he began to weep for his (evidently dead) father and mother. He then heard a voice, which told him to go into Bhambharolī, where there was a holy man called Mawlānā Ismā'īl, and to do what he would be told by him (the name suggests that he was yet another member of the Lāhawrī family of the compiler of the text).

[20] I am grateful to Mr Z.A. Desai (see note 16 above) for this reconstruction of the name, which also appears, corruptly written, in another anecdote (no. 43). Mr Desai also suggested Mahoba in Hamirpur District, mentioned in proximity to Bhambharolī in a passage discussed below.

[After going into the settlement,] Gurg beheld a *pīr* with spiritual authority (*ṣāḥib wilāyat*) standing before the door. The *pīr* greeted Gurg as soon as he saw him, and he said: 'O brother in the faith, it is good you have come! It is nearly ten years that I have been waiting for you. Take this letter to the hill where the lamp is burning, and deliver it to Khwāja Khiżr. He will tell you whatever is to be!'

Gurg felt longing and pain and exaltation, and immediately set out. He came to the foot of the hill where the light burnt. Before the hill there was a vast expanse of water. He drank of the water and climbed the hill. There he found an old man performing his prayers on a prayer carpet. He greeted him and placed the letter in front of him. Khwāja Khiżr (for it was he) pronounced: 'Verily the time has now come! God has called you His own *abdāl*.[21] Go back to Kara and drink the wine that is reprobated by people, and turn it into rosewater!'

[21] For ideas and anecdotes of *Abdāls* in the Dehlī Sultanate, see S. Digby, 'Qalandars and Related Groups', in *Islam in Asia*, ed. Y. Friedmann, Jerusalem: Hebrew University, 1984, pp. 80–1 [*L&WSD* III.7; this volume, pp. 213–15]; Digby, 'The Sufi *Shaykh* as a Source of Authority', p. 62 [*L&WSD* III.1; this volume, pp. 13–14]. One further anecdote indicates suspicion and confrontation (no. 131). A Qalandar brought wine to Gurg, who after sipping it poured it upon the ground. The implication may be that the wine was poisoned or drugged. Gurg then said that he would meet the Qalandar at the prophet's tomb at Medina and the Qalandar fell at Gurg's feet. However, peripatetic Qalandars may be distinguished from settled local *majdhūbs*. In an anecdote in *Asrār al-majdhūbīn* (no. 9; translated in Digby. 'Qalandars and Related Groups', p. 98; this volume, pp. 236–7), a group of Qalandars attacked Khwāja Gurg while he slept. Other anecdotes show Qalandars and Ḥaydarīs (members of the groups also being called *zhinda-pōsh*) consorting with Gurg and showing him respect (nos. 94, 149, 150, 157, 176). In the last of these anecdotes, Khwāja Gurg also meets *abdāls* at the Ka'ba. In another anecdote of Gurg's power of bilocation, Gurg rescues a Qalandar called Shīrīn Gōyā ('Sweet singer') from ghouls who are seated beneath a great shady tree on a distant road (anecdote no. 103). In another anecdote, the same Qalandar is passing time in Gurg's company (no. 153). A Qalandar meeting Gurg addresses him as 'Emperor of *abdāls* ... naked Gurg' (anecdote no. 147).

Gurg bent his head low, and set off back to Mawlānā Ismā'īl. [When he entered his presence,] he saw that the latter was seated with two personages. He greeted them and they answered his salutation. He then sat down politely on his knees. After a while he asked his preceptor for wine, who said to him that it was 'over there'.

'In Ḥaẓrat's cell?' Gurg asked.

Mawlānā Ismā'īl replied, 'Go yourself and get it!'

Gurg, in telling this anecdote, remarked that the wine he found was in the very same vessel that Khwāja Khiẓr had shown him. After this, Gurg took his leave from his *pīr* and came to Kara. From that day on, he states, he found the scent of rosewater in wine; and till the day when he was speaking in all that he drank Gurg found the scent of the Friend (God), and this inspired the thought of Him.

In the whole of the *Asrār al-majdhūbīn*, this strange account is the only passage of sustained and allegedly autobiographical narrative; and it has to be said that, like almost every other anecdote in the work, it is hard to accept it as a realistic account of objective happenings. We may add here the sole concrete item of information regarding Gurg's life to be found in the work, namely the date of his death as given in the final anecdote (no. 210). On Saturday, 3 Rajab AH 700 (15 March 1301), Gurg, when he was brought his morning wine, contrary to his wont, poured it on the ground. He passed away in the middle of the following night.

The majority of the anecdotes show the same aberrant sense of mission that is revealed in the narrative of his call to the spiritual life. The formulaic anecdotal pattern displays Gurg seated 'in the bazaar', sometimes in the town mosque, occasionally visiting the boys' school or the house of his patrons and devotees of the Lāhawrī family. Occasionally, he is wandering outside the city or even bathing in the Ganges, which he calls the local Dijla or Euphrates. Most often, he is sitting at the liquor shop. There were evidently two of these alcoholic establishments, run by Hindus called Bholā and Bāndī (Pāndēy?). Bholā, we are told, was childless, but through the intercession of Khwāja Gurg, he later had sons by his three wives, and this led to his conversion to Islam; but he evidently did not abandon his profession of wine-selling.

Many of the anecdotes testify to the belief that the wine consumed by Khwāja Gurg changed to *gulāb* (rosewater) and honey. Its sweet fragrance scented whole adjacent areas of the bazaar. Yet in other anecdotes Gurg, evidently inebriated, is represented as having fallen down unconscious and naked (no. 176). His companions under the influence of *sharāb* sometimes turned violent and even laid hands upon the *khwāja* himself. The local *sharāb* is therefore represented as a strong physical intoxicant; and if these anecdotes can be taken as historical evidence, there was evidently a problem of lower-class urban alcoholism in northern India in the thirteenth century. As also in a well-attested poem of Kabīr which we must assign to around the fifteenth century, in this text there are references to the fiery *bhaṭī* in which strong liquor is distilled.[22] Into the fire of a still from which the liquor was dripping, Gurg is said to have thrust the *khirqa* (cloak) despatched to him by Shaykh Niẓām al-Dīn of Dehlī, though it was afterwards taken out and sent back unharmed (anecdote no. 196, f. 80).

As Gurg sits drinking his wine, he is joined by visitors (more anecdotes start in this way than in any other). Some of the visitors are hostile. Among them there are men of education (*muta'allimīn*), a royal official who wishes to chastise Gurg for drinking wine, Qalandars, and mere troublesome drunkards. What is built into the pattern of

[22] Cf. *Kabīr-granthāvalī*, ed. Pārasnāth Tiwārī, Prayāg: Hindī Parishad, 1961, *pada* 56, p. 32. Cf. also *Kabīr Bījak, śabda* 12.2, 29.3; ed. Sukdev Siṅh, Ilahabad: Nīlābh Prakāśan, 1972, pp. 115, 122; tr. Rev. Ahmad Shāh, repr., Delhi: Forgotten Books, 1990, pp. 100, 110.

these anecdotes is the outcome that Khwāja Gurg will triumph over his opponents. The arguments and criticisms of the verbose men of learning are confounded. The royal official repents and becomes *sāqī* or cupbearer to the khwāja (anecdote no. 172). The violent Qalandars and drunkards are paralysed and rendered powerless (anecdote no. 91). The tendency of the anecdotes is on the whole merciful rather than wrathful. Khwāja Gurg's opponents are usually given the opportunity to repent, and from the paralysis or blindness that has struck them, they are often restored to the use of their faculties.

Such anecdotes are often accompanied by homilies by Gurg on Islam or *taṣawwuf* and spiritual love, or by tales of the Prophet of Islam and his times. The homilies and tales are on the whole of a sobriety which contrasts favourably with the setting and wild superstitious atmosphere and unconvincing detail of many of the anecdotes. *Āyas* of the Qur'ān and *ḥadiths* are frequently and correctly quoted. The anecdotes often end with the khwāja reciting a quatrain of his own composition.

Other visitors to Khwāja Gurg, who believed in his paranormal powers, sought his aid. They bore offerings, often money that was immediately spent upon wine, or sometimes wine itself. A Hindu who wanted a son brought a flower, and he was told that he would have two sons (no. 110). Many other men wanted sons, but two other suppliants, one a traveller, came to collect money for the marriage of their daughters (nos. 146, 154). Yet another man asked for money 'because he [had] no sustenance'. Gurg gave him five gold *ṭankas*, telling him to spend four and keep one for a day of need (no. 165).

A number of anecdotes testify to the belief in Khwāja Gurg's ability to produce gold at need.[23] For those who

[23] Anecdotes of the power of Sufi shaykhs and of other Indian wonder-workers over gold are considered in a forthcoming study by the present

wanted money, the Khwāja used to put his hand into a pot (no. 63) or to strike the ground (nos. 53, 114, 127), and gold or silver coins were produced. It is a feature of such gold-producing anecdotes that the gold is always bestowed or spent on suppliants, never used for the needs of the wonder-worker himself.

Conforming to an anecdotal pattern found elsewhere in Indian Sufi hagiography, of shaykhs displaying a river of gold, are two anecdotes which associate this power of Khwāja Gurg with the most conspicuous geographical feature of Kara, the great river Ganges on whose banks the settlement stood. One of these anecdotes concerns Khwāja Gurg's alleged relations with Sultan 'Alā' al-Dīn Khaljī, considered below. The other is a long and exuberant anecdote (no. 113), in which Khwāja Gurg is represented as drinking wine with sixteen other people from the mid-morning prayer to the afternoon prayer, without the measure (*man*) of wine ever diminishing. He then bade them follow him and himself sat down in the water of the Ganges. The sixteen followed him. Then he asked them what they all desired. One said:

'I have need of two *ṭankas* of gold.'

[Khwāja Gurg] put his hand into the Ganges and drew them out. The second said: 'A *ṭanka* of silver'. He drew it out and gave it to him. [...]

From the waters of the Ganges, nuts, a cup of sherbet and sugar followed, roasted wheat and *kabāb* and *sharāb*, a veil and more 'current coin' (*ṭanka-i rā'ij al-waqt*). One of the sixteen wished to be brought to God and [in a naïve and irreverent response to this wish] he was thrown up into the sky. From the river the various demands of the whole band were satisfied.[24]

---

writer [see David Lunn, ed., *The Life and Works of Simon Digby, Volume II: Encounters with Jogīs in Indian Sūfī Hagiography*, New Delhi: Primus Books, 2025, chapter 5, 'Proffered Gifts: Power over Gold' and class 4, 'Anecdotes of the Refusal of the Proffered Gift' ~DL].

[24] MS ff. 49b–50a.

In another anecdote (no. 11), Gurg, sitting in the Ganges, brings out of the water for members of the party accompanying him sherbet, halwa and milk, and finally honey, the last at the request of a girl.

The Ganges flowed between the towns of Kara and Manikpur. Like the Buddha before him, Khwāja Gurg is shown walking upon its water to the other side (no. 68):

It is related that Khwāja Gurg ... was sitting [in his usual place in the bazaar at Kara] when a man came and said, 'The Mad Boy has died at Manikpur.'

Khwāja Gurg rose and said, 'Come, we shall go to Manikpur and visit [his burial]!'

Slave-like, the man fell at the khwāja's feet; and he left with him, the khwāja in front and the man following. When they arrived at the crossing there was no boat there. 'What do you want with a boat?' the khwāja said. 'Come along with me!'

The khwāja took his hand and they went across the level surface of the water just as if it was dry land. Most of those who were at the crossing trembled and said: 'Hurrah for the spiritual authority (*wilāyat*) that the khwāja has!' They arrived at Manikpur when the Mad Boy was about to be taken out [to be buried] ... So when the Mad Boy had been taken out and buried, the khwāja stayed for a while, and then he went back to Kara in the same manner.[25]

Of Khwāja Gurg's clientèle, some visitors resorted to him because they had a wife or relation afflicted by evil spirits, *parīs*, or *devs* (nos. 88, 155, 169); or, less commonly, were themselves afflicted (no. 92). Khwāja Gurg used to chase

[25] MS f. 30a. For the Buddha's walking across the Ganges, see *Mahāparinibbānasutta*, chapter I, § 34 [see translation by T.W. Rhys Davids, *Buddhist Suttas*, Oxford: Oxford University Press, 1881; repr., Delhi: Motilal Banarasidass, 1965, pp. 21–2 ~DL]; *Divyāvadāna*, legend III, ed. E.B. Cowell and R.A. Neil, Cambridge: Cambridge University Press, 1886; repr., Delhi: Indological Book House, 1987, p. 56; J. Ph. Vogel, *Indian Serpent Lore, or the Nāgas in Hindu Legend and Art*, repr., Varanasi: Prithivi Prakashan, 1972, p. 172.

these spirits away, in one instance forbidding the spirit ever to come back within the boundaries of Kara. In two cases, the *parī* volunteers that he will not remain longer in the town (nos. 88, 169); in yet another, the king of the *parīs* promises that they will no longer roam 'round and about the settlement of Kara' (*gird u payrāmūn-i ḥavālī-i kara*; no. 205).

Perhaps the most notable of all the gift-bestowing powers credited to Sufis in medieval India and elsewhere in the eastern Islamic world is that of bestowing kingship on aspirants to power. The tale was widely believed that Khwāja Gurg had prophesied the rise to the throne of 'Alā' al-Dīn Khaljī when the latter was governor (*muqṭa'*) of Kara. 'Iṣāmī, who wrote in the Deccan twenty years before the composition of the *Asrār al-majdhūbīn* has a story regarding this bestowal.[26] Our text has a number of anecdotes about the special relationship between Khwāja Gurg and Sultan 'Alā' al-Dīn.

When 'Alā' al-Dīn was first appointed governor of Kara, he rode past Khwāja Gurg and some Qalandars as they were drinking wine. The future sultan dismounted and fell at Khwāja Gurg's feet, whereupon Gurg told him that he had given him the kingdom of Dehlī. After he had attained the throne, he offered five trays of gold coins and five of silver to Gurg, but the khwāja took him by the hand and led him to the banks of the Ganges, where he told him to close his eyes. When the Sultan opened his eyes he saw that the whole great river was flowing with gold and silver (Anecdote no. 136).

When the Sultan opened his eyes, the *Khwāja* asked: 'What do you see?'

The Sultan said: 'The whole of the river is flowing with gold and silver. It is saying, "Here I am, Gurg! Here I am!"'

[26] See S. Digby, 'The Sufi *Shaykh* and the Sultan', *Iran*, vol. 28, 1990, p. 76 [*L&WSD* III.2; this volume, pp. 67–8]; *Futūḥ al-salāṭīn*, Madras: University of Madras, 1948, p. 229.

The khwāja remarked: 'This is the treasure of My Friend [God], so it belongs to me. I do not need to look towards others.'

In 'Alā' al-Dīn's mind, great awe took hold, and like a slave he asked pardon at the foot of the khwāja. To set his mind at rest, the khwāja accepted a single silver *ṭanka* from him.[27]

'Alā' al-Dīn rose to supreme power by the treacherous murder of his uncle, Sultan Jalāl al-Dīn Fērōz, at a meeting arranged on a boat on the Ganges. The *Asrār al-majdhūbīn* contains a version of this incident, which is a disingenuous attempt to absolve 'Alā' al-Dīn from all blame while exalting the role of Khwāja Gurg. According to this version, Jalāl al-Dīn, being afraid of his nephew (who was also his son-in-law), had tried to persuade his daughter, 'Alā' al-Dīn's wife, to poison the latter. But husband and wife fled; and with Khwāja Gurg's advice and blessing, 'Alā' al-Dīn brought back treasure from his successful raid on Dēvgīr (in this source called Khāragarh). After his return, at the meeting between uncle and nephew in the boat on the Ganges, it was (according to this unconvincing account) Jalāl al-Dīn who had plotted treachery against his nephew. There were eight armed men hidden under his throne on the boat; but when these rushed out, dagger in hand, the appearances of Jalāl al-Dīn and 'Alā' al-Dīn were miraculously reversed. It was Jalāl al-Dīn whom the armed men stabbed to death in error (anecdote no. 196).[28]

[27] MS f. 57a.

[28] The historian Farishta, writing at the end of the sixteenth century, has an anecdote of Khwāja Gurg's 'bestowal' of kingship on Sultan 'Alā' al-Dīn Khaljī which does not derive from the *Asrār al-majdhūbīn* or from 'Iṣāmī. Before the confrontation between uncle and nephew on the boat in the Ganges, 'Alā' al-Dīn went to pay his respects to 'Shaykh KRK the *majdhūb* buried in Kara. The *majdhūb* raised his head [from meditation] and said:

har kas kih bikunad bā tu jang
sar dar kishtī tan dar gang

There are many miraculous anecdotes of familiar patterns in the *Asrār al-majdhūbīn*. Bilocation is even more common than the production of gold. Khwāja Gurg, after dramatic and exhausting encounters in the bazaars of Kara, would suddenly disappear for days on end; and his adherents then believed that he had been away in distant holy places or the world of the unseen. On Friday eves he was supposed to be present at the Ka'ba (no. 144) or the tomb of the Prophet (no. 149). One particularly extravagant anecdote is the alleged testimony of a man at whose house Khwāja Gurg was passing the night. Outside, he suddenly saw a great light, and beheld a camel and its rider descending from the sky, escorted by two angels (anecdote no. 4, folio 4b). This was to bear Gurg away to Mecca.[29] The man hung onto the tail and was afterwards stranded in the holy city. Never mind, the servants of the *Ḥaram* assure him, Gurg will be back next Friday, and he can hang onto the tail for the return journey. On distant roads, Gurg would appear before travellers in peril, to save them from dacoits, ghouls, or wild beasts (nos. 62, 86, 103, 146).

Many anecdotes are part of the extended folklore of Sufi piety and Sufi powers, and they are also found in other hagiographical works and in oral tradition attached to the

---

> Whosoever makes war upon you—
> Head in the boat, body in the Ganges!'

Firishta, *Ta'rīkh-i Firishta*, vol. I, Bombay: Government College Press, 1831–2, p. 174; vol. I, Kanpur: Naval Kishor, p. 100. Niẓām al-Dīn Aḥmad, *Ṭabaqāt-i Akbarī*, Calcutta: Baptist Mission Press, 1937, vol. I, p. 136, merely reproduces the work of Farishta.

[29] A similar anecdote of the flying camel standing ready to take Shaykh Niẓām al-Dīn Chishtī of Dehlī to Mecca is found in an early and reputable source: Khwurd, *Siyar al-awliyā'*, p. 143; Lahore repr., p. 153; for Shaykh Sharaf al-Dīn Aḥmad Manērī's presence in Mecca on Fridays, see Shaykh Shu'ayb bin Shaykh Jalāl Manerī, *Manāqib al-aṣfiyyā'*, Calcutta: Nūr al-Afāq Press, 1895, p. 142.

names of other shaykhs. A very widely distributed story which finds a place in the *Asrār al-majdhūbīn* is that of the spiritual challenger who comes with wrathful aspect, riding a lion or a tiger and brandishing a snake as a whip, only to be confronted and discomfited by the local resident holy man, who rides forward on the wall on which he has been sitting (anecdote no. 183). Numerous Indian versions have been recorded, and it has been found far afield, among the Kurds in 'Irāq, and among the Bektashīs in Anatolia.[30] There are anecdotes of a talking horse and of a talking snake, each of which obeys the commands of Khwāja Gurg to moderate its behaviour. The anecdote of the talking snake is a long one, recognizably modelled on popular *dāstān* literature, in which Gurg travels to a distant region to recover the mate of the snake from the king of the *parīs* (anecdote no. 84). To the historical folklorist, this suggests that the *parīs* of thirteenth-century Kara were ancient Indian *nāgas* but thinly disguised.[31]

If the *parīs* are recognizably *nāgas*, an identity of name (derived from the common Aryan linguistic heritage) ensured that the *dēvs* ('demons') of Persian folklore were yet more easily identified as local deities (*dēv*, *dēva*) in worship in the vicinity of Kara. In one anecdote, Gurg is shown seated at the shop of a cloth-merchant (*bazzāz*) called 'Alī. He reproached him, asking why he kept Hindus in his house (the implication seems to be that 'Alī himself was a householder who was a convert to Islam, but members of his household had not converted). It then transpired that 'Alī himself went

[30] M. Van Bruinessen, 'Hajji Bektash, Sultan Sahak, Shah Mina Sahib and Various Avatars of a Running Wall', *Turcica, Revue d'Études Turques*, vol. 21–3, 1991, *Mélanges offerts à Irène Mélikoff*, pp. 55–69 [See Digby's extended treatment of this theme: 'To Ride a Tiger or a Wall? Strategies of Prestige in Indian Sufi Legend', in *According to Tradition*, ed. Winand Callewaert and Rupert Snell, Weisbaden: Harrassowitz, 1994, pp. 99–129/*L&WSD* III.6. ~DL].

[31] See Vogel, *Indian Serpent Lore*, *passim*.

out every Sunday with flowers and a lamp to worship a *dēv*, who would trouble him if he did not appear. Khwāja Gurg proceeded to rid him of the *dēv*, saying that he had sent him off and 'burnt' him; and 'Alī was troubled no more by the *dēv*. In the same way, one may reflect, the *muḥtasib* had sent troublesome Qalandars out of town (anecdote no. 9).

These exorcisms of vexing spirits, in one case specifically required to dwell beyond the boundary of the town, again show local loyalty to the Muslim settlement of Kara. And it was not only against ghostly adversaries that Gurg's aid was sought. The *shiqqdār* or governor of Kara was engaged in a campaign against local insurgents at Bhambharolī and Mahoba. Ten days of fighting had brought no gains. He then despatched a messenger to Gurg, saying that he had been told by Sultan 'Alā' al-Dīn to resort to him in case of difficulties. As a result of Gurg's prayers, he conquered the village which he had been besieging (anecdote no. 43). Though the terms of Gurg's appointment by Khwāja Khiżr to sit and drink wine in the bazaar may lack the grandeur of the delegated authority of the great shaykhs of the major *silsilas*, it is a claim of the conferral of a territorial *wilāyat* (dominion).[32] It is from the *wilāyat* of Kara, also called his own *wilāyat* (*wilāyat-i man*) that Khwāja Gurg bids the *parīs* depart (anecdote no. 205). A large portion of the anecdotes of the *Asrār al-majdhūbīn* endeavour to present Khwāja Gurg as engaged in maintaining the well-being of the place which has been entrusted to him and of its inhabitants, by his actions, his advice, and his spiritual power (*barakat*).

It cannot be claimed that the *Asrār al-majdhūbīn* is of great value for its factual or historical evidence, but it provides some information regarding the social life of a Muslim settlement in northern India in the thirteenth century,

[32] See Digby, 'The Sufi *Shaykh* as a Source of Authority in Medieval India', pp. 62–3 [this volume, pp. 14–17].

for which other evidence is lacking. The work lacks any profound or subtle spiritual content, while providing many instances of extreme credulity and of antinomian behaviour. Yet it remains of value as a recognizable addition to the early corpus of biographical literature regarding Sufis of the Dehlī Sultanate, and as evidence of levels of popular Muslim belief, practice, and states of mind in a provincial urban community of the period.[33]

[33] A first draft of this paper was presented at the International Seminar on Sufism organized by the Government of India in New Delhi to commemorate the centenary of Mawlānā Abu'l Kalām 'Āzād's birth. I could not rival the lofty and wide-ranging surveys of Sufi doctrine or of Sufi influence on Indian society boldly offered by other delegates, and instead I drew attention to this surviving hagiographical work which must have seemed less than edifying to my audience in current political circumstances.

My paper was submitted late, and I was disconcerted when it was returned from the Secretariat of the Indian Council for Cultural Relations, on the morning of its presentation and distribution, photocopied rather than typed. But I then reflected that this was one of the curious but apt coincidences that so frequently occur in the patterns of Sufi anecdotes. The paper refers to the hazards of manuscript transmission, and it was circulated in reproduced handwritten form. Likewise, the story that I tell in it concerns a missing manuscript leaf, and in the original circulated form there was an error in the enumeration of the pages, whereby p. 11 appeared to be missing.

My paper's timing in the course of the Proceedings of the Seminar also had a symbolic value. This paper concerns a *majdhūb*: and the Indian Sufi biographical *tadhkiras* sometimes notice this category of devotees in a section towards the end of the work reflecting their lower status, after the notices of grander or more conformist shaykhs (cf. note 12 above). Hence, it was appropriate that my contribution should have been presented at the tail-end of the deliberations of the seminar. I am grateful to the Convener on behalf of the Government of India, Shri Burney [= Baranī], whose very name evokes a potent shade of the Dehlī Sultanate, and to my Chairperson, Shrimati Kapila Vatsyayan, whose already wide tolerance may have been stretched further by the persona of the man of religion who was my subject.

10

'Abd al-Quddus Gangohi, AD 1456–1537

The Personality and Attitudes of a Medieval Indian Sufi

The emphasis put in recent historical writing upon the individual aspects of medieval Indian Sufis has induced the present writer to attempt, within the compass of a short monograph, to present a more rounded study of the diverse and sometimes conflicting activities of a single Sufi shaykh. 'Abd al-Quddus Gangohi is generally held to be in the second rather than the first rank of Indian Muslim religious figures. His theological writings, particularly the *Rushd-nama* (of which a detailed examination is presented in section VI of this study), are repetitious and somewhat lacking in intellectual distinction. He was a minor rather than a major poet in Persian and in Hindi and the role which he played as a recorder of Hindi verses current at the end of the fifteenth century is also of some importance to the historian of literature. His recorded behaviour does not show outstanding nobility of character, or wideness of human sympathies or fortitude, although such qualities

* Originally published in *Medieval India: A Miscellany*, vol. III, Aligarh: Aligarh Muslim University, 1975, pp. 1–66. It included the following opening note: 'The transliteration system followed by the author, though different from the one adopted for the Miscellany, has not been disturbed'; nor has it been here.

may be discerned in other Indian Sufi shaykhs when they have been stripped of the adornments of hagiographic piety. 'Abd al-Quddus' life and personality are worth examining in detail because he is a representative figure, in whom many of the sometimes-conflicting tendencies and aspects of Indian Islam find expression, and about whom we have copious and contemporary, therefore fairly reliable, biographical material. In his behaviour and in the contradictions in it we see at work a number of the processes of adaptation and conflict generated by the Muslim presence in medieval India.

Life of 'Abd al-Quddus

Shaykh 'Abd al-Quddus bin Shaykh Muhammad Isma'il bin Shaykh Safi al-din Hanafi Ghaznavi Chishti Gangohi was among the most prominent Sufi shaykhs of the Sabiri branch of the Chishti *silsila*, and indeed of late fifteenth- and early sixteenth-century north Indian Sufism. Biographical notices of him are common in later Sufi *tadhkiras*;[1] and a copious collection of anecdotes regarding him was compiled in his lifetime and immediately after his death by his son and successor (*sajjada-nashin*), Shaykh Rukn al-Din Quddusi.[2] A few years ago a lengthy modern biography in Urdu, which

[1] 'Abd al-Haqq Muhaddith Dehlavi, *Akhbar al-Akhyar*, Dehli: Mujtaba'i Press, 1309, pp. 215–17; Ghulam Sarvar, *Khazinat al-asfiyya*, Kanpur: Naval Kishor Press, 1332/1914, I, pp. 416–18.

[2] Rukn al-Din Quddusi, *Lata'if-i Quddusi*, Delhi: Mujtaba'i Press 1311/1894, hereafter cited as *Lata'if*. The portion composed by Rukn al-Din was begun in the lifetime of his father and completed two months after his death, in Sh'aban 944/1538—see p. 71. Further anecdotes were added by an Afghan *murid* Dattu Sarvani, evidently around 953–4/1546–7, see Simon Digby, 'Dreams and Reminiscences of Dattu Sarvani, a Sixteenth Century Indo-Afghan Soldier' in *The Indian Economic and Social History Review*, vol. II, 1965, pp. 52–7 [see *L&WSD* I, *Against the Mughals*, for Digby's book-length expansion of his 1965 study].

draws upon some minor inaccessible sources was published by a descendant of the shaykh.[3]

'Abd al-Quddus was born near Rudawli in the modern Barabanki district of the United Provinces (UP),[4] probably in the year 860/1456,[5] in a family who, although they had Sufi allegiances of the type common in medieval India, were more distinguished as '*ulama*' expounding the traditional Islamic sciences.[6] They claimed descent from the Imam Abu Hanifa and were said to have migrated from Ghazni to Dehli. The connections of the family appear to have been with the metropolitan city of Dehli itself until, probably during the disorders of the late fourteenth century, one Shaykh Nizam al-Din moved eastwards towards the rising

[3] I'jaz al-Haqq Quddusi, *Shaykh 'Abd al-Quddus awr un ki ta'limat*, Karachi: Academy of Educational Research, 1961, hereafter referred to as *Shaykh 'Abd al-Quddus*.

[4] H.R. Nevill, *Barabanki: A Gazetteer. District Gazetteers of the United Provinces*, vol. XLVIII, Allahabad: Government Press, 1904, pp. 258–60. Rudanli (Rudawli) is a few miles south of the present course of the river Gogra, about 38 mi. east from Barabanki, lying close to the main roads from Lucknow and Barabanki to Fyzabad. It is described as 'a large Musalman town' which in 1901 possessed 3,292 houses.

[5] *Shaykh 'Abd al-Quddus*, p. 168. Citing *Adhkar al-abrar*, possibly the Urdu translation of Muhammad Ghawthi's *Gulzar-i abrar*; no mention of his date of birth is found in the manuscript of Ghawthi's *Gulzar-i abrar* in the John Rylands Library, Manchester (Lindesiana No. 185), f. 152a. The date AH 860 for his birth is not inherently improbable. At his death 'Abd al-Quddus would have been 84 Muslim or 81 solar years old. His eldest son was 11 years old in 896/1491—see *Lata'if*, p. 31. 'Abd al-Quddus would therefore have been 25 years old when the latter was born.

[6] The difference between these two Muslim traditions is depicted in *Lata'if*, pp. 6–7. When 'Abd al-Quddus took to the ecstatic way of life of the Sufis, one Shaykh Fath Allah objected saying, 'You are the son of a *danishmand* [man of learning] Shaykh Isma'il and the grandson of a *danishmand* Qadi Safi al-Din, and the brother of a *danishmand*, 'Abd al-Samad.' His mother also complained in similar terms—see p. 7, cf. also p. 9.

power of Jawnpur. This Shaykh Nizam al-Din is described as a *murid* (Sufi disciple) of Mawlana Khvajagi, who was a *khalifa* (successor) of Shaykh Nasir al-Din Mahmud 'Chiragh-i Dehli', the principal Sufi of the Chishti *silsila* in the capital city in the middle years of the fourteenth century. Shaykh Nizam al-Din came eastwards to Jawnpur in the company of the celebrated *'alim* Qazi Shihab al-Din Dawlatabadi, author of the *tafsir Bahr-i mavvaj.*[7] The son of Shaykh Nizam al-Din, Shaykh Nasir al-Din was given lands at Phagawli, described as very close to Rudawli,[8] by Sultan Ibrahim Shah Sharqi of Jawnpur (r. 804–40/1402–36). The lands were enjoyed by his son Shaykh Safi al-Din and his grandson Shaykh Muhammad Isma'il. The last married the daughter of one Qazi Khan, sister of Qazi Daniyal, both of whom filled the office of 'Hakim' of Rudawli; by this lady he had four sons, of whom the third was 'Abd al-Quddus.[9]

[7] 'Abd al-Haqq, *Akhbar al-akhyar*, pp. 175–6; C.A. Storey, *Persian Literature: A Bio-Bibliographical Survey*, London: Royal Asiatic Society, 1977, vol. I, part i, pp. 9–10; Muhammad Ghawthi, *Gulzar-i Abrar*, Manuscript, John Rylands Library, Manchester, Lindesiana no. 185, n.d., ff. 88a–b.

[8] So in *Shaykh 'Abd al-Quddus*; the name is not to be found in the *Barabanki Gazetteer.*

[9] This account of the immediate ancestors of 'Abd al-Quddus is taken from *Shaykh 'Abd al-Quddus*, pp. 145–68, who gives as his source a MS entitled *Anvar al-safa*, which is evidently a late nineteenth-century composition—see p. 167, n. 1. All the details here quoted are plausible. But Nizam al-Din and his son Nasir al-Din are stated to have come from Ghaznin to Dehli in the reign of 'Ala' al-Din Khilji (695–715/1295–1315—see p. 145). This is about a century before the same pair moved to Jawnpur. Shaykh Muhammad Isma'il is stated to have been born in AH 789 (p. 162) and to have died in 860 (p. 197). In this case four generations would have travelled together on the move from Dehli to Jawnpur; and Muhammad Isma'il would have been 71 Muslim years of age in the year of the birth of 'Abd al-Quddus. Moreover, though he is there stated to have died in the same year, in the immediately preceding anecdote he is said to have been 78 years old. An anecdote in *Lata'if*, p. 5 (also quoted in *Shaykh 'Abd*

Shaykh 'Abd al-Quddus, as a member of a family of *'alims*, began the curriculum of formal Islamic learning: but he had not pursued this very far when he was overtaken by the love of God, and destroyed the copy of the *Kafiyya*, with Qazi Shihab al-Din Dawlatabadi's commentary, which he had been studying.[10] His ability later in life to teach and write upon the *ulum-i zahiri* (i.e. the non-Sufi branches of Muslim theological learning) was ascribed to divine inspiration.[11] After being turned back by a *darvesh* whom he had met upon the road when he attempted to leave Rudawli, Shaykh 'Abd al-Quddus went to the local *khanqah* founded by Shaykh Ahmad 'Abd al-Haqq (d. 837/1434).[12] 'Abd al-Quddus himself gives a rather different account of the immediate circumstances which led him to enter the *khanqah* of Shaykh Ahmad 'Abd al-Haqq, stating that he left his family while suffering the pangs of human love.[13] Ahmad 'Abd al-Haqq

---

al-Quddus, pp. 168–9) also shows that he was alive at the time when his sons were able to read and write: the following anecdote, *Lata'if*, p. 6, refers to 'Abd al-Quddus talking to his father: but he evidently died before 'Abd al-Quddus abandoned his studies, ibid., p. 7. Ghawthi describes 'Abd al-Quddus as the son of Shaykh Safi al-Din's daughter (Ghawthi, *Gulzar-i abrar*, f. 152a). This is incorrect as Shaykh 'Abd al-Quddus gives his pedigree on several occasions as "Abd al-Quddus, son of Isma'il, son of Safi, the Hanafi, the Ghaznavi' (*Anwar al-'uyun*, Lakhnau: Gulzar-i Muhammadi Press, 1296, p. 4: letters to Babur and Humayun, see *Shaykh 'Abd al-Quddus*, pp. 453, 457). For an anecdote concerning the maternal uncle and maternal grandfather of 'Abd al-Quddus, Qazi Daniyal and Qazi Khan, and their relations with Ahmad 'Abd al-Haqq, see *Anwar al-'uyun*, p. 108.

10 *Lata'if*, p. 6.

11 Ibid., p. 8. Details in the anecdote suggest that 'Abd al-Quddus in later life progressively mastered the studies which he had neglected in youth. This was apparent also to Ghawthi (Ghawthi, *Gulzar-i abrar*, f. 152b).

12 Ilahdiya Chishti, *Siyar al-aqtab*, Lakhnau: Naval Kishor Press, 1306/1889, p. 222; *Shaykh 'Abd al-Quddus*, p. 138.

13 *Anwar al-'uyun*, p. 108. *Dar napak 'ishq uftada bud*: but possibly in *napak na* may be a copyists' error, in which case there is no conflict with the account of the *Lata'if*.

belonged to a relatively obscure line of the Chishti *silsila*, which has however attained great prominence in later Indian Sufism. His spiritual pedigree was traced with only two links—through Shaykh Jalal al-Din Kabir al-Awliya' Panipati and Shaykh Shams al-Din Turk Panipati—to Shaykh 'Ala al-Din 'Ali Ahmad Sabir, identified with a *khalifa* of Shaykh Farid al-Din 'Ganj-i shakar' Chishti of Ajodhan (AD 1175–1265), a central figure in the religious traditions of the Dehli Sultanate.[14] The *shajara* is weak, in that the number of links appears too few, probably in the connection between Jalal al-Din and Farid al-Din.[15]

[14] For Shaykh Farid al-Din, see K.A. Nizami, *Life and Times of Shaykh Farid-u'd-din Ganj-i-shakar*, Aligarh: Aligarh Muslim University, 1955. For the identification of 'Ala' al-Din 'Ali Ahmad Sabir with 'Ali Sabir, see ibid., p. 78.

[15] *Lata'if*, p. 29, gives the complete *shajara*. 'Abd al-Quddus confirms that Ahmad 'Abd al-Haqq was the disciple of Jalal al-Din Panipati, *Anwar al-'uyun*, pp. 14–18. Some seventeenth-century and later *tadhkiras* give 765/1364 as the date of the death of Jalal al-Din Panipati, which is improbable in view of the fact that Ahmad 'Abd al-Haqq was still alive in 837 (the date 765 is found in Sarvar, *Khazinat al-asfiyya'*, vol. I, p. 365, also *Shaykh 'Abd al-Quddus*, p. 120). However, the *Siyar al-aqtab* does not mention the year of Jalal al-Din Panipati's death but makes it clear that it occurred after that of his namesake Jalal al-Din Makhdum-i Jahanian, which it mentions occurred in AH 785 (AD 1384, p. 213). 'Abd al-Quddus in his narrative, which is much the earliest source, refers to the flight of Jalal al-Din Panipati and Ahmad 'Abd al-Haqq before a major Mongol invasion which devastated Dehli, *Anwar al-'uyun*, p. 21: this can only be the invasion of Amir Taimur in 801/1398.

Of Jalal al-Din Panipati's predecessors, Shaykh Shams al-Din Turk Panipati is said in seventeenth-century *tadhkiras* to have died in 715/1315 or 718/1318; the discrepancy is noted in Sarvar, *Khazinat al-asfiyya'*, vol. I, p. 324. The same work, depending on the seventeenth-century *Ma'arij al-wilayat*, gives 690/1290 as the year of the death of 'Ala' al-Din 'Ali Ahmad Sabir, ibid., vol. I, p. 319. *Shaykh 'Abd al-Quddus* wrongly transcribes 696, p. 112, while the *Siyar al-aqtab* states that he died in 664/1265–66, p. 184. 'Abd al-Haqq, writing at the close of the sixteenth century, doubted the identity of this Shaykh, buried at Kalyar

Shaykh Ahmad 'Abd al-Haqq was from a family claiming Faruqi descent, who had evidently settled at Rudawli in the second half of the fourteenth century.[16] In his youth he left Rudawli to go and study in Dehli, but he was overtaken by mystical love and soon abandoned these formal Islamic studies.[17] He then became a disciple of Shaykh Jalal al-Din at Panipat.[18] He had visited Bhakkar and Sind, and he resided for a while at Sannam in the Panjab, evidently in the last years of the fourteenth century.[19] He returned eastwards in the disturbances which followed the invasion of Amir Taimur (801/1398) and visited Pandwa, the capital of the Sultans of Bengal.[20] After a sojourn of some months in Bihar during

---

near Rurki (Rourkee), with the 'Ali Sabir mentioned as a *khalifa* of Shaykh Farid in the fourteenth-century Chishti *tadhkira* of Amir Khwurd (*Siyar al-awliya'*, Dehli: Muhibb-i Hindi Press, 1302, p. 185; see 'Abd al-Haqq, *Akhbar al-akhyar*, p. 69). But there is no doubt that 'Abd al-Quddus and Ahmad 'Abd al-Haqq saw themselves as shaykhs of the Chishti *silsila*, and, in default of a more obvious connection, the identification is not improbable. However, the *shajara* given in the *Lata'if*, as well as in the *Siyar al-aqtab* and most subsequent works, has suspiciously few generations between Shaykh Jalal al-Din and Shaykh Farid al-Din.

[16] The *Anwar al-'uyun* does not mention where Ahmad 'Abd al-Haqq was born or brought up previous to his departure for Dehli, but a reference to his returning home (*su'e vatan-i khvud*) after his visit to Bengal implies that he was raised in Rudawli (p. 26). 'Abd al-Haqq Dehlavi was clear that Rudawli was his place of birth (*mawlid*) as well as of burial (*murqad*), 'Abd al-Haqq, *Akhbar al-akhyar*, p. 182. I. Quddusi gives from an unspecified source the additional information that his father's name was 'Umar and his grandfather's Da'ud. The family claimed Faruqi descent. His grandfather had professed *bay'at* to Shaykh Nasir al-Din 'Chiragh-i Dehli', and had received instruction from him. Later he settled in Rudawli (*Shaykh 'Abd al-Quddus*, p. 126).

[17] *Anwar al-'uyun*, pp. 11–14.

[18] Ibid., pp. 14–18.

[19] Ibid., pp. 70, 19–20.

[20] Ibid., pp. 22–5. For the visit of Shaykh Safi al-Din to Pandwa, see *Shaykh 'Abd al-Quddus*, p. 159, citing *Anwar al-safa*.

which his spiritual claims and his reputation as a shaykh increased, he returned home to Rudawli.[21]

He was offered by Sultan Ibrahim Shah Sharqi a grant of four villages and 1,000 *bighas* of land near Rudawli, but evidently refused this.[22] At some later date he visited Jawnpur, where through the agency of Qazi Shihab al-Din Dawlatabadi (whose connection with the family of 'Abd al-Quddus has already been mentioned) a meeting between the shaykh and the sultan took place.[23] According to 'Abd al-Quddus, no formal grants for the maintenance of the *khanqah* had been accepted from sultans or noblemen down to the time of Shaykh Muhammad's incumbency when he was writing:[24] but 'Abd al-Quddus also mentions that from the time of his refusal of Sultan Ibrahim's grant, Ahmad 'Abd al-Haqq's way of life had been 'princely' (*chun mulukan*).[25] It must have been maintained by a substantial flow of day-to-day offerings (*futuhat*) reflecting the esteem in which the shaykh and his shrine were held.

When Shaykh 'Abd al-Quddus was received into the *khanqah* of Shaykh Ahmad 'Abd al-Haqq, the incumbent (*sajjada-nashin*) was the grandson of the latter, Shaykh Muhammad bin Shaykh 'Arif. He was a boy of the same age as 'Abd al-Quddus; and 'Abd al-Quddus, although he made a profession of discipleship (*bay'at*), showed little of the intense respect and subservience to his *pir* which is inculcated by Sufi manuals and collections of anecdotes of the late medieval period.[26] Instead, we are told that subsequently Shaykh Muhammad showed the greatest respect towards 'Abd al-Quddus.[27] 'Abd al-Quddus

[21] Ibid., pp. 26–8.
[22] Ibid., pp. 31–3.
[23] Ibid., pp. 33–4.
[24] Ibid., p. 39.
[25] Ibid., p. 35.
[26] *Lata'if*, p. 10.
[27] Ibid.

claimed that spiritual grace had come to him directly from Shaykh Muhammad's deceased grandfather. According to the *Lata'if-i Quddusi*, when he had intended to go elsewhere to profess *bay'at*, each time that the thought occurred the spirit of Ahmad 'Abd al-Haqq had appeared before him to forbid it. Finally Ahmad 'Abd al-Haqq had come forward in bodily form[28] and consigned 'Abd al-Quddus to his grandson, to whom he professed *bay'at*. Another early account adds that there were many people present when the tomb of Shaykh Ahmad 'Abd al-Haqq split open and the deceased shaykh came out in corporeal form, sat upon the *chabutra* or platform of the *khanqah* courtyard where 'Abd al-Quddus happened to be, took him by the hand and announced that he had brought him to God.[29]

'Abd al-Quddus' own account of his entry into the *khanqah* of Ahmad 'Abd al-Haqq contains no mention of his intention to profess *bay'at* elsewhere: nor does it allude to such a crude miracle as the deceased shaykh coming out of his tomb to welcome him. In this account it is not difficult for us to accept that the supernatural voices, of the *'alam-i ghayb* ('world invisible'), were a part of the subjective experience of this shaykh and those who lived in a similar religious environment; later in this chapter we shall revert to the mystical experiences of 'Abd al-Quddus.

[28] Ibid. *ba juththa-i zabri hazir shudand*; in contrast to earlier occasions when it was *dar mu'amala-i batin*, 'in a dream'—for this usage see ibid., pp. 63, 67.

[29] Reproduced in the nineteenth-century preface to the smaller collection of 'Abd al-Quddus' letters (see note 92 below), p. 3. Also reproduced verbatim in the concluding matter of the lithograph of *Anwar al-'uyun*, pp. 131–2. The source is a collection of *malfuzat* (*Malfuzat-i Qutb-i 'Alam*, possibly not the actual title) compiled by 'Abd al-Sattar Saharanpuri, *khalifa* of 'Abd al-Quddus (d. 950/1543–44), for whom see *Shaykh 'Abd al-Quddus*, p. 596, citing *Nuzhat al-khawatir*, vol. IV, pp. 177–8.

'Abd al-Quddus remarks that the sound of the name of God, *Haqq*, used to be heard by the *murids* (disciples), around the *khanqah*, a sign of the awesome potency of the *wilayat* (spiritual jurisdiction) of Shaykh Ahmad 'Abd al-Haqq. He himself had heard it in the following circumstances.

At the beginning of his entry into the Sufi life, he was sitting amid a gathering of friends. He had abandoned his own household and his dear mother, and had fallen into an impure or worldly love (*'ishq-i napak*).[30] His elder brother then came and admonished him, gave him much advice, and led him by the hand back home. It was one of the nights of the blessed month of Ramazan and in the spring (*bahar*). The moon had risen in a clear sky free of dust, and 'Abd al-Quddus was sitting upon the charpoy of his mother. Suddenly there arose from the unseen the cry of '*Haqq!*' from a westerly direction. 'Abd al-Quddus' head had been bowed from his affliction with the pangs of love. He now raised his head; and a while passed and again the name '*Haqq!*' was heard from between the north and west. He then went out into the courtyard of the house. His mother and all the members of the household had been wakened. Not much time elapsed before the cry of '*Haqq!*' again came from the unseen world in the north, in such a manner that all heard it. 'When we investigated it,' 'Abd al-Quddus adds, 'we found that there was no one around the outside of the house.' About half the night had passed when 'Abd al-Quddus asked his mother to forgive him, because he was not master of his own actions. The *wilayat* of Shaykh Ahmad 'Abd al-Haqq was drawing him away to itself, and she should release and excuse him.

'Abd al-Quddus then settled down to worship and austerities. Every night when two thirds of the night had

[30] See note 13 above.

passed, a world of revelation (*'alam-i fayz*) blazed upon him. It was as if the mountains of the world had been placed upon his head, or as if he had been carried away to the depths of the ocean. Then, as a sign of the intercession and of the plenitude of the *wilayat* of Shaykh Ahmad 'Abd al-Haqq, the cry of '*Haqq!*' would come from the unseen, and he would arise and perform the *tahajjud* prayers.[31]

After his reception at the *khanqah*, 'Abd al-Quddus was engaged in austerities and in the menial tasks customarily undertaken by the *murids* in such establishments.[32] He evidently spent much time in the company of a privileged old servant of Shaykh Muhammad's father, called Shaykh Piyare, who was attracted to 'Abd al-Quddus on account of the latter's mystical impassioned state (*hal-i jadhba*). A suspicion of levity attaches to the association, as his biographer explains that during the time he apparently spent with Shaykh Piyare, 'Abd al-Quddus was in reality receiving inward graces from Shaykh Ahmad 'Abd al-Haqq.[33] Shaykh Piyare appears to have influenced and encouraged the taste of 'Abd al-Quddus for both Persian and Hindi poetry. Another member of the same circle was a tailor called Bhikan who experienced mystical illuminations. After his own house was burnt down, 'Abd al-Quddus went to live with him.[34] Against his own professed desire to be free from earthly attachments, 'Abd al-Quddus' marriage was arranged with a younger sister of Shaykh Muhammad, granddaughter of Ahmad 'Abd al-Haqq.[35]

'Abd al-Quddus had visited Siddhawr, some 15 mi. due west of Rudawli, where he had studied under Shaykh

[31] *Anwar al-'uyun*, pp. 107–9.

[32] *Lata'if*, pp. 10–11; *Shaykh 'Abd al-Quddus*, pp. 183–6.

[33] *Lata'if*, pp. 9–10.

[34] Ibid., p. 19.

[35] Ibid., pp. 11–12; *Shaykh 'Abd al-Quddus*, pp. 199–202.

Khvajagi.[36] He had also roamed through the deserted places of the nearby countryside,[37] and, when young, may have been in the habit of visiting Jawnpur:[38] but he appears to have spent the first thirty-seven (Muslim) years of his life without ever going far afield from Rudawli. Rudawli had suffered devastation a number of times in the wars between Bahlul Lodi and Husayn Shah Sharqi around or before 884/1479.[39] In the following decade, when 'Abd al-Quddus had reached maturity and Rudawli was under the rule of the Lodi sultans, 'Abd al-Quddus began to receive the Afghan disciples who figure prominently in his biography, soldiers in the Lodi tribal army. At the beginning of the last decade of the fifteenth century Rudawli temporarily passed out of the control of the Lodi sultans. The *Lata'if-i Quddusi* states that the Kafirs had gained power in Hindostan (i.e. the Gangetic plain eastwards from Dehli) and the *pargana* of Rudawli was under their administrative control (*'amal*).[40] The Kafirs in question appear to be the Bachgoti Rajputs who caused a considerable disturbance in the eastern UP following Sikandar Lodi's accession (894/1489) and his war with his brother Barbak Shah.[41]

36 *Lata'if*, p. 7. For Siddhaur (ancient Sidhapura) see Nevill, *Barabanki*, map facing p. 1 and pp. 270–1.
37 *Lata'if*, p. 18, anecdote 26.
38 Casual visits to Jawnpur are implied in ibid., pp. 22, 24.
39 Ibid., pp. 23, 100. For the terminal date of the war, that of Husayn's flight to Bihar, see K.S. Lal, *Twilight of the Sultanate*, Bombay: Asia Publishing House, 1963, p. 151 and n. *Anwar al-'uyun*, pp. 40–1, states that Rudawli was devastated several times (*chand karat*) in the disturbances of Husayn Shah Sharqi's reign and later mentions a very recent sacking of the place (p. 102).
40 *Lata'if*, pp. 30–1.
41 The beginning of this anecdote makes a reference to the succession of Sikandar Lodi to the throne, which occurred in 1489, and the war with Barbak Shah: later in it the birth of the author, one year after the move

Under Hindu rule pork was openly sold in the bazaar and 'Abd al-Quddus was distressed (*dilgir*). In these circumstances he went to visit an influential disciple, 'Umar Khan Sarvani, a military leader in one of the most important Afghan tribes of the Lodi Sultanate.[42] At 'Umar Khan's invitation, 'Abd al-Quddus moved in 896/1491 from his ancestral home at Rudawli to Shahabad in the Karnal district of the eastern Panjab on the west bank of the Jamuna—a journey of between 400 and 500 mi. to the north-west.[43] He was to spend three and a half decades mainly in Shahabad; and his children grew up there.[44] One anecdote in the *Lata'if* mentions a pilgrimage to Dehli;[45] he certainly made a long stay at Dehli when his son Rukn al-Din was studying there, probably between AD 1505 and 1510.[46] At least once in the years at Shahabad 'Abd al-Quddus went on a pilgrimage to Ajodhan and Multan by way of Dipalpur.[47]

Disturbed political conditions also led to 'Abd al-Quddus' final change of residence. Another of his Afghan *murids*, 'Uthman Karrani, was established at Gangoh in the Saharanpur district of the modern UP, which is about 40 mi. south-east of Shahabad across the river Jamuna.[48] At this

---

from Rudawli in the year 897/1492, is mentioned. For the Bachgoti revolt, see Lal, *Twilight of the Sultanate*, pp. 167–8.

[42] For the tribal basis of the military machine of the Lodi Sultanate, see Digby, 'Dreams and Reminiscences of Dattu Sarvani', pp. 52–60.

[43] *Lata'if*, p. 31. For the town of Shahabad in the Thanesar *tehsil* of Karnal district, East Panjab, see R.C. Burn, *Imperial Gazetteer of India: Provincial Series: Punjab*, Calcutta: Superintendent of Gevernment Printing, 1908, vol. I, p. 318.

[44] *Lata'if*. Hamid al-Din was 11 years old at the time of the move to Shahabad. Rukn al-Din, as mentioned above, was born one year after it.

[45] For an anecdote mentioning a pilgrimage to Dehli, see *Lata'if*, p. 41.

[46] Ibid., pp. 46, 48, 61.

[47] Ibid., p. 39.

[48] H.R. Nevill, *Saharanpur: A Gazetteer, District Gazetteers of the United Provinces and Oudh*, vol. II, Allahabad: Government Press, 1909, pp. 240–2.

murid's invitation 'Abd al-Quddus had despatched his son Rukn al-Din to take up residence there, probably in AD 1524, two years before the First Battle of Panipat.[49] The tenor of the anecdote which relates this suggests that 'Abd al-Quddus agreed to this arrangement with the thought in his mind of a safer refuge for the whole of his household and entourage in a place which was not, like Shahabad, upon the main road of any army advancing southwards towards Dehli. A year before Babur's successful invasion 'Abd al-Quddus moved to Gangoh 'out of fear of the Mughals'.[50] Shortly after the move there was a disastrous fire in Gangoh, in which the shaykh narrowly escaped being burnt. The same night he heard the voice of God urging him not to be despondent and proclaiming that He had bestowed on him the rank of *Qutb* and created him *Qutb al-Aqtab*.[51]

When Babur's anticipated invasion occurred and the Mughal and Lodi armies confronted one another outside Panipat, 'Abd al-Quddus, like most of the rest of the population of the nearby countryside, attempted to flee southwards well behind the Afghan lines. But he only succeeded in reaching Kutana, on the eastern bank of the Jamuna level with Panipat on the western side, when he was summoned by Sultan Ibrahim Lodi to bless his army by his presence. He had to obey the command, but—obliquely prophesying disaster—he ordered most of the rest of his family to leave him and go onwards 'towards Hindostan'.

[49] *Lata'if*, p. 62.

[50] *Lata'if*, p. 64. The widespread alarm felt before this final successful invasion of Babur is witnessed by two dreams recorded in the *Lata'if*, of the wife of 'Abd al-Quddus (p. 63) and of Dattu Sarvani (pp. 71–2).

[51] *Lata'if*, pp. 64–5. *Qutb* (polestar) and *Qutb al-Aqtab* (polestar of polestars) indicated in Sufi parlance the supreme member of a hierarchy of divinely appointed beings who guarded and watched over the mortal world. See for instance al-Hujwiri, *Kashf al-mahjub*, tr. R.A. Nicholson, Leiden: Brill, 1911, p. 214.

With Ibrahim's defeat and death, 'Abd al-Quddus fell into the hands of a Mughal; and this elderly and honoured figure was led away on foot from Panipat to Dehli, a distance of some 40 mi., with his son Hamid and his servant Sayyid Raja tied to the saddle of their captor's horse by the long, black woollen turban of the shaykh.[52]

He was released at Dehli; and he was settled for the remaining eleven years of his life at Gangoh. He was evidently at the fort of Agra at a date between April and July AD 1537, where he must have been waiting upon the Mughal emperor Humayun.[53] His connections with his Afghan soldier *murids* were maintained after the downfall of the Lodis; they regarded him as a valuable spiritual aid in the continued struggle against the Mughals.[54] At the same time 'Abd al-Quddus seems rapidly to have formed connections with the Mughal conquerors. His letter to Babur, discussed below, does not indicate that he enjoyed any standing with that monarch, but he appears to have received the esteem and offerings of Humayun, both before and after he came to the throne,[55] as

[52] *Lata'if*, pp. 63–4.

[53] Ibid., p. 71. The Afghan soldier Dattu Sarvani says that he met 'Abd al-Quddus at the fort of Agra, after his own return from Gujarat. The emperor Humayun was probably in residence at Agra from June or July 1536 to the end of July 1537, when he set out for Bengal. Dattu Sarvani can hardly have come to Agra before April 1537: see Digby, 'Dreams and Reminiscences of Dattu Sarvani', pp. 56, 61, 75 n. 25, 79 n. 45, 179 and 192 n. 47, in which the chronology of Humayun's movements and those of Dattu is discussed at length; see also 'Humayun' in *Encyclopaedia of Islam, 2*, which embodies the conclusions of the writer regarding the chronology of the reign. Rukn al-Din may be referring to this or an earlier visit of 'Abd al-Quddus to Agra, when he describes a meeting 'after a long interval' with Miran Sayyidi Ahmad there, whom he had previously encountered in Sikandar Lodi's reign: *Lata'if*, pp. 54–5.

[54] See Digby, 'Dreams and Reminiscences of Dattu Sarvani', passim.

[55] The contents of the letters to Babur and Humayun are discussed in detail below (see pp. 350–4). Further evidence of the attachment of

well as of the Mughal commander Tardi Beg.[56] Abu'l-Fazl mentions that Humayun was in the habit of visiting the *zaviya* of 'Abd al-Quddus (possibly rooms occupied by him at Agra rather than the *khanqah* at Gangoh), suitably attended by men of learning, and of holding discussions with him.[57]

'Abd al-Quddus died at Gangoh on 23 Jumada II 944/28 November 1537.[58] The substantial sixteenth-century domed tomb in his *khanqah* may have been completed in the last year of his life.[59] The *khanqah* is still in the possession of his descendants.[60] Perhaps the most famous of these was

---

Humayun to 'Abd al-Quddus is found in an anecdote in which when 'Abd al-Quddus wished to abandon his family and live elsewhere, he was stopped by the *darogha* of Gangoh, who pleaded that Humayun would think that the Shaykh had left on account of his ill-treatment of him, and would probably kill him: *Lata'if*, p. 60.

[56] See below, p. 349.

[57] *A'in-i Akbari*, Calcutta, 1877, vol. II, p. 223; English tr. by Jarrett and Sarkar, Calcutta, 1948, vol. III, p. 417. The continuative past tense of the verbs *shude*, *padhi-rufte* in Abu'l-Fazl's note imply that Humayun was in the habit of visiting the Shaykh.

[58] *Lata'if*, p. 70. Ghawthi states, incorrectly, that he died in AH 950 (*Gulzar-i abrar*, f. 152b).

[59] Nevill, *Saharanpur*, p. 241 states that the tomb was built by Humayun in 944/1537. If there is an inscription which mentions that it was built in that year, it will in all probability mention Humayun as the reigning monarch (cf. epigraphs of AH 944 and AH 946 in *Epigraphia indo-moslemica*, 1933–4, pp. 19–20). But in view of Humayun's long connection with the shaykh, and the shaykh's visit to him in the last year of his life, said to be that of the building of his tomb also, it is not impossible that it was built or at any rate completed from a donation from Humayun for this purpose. See also *Shaykh 'Abd al-Quddus*, pp. 400–1 and frontispiece, showing the tomb. It is a large square *maqbara* for which a date of completion of AD 1537 is acceptable. The building of their tombs in their own lifetimes had become quite common in India before this time, among both noblemen and Sufi shaykhs.

[60] *Shaykh 'Abd al-Quddus* has (facing p. 402) a photograph of the *sajjada-nashin* and his predecessor.

his grandson Shaykh 'Abd al-Nabi bin Shaykh Ahmad, the *sadr al-sudur* of the early years of Akbar's reign who later excited that monarch's wrath; he also caused scandal in respectable and learned Indo-Muslim circles by attacking the practice of his own relations in the matter of *sama'* or listening to music.[61] Nevill states that in the early years of this century many of the *pirzadas* or descendants of Shaykh 'Abd al-Quddus resident at Gangoh were Wahhabis.[62] At the same time the *'urs* or death anniversary of the shaykh was celebrated with great ceremony; perhaps the term Wahhabi is to be taken in a loose nineteenth-century Anglo-Indian sense. However, at Deoband, in the Saharanpur district not far from Gangoh, the celebrated *dar al-'ulum* was founded in AD 1867,

[61] 'Abd al-Haqq, *Akhbar al-akhyar*, p. 216. 'Abd al-Haqq Dehlavi in his notice of 'Abd al-Quddus is more concerned with the demerit of his grandson than with the excellences of the Shaykh. Cf. also Badayuni, *Muntakhab al-tawarikh*, Calcutta: Asiatic Society, 1865–69, vol. II, pp. 71, 255, 311; vol. III, pp. 79–83. Although they must have been personally acquainted with him, both Badayuni and 'Abd al-Haqq seem to be mistaken regarding his parentage. Badayuni (vol. III, p. 79) states that he was the son of Shaykh Ahmad, son of Shaykh Rukn al-Din, son of Shaykh 'Abd al-Quddus. 'Abd al-Haqq describes him as 'one of the offspring' (*yakeaz ubna*) of Rukn al-Din. In fact, the third son of 'Abd al-Quddus was called Ahmad and was evidently considerably younger than Rukn al-Din: his childhood and that of his still younger brother is mentioned in the *Lata'if*, p. 35. I. Quddusi, who had in his possession *shajaras* of the family, describes 'Abd al-Nabi as the son of this Ahmad, who died in 1000/1591–2 (*Shaykh 'Abd al-Quddus*, p. 507). The *shajaras* are unlikely to be wrong in this matter, and the confusion of 'Abd al-Haqq and Badayuni may be the result of a considerable difference of age between Shaykh Rukn al-Din and Shaykh Ahmad. I. Quddusi also mentions the composition by this Shaykh Ahmad of a treatise on the lawfulness of *sama'*, the point on which, according to 'Abd al-Haqq, 'Abd al-Nabi denounced his father. Ghawthi, who wrote between AD 1602 and 1613, confirms that 'Abd al-Nabi was the son of Shaykh Ahmad (*Gulzar-i abrar*, f. 153a).

[62] Nevil, *Saharanpur*.

and this was under Wahhabi influence from south Arabia.[63] Mawlavi Rashid Ahmad Gangohi, a descendant of 'Abd al-Quddus, was among the founders of the *dar al-'ulum*; and his own descendants have since played a prominent part in it.[64]

Turning from the descendants of 'Abd al-Quddus to his and their *khalifas* in the Chisiti Sabiri *silsila*, we find a number of figures prominent in the subsequent development of Indian Sufism and Indian Islam, with a wide spectrum of theological opinions. Among the *khalifas* of 'Abd al-Quddus who exerted influence in the reign of Akbar were Shaykh Jalal al-Din Thanesari, author of a treatise defending the rights of Muslim settlers over land against the encroachments of the sovereign;[65] and Shah 'Abd al-Ghafur A'zampuri, friend of the historian Badayuni and ancestor of a line of Qazis.[66] 'Abd al-Ahad, father of the 'Mujaddid' Shaykh Ahmad Sirhindi, was a *khalifa* of Rukn al-Din Quddusi.[67] Through 'Abd al-Ahad the powerful but unorthodox line of Pir Pagaru in Sind trace a connection.[68] Later *khalifas* in the *silsila* descending from 'Abd al-Quddus include Shah Muhibb Allah, the advocate of *wahdat al-wujud* in the reign of Shah Jahan;[69] and Haji Imdad Allah, who had travelled

63 Murray T. Titus, *Islam in India and Pakistan*, Calcutta: Y.M.C.A. Publishing House, 1959, p. 78. Titus describes Deoband as 'the most important *madrasah* in the Muslim world, next to *Al-Azhar* in Cairo'.

64 *Shaykh 'Abd al-Quddus*, pp. 556–61. It is not mentioned there that he was of the *awlad* of 'Abd al-Quddus.

65 Ibid., pp. 535–40; Badayuni, *Muntakhab al-tawarikh*, vol. III, pp. 3–4; K.A. Nizami, *Tarikh-i mash'aikh Chisht*, Delhi: Nadvat ul-muṣannifīn, 1953, pp. 224–5. Shaykh Jalal al-Din Thanesari, *Tahaqquq-i aradi-i Hind*, Arabic text edited with Urdu translation by S.S.A. Nadvi, Karachi: Da'irah-i mu'in al-ma'arif, 1963.

66 *Shaykh 'Abd al-Quddus*, pp. 573–4; Badayuni, *Muntakhab al-tawarikh*, vol. III, pp. 42–3.

67 *Shaykh 'Abd al-Quddus*, pp. 503–5.

68 Ibid., p. 503 and n.

69 Ibid., pp. 543–53.

in Wahhabi Arabia in the early years of the nineteenth century.[70] His *khalifas*, Rashid Ahmad Gangohi mentioned above, and Mawlanas Muhammad and Muhammad Ya'qub of Nanawta, were among the principal founders of the Deoband *dar al-'ulum*.[71] The expressed attitudes of 'Abd al-Quddus himself were very far from the climate of theological opinion at Deoband and have been a source of some embarrassment to descendants of his connected with this institution.[72]

The Literary Works of Shaykh 'Abd al-Quddus

Shaykh 'Abd al Quddus was often seen by his son engaged in literary composition.[73] I. Quddusi mentions seventeen compositions of the shaykh, many of which are no longer extant.[74] Of lost works to which reference is made in the *Lata'if-i Quddusi* or other near contemporary sources, three treatises—(1) *Bahr al-inshi'ab* on Arabic grammar; (2) a *sharh* on the *Misbah*; and (3) a *hashiya* on the *Sharh-i saha'if*—can be classed as *juvenilia* in which 'Abd al-Quddus embodied the lessons which he was receiving as a young student.[75] Other apparently lost works include (4) *Fava'id al-qira'a* on Quranic recitation, composed as a result of his association

[70] Ibid., pp. 554–6; Nizami, *Tarikh-i masha'ikh*, pp. 232–4. See also Hajji Imdad Allah, *Ziya' al-qulub*, Dehli: Mujtaba'i Press, 1284, p. 61.
[71] *Shaykh 'Abd al-Quddus*, pp. 561–70; Imdad Allah, *Ziya' al-qulub*, p. 60.
[72] Cf. a letter from a grandson of Rashid Ahmad Gangohi reproduced in *Shaykh 'Abd al-Quddus*, pp. 312–20.
[73] *Lata'if*, p. 8: *tasanif-i bisyar kard.*
[74] *Shaykh 'Abd al-Quddus*, pp. 421–33. See also Storey, *Persian Literature*, No. 1279, p. 968; N.D. Marshall, *Mughals in India*, Bombay: Asia Publishing House, 1968, no. 58, pp. 20–1; Nizami, *Life and Times of Shaykh Farid-u'd-din*, p. 221; and recently published catalogues of MSS listed in the following notes.
[75] *Lata'if*, p. 6.

with Shaykh Sulayman Mandavi,[76] and (5) *Nur al-ma'ani*, a *sharh* on the *qasida-i Amani*, the preface of which treated of *wahdat al-wujud* and drew the shaykh into a controversy with Miran Sayyidi Ahmad Multani.[77] Both of these works were probably written at Shahabad. An early seventeenth-century source refers to the shaykh's *sharhs* on (6) the *Fusus al-hikam* of Ibn al-'Arabi and (7) upon the *Istilahat-i Kashi*.[78] I. Quddusi thought that there was a volume of the Shaykh's Persian poetry (*majmu'a-i kalam-i farsi*) collected in the Shaykh's lifetime, but the reference he gives to the *Lata'if* does not support him;[79] it is indeed probable from the superscription to the *ghazals* included at the end of the *Lata'if* that no such collection had been made.[80] However, the *Lata'if* quotes from and describes (8) a translation into Persian verse of Mawlana Da'ud Dalama'i's Avadhi poem *Candayan*, which was made by 'Abd al-Quddus before AD 1479, but had not been completed before the time of its destruction.[81]

Extant works of the shaykh include (9) an Arabic *sharh* on Suhrawardi's *'Awarif al-ma'arif*, of which one manuscript has been recorded.[82] This was a work of his maturity, on which he set considerable store.[83] One

[76] Ibid., p. 41.
[77] Ibid., pp. 54–5.
[78] Ghawthi, *Gulzar-i abrar*, f. 152a. The *sharh* on the *'Awarif al-ma'arif* is also mentioned by him (for which see below) and these works are described as 'profitable' (*sudmand*).
[79] *Shaykh 'Abd al-Quddus*, p. 429, referring to *Lata'if*, p. 100.
[80] *Lata'if*, pp. 96–9. Heading: *baze abyat-i hazrati qutbi u shaykhi ki mutafarriqa budand dar inja jam karda shudand*—'Some of the verses of 'Abd al-Quddus which were scattered have been collected here.'
[81] *Lata'if*, p. 100. Mawlana Da'ud Dalama'i, *Candayana*, ed. P.L. Gupta, Bombay: Hindi Granth Ratnakar, 1964; *Canadyana* [sic], ed. M.P. Gupta, Agra: Pramanik Prakashan, 1967.
[82] *Fihrist-i kutub*, Hyderabad: Kutubkhana-i Asafiyya-i Sarkar-i 'Ali, AH 1332–47/AD 1914–28 vol. I, p. 172, no. 881.
[83] *Lata'if*, pp. 8, 68.

manuscript is recorded of (10) the *Risala-i Qudsi*, probably the work on *'ilm-i ma'rifat*, which he composed for Shaykh Sulayman Mandavi;[84] (11) a *risala* called *Mazhar al-'aja'ib* is referred to by Professor Nizami,[85] and (12) another short Sufi treatise partly in the form of questions and answers, *Ghara'ib al-fava'id*, exists in lithograph.[86] Two further *risalas* on Sufi doctrine, entitled respectively (13) *Nur al-huda* and (14) *Qurrat al-'ayn* or *Qurrat al-a'yun* are extant in manuscript.[87]

(15) *Anwar al'uyun fi asrar al-maknun* is a biographical *tadhkira* concerning Shaykh Ahmad 'Abd al-Haqq of Rudawli. It was probably composed within a few years after 887/1482, when 'Abd al-Quddus was still resident at Rudawli.[88] It is a work of much interest for its record of Sufi practice and for its references to political and social conditions in the eastern UP in the first half of the fifteenth century. One

[84] M.B. Husayn, *Fihrist-makhtutat-i Shayrani*, Lahore, 1968–69, vol. II, p. 224, no. 1236. The work is referred to in *Lata'if*, p. 41.

[85] Nizami, *Tarikh-i masha'ikh*.

[86] No manuscripts are recorded. Lithographed edition: *Ghara'ib al-fawa'id*, 'under the care of Ghulam Ahmad Khan "Biryan"', Jhajjar: Muslim Press, n.d. [*circa* 1314/1896–97]; mentioned by Nizami, *Tarikh-i masha'ikh*; not in the British Museum or India Office catalogues, but a copy is in the writer's collection.

[87] Ethé, *India Office*, vol. I, no. 1924, p. 1075, items 14 and 16 on folios 107–13, 115–61. In this manuscript the second title is given as *Qurrat al'a yun*; but Hafiz Mahmud Shayrani, who may have had a manuscript of the treatises in his own rich collection, calls it *Qurrat al'uyun*, see Hafiz Mahmud Shayrani, *Panjab men Urdu*, Lahore, 1st edn., n.d. [*circa* 1928], pp. 162–3.

[88] Cf. *Anwar al-'uyun*, p. 39, 'and to the present day when fifty years have passed from the death of Hazrat-i Shaykh'—which occurred in AH 837; also p. 41, which indicates that at the time of writing Rudawli had recovered from the devastation of the war which came to an end in AD 1479 (see note 39).

manuscript has been recorded and it has been lithographed at least three times.[89]

(16) *Rushd-nama* or *Risala-i Rushdi*, is the short Sufi tract whose contents are examined later in this chapter. There survive at least seven recorded manuscripts, and it has once been lithographed.[90]

Collections of letters and of anecdotes of the shaykh remain to be considered. His letters survive in (17) a collection of 193 letters, called *Maktubat-i Quddusi* or *Makatib-i Quddusi*, extant in at least three manuscripts and a lithographed edition.[91] This collection was made shortly

[89] Asafiyya, *Fihrist-i kutub*, vol. I, p. 486, no. 575 (?); there called *Malfuz-i Shaykh Ahmad 'Abd al-Haqq*. Lithographed editions: (i) with a Persian preface by Chawdhari Khalil al-Rahman and other matter at close, Lakhnau: Gulzar-i Muhammadi Press, 1295/1878 (copy in the writer's collection); (ii) 'Aligarh: Ahsan al-matabi', 1905 (copy in the IO Library); (iii) 'with Urdu translation by Khalil al-Rahman Chawdhari', Lakhnau: Mujtaba'i Press, 1909 (IO Library).

[90] Princeton, no. 113; 'Aligarh (Subhan Library), p. 16, no. 75; Tuebingen, Staatsbibliothek, Or. Sprenger 827, evidently the copy formerly in the library of the Kings of Oude; M.B. Husain and M.K. Shairani, *Fihrist-i makhtutat-i Shayrani*, Lahore: Danishgah-i Panjab, 1968, vol. II, p. 226, nos. 1246 and 1247 (no. 1248, entitled *Rushd nama ya irshad nama* is probably a different work); S.S.A. Rizvi, *Makhtutat-i anjuman-i taraqqi-i urdu*, Karachi: Anjuman-i Taraqqi-i Urdu, 1967, p. 86, no. 848; Nizami, *Tarikh-i masha'ikh*. A MS listed as *Rushd-nama* without identification of author is found in *A Descriptive Catalogue of the Persian Manuscripts in the Government Museum, Alwar*, Jaipur: Dept. of Museums and Archaeology, n.d., p. 109, no. 491. I. Quddusi has used a manuscript copied from the lithographed edition, in the possession of Sufi Bashir Ahmad (pp. 40–1,425). Lithographed edition, *Rushd-nama muhashsha*, ed. Ghulam Ahmad Khan 'Biryan', Jhajjar: Muslim Press, 1314/1896–97 (British Library; writer's collection), henceforth referred to as *Rushd-nama*.

[91] Ethe, *Bodleian*, no. 1275; Ethe, *India Office*, no. 1873, p. 1041; IO Dehli Persian no. 1041. Lithographed edition: *Makhtubat-i Quddusiya*, Dehli: Ahmadi Press, 1287/1870 (British Library and India Office Library).

after the death of 'Abd al-Quddus by Shaykh Khizr Budhan bin Rukn Jawanpuri, known as Miyan Khan.

(18) A smaller anonymous selection of fifty-four letters, called *Muntakhab-i Maktubat-i Quddusi* survives in a manuscript in private hands and has once been lithographed.[92]

Of anecdotal or biographical works dealing exclusively with the acts and conversations of Shaykh 'Abd al-Quddus, extensive use has already been made in this chapter of (19) *Lata'if-i Quddusi* by Shaykh Rukn al-Din, son of 'Abd al-Quddus. One manuscript is recorded and it has once been lithographed.[93] Two similar nearly contemporary works are known only from literary references: (20) *Asrar al-'aja'il* by Shaykh Khizr Budhan Jawnpuri, collector of the *maktubat* noticed above;[94] and (21) a compilation possibly called *Malfuzat-i Qutb-i 'alam* by Shaykh 'Abd al-Sattar Saharanpuri.[95]

Religious Attitudes and Behaviour

Historical writing about Islam in India has tended to produce some very simple stereotypes of the attitudes and activity of Sufi shaykhs, who are often summarily divided into the liberal and the strictly orthodox, those who made concessions

[92] See *Shaykh 'Abd al-Quddus*, p. 430, who states that the manuscript used for the preparation of the lithograph used to be in the possession of his grandfather: it was evidently copied in 1159/1746–47 (see preface to the lithograph, p. 8). Lithographed edition: *Muntakhab-i maktubat-i Quddusiya*, with a short, evidently nineteenth-century, biographical preface by Mushtaq Ahmad Ambethavi Chishti, Dehli: Mujtaba'i Press, 1312/1894–95 (writer's collection).

[93] IO Dehli Persian, no. 1099. Lithographed edition: *Lata'if-i Quddusi*, Dehli: Mujtaba'i Press, 1311/1894 (British Library; writer's collection).

[94] [This footnote was omitted from the original publication; I have not been able to restore it from Simon Digby's papers. ~DL]

[95] For details see note 29, above.

to their Indian environment and those who did not. They are then commended or blamed according to the viewpoint of the writer. The historical reality is of course much more complex than this, and a detailed study of a medieval Sufi shaykh will often reveal apparent inconsistencies of attitude, character, and behaviour. Acceptance of a Sufi in his lifetime as a great shaykh depended on the recognition that he possessed, to an impressive degree, qualities which indicated that he was an especial recipient of Divine Grace. The balance of these qualities embodied in a single shaykh might vary, just as a winning hand at cards may be stronger in some suits than others. Descent from the Prophet, his companions or other *ashraf*; connection with a Sufi *silsila* of already established local prestige; a reputation for strict orthodoxy; meticulous performance of Islamic duties; austerities sometimes of a more and sometimes of a less orthodox character; a mastery of Islamic doctrinal and Sufi texts or an abundance of literary compositions; the working of miracles together with a careful avoidance of the vulgar display of them; a reputation for inaccessibility and dislike of human society, often combined with a care for disciples and accepted hangers on; visible ecstasy, often of a shamanistic type and often also linked with a refined sensibility to poetry and music—all these qualities were held to be evidence of the especially close relations of the shaykh with the Deity and all contributed to his prestige and to the winning of devotees. 'Abd al-Quddus exhibits many of these qualities and also some of the inconsistencies which result from striving after such different excellences.

The orthodox Islamic element in 'Abd al-Quddus' activities and character is strongly attested. 'It is apparent', his son writes,

> that in conforming to [the example of] the Prophet [and] in the [observance of] the *shar'* of the Prophet he was so strict that he

did not allow the most minute departure from it to be permissible in either exterior or interior matters—as regards himself or others. If he got to know of any departure from the *shar'* by anyone, he showed dissatisfaction and wished to avoid his company; and he did not allow him to come near him. However much Hazrat-i Qutbi ['Abd al-Quddus] had associated with all kinds of men, company which was hostile to the faith had no effect upon his nature; but rather others from the effects from his company returned to the narrow path (*sirat-i mustaqim*).'[96]

One may note the defensive tone of his biographer and the reference to his 'association with all kinds of men'.

A large part of the time of 'Abd al-Quddus was spent in prayers and devotions, of which those not actually enjoined by Islam were above any criticism on the grounds of orthodoxy. At the beginning of his religious life he was in the habit of performing 400 *rak'ats*, additional to those which are obligatory, every day and 400 more every night.[97] He was never distracted from his prayers by the mice, ants, and snakes which shared his cell.[98] Through the coldest of winters and in his old age his *wazu* was performed with unheated water.[99] He fasted during the day at all times apart from the prohibited days, and at night he ate little except when he was so carried away discoursing upon *'ilm-i ma'rifat* that he ceased to notice how much he was eating.[100] Ramazan, the *shab-i barat*, and other Muslim festivals were occasions for supererogatory prayers; but on such occasions 'Abd al-Quddus, although he was a *hafiz* of the Qur'an, was too overcome to recite himself before the *mihrab*.[101] Among Sufi devotions, for years he was in

[96] *Lata'if*, p. 19, also pp. 35–6.
[97] Ibid., p. 15, anecdote 21.
[98] Ibid., p. 15, anecdote 20.
[99] Ibid., pp. 15, 66.
[100] Ibid., pp. 69–70.
[101] Ibid., p. 42.

the habit of passing the night from the *'isha* prayer to the dawn in *dhikr-i jahr*.[102]

Although 'Abd al-Quddus urged the necessity of strict orthodoxy,[103] he held several opinions which conflict with the consensus of Sunni belief. Throughout his life he remained a vigorous advocate of the doctrine of *wahdat al-wujud*, the unity in essence of the Creator and the created. The *Rushd-nama* constantly returns to this theme. In later life he developed arguments of greater subtlety, but his beliefs remained unchanged.[104] At Gangoh he argued with Miran Sayyidi Ahmad, a theologian from Multan, upon this doctrine, 'for five or six months', until he had persuaded him to accept it.[105] When his sons questioned his doctrine, he was so grieved that he set out from Gangoh to take up residence with one of his *khalifas*, whom he believed, rightly as it turned out, to be convinced upon the point.[106]

'Abd al-Quddus also urged very strongly the claims of the *pir* as Perfect Man (*insan-i kamil*) and as the mirror of God. In the *Rushd-nama* he argued that the *murid* (disciple) had an actual obligation to perform *sijda* (prostration) before his *pir* as before God.[107] In the *Anwar al-'uyun* he expressed the curious doctrine that the *wilayat* (spiritual influence over earthly affairs) of a Pir endured for forty years after his death, but that of Shaykh Ahmad 'Abd al-Haqq would endure until the day of judgement.[108]

The Chishti *silsila* in India was noted for its attachment to *sama'* (listening to music). *Sama'* and *raqs*, the ecstatic

102 Ibid., p. 15, anecdote 22.

103 *Rushd-nama*, p. 14, quoting a verse of Sakhshabi, cf. the remarks on *shar'* quoted above.

104 *Lata'if*, p. 58.

105 Ibid., p. 55.

106 Ibid., p. 58.

107 See the synopsis of the doctrinal content of the *Rushd-nama*, below.

108 *Anwar al-'uyun*, p. 110.

dancing which often accompanies it, are often described in the biography of ‘Abd al-Quddus.[109] The question of the lawfulness of *sama‘*, together with that of the opinion of *wahdat al-wujud* were the two major points of contention between the more extreme but respectable Sufis and the stricter Sunni *‘ulama* in medieval India. In a later addition to the *Lata’if* a conflict is described between ‘Abd al-Quddus and a *muhtasib* appointed by Sikandar Lodi, concerning the holding of *sama‘*; naturally the anecdote ends with the subjection of the *muhtasib*.[110] ‘Abd al-Quddus pursues a rather unusual line of argument regarding *sama‘*, beyond the ordinary defence that when the musical instruments classed as *mazamir* are banished from the accompaniment of the singer, *sama‘* is lawful.[111] ‘Abd al-Quddus in the *Rushd-nama* maintained that purely instrumental music without singing is unlawful, because it lacks the words which will recall the Divine Beauty to the hearer. Such instrumental music is animal (*hayavani*) while singing is human (*insani*). *Sama‘* draws out the Divine secrets which are concealed in the human heart.[112]

Another point on which the opinions of ‘Abd al-Quddus are questionable from a point of view of Sunni orthodoxy is his advocacy and practice of the *salat-i ma‘kusa* or *namaz-i ma‘kus*, devotions performed upside down while hanging suspended by a rope tied to the heels. This is a practice which may be found among some non-Muslim Indian ascetics and will be considered again when Yogic influences upon ‘Abd al-Quddus are discussed. Nevertheless, the practice is first recorded among Sufis before the Muslim conquests in India. Abu Sa‘id b. Abu’l-Khayr, the celebrated late tenth-

[109] *Lata’if*, pp. 11–12, 49, 60–5.
[110] Ibid., pp. 107–10.
[111] Khwurd, *Siyar al-awliya’*, *bab* 9, *dar sama‘*, p. 492.
[112] *Rushd-nama*, p. 25.

century shaykh of Mayhana in north-west Khurasan (modern north Afghanistan), is said by an early biographer to have performed it.[113] Among Chishti shaykhs in India, Farid al-Din performed this devotion. His *khalifa*, Nizam al-Din Awliya', in a conversation of the early fourteenth century, also stated that Shaykh Abu Sa'id (mentioned above) had said that the Prophet himself used to perform it.[114] Among all Chishti shaykhs, 'Abd al-Quddus himself would appear to have been the most frequent practitioner of the *salat-i ma'kusa* and the most fervent advocate of the practice. In the *Rushd-nama*, after describing the attainment of a state of proximity to God, he states that 'anyone who has grown firm in this condition will achieve the upside-down prayers which are in reality the right way up' (*salat-i ma'kusa mustavi al-ma'na*). In support of this proposition he quotes two couplets of a *ghazal* of Bu 'Ali Qalandar[115] beginning:

> A prayer which I who am drunk from the tavern perform
> has in it neither standing nor kneeling not prostration.[116]

[113] Muhammad bin Munawwar, *Asrar al-tawhid*, ed. Dh. Safa, Tehran: Amīr-i Kabīr, 1332 Shamsi, pp. 33–4; R.A. Nicholson, *Studies in Islamic Mysticism*, Cambridge: Cambridge University Press, 1921, p. 15; see also Nizami, *Life and Times of Farid-u'd-din*, p. 25 and n. 1.

[114] Amir Hasan Sijzi, *Fawa'id al-fu'ad*, Dehli: Fakhr al-matabi', AH 1272, pp. 8–9. Cf. the manner in which cow slaughter is condemned in a bogus *malfuz*, *Anis al-arwah*, Dehli: Mujtaba'i Press, 1312, p. 21. The condemnation is presented in the form of a *hadith* related by 'Abd Allah bin Mas'ud.

[115] Near-contemporary information about this shaykh of the Chishti *silsila* of the thirteenth century is scanty and subsequent biographical accounts are divergent. The *Siyar al-aqtab* mentions his association with Khwaja Shams al-Din Turk, also of Panipat, who figures in the *shajara* of 'Abd al-Quddus (pp. 159–60). See also Sarvar, *Khazinat al-asfiyya'*, vol. I, pp. 326–8, and a very fanciful seventeenth-century biography by Hamid al-Din bin Shah Budh, *Sharaf al-manaqib*, Urdu tr. by Munshi Jaganath, Dehli: Afzal al-matabi', n.d. [nineteenth century].

[116] *Rushd-nama*, p. 18.

It scarcely needs to be observed that these ritual actions are not performed by a worshipper suspended from the heels. Elsewhere in the *Rushd-nama* the Hindi verse occurs:

> *Kara jura sira dhara pav sanehara lagu re*
>
> Joining hands, place your head at the feet: apply yourself to love.

The marginal commentary by Rukn al-Din maintains that the inner meaning of this is that the *murid* should perform *namaz-i ma'kus*.[117]

An anecdote in the *Lata'if* describes 'Abd al-Quddus' own performance of the *namaz-i ma'kus*. It opens with the remark that, whereas for other men the time for work was in the day, for 'Abd al-Quddus it was during the night. For years through the nights he used to perform the *namaz-i ma'kus*. After the *'isha* prayers he would hang himself upside down and thus spend the night until the dawn. 'One night I was in *namaz-i ma'kus*', he had related,

> when the *sultan-i dhikr*[118] manifested itself and put to flight my external existence. A state of obliteration (*mahviyat*) came to pass and there was no consciousness apart from my consciousness of myself. In that state I had to pass beyond this consciousness of myself and reach the annihilation of annihilation (*fana' al-fana'*). By God's grace this came to pass and the world of eternality (*baqa'*) was revealed. When I had descended from this state, a man appeared from the unseen (*az ghayb*)[119] and said, 'Blessed be it, at this time you were united with God (*wasil bi-haqq*)!' He then vanished.

[117] Ibid., p. 13, marginal commentary.

[118] See below.

[119] *Az ghayb*. The *mardan-i ghayb* or *rijal al-ghayb* figure in many Indian Sufi hagiographical anecdotes.

Rukn al-Din, the recorder of the anecdote, asked who the man was, but 'Abd al-Quddus did not reply.[120]

The *sultan-i dhikr* mentioned in this passage is described by Rukn al-Din as the especial characteristic of the religious practice (*khassa-i mashrab*) of 'Abd al-Quddus. He says that whereas other Sufi works do not treat of it, the term is taken from the *Risala-i Makkiya*, of which he quotes a short passage.[121] It is evident from Rukn al-Din's description that *sultan-i dhikr* is not in itself an ordinary *dhikr*, that is to say the recitation of a short religious formula to a fixed bodily rhythm, intended to produce an extension of consciousness or other spiritual powers in the reciter. The term does not seem to be found in earlier Chishti works which describe *dhikr*, although it occurs in some later works which bear other traces of the influence of the *Rushd-nama*.[122] As used by 'Abd al-Quddus and Rukn al-Din, the meaning of *sultan-i dhikr* appears to be 'the dominance of *dhikr*', referring to the psycho-physical condition produced by the repetition of *dhikr*, whether silent or spoken; or by other practices intended to relax the normal bounds of consciousness, such as the *namaz-i ma'kus*.

The alarming quality of *sultan-i dhikr* is much emphasized by Rukn al-Din. 'Abd al-Quddus used to say that in the early years of his spiritual life, when *sultan-i dhikr* often overcame him and gave him no respite, he feared that he was about

[120] *Lata'if*, p. 18, anecdote 24.

[121] Possibly the *Futuhat-i Makkiya* of Ibn al-'Arabi rather than the comparatively rare Sufi work called *Risala Makkiya* listed by Brocklemann.

[122] Cf. Nizam al-Din Awrangabadi, *Nizam al-qulub*, Dehli: Mujtaba'i Press, 1309, especially pp. 5–8. For a description of the *dhikrs* earlier in use among the Chishtis, see Sayyid Muhammad Gesudaraz, *Takmila-i Sharh-i Adab al-muridin*, translated into Urdu as *Ruh-i tasawwuf* by Shabbir Hasan Chisht Nizami, Dehli: Zawia Publishers, n.d. [c. 1955], pp. 216–25. For recurrence of the term see Imdad Allah, *Ziya' al-qulub*, pp. 20–1.

to lose his reason and that he would lapse into a permanent state of madness (*jununiyat*).

Rukn al-Din equates the phenomenon of *sultan-i dhikr* with *wahy* or Prophetic inspiration. In support of the identification he quotes the well-attested *hadith* that the Prophet, when questioned as to how *wahy* worked upon him, replied, 'It is like the ringing of a bell, but more violent upon me.'[123] The *wahy* of the prophets is the *ilham* (supernatural guidance) of the saints; this in turn is equated with the sensation of *sultan-i dhikr*, which is also said to be like the state described in the opening verses of the Sura of the Earthquake: 'When the earth is shaken with her (final) earthquake and the earth yieldeth up her burdens, and man saith, "What aileth her?"' (Qur'an, XCIX, 1–3).

The time of the appearance of *sultan-i dhikr* is between sleeping and waking, when the external senses are weak; but after internal spiritual discipline has been established, waking and sleeping are alike, and sometimes *sultan-i dhikr* occurs during complete wakefulness. At the beginning of one's spiritual life, *sultan-i dhikr* is completely terrifying; but a familiarity or liking is engendered by its repeated occurrence, the terror diminishes and the subject comes to long every moment for this condition. Consciousness of the world and its inhabitants departs, but some consciousness of self remains; and the subject knows that the condition has befallen him. But sometimes consciousness of self is also obliterated, and in this immersion occurs the *fana' al-fana'* or 'annihilation of annihilation'.[124]

A description of the actual sensation of *sultan-i dhikr* is difficult because the spiritual world cannot be described: one can only indicate it by similes. It is as if a strong and blustering wind has engulfed a tree already ravaged by

123 *Lata'if*, p. 16.
124 Ibid., pp. 16–17.

autumn, and shakes it till the roots quake in the earth; and no leaf or branch is left in peace but quivers and sways to left and right. When *sultan-i dhikr* occurs there is a roaring as of thunder and one's fear is the fear that the whole of heaven is falling on one's head. While the ears are filled with thunder a quaking and a trembling occurs through the whole body. *Sultan-i dhikr* rising inside the human frame purifies it of darkness. Or it is as if a weak man has fallen into a river in flood and the force of the waters gives him no chance to return. The racing waters produce a terrible noise, which engulfs the orifices of his ears while his whole being is dashed to pieces by the forces of the waves.[125]

The experiences of *sultan-i dhikr* evidently occupied a dominant position in the mystical life of 'Abd al-Quddus, but his son and biographer also describes other conditions of ecstasy which were not directly induced by *dhikr* or other austerities, in which the shaykh was overwhelmed with emotion, often as a result of a combination of religious and aesthetic sensibilities. Similar anecdotes to those related of him are found in the biographical literature concerning the great shaykhs of the Chishti *silsila* in India during the thirteenth and fourteenth centuries; and a general resemblance to patterns of behaviour established among the Sufis of Khurasan in the tenth and eleventh Christian centuries can easily be discerned. The fact that such ecstatic behaviour is canalized or stereotyped and common to a large number of people does not necessarily affect the experience for the subject and those who associated with him: but expectations of phenomena in a community help to induce and condition such phenomena. Writing around AD 1880 on an allied topic, Sir Richard Temple observed, 'Saints and holy men are still a living power in the India of today, and miracles are worked all round as a matter of daily occurrence

[125] Ibid., pp. 17–18.

and not of much wonder.'[126] In pre-Mughal India, within the Muslim community Sufi shaykhs were leaders in fashions of religious sensibility, in which piety is with difficulty distinguished from aesthetic reaction to literary and musical forms: and the violent tenor of life and wasteful distribution of the resource of the society in which they lived greatly encouraged such sensibility. From the limited and one-sided biographical evidence which survives to us it sometimes seems as if the social scene of the Dehli Sultanate was largely populated by madmen of a religious turn of mind and by Sufi shaykhs who, although subject to the same symptoms of ecstasy and mental derangement, did not sink into this class of *divanagan* mainly as a consequence of their superior education and social status. States of mystical intoxication, held in check by learning and a concern for the appearance of Muslim orthodoxy, were almost essential to the reputation of a medieval *pir*.

'Abd al-Quddus in his boyhood used to frequent the company of 'a gathering of accomplished people' (*majma'i afazil*) also described as 'several naked madmen, men of God', and these used to shout Persian verses at him.[127] He also sought out the company of other 'madmen' (*divanagan*).[128] On instructions conveyed to him in a dream by Shaykh Ahmad 'Abd al-Haqq, he took up residence in the house of a tailor subject to mystical illuminations.[129]

Till quite late in life 'Abd al-Quddus was in the habit of setting out to roam the hills and jungles, partly impelled by a distaste for those in worldly employment (*ahl-i dunya*) but also in a high state of mystical excitement. On some of these occasions groups of disciples used to follow him, not

[126] Sir Richard C. Temple, *The Legends of the Panjab*, Bombay: Education Society's Press, n.d., vol. I, p. xv.

[127] *Lata'if*, p. 8.

[128] Ibid., pp. 9–10.

[129] Ibid., p. 19.

daring to approach him in order to turn him back to the *khanqah*, or risking a terrible sight if they did so.[130] Once on such a sortie he was approached by Afghan disciples, the sons of 'Umar Khan Sarvani (who had established him at considerable expense in the *khanqah* at Shahabad); 'Abd al-Quddus' condition 'changed', his eyes turned up until only the whites were visible and he fell down unconscious. The unfortunate young Afghans retired, fearing that either the shaykh would expire or harm would befall themselves. After their departure he spent the night at the place where they had accosted him, speaking *shathiyat* (Sufi ecstatic outpourings). Only after the following day did he return to the *khanqah*.[131] Other rambles in the jungle lasted for two or three days.[132]

His states of mystical intoxication (*hal-i sukr u masti*) frequently reduced 'Abd al-Quddus to an inability to speak; but this was sometimes followed by a torrent of speech regarding divine mysteries.[133] In this latter state on one occasion he expounded *tafsir*, but not according to any of the known commentaries upon the Qur'an.[134] Such of his *shathiyat* or outpourings when in this state of mystical intoxication as are recorded in the *Lata'if* are of a somewhat conventional nature; at least one of them had previously been among Ahmad 'Abd al-Haqq's *shathiyat*. 'I can strike the sky down to the ground.' 'If God wills, I will take my tent to paradise.' 'The umbrella of royalty is over the heads of my children.'[135] 'O friends, the veil remains not! Jibra'il says, God's command is one of mercy!' Most of these utterances were during *sama'*. On one occasion he testified that he was

[130] Ibid., pp. 18–19.
[131] Ibid., p. 39.
[132] Ibid., pp. 18–19.
[133] Ibid., p. 60.
[134] Ibid.
[135] Cf. *Anwar al'-uyun*, p. 103.

present when Moses conversed with God; and then added, 'I do not say [this]: with my tongue God says "I".' On another occasion he announced that he had bestowed paradise upon the *qawwal* who was singing before him.[136]

The relation between religious and aesthetic sensibility in such ecstasies and the physical and social consequences of their occurrence are illustrated by two anecdotes of the period when Rukn al-Din was studying at Dehli and his father had come from Shahabad to join him.

On one occasion, the Friday prayers were being performed in a mosque in Dehli, the administration of which had been entrusted to Rukn al-Din or to him and his father jointly. The Khatib was not present, and Rukn al-Din therefore read the *khutba* himself. This was a composition of 'Abd al-Quddus and his son in reading it was somewhat overcome by emotion. 'Abd al-Quddus then passed into an ecstatic state and gave a painful shriek (*na'ra-i dardnak*). In this state of spiritual intoxication he correctly performed the Friday prayers. At their conclusion he saw among the congregation another shaykh who was accompanied by two of his own *qawwals*. 'Abd al-Quddus seized him in his embrace and the *qawwals* began to sing, and to this accompaniment they set out on a several-mile pilgrimage to the tomb of Qutb al-Din Bakhtyar Kaki,[137] passing time in *sama'* and *raqs* (mystical dancing) through the bazaar of Dehli towards the Baghdad

[136] *Lata'if*, pp. 60–2.

[137] The *dargahs* of Shaykh Nizam al-Din Awliya' and Khwaja Qutb al-Din Bakhtyar Kaki were the two holiest Sufi shrines of Dehli. The especial significance of the intention of 'Abd al-Quddus to perform pilgrimage (*ziyarat*) to this *dargah* when in such an elevated state derives from the circumstances of the death of Qutb al-Din, who in the year 633/1235–36 passed away after an ecstasy of four days, induced by the singing of a couplet from a *ghazal* attributed to Ahmad-i Jam: see Khwurd, *Siyar al-awliya'*, pp. 55–6; Jamālī, *Siyar al-'arifin*, Dehli, 1893, p. 30; Chishti, *Siyar al-aqtab*, p. 160.

Gate. But on the way one Shaykh 'Abd al-Samad Jawnpuri came out into the street, grasped 'Abd al-Quddus and led him inside his own *khanqah*. Many *qawwals* were there and scenes of increasing rapture took place until the break for the night prayer. 'Abd al-Quddus then argued with 'Abd al-Samad concerning the execution of Mansur ibn al-Hallaj (the tenth-century Sufi martyr of Baghdad), saying that had he been alive at the time he would not have permitted it: and he was driven to renewed ecstasy by the thought that both the blood of Mansur and the ink of the Imam Yusuf who condemned him fell in drops which formed the shape of the letters of Allah's name.[138]

On another occasion during this stay in Dehli, at Rukn al-Din's suggestion 'Abd al-Quddus went to hear a certain Mawlana Shu'ayb, famous for his sweet voice, expounding *tafsir* from the *mimbar* (pulpit). Hearing his discourse 'Abd al-Quddus fell into an ecstasy and himself began to explain Divine mysteries, while Mawlana Shu'ayb waited in vain for an opportunity to continue. But 'Abd al-Quddus' ecstasy did not come to an end and in this condition Rukn al-Din mounted him upon a horse and took him away. They stopped for the evening prayer at the mosque of one Shaykh Nasir al-Din Danishmand. When those who were present there observed the trembling and bodily agitation of 'Abd al-Quddus, they inquired from his son what the illness was from which he was suffering and why he had left his house when he was so unwell? But in spite of these symptoms 'Abd al-Quddus performed with propriety his ablutions and prayers.[139]

[138] *Lata'if*, p. 48. A drop of ink or coloured liquid falling at an oblique angle upon paper or some similarly absorptive surface makes a stain, rounded at the base and sharply crested at the top, which resembles the Arabic letters of the name Allah. The same conceit is found with regard to the blood spurting from the roots of the hair of Qutb al-Din in the account of his death in Chishti, *Siyar al-aqtab* (note 137, above).
[139] *Lata'if*, p. 61.

The state of mystic intoxication (*sukr*) depicted in these anecdotes is balanced in other anecdotes by the account of the fulfilment by 'Abd al-Quddus in his sobriety (*sahw*) of the social role and obligations incumbent upon a Sufi shaykh of note. As a *pir* he took his duty of instructing his *murids* very seriously. The range of his teaching extended to formal Islamic subjects which he had neglected in his own youth.[140] Muhammad Ghawthi remarks on the 'utility' of the commentaries which 'Abd al-Quddus wrote upon standard Sufi works.[141] He took pains also in teaching to his disciples the physical techniques which produced mystical states of consciousness.[142]

Though he urged the importance of remaining unattached to one's family (*ahl-i khana*),[143] the only hardships to which he subjected his own wife and children were of a mild character;[144] 'Abd al-Quddus' wife is mentioned by his son and biographer as 'one of the saints of God' and she evidently enjoyed some celebrity for her dreams foretelling the future.[145] From Rukn al-Din's account it would also appear that the sons of 'Abd al-Quddus had a warm personal affection for him. The additions to the *Lata'if* made by Dattu Sarvani also [indicate] that 'Abd al-Quddus' relations with the Afghan soldiers who became his *murids* were not merely those of a personally remote *pir* of formidable charisma. He listened with sympathy to their accounts of their affairs, which may have been very

[140] See above, note 11.
[141] Ghawthi, *Gulzar-i abrar*, f. 152a.
[142] *Rushd-nama*, p. 16, note 3 of marginal commentary.
[143] Ibid., p. [omitted].
[144] *Lata'if*, pp. 12–13: an anecdote of lack of food in the house and 'Abd al-Quddus suggesting to his eldest son that they might be going to paradise.
[145] *Lata'if*, p. 63.

remote from anything in his own personal experience, and he gave them reassurance.[146]

Nevertheless, there is little evidence in the *Lata'if* of the delicacy of moral feeling, extended sympathy with suffering humanity and overflowing sensibility (*dard*) which had characterized the behaviour of the great Chishti shaykhs of the earlier Dehli Sultanate; and the hagiography of Ahmad 'Abd al-Haqq by 'Abd al-Quddus himself nowhere contains a mention of these characteristics. Instead, the elements of ecstasy and *jalal*, a kind of wrathful splendour, predominate. In anecdote after anecdote those who act contrary to the dignity of Ahmad 'Abd al-Haqq, even though unintentionally, are quickly visited with disaster and death. His wife is continually weeping for their children, whom he has caused to depart to another world because the noise of their playing disturbed him at his devotions.[147] One would-be disciple, when he encounters the awesome glance of the shaykh, is driven crazy and dies.[148] The ecstasies and the miracles of Ahmad 'Abd al-Haqq are usually frightening; and there is no sign that he possessed any moral virtues unconnected with his devotions. The standards of morality prevailing in his *khanqah* are somewhat unhappily illustrated by an anecdote of how Ahmad 'Abd al-Haqq went out into the jungle with some of his disciples and there appeared to die: the immediate reaction of his disciples was not grief, but terror lest they should be accused of having murdered their *pir* for the sake of some particularly large offering from a passer-by.[149] Rukn al-Din's anecdotes of 'Abd al-Quddus,

[146] Ibid., p. 71 and other anecdotes told by Dattu Sarvani: see Digby, 'Dreams and Reminiscences of Dattu Sarvani'.

[147] *Anwar al-'uyun*, pp. 50–1; for anecdotes of retribution, see pp. 45–9, 54.

[148] Ibid., pp 100–1.

[149] Ibid., pp. 52–3.

while they are similarly devoid of any account of acts of disinterested and general benevolence, show that 'Abd al-Quddus' ordinary human relationships were generally of greater benignity than those of his exemplar.

Political Attitudes

'Abd al-Quddus also appears to have departed from the practice of Ahmad 'Abd al-Haqq in his relationships with the Muslim ruling classes of northern India. His account particularly commends Ahmad 'Abd al-Haqq's refusal to accept, for the maintenance of the Rudawli *khanqah*, any grant of land from Sultan Ibrahim of Jawnpur.[150] This is in the earlier tradition of the Chishti *silsila*, whose disinterestedness is much praised by medieval hagiographers. Chishti standards were often satisfied by a refusal of direct contact with the sultan and of permanent grants of maintenance, which was compensated by the acceptance of *futuhat*, non-recurrent gifts, sufficing to provide on a day-to-day basis for the sometimes extensive *khanqah* establishments and their hangers-on. It has been noted earlier that no land grants were accepted by Ahmad 'Abd al-Haqq's successors at Rudawli in the following fifty years; but, on 'Abd al-Quddus' testimony, the flow of *futuhat* must have been constant.[151]

'Abd al-Quddus in his practice does not show the same scrupulosity as he attributes to his predecessors. His letters to Sikandar Lodi, to Babur, and to Humayun contain allusions to the consternation of the religious classes at the cancellation of their permanent *waza'if* (grants, though whether of allotment or stipend is not clear), to the abominable innovation of collecting *'ushr* and other dues on land held by them, and

[150] Ibid., pp. 31–3; above, p. 315.
[151] Ibid., p. 35.

to the importance, while making grants of land to them, of giving them in tax-free tenure.

Though they are filled with moral exhortations, 'Abd al-Quddus' letters to the rulers of Hindostan and to their high officers are not immediately edifying to the modern reader; but it is nevertheless important to understand the point of view of the writer, which is still widely held in old-fashioned Muslim circles in India. God created the world in order that He might be known. The finest flower of creation, the figure for whom creation was created, was the Sufi who 'knew' God. Hence for those who held worldly power and worldly possessions the best of all pious acts was to cherish the Sufi and to see that he had clothing, food, peace, and freedom from worldly cares. The 'poor' (*fuqara'*) and the 'weak' (*zu'afa*) when they are mentioned in the letters of 'Abd al-Quddus, often with the Prophet's injunction to care for them, are not the underprivileged masses. They are identified with the 'learned' (*'ulama*), the 'pious' (*sulaha*), and the shaykhs (*masha'ikh*) in addition to such synonyms (strangely convergent) as *ghuraba'* and *masakin.*[152] All these are a single 'group' (*ta'ifa*) and the terms are in fact used almost interchangeably for the Muslim religious population—those who were permanently on the premises of *khanqahs*, schools, and mosques, headed by such men as 'Abd al-Quddus himself, playing a varied role as a Sufi of powerful *barakat* with direct 'knowledge' of the deity, an *'alim* or scholar of traditional Islamic disciplines, an inculcator of morals in the community, and an organizer of elementary religious instruction and communal prayers. The contradictions between these roles did not prevent Sufi shaykhs from undertaking them all. In the medieval Muslim community such charismatic figures had a widely recognized

[152] Both words are used indiscriminately in the sense of 'poor'; they have more specific meanings of 'foreigners' and 'settled population'.

claim to extensive financial support. The provision of such support was thought to bring fortune in this world and in the world to come. Beside such an earlier figure as Shaykh Ahmad-i Jam, 'Abd al-Quddus does not appear greedy or undignified in his demands from the rich and the powerful.[153]

The letters of 'Abd al-Quddus to rulers and their officers are of varying length but mostly very like one another in their main content, the same Persian phrases and the same *hadiths* appearing again and again. The circumstances of the composition of three of the letters to noblemen are somewhat unusual. The first of these is a letter of introduction for Shaykh Khan Khizr Jawnpuri (the compiler of the collection of letters) addressed to Masnad-i 'Ali Shaykh Sulayman Farmuli, evidently a Lodi military commander. The bearer has come to the army for a special reason (*zarurate*). For many years he has enjoyed the benefits of the company of 'Abd al-Quddus and his teaching and he is his *khalifa*. He is very holy (*bi-ghayat buzurgwar-and*) and very much occupied with God. If the recipient of the letter meets with him it will be as if he was meeting 'Abd al-Quddus himself.[154]

Another of the less usual letters of 'Abd al-Quddus is addressed to Dilavar Khan, son of Mian Bhu'a, the chief minister of Sikandar Lodi. It alludes to a personal predicament of the writer. As mentioned above, 'Abd al-Quddus was in Dehli for a while in the first years of the sixteenth century, when Rukn al-Din was a student there; they had charge of a congregational mosque, probably the *Moth ki masjid* built

[153] Sadid al-Din Muhammad Ghaznavi, *Maqamat-i Zhinda pil*, ed. Heshmat Moayyed, Tehran: Intishārāt-i Bungāh-i Tarjumah va Nashr-i Kitāb, 1961; cf. the sketch of the character of the shaykh in the introduction of the editor, pp. 16–19.

[154] *Maktubat-i Quddusiya*, Dehli: Ahmadi Press, 1287, pp. 40–1, *maktub* 29 (for edition see note 91); reproduced in *Shaykh 'Abd al-Quddus*, pp. 451–2.

by Mian Bhu'a.[155] After Mian Bhu'a's death it is evident that his son made no provision for the maintenance of 'Abd al-Quddus and his establishment at Dehli.

The late Mian Bhu'a, 'Abd al-Quddus wrote to Dilavar Khan, was a friend of God and of the friends of God and the heavens and the earth grieve at his loss. Inevitably the writer had great hopes and was staying at this place on account of his kindness. He has now no other resource than patience and, reciting 'I am God's and unto Him I am returning', will have to go his own way (the Qur'anic quotation neatly conveys the additional impression that Dilavar Khan has brought him to death's door by his stinginess).[156]

Another departure from the normal content of the letters to secular dignitaries is one of several addressed to Khavass Khan, which expresses with warmth the desire of 'Abd al-Quddus for a meeting. A possibility which is not made explicit in the letter is that the meeting desired was with the sultan, Sikandar Lodi, rather than Khavass Khan, who may have been acting as the royal chamberlain.[157]

A letter addressed to Haybat Khan Sarvani acknowledges the receipt of a letter with news of Haybat Khan's safe return from a military campaign. It exhorts him to turn from the army of this world to heavenly command (*sipahbudi-i jahan-i baqi*) and to the 'cultivation of hearts' (*'imarat-i dilha*).[158] A letter of 'Abd al-Quddus was sent to the Mughal commander Tardi Beg, evidently on the occasion of his safe return to court after a campaign against rebels (*zaliman u mufsidan*).[159]

[155] Cf. *Lata'if*, pp. 46, 48, 61 for this period in Dehli.

[156] *Maktubat-i Quddusiya*, no. 62; *Shaykh 'Abd al-Quddus*, pp. 449–51.

[157] *Maktubat-i Quddusiya*, pp. 41–2, no. 30; *Shaykh 'Abd al-Quddus*, p. 445.

[158] *Maktubat-i Quddusiya*, pp. 12–15, no. 10; *Shaykh 'Abd al-Quddus*, pp. 439–42.

[159] *Maktubat-i Quddusiya*, pp. 255–6, no. 131; *Shaykh 'Abd al-Quddus*, p. 460.

Another to the same commander clearly acknowledges the receipt of a gift.[160] The remainder of the correspondence of 'Abd al-Quddus addressed to royal officers appears to be reminders, wrapped in elegant and sanctified phrases, of their obligation to support men of religion; and of the benefits which will accrue to them in this world and the next when they do so.

A letter to Humayun before his accession really belongs to the same class. It states that 'Abd al-Quddus has heard of the prince's attainments, of his consultation with men of learning and of peace, and of his regard for Sufis. The writer renders thanks to God and offers up prayers for Humayun's preservation.[161]

There remain three letters addressed to reigning monarchs, to Sikandar Lodi, Babur, and Humayun. These are also reminders of the obligations of the holders of worldly power to Muslim men of religion, but the first two of them express at greater length than elsewhere the political philosophy of 'Abd al-Quddus. The earliest, addressed to Sikandar Lodi, begins with the reflection that monarchy is the noblest of worldly occupations. The operation of justice (*'adl*) by a ruler for a single moment is better than sixty years of worship (*'ibadat*). Now that the sultan has chastised the rebellious and the wicked with the sword and peace reigns, he should honour the Muslim religious classes (*ta'ifa-i a'imma u 'ulama' u zu'afa*) in such a way that they attain a loftier dignity in his kingdom than in any age or clime. But instead of this they are plunged into the deepest grief and are on the verge of extinction on account of his wicked action in cancelling their permanent grants (*waza'if*). They have none other

[160] *Maktubat-i Quddusiya*, p. 224–5, no. 119; *Shaykh 'Abd al-Quddus*, pp. 459–60.

[161] *Maktubat-i Quddusiya*, pp. 337–8, no. 170; *Shaykh 'Abd al-Quddus*, p. 457.

to whom they can appeal. If he neglects to cherish this class—which God forbid!—a cry for redress (*damar*, literally 'smoke') will arise (the implication is that worldly events are influenced and kings are made and unmade by access to supernatural powers of the Man of God).[162] Fortune in this world and felicity in the world to come depend upon two acts: the service of God with sincere devotion and the service of man with all one's power (it has been noted above that the 'service of man'—*khidmat-i khalq*—, or of the poor, the weak, etc., is taken in the peculiar and limited sense of the Muslim religious 'poor'). The most perfect conjunction of these two acts is in kingly rule (*saltanat*), to attain which the high virtue of *futuwwa* (generosity, with many other 'chivalric' connotations)[163] is necessary. With high resolution, therefore, the sultan should proffer to 'the poor and the pious' money and station, so that in their service he may attain this felicity.[164]

In the letter to Babur, whom possibly he regarded as a conqueror from the lands of Islam who would make a clean sweep of existing abuses, 'Abd al-Quddus developed some of the themes which have appeared in the letter to Sikandar Lodi. In the opening phrases after the royal titles, 'Abd al-Quddus introduces himself in the manner of a *darvesh*. He then commends the emperor for having acted in accordance with the opinions of the *'ulama'* and for having shown attachment to Sufis and made provision for them. Thus the emperor has recognized the worth of the religious classes (*arbab-i 'ilm u m'arifat*) and the writer has full hopes that his own expectations will be fulfilled. The emperor should

[162] A numerous class of anecdotes concerns the bestowal of kingship by Sufi *pirs*, and the deposition of monarchs who had offended against their dignity.

[163] See *Encyclopaedia of Islam 2, s.v. futuwwa.*

[164] *Maktubat-i Quddusiya*, pp. 44–6; *Shaykh 'Abd al-Quddus*, pp. 437–9.

so honour the Muslim religious classes (*ta'ifa-i 'ulama' u a'imma u zu'afa'*) that they will reach a loftier dignity than in any age and clime; and he should hold impermissible and abominable the imposition of *'ushr* upon (the lands of) their livelihood. From such an abominable imposition the world will grow dark, and a calamity and wrathful visitation will be engendered when the cry for redress (*damar*) rises up from the *faqirs*. No wise man will fall into this pit and perish.

May the emperor remit this and no ill will befall. The religious classes will dwell at ease, occupied with prayers for the emperor and for the wellbeing of all Muslims. God has given Babur sovereignty; if he neglects to care for the Muslim religious classes (*fuqara' u zu'afa' u 'ulama' u sulaha' u masha'ikh u masakin*) a cry for redress (*damar*) will rise up from the land. Fortune in this world and in the next lies in the ease of this class (*ta'ifa*).

The *'arif* ('knower' of God) cares nought for this world. The love of the world and of its good has many evil consequences: but when these goods are spent in God's work and are preferred for the wellbeing of the people of God (*ahl-i Haqq*), a great reward will be laid up in the world to come. The shadow of the royal justice should be cast over mankind and none should oppress anyone. The army should remain firm in the commandments and prohibitions of the *shar'*; prayers should be performed in congregation; learning and men of learning should be cherished; censors (*muhtasiban*) should patrol the bazaars of every city to enforce the *shar'*.

In this auspicious reign the acts of government should be above suspicion (of departure from the prescriptions of Islamic law) just as they were in every respect in the time of the just Caliphs (*khulafa'-i rashidin*). Muslims of pure and zealous faith should be appointed to posts of government in the countryside (*dar vilayat*: the next sentence makes it clear that 'Abd al-Quddus' mind was running on taxes farmed out to Hindu financiers and the filling of clerkly posts by Hindus). In a Muslim administration and an Islamic polity no non-Muslim (*kafir*) should enjoy a governmental post or an assignment of revenue (*vajh*). Non-Muslims should not wield the pen in offices and they should not be commanders and tax-gatherers. In the *shar'* the subordination of *kafirs* is enjoined; and in accordance with it they should be humbled, subordinated, and made to pay tax. *Jizya* and *zakat* upon their property should be collected according to the prescriptions of the *shar'*. *Kafirs* should be forbidden to dress like Muslims to conceal their unbelief and they should be prohibited from practising heathen observances ostentatiously and publicly. In this manner the light of Islam will be maintained in its full glory.[165]

The letter to Humayun as a reigning monarch is comparatively brief. It alludes to his victorious return from a campaign. This may be the Gujarat campaign of AD 1535, although only by a stretch of the imagination can this be described as victorious;[166] we know that 'Abd al-Quddus waited upon Humayun at Agra in AD 1536.[167] Another possible occasion is at the outset of his reign, on his return from his campaign against the Raja of Kalinjar in AD 1531.[168] This letter again expresses the hope that under this sovereign the religious classes (*ta'ifa-i a'imma u fuqara'*) will be so secure and prosperous that they will reach a loftier station than in any age or clime. Whatever is bestowed upon them ought to be in tax-free tenure (*marfu' al-qalam*) to prevent trouble being caused to them in their

[165] *Maktubat-i Quddusiya*, pp. 335–7, no. 169; *Shaykh 'Abd al-Quddus*, pp. 453–6.

[166] The Gujarat campaign led to no permanent gains and Humayun's return to Agra was a rush to prevent Askari arriving before him.

[167] Digby, 'Dreams and Reminiscences of Dattu Sarvani', pp. 56, 61; *Lata'if*, p. 71.

[168] Probably in 1531 after Humayun's ascent of the throne, and not before it as in some sources.

devotions by base people (*na-ahlan*). So, day by day the light of Islam will be increased.[169]

Attitudes towards the Indian Environment

The straightforward antithesis in patterns of personality which used to be assumed by most writers on medieval Indian Muslim history—between narrow-minded and bigoted Sunnis on the one hand and Sufis who were considered broad-minded pantheists interested in Hinduism on the other—is seldom found in this simple form. A survey of the activities and attitudes of 'Abd al-Quddus has revealed him as an advocate of Sunni orthodoxy to whom a strong suspicion of heretical practices and beliefs must cling. He was a believer in the immanence of God in Creation, who at the same time advocated the severest application of Muslim legal theory in the treatment of Hindus. But, while expressing this last attitude, 'Abd al-Quddus drew upon yogic tradition in his own practice of techniques for the attainment of ecstasy; his explanations of these techniques given to his disciples are conceived partly in terms of yogic physiological concepts, as will be made clear below. His own interpretations of Nathapanthi Yogic traditions are also of interest, differing from those found elsewhere. He was a poet of some merit in Hindi and many of the verses he quoted show a fondness for the love poetry of the north Indian countryside. Is there any simple explanation of the marked contrast between these sympathetic attitudes and the intolerant views expressed in the letter to Babur?

Medieval Indian Muslims found themselves in their relationship with the non-Muslim Indian environment in what

[169] *Maktubat-i Quddusiya*, pp. 338–9, no. 171; *Shaykh 'Abd al-Quddus*, pp. 458–9.

has recently been called 'the alternating and simultaneous processes of mutual attraction and repulsion'.[170] An anecdote in the *Lata'if-i Quddusi* recording an experience of the Afghan soldier *murid* Dattu Sarvani well illustrates the instability of this relationship. In Bihar in AD 1528 Dattu became friendly with a *sannyasi* called Anant Guru, who was then attending to the defeated Afghan forces and promising them spiritual aid in their struggles against the Mughals. 'He talked well about God being One'; but 'Abd al-Quddus appeared in a dream to Dattu and warned him that he was a heretic (*zindiq*) and 'not near to God'.[171]

The tale may be considered a projection of the soldier *murid*'s subconscious rather than an expression of 'Abd al-Quddus' own attitude. However, a condemnation of Jogis occurs in an important discussion of *wahdat al-wujud* in the main part of the *Lata'if*, and this probably represents a discourse of 'Abd al-Quddus noted down at the time when it was delivered:

> The manner in which certain unbelieving Jogis, who have not a trace of Islam in them, relate knowledge of spiritual matters and of the Divine Unity (*'ilm-i ma'rifat u wahdat*) and the way in which they gain control over their breath and display miracles is not hid from the wise: but do you not see how Pharaoh also—curses be upon him!—as he was possessed of supernatural powers claimed divinity?[172]

An interesting line of argument is also found in Rukn al-Din's marginal notes to the *Rushd-nama*, in which he quotes an explanation by his father that the Jogis have misunderstood a point in their own physiological

170 Aziz Ahmad, *Studies in Islam in the Indian Environment*, Oxford: Oxford University Press, 1964, p. vii.
171 *Lata'if*, p. 74; Digby, 'Dreams and Reminiscences of Dattu Sarvani', pp. 64–5.
172 *Lata'if*, p. 20.

doctrines.[173] This echoes the remarks of an important shaykh of the fourteenth century, Sharaf al-Din Ahmad Maneri, who on one occasion maintained that the Jogis of his own day did not understand the traditions of mystical knowledge which had been handed down to them.[174] But on the evidence of the passage cited above we cannot convict ‘Abd al-Quddus of being over-sympathetic to the claims of living Jogis.

Are the contradictions in ‘Abd al-Quddus’ attitudes towards Jogis and other classes of Hindus the result of changes in his opinions in the course of his life? The basis for such conjecture would be that the *Rushd-nama* is a work of his youth, while the letter to Babur and the remarks about Jogis quoted above were the products of his old age. But such a view must be rejected on the evidence of Rukn al-Din’s marginal glosses to the *Rushd-nama* as well as that of his concluding note to it.[175] In his latter years ‘Abd al-Quddus used to teach the *Rushd-nama* to his disciples and used to impart to them yogic techniques and doctrines which are examined below. Many years after the move to Shahabad he taught the Arabic or Persian adaptation of the *Amritkund*, a yogic manual, to Shaykh Sulayman Mandavi in return for lessons in Qur’anic recitation.[176] Within a few years of writing the *Rushd-nama*, he had felt impelled to leave his ancestral home because it had come under Hindu domination.[177] Yet

[173] See below.

[174] Zayn Badr ‘Arabi, *Mukhkh al-ma‘ani*, MS, private collection, f. 100b [the reference is presumably to the manuscript in Digby’s own collection: Sharaf al-Dīn Ahmad Manerī, *Mukhkh al-ma‘ānī*, Bodleian Library, University of Oxford, MS S. Digby Or. 6, n.d. ~DL].

[175] *Rushd-nama*, pp. 35–6.

[176] *Lata’if*, p. 41, anecdote 45; see Yusuf Husain, ‘*Haud al-hayat*: la version Arabe de l’Amratkund’, *Journal Asiatique*, vol. CCXIII, pp. 291–344. The relationship between the various Arabic and Persian versions of this Yogic manual have not yet been the subject of detailed research.

[177] *Lata’if*, pp. 30–1; see above.

in the letters of the Shahabad period he continued to quote Hindi verses in his letters,[178] and quite late in life he still used to fall into ecstasy at the singing of Hindi verses, in one instance those sung behind the walls of a house in the same *muhalla* by a Hindu woman.[179] The available evidence in fact suggests that throughout his life, 'Abd al-Quddus' attitudes towards the non-Muslim Indian environment were complex and contradictory—as are those of most educated human beings living in a background of mixed but divergent cultures and communities.

Yogic Elements in the Teachings of 'Abd al-Quddus

Some of the yogic influences on the thought of 'Abd al-Quddus may be the result of direct contacts with Jogis, and Rukn al-Din may have been referring to such contacts when he mentions his father's association with 'all kinds of men'.[180] A later source relates an encounter between 'Abd al-Quddus and a Jogi previously in residence at Gangoh, whom he subdued by superior magical powers and converted to Islam;[181] little reliance is to be placed on the historicity of this anecdote, which is in a familiar hagiographical pattern.[182] There may have been centres of Natha-panthi

[178] Ibid., p. 62.
[179] Ibid., p. 108.
[180] Ibid., p. 19; see above.
[181] Muhammad Akram Barasawi, *Iqtibas al-anwar*, Lahore: s.n., 1895, p. 237.
[182] For an analysis see the present writer's forthcoming paper, 'Anecdotes of Jogis in Sufi hagiography', in the *Proceedings of the Seminar on Aspects of Religion in South Asia* held in London, 1970–1 [the *Proceedings* were never published. Digby's book-length version of his widely-circulated and -cited but previously unpublished paper is included in this series:

or other yogic traditions in the countryside near Rudawli: the name of Siddhawr, ancient Siddhapura where 'Abd al-Quddus went for elementary Islamic teaching, is suggestive. But the *Rushd-nama* accommodates and adapts yogic concepts with considerable skill to fit them into a Sufi theological framework. It is a production of 'Abd al-Quddus in his youth. Both these factors suggest that he was drawing upon a tradition already current in the Rudawli *dargah*.

In the *Anwar al-'uyun* there are three anecdotes which may indicate that Ahmad 'Abd al-Haqq adopted yogic ideas or practices not previously found in his branch of the Chishti *silsila*. When Ahmad 'Abd al-Haqq, travelling eastwards after Timur's invasion of AD 1398, arrived at Pandwa, the capital city of the Sultans of Bengal, he resided with other *darveshs* and Qalandars upon the banks of the river, side by side with bands of Jogis. The Sultan of Bengal, struck by the better treatment which, when roaming around in his disguise, he had received at the hands of the Jogis, threatened to drive out the Sufis and Qalandars.[183] The sultan's wanderings in disguise and his threat probably belong to legend, but the dwelling of the Sufis and the Jogis side by side is not unlikely (from other anecdotes of Ahmad 'Abd al-Haqq's eastern wanderings it appears that he was living in great poverty, held in little esteem.[184] His extensive association with these Jogis, whose generosity in sharing their food with all comers is mentioned in the anecdote, is not improbable).

On his return from Bengal to his birthplace of Rudawli an event took place which suggests that Ahmad 'Abd al-Haqq had profited from his recent association with these Jogis: in Bihar he was buried alive for six months. On his emergence

---

The Life and Works of Simon Digby, Volume II: Encounters with Jogīs in Indian Sūfī Hagiography ~DL].

[183] *Anwar al-'uyun*, pp. 23–5.

[184] Ibid., pp. 26–7, 53–4.

from the earth we are told that he assumed authority as a Sufi shaykh and began to incite allegiances.[185] Ahmad 'Abd al-Haqq is also described by 'Abd al-Quddus as causing a disciple to be buried alive, sitting on a mat on the ground in which he was buried and, after a fortnight had elapsed, taking the disciple out of the ground and bestowing his *khilafat* upon him.[186] This practice of burial alive and resuscitation does not, to my knowledge, appear elsewhere in Sufi literature; but it is a striking and familiar Natha-panthi yogic practice, examples of which are still occasionally reported in Indian newspapers. Such burials alive are generally undertaken amid considerable publicity and in circumstances which suggest that one object of the exercise is to secure a hold upon the devotions of the local population.[187]

A further parallel of the Rudawli tradition with yogic practice may be coincidental. The followers of Ahmad 'Abd al-Haqq, when they met, did not use the Qur'anic greeting '*salam 'alaykum*'. Instead of this they cried out '*Haqq, Haqq, Haqq!*' (*Haqq*, 'the Truth', is both a prominent attribute of God and an allusion to the name of the shaykh). In the Islamic world Qalandars had been in the habit of shouting '*Haqq, Haqq*', but the use of the repeated word as a greeting recalls the '*Alakh, alakh*' or '*Ades, ades*' used by the Jogis.[188]

The evidence is not conclusive but, in spite of the reference to his association with 'all kinds of men', the Yogic traditions

[185] Ibid., pp. 27–8: *bi-kamal rasidand u ba khalq bi-da'vat u mashaykhat mashghul shudahnd.*

[186] Ibid., p. 90.

[187] G.W. Briggs, *Gorakhnath and the Kanphata Yogis*, Calcutta: Y.M.C.A. Publishing House, 1938; W. Crooke, *Things Indian*, London: J. Murray, 1906, pp. 201–2; M. Eliade, *Yoga: Immortality and Freedom*, New York: Pantheon Books, 1958, p. 57n.

[188] *Anwar al-'uyun*, pp. 104–5; Briggs, *Gorakhnath and the Kanphata Yogis*; Nur Ahmad Chishti, *Tahqiqat-i Chishti*, Lahore: Hamidiyya Steam Press, 1323/1907, p. 486.

with which ‘Abd al-Quddus was familiar may in fact have been handed down in the intimate and Muslim milieu of the Rudawli *dargah*. It is possible that this tradition may have been transmitted to him mainly by Shaykh Piyare who in other ways exercised an influence upon his development.

The *Rushd-nama* is a fairly short example of a class of composition popular among Indian Sufis, a *risala* or treatise in ornate Persian prose interspersed with Arabic quotations and Persian verses. It differs from other examples of the genre not only in the traces of yogic influence which it reveals, but also in the number of Hindi verses which are inserted in the text. Although it is a comparatively short work, it lacks any strong connected chain of argument. It is a series of exhortations addressed to the *talib* or student of the *tariqa* concerning the Unity of Being, God's purpose in creating the world, the necessity of entering the Sufi Path, the reassumption of created into Creator, and other main ideas of the Sufi way of life. It has no description of successive stages along the Sufi Path (*maqamat, manazil*) or of the gradual progress of the *talib* along them. It merely advocated the necessity of embracing this Path.

At the opening ‘Abd al-Quddus, ‘the sweeper of the dust of the *khanqah* of ‘Abd al-Haqq’, states his intention of compiling an account of *tawhid* (the Divine Unity) in accordance with the words of his *ustad-i tariqat* (Master in the Sufi Path). If this phrase is not purely conventional, it can hardly refer to his nominal *pir*, Shaykh Muhammad—a youth of his own age; possibly it refers to his communion with Ahmad ‘Abd al-Haqq, then forty years in his grave; or his *ustad-i tariqat* may have been neither his living nor his dead *pir*, but rather his companion and instructor in the *dargah*, Shaykh Piyare. ‘Abd al-Quddus states that he will bring into his account of *tawhid* ‘the word of every sect’ (*sukhun bar ta‘ifa*) in accordance with the *hadith*, ‘The Knower [‘*arif*, i.e. the mystic] knows the Lord in all things, as all things are within the knowledge of the Lord.' By this he meant that he was about to adduce non-Muslim as well as Muslim testimony in support of his view of the Divine Unity.

In the exhortations which follow, 'Abd al-Quddus advances in support of each of his propositions verses (*ayats*) from the Qur'an, examples of *hadith-qudsi* or statements attributed by earlier Sufi mystics to God Himself, *hadiths* of the Prophet Muhammad, and Persian and Hindi verses. While the Persian verses are almost all of an easily recognizable Sufi content, those in Hindi belong to a number of different or mixed traditions of religious or amatory poetry. The Hindi verses usually bring a particular exhortation to its close. A related topic is then introduced, often with the opening words 'O brother!' (*ay biradar*). There are, however, infrequent departures from this order, where the Hindi verses are succeeded without a break by further quotations in Arabic or Persian.

Although the *Rushd-nama* does not present a coherent argument, the following synopsis may be offered of the chain of thought of its contents:

1. God's purpose in Creation in the revelation of the hidden treasure of the Divine Nature (p. 2);
2. The creation of Adam; Man is the *khalifa* (deputy) of God; Man's blindness in failing to recognize that he himself is pure Spirit (p. 4);
3. A *pir* is necessary for guidance in the attempt to remove this blindness and to see God (p. 5);
4. The plight of those who have no *pir* and therefore go astray (p. 5);
5. Man is created for the service (*'ibadat*) of God: the quest for God is therefore his duty. This quest is the *'ilm-i tawhid* or science of the Divine Unity. *Tawhid* is the release by means of *'ilm-i ma'rifat* (mystic knowledge) and *talab* (quest) from Duality: it is the realization of the identity of Man with God (pp. 5–7);

6. Man, the created, is to God as the drop to the ocean; this doctrine is a secret revealed (p. 7);
7. Exhortation to the drop to merge into the ocean, the Sufi *talib* is to seek absorption into the Divine (p. 8);
8. Nothing in the interior or exterior world is to be considered as apart from God (p. 8);
9. God considered as a royal falcon (*shahbaz*). Exhortation to the pigeon to fly up from the perishable world to the world which endures, there to become a morsel for this falcon (p. 9);
10. Unless you die to the world before your death you will never reach the everlasting Beloved (p. 9);
11. Remember your home and look to your origin! The vital breath (*nafas*) is installed by God (p. 10);
12. The place where you dwell is a prison, the world a house of misfortune (p. 10);
13. You should travel: hasten to your own country and find that which you desire (p. 10);
14. You should guard your goods so that they arrive safely from the perishable world to the world enduring (p. 11);
15. The benefit of spiritual and physical wakefulness, which induce a mystic state (p. 11);
16. The state of those 'killed with the dagger of Love' (p. 12);
17. The necessity of *sama'*: music which is purely instrumental has in it no attraction to the Divine and is therefore forbidden: it is animal where song is human. From song Love dominates the heart and Divine secrets are revealed. From this attraction mystic dance (*raqs*) is engendered (p. 12);
18. Enter this day into the quest for God: if you do not do so now you will be sorely vexed by the inquiring angels at the Judgement (p. 12);
19. Those who enter not into the Love of God and seek not the intercession of His Prophet this day shall not do so later. As you sow, so shall you reap (p. 13);

20. Waste not your time upon that which is without meaning, lest injury befall you (p. 14);
21. Preaching is vain, unless the hearer listens with his heart and acts upon it;
22. (no break in text) The *talib*, when he possesses sincerity and faith and acts inwardly and outwardly according to the straight path, attains the degree of *pas-i anfas*. He then turns back the three breaths of his body into a single breath. He will then reach the station of everlasting life (p. 15);
23. This is a Divine mystery which must not be put to worldly purposes (p. 16);
24. Reading and writing are commendable but the Path of the Sufi is quite different (p. 16);
25. All three stages (*maqams*—here equated with the three 'breaths') are within you (p. 16);
26. Concerning the *Ruh* or Spirit (breath) of God pervading creation (p. 18);
27. (no break in text) On the necessity of *salat-i ma'kusa* (p. 18);
28. Look not to aught but God! Similes from grammar: God as the *masdar* or noun of action, and as the cause (*asl*) of the consequence (*far'*); God's regard for His servants (p. 19);
29. The understanding of the vital principle (*nafs*) or breath (*nafas*) is the condition (*shart*, 'conditional clause') for the quest of the knowledge of God (p. 21);
30. Similes based upon syntax (*nahw*). The importance of *samt* (direction, 'sentence order'): the direction towards God. God is exalted (*marfu'*, 'nominative'): all else is redundant. The act (*fi'l*, 'the verb') is occupation with God: God is the Beginner (*mubtadi*, 'the subject') (p. 23);
31. God is without qualification (*fa'ida*, 'a qualifying phrase') in His Essence (*dhat*); man is the edifice (*'imarat*) of the Lord (p. 24);

32. Water is not drawn from the well till there is a drawer. The Divine mysteries in the human heart are drawn out by *sama'*. The lawfulness of *sama'* for those to whom it pertains (*li ahlih*): concerning *raqs* (p. 25);
33. *Sijda* (prostration) in front of anyone other than God is unlawful: but there is naught created which is apart from God, and therefore in whatsoever direction you perform *sijda* it will be lawful. Adam first prostrated himself before stars and moon, and eventually before God without form: God's immanence (p. 27);
34. *Sijda* before a *pir* has an especial significance. All creation, beautiful and vile alike, is the manifestation of God, but the perfection of creation is Man. Man is of two kinds: the man who is human in outward form and the man who is so in truth. The true Man is an example for the whole creation, 'the good tree' (*shajara-i tayyiba*) whose roots are firm, whose branches are in the sky. That Man, fair outside and pure within, is Perfect Man (*insan-i kamil*): He is no other than the *pir*, the Guide imbued with the attributes (*sifat*) of God Himself. The *pir* is like a king visiting the house of a subject. Rabia of Basra, the *pir* of her age, was circumambulated by the Ka'ba, which also performed *sijda* before her. The heart of the believer, who is the *pir*, is the *haram* of God. Man's heart, the heart of the *pir* is the mirror of God (pp. 30–2);
35. The *pir* is the mirror: when the splendour of God is manifest in the *pir*, he is himself turned to naught and naught but God remains (p. 32);
36. When the secrets of the nature of the *pir* are proven true, the *sijda* of his *murid* before him becomes not only permissible but obligatory. *Sijda* was incumbent upon bygone *ummats* (communities of believers), who prostrated themselves before father and mother, teacher, sultan, and *pir*. With the coming of our Prophet, *sijda* ceased to be obligatory, except to God;

but it remains permissible, like the mid-monthly fasts (*ayyam-i bayz*). When you possess this great secret, you must not reveal it, else you will be unworthy of another secret (pp. 32–3);

37. It is forbidden to reveal the secrets of Maliks and Khans, but this is the secret of God Himself, and if any man reveals it he is worthy of death. Although during the height of pleasure and in the intoxication of love, one cannot restrain oneself, one must not be negligent in letting God's secrets fall into unworthy ears; yet they should not be concealed from the true seeker who is worthy of them (p. 33);
38. You must look in one direction only in order to pass safely along this road. Know that you will surely come to Siri[189] (one of the cities of Dehli: also *sayre*, 'an excursion') and Mahmudabad: there you will see Sultan Nasir. You will come out of Siri: journey in Dili (Dehli; *dile*, 'a heart') until you come to Mahmudabad: there you will see Sultan Mahmud, who is King of Dili, as indicated in the word of God, 'A praiseworthy station and a victorious dominance' (the place Mahmud and Sultan Nasir) (for the explanation of this complicated simile based upon a Qur'anic phrase and a pun upon *Dili*, see below). This is the stage of faith (*taslim*, submission) and it is not attained except by the grace of God. Until you are wholly immersed in the river of the Divine Unity,[190] you will never reach the stage of faith: this is the Reality (p. 34).

[189] Siri was the city built by 'Ala' al-Din Muhammad Khilji (AD 1296–1313), the most westerly section of the walled triple city of fourteenth-century 'Old' Dehli, contrasted with Ferozabad, the garden city of Feroz Shah Tughluq (AD 1351–88), which probably provides a model for Mahmudabad, there being no actual city of Dehli known by this name.
[190] The texts read Sultan Nasir in place of Sultan Nasir which the Qur'anic phrase requires [as published; should possibly read 'in place of

This synopsis of the contents of the *Rushd-nama* reveals the preoccupations which have already been noted in the discussion of the religious practice of 'Abd al-Quddus. *Wahdat al-wujud*, *sama'*, and *salat-i ma'kusa* are all strongly urged upon the *talib*. Apart from the Hindi verses (examined later in this chapter) two sections (15 and 22) show a strong influence of yogic ideas in their doctrinal content. The conclusion (38) seems to support, in oblique and allusive language, the view expressed in the *Lata'if* that what 'Abd al-Quddus called *sultan-i dhikr* was the height of mystical experience, the goal to which the efforts of the *talib* led.

The conclusion is somewhat obfuscated by the geographical simile and plays upon words, probably deliberately so with the intention commended in the previous section (37) of preventing the secrets of God from falling into unworthy hands. The context of *maqaman mahmudan wa sultanan nasiran* (Qur'an, XVII, concluding words of 79, 80) seen through a long tradition of pietistic and Sufi exegesis, would be familiar to the *talib* to whom the *Rushd-nama* is (in theory) addressed.

And watch (some part) of the night in the same, as a work of supererogation (*nafila*) for thee; peradventure thy Lord will raise thee to an honourable station. And say, 'O Lord, cause me to enter as a favourable entry and cause me to come forth with a favourable coming forth; and grant me from Thee an authority which prevails'.[191]

---

sultanan nasir' ~DL]. Nasir al-Din and Mahmud being found among the royal names and titles of the Dehli sultans (e.g. Nasir al-Din Mahmud Shah, the last Tughluq sultan), this may have set 'Abd al-Quddus' mind running on this strange punning allegory. If the geographical allegory is still adhered to, the cities of Dehli are set at varying distances from the Jamuna (Jun): cf. the simile of the river in flood for *sultan-i dhikr* above.

[191] Sale translates 'an honourable place' and 'an assisting power'; Pickthall, 'a praised estate' and 'a sustaining power'; Arberry, 'a laudable station' and 'authority to help me'. A worse problem is to find a translation of the phrases not in their context and in a rationalist

The first of these two verses is a standard justificatory text for the performance by Sufis of supererogatory devotions and austerities. *Maqaman mahmudan* is taken according to tradition to be the station of intercession for others;[192] in Muslim exegesis the following verse is often taken to refer to the Prophet's victorious re-entry into Makka, and this interpretation may have influenced 'Abd al-Quddus in his adoption of an elaborate geographical simile.[193] 'A favourable (or just) ingoing' and 'a favourable (just) outgoing' can here be taken as referring to the ingoing and outgoing breath in the performance of *dhikr* and the practice of breath control (*habs-i dam, pas-i anfas*). The conclusion of the *Rushd-nama* is that beyond that stage there lies 'the immersion in the river (or sea) of Divine Unity'.

The section of the *Rushd-nama* which urges the benefits of wakefulness as an aid to achieving ecstasy (15) reveals yogic influences. After remarking, 'Therefore you must turn from negligence to awareness, and in your behaviour towards men (*kar-i khalq*) must remain ever immersed in the Divine Presence: and you must know that the place of sleep is in the head', 'Abd al-Quddus quotes the following Hindi verses:

gagana asthanai magana dvara
tahan basai nindra ghora andhara
bijli ki camaken avai jai
panca tanta liye gagana samai[194]

In the court of heaven is the gateway of joy
and there dwells the sleep of deepest darkness;

---

exegesis of the Qur'an, but in the metaphysical sense which they are made to bear in medieval Sufi teaching.

[192] G. Sale, *The Koran*, New York: A.L. Burt, 1892, p. 214n.

[193] Ibid.

[194] *Rushd-nama*, p. 12; P.D. Barthwal, ed., *Gorakha-bani*, Prayag: Hindi Sahitya Sammelan, 1946, p. 60, no. 176; see below pp. 392–3 and note 275.

flashes of lightning come and go
and the five senses are taken up and absorbed in heaven.

'O brother', the *Rushd-nama* continues, 'this alludes to those slain by the dagger of love,[195] who, being exclusively devoted to God, have turned their gaze unto him and perceive not themselves in between.'

To those unfamiliar with *hatha-yoga* or Natha-panthi literature the Hindi quatrain requires some explanation. Yoga is largely conceived by the Natha-panthis and other allied sects as a physiological process towards the attainment of perfection, and many of their exercises are designed to reverse the processes of nature from which the human frame decays. The *bindu-rasa*, seminal fluid or vital juice, drops down from a cavity in the skull above the throat to be consumed by the raging fire of *rajas*, situated close to the naval. When the loss of this and other vital fluids is prevented by the mastery of austerities, a dormant force, symbolized as a coiled serpent called *kundalini* and also *sakti*, is persuaded to rise through a succession of *chakras* (wheels, lotuses) in the spine till it attains union with *siva*, the force responsible for the production of the *bindu-rasa* within the skull. The ordinary nine orifices of the body have by now been sealed; the final stage in the achievement of immortality is the opening, by the united *siva* and *sakti*, of the orifice at the top of the skull, the *brahmarandhra* or fontanelle, the hidden 'tenth door'.[196] This is the *magana*

[195] The phrase echoes the couplet at the singing of which Khwaja Qutb al-Din Bakhtyar Kaki died in ecstasy: 'For those slain with the dagger of faith (*taslim*), every moment from the Unseen there is new life.' See above, notes 126 and 127.

[196] See Briggs, *Gorakhnath and the Kanphata Yogis*, ch. XV, 'The more important physiological concepts', pp. 305–21 and for the Brahmarandhra especially pp. 316–17.

dvara, 'the gateway of joy' of the verses quoted by 'Abd al-Quddus; the great latent forces of the body have been united and the deep darkness of unknowing is illuminated by flashes of lightning, the prelude of the liberation to be achieved through this final door. In common with other Khurasani and Indian Sufis, 'Abd al-Quddus was an advocate of the physical deprivation of sleep as an aid to ecstasy; but here the allusion is also to another more mystical awakening to which the *talib* must attain—'in the place of sleep which is in the head'.

The Hindi lines are identifiable in surviving Natha-panthi tradition, being one of two *caupais* or quatrains common to the *Rushd-nama* and the *Gorakha-bani*, the set of Hindi verses most widely accepted among Natha-panthi Jogis.[197] The flashes of lightning suggest the presence of the thunder which in this literature describes the *anahada sabda*, the 'unstruck sound'; and in the *caupai* which follows this in the *Gorakha-bani*, 'the *anahada sabda* thunders in heaven' (i.e. in the skull).[198]

The second point at which yogic ideas intrude into the Persian prose of the *Rushd-nama* is in the section (22) concerned with the control of the breath (*pas-i anfas*). When the *talib* has reached the stage of sincerity and faith,[199] and when he acts inwardly and outwardly on the straight path (*sirat-i mustaqim*), not inventing of himself any innovation (*bid'at*) and not behaving otherwise than as God and His Prophet have commanded, and when he reaches, in the degree (*martaba*) of conservation of the breaths (*pas-i anfas*) a state (*maqam*) where all three breaths which are in the body are turned back into a single breath, he attains the fountain of life and drinks out of it. Then he will reach the

[197] See notes 194 and 275.

[198] Barthwal, *Gorakha-bani*, no. 177.

[199] *Sidq u yaqin*.

station of everlasting life. His lot will be the station of Idris and he will enjoy the company of Khizr.[200]

This is a very curious train of thought for a Muslim who has been counselling against *bid'at* (innovation, heresy) only a sentence before. What the Jogi strove for, by a reversal of the physiological processes of decay, was the physical immortality of his body. This was the concomitant of his ecstasy and achievement, of his arrival at the 'tenth door'. Now Idris and Khizr among Muslim prophets did not suffer death. But at this point in his meditation 'Abd al-Quddus checks himself and adds, 'Such [everlasting] life is in proximity to God, and is in the category of life in the next world, not mere life in this world—lest you fall into the error of the *malahida* (heretics).'[201]

To the same section of the *Rushd-nama* (22) there is an important gloss by Rukn al-Din, which evidently records 'Abd al-Quddus' oral teaching regarding the three breaths here described:

> It is recorded from the author (God's mercy be upon him!) that one breath comes out upwards and another breath goes downwards, and a third breath comes out from the whole of the body along the roots of the hairs of the body. These three breaths should be turned back into a single breath, just as the Guide of the times ['Abd al-Quddus] states.[202]

Of the three breaths described by 'Abd al-Quddus, the breath going upwards is clearly—in the yogic physiology of the *Goraksa sataka* and similar Natha-panthi treatises—the *prana*, while the breath going downwards is the *apana*.

[200] The extensive post-Qur'anic cycles of stories around these two figures in each case emphasize their immortality on earth: see *Encyclopedia of Islam* 1, s.v. *Idris, al-Khadir.*

[201] The term *mulhid* (pl. *malahida*) is very loosely applied in the usage of the Dehli Sultanate to any variety of obnoxious heretic or unbeliever.

[202] *Rushd-nama*, p. 15, marginal note 3.

An element of confusion seems to exist, not only in 'Abd al-Quddus' exposition, between the *apana* as the wind expelled through the lower orifices of the body and the downward intake of breath, which should be entirely an act of the *prana*. 'In Yogic practice', Briggs writes, 'these two, *prana* and *apana*, are to be joined. The knowledge of how this is to be done is of great importance to Jogis and belongs to the highest knowledge, delivering from old age and death.'[203] 'Abd al-Quddus' third wind, which is already in operation in the human frame before the joining, rather than engendered by the other two, is a departure from standard yogic expositions, but seems to be found in the traditional Sikh exegesis which Macauliffe drew upon in the translation cited below. It should probably be identified with the first and most important of the additional eight winds found in the common Natha-panthi texts: 'The *samana* (*samvayu*), whose chief seat is in the navel, is the function of digestion. This air, or intestinal fire resides also in all the limbs and makes the body dry.'[204]

In section 25 of the *Rushd-nama*, 'Abd al-Quddus returns to the three breaths. Here they are considered as *maqams* (places, 'stations'). 'O Brother, all three *maqams* are within you.' He quotes the words of the Qur'an, 'And do you not regard within yourselves?'[205] A Hindi verse follows:

thirai tikuti ... sandhu
mula dvara pavana bandhu[206]
Firmly unite ... in (?) the *trikuti*;
Close the wind in the *muladvara*.

[203] Briggs, *Gorakhnath and the Kanphata Yogis*, pp. 306–7.
[204] Ibid.
[205] *Rushd-nama*, p. 16.
[206] The correct reading of the missing word is not clear: for the collation of the manuscripts by Mr Simon Weightman and myself, see note 255.

Trikuti has the etymological sense of 'three corners', 'three directions'. In yogic terminology it is often applied to the point of junction of the cords *ida* and *pingea*, from which the *kundalini* may pass up the third central cord *susumna*. *Prana* and *apana*, the vital winds, are considered as travelling up and down the first two of these cords. There is, however, considerable terminological confusion. Macauliffe, probably relying upon a Sikh verbal tradition of exegesis, when the phrase *trikuti sandhi* occurs in a verse of Kabir in the *Adi Granth*, renders it as 'at the union of the three breaths';[207] this clearly corresponds with 'Abd al-Quddus' own exposition. The *trikuti* is sometimes conceived of as the penultimate *cakra* situated above the eyebrows,[208] but it is also, and particularly in relation to the movement of the vital winds, thought to be located near the solar plexus, in the navel where the winds are knotted together.[209] As such, it is the *madhya sunya*, the 'middle void', *sunya*, 'the Void' being used to express final liberation.[210] In the form *suni madhe* this expression occurs in verses quoted shortly afterwards by 'Abd al-Quddus;[211] but in view of his earlier statement regarding 'the place of sleep in the head' it is not unlikely that he, like most Jogis, was in some confusion as to where the junction of the *trikuti* was. However, he quoted a Hindi verse and, later, a *hadith*, emphasizing the importance of this mystic point within the human frame:

[207] *Adi Grantha, Kabir*, Rag Bilawal, no. 11; R.K. Varma, *Santa Kabira*, Ilahabad: Sahitya Bhavana Limited, 1967, p. 162; M.A. Macauliffe, *The Sikh Religion: its Gurus, Sacred Writings, and Authors*, 6 volumes, Oxford: Clarendon Press, 1909, vol. VI, p. 232.

[208] E.g. Varma, *Santa Kabira*, p. 483, cf. E. Wood, *Yoga*, Harmondsworth: Penguin, 1962, p. 164.

[209] Cf. C. Vaudeville, ed. *Kabir Granthavali (Doha)*, Pondicherry: Institut Français d'Indologie, 1957, p. 101, n. 21; p. 116, n. 255.

[210] Ibid., p. xx. The literature on Yogic subjects is very extensive and one can only begin to touch its outer fringes in this study of 'Abd al-Quddus.

[211] *Rushd-nama*.

heren bhitara hai hiya tina mahan kanta basai
tahan basera jo karai so bhi piya milai[212]

Within the flesh there is a heart, where my lord takes his residence.
He who makes his lodging there meets with his lord.

Hadith: Lo, in the body of Adam there is a lump of flesh, and in that lump of flesh a secret, and in that secret am I.[213]

The verse concerning the *trikuti*, situated between these two quotations, has two important marginal glosses by Rukn al-Din, the first of which discusses its general import:

This is an account of the occupation of the *talib* of God. Being employed in this activity, he achieves perfection. This is the activity of breath control (*dam-sazi*).[214] In the language of the Jogis they call it *bhuvangam*, which means 'the snake', as it is breath control for the snake [?].[215] The *talib* should practise such breath control, the technique of which is conveyed by his *murshid* [*pir*].[216]

The second and longer gloss concerns the meaning which 'Abd al-Quddus attached to the *muladvara*. It suggests the extent to which the yogic exegesis of 'Abd al-Quddus had departed from more commonly held Natha-panthi doctrines. '*Muladvara*', Rukn al-Din writes,

refers to the three breaths. The first breath is upwards and the second downwards and the third in the whole body. The joining together of these breaths is a firm work: all three breaths should

212 Ibid., p. 16.
213 Ibid., p. 17.
214 Thus, usage of *dam-sazi* is not found in Persian lexicons, but occurs also in the passage of *Nizam al-Qulub*, cited below, note 226.
215 The meaning is obscure to me and the text possibly corrupt. The Aligarh MS, which also has Rukn al-Din's glosses, does not vary here from the lithograph.
216 *Rushd-nama*, p. 16, marginal note 3.

be closed in the *muladvara*. The Guide of the time ['Abd al-Quddus] says, 'Let him conserve his breath as far as he can: and for meditation (*fikr*) in his heart let him visualise his own interior state.'[217] The Jogis say something different. According to them the *muladvara* is the podex: but it has been ascertained from the author of this *Rushd-nama* that *muladvara* means the crown of the head, which is the place of the brain and of the gathering of the seminal fluid. When a child is bound up there, [we] may see it beneath the skin on the crown of the head: this is the *muladvara*. When the breath is bound up there, and when from the heat of the breath the seminal fluid becomes like clear water, [it] suffuses through the whole body. The traveller (*salik*, synonym of *talib*) feels it like a cloud which is raining. This is the time when the upside-down breath comes inside his body. As a wise man (*'alime*) says in Hindavi, *ultai sakti carhai prabandha* (the *sakti* is turned upside down and the process ascends): that is to say the reversed[218] breath goes back the opposite way and suffuses the interior. Then the body of the traveller (*salik*) becomes subtle (*latif*): the state (*maqam*) of levitation (*tayr*) is engendered. Illuminations of Divine mysteries and the mysteries of the unseen world are revealed. Annihilation (in God) and the obliteration of all else is brought to pass. For this exercise two things are necessary: emptiness of the stomach from food and drink, and perpetual seclusion.[219]

Assuming that Rukn al-Din has correctly reported his father, 'Abd al-Quddus has here departed far from commonly accepted Natha-panthi exegesis. *Muladvara* would appear to be an unlearned version of *muladhara*, the 'fundamental base'. The *sphincter ani* in the region where, in Natha-panthi tradition, the *muladhara* is situated, is an orifice, a *dvara* or 'door' of the human body.[220] *Muladvara pavana bandhu*

[217] The Aligarh MS reads *giraftan* for the lithograph's *guftan*. I have amended *khayal*, found in both, to *hal*.

[218] Aligarh MS, *ma'kusa*; lithograph, *makuta* (*sic*).

[219] *Rushd-nama*, p. 16, marginal note 4.

[220] Briggs, *Gorakhnath and the Kanphata Yogis*, pp. 311–13.

in the verse quoted would in this case refer to the closing and containment there of the *apana*, the downward wind, in accordance with the general reversal of physiological processes as a prelude to the attainment of mystic powers. But *mula*, 'root', 'ground', 'essence', is also used, in the personalized mysticism of some of the Hindi verses of the *Rushd-nama*, as a term for God immanent in His creation:

jala tain upana bulbula jalahin mahin bilai
taisa yaha sainsara sabha mulahi jai samai[221]

The bubble was formed from water: in water it disappears:
In the same way the whole Universe is contained in the *Mula*.

If *mula* is understood in this sense, the *muladvara* is no longer the ordinary *muladhara* of Natha-panthi teaching, because it has been reidentified with the *brahmarandhra*. It is the 'gate of the Essence', the door to liberation and, in this personalized mysticism, to union with God. In the interpretation of 'Abd al-Quddus, the binding or closing of the wind there refers not to the beginning of the psycho-physical process of Hatha Yoga, but to the immediate prelude to its successful conclusion.

In 'Abd al-Quddus' doctrinal expositions in Persian, yogic concepts are described in a shadowy and allusive manner and their presence has been made more explicit by the glosses of Rukn al-Din. This suggests that the extent of Yogic influence on his religious thought may have been wider than has been allowed to appear in his own exegesis. In particular, his emphasis upon two favourite aspects of the mystical life, the utility of *salat-i ma'kusa* and the importance and nature of *sultan-i dhikr*, may reflect the concealed influence of Natha-panthi Yogic beliefs. As regards the former, hanging upside

221 *Rushd-nama*, p. 9.

down is the most conspicuous ascetic practice of a group of '*sadhus*' (in the broad sense of the term) called *urdamukhi.*[222] The terms *ardha-urdha*, 'downwards-upwards' and *ulta*, 'upside-down', are very frequently found in Hindi Yogic texts and refer, at one level of exposition, to the reversal of the physical processes:[223] being hung upside-down is an obvious contribution to such a reversal. The author of the *Dabistan* refers to this practice among a group of *sannyasis* as *namaz-i ma'kus.*[224] With regard to *sultan-i dhikr*, the emphasis upon its physical symptom may reflect Natha-panthi influence. In spite of the analogy drawn between *sultan-i dhikr* and *wahy* (Prophetic inspiration),[225] it is likely that 'Abd al-Quddus was influenced by the yogic idea of the *anahada sabda*, the 'unstruck sound'. Though the term is not mentioned in the *Lata'if* or the *Rushd-nama*, the *Nizam al-qulub*, a late seventeenth-century Chishti Sabiri treatise on techniques of *dhikr*, which includes sentences deriving from this section of the *Rushd-nama* and the accompanying gloss and probably conserves oral teachings handed down in the *silsila*, identifies the *sawt-i sarmadi* (sound of eternality) produced by breath control (*pas-i nafas*, *habs-i dam*) with the *anahada* of the Jogis.[226] The identification of *sultan-i dhikr* with the *anahada* is made by an important *khalifa* of the *silsila* descending from 'Abd al-Quddus, Hajji Imdad Allah, in the early nineteenth century; his description of the sensation also echoes the passage in the *Lata'if.*[227]

The crude physical concepts of the Jogis are allegorized and refined in 'Abd al-Quddus' references to them. This appears to be in accord with his more general tendency to

[222] J.C. Oman, *The Mystics, Ascetics, and Saints of India*, p. 45.

[223] Vaudeville, *Kabir Granthavali*, p. 101, n. 21.

[224] *Dabistan al-madhahib*, Bombay: Lachman Press, 1262/1846, p. 170.

[225] See above.

[226] Awrangabadi, *Nizam al-qulub*, pp. 6–8; see also Shah Kalim Allah Jahanabadi, *Kashkul-i Kalimi*, Dehli: Mujtaba'i Press, June 1891, p. 39.

[227] Imdad Allah, *Ziya' al-qulub*, pp. 20–1.

elevate and regularize the Sufi tradition which he inherited—his more cultivated behaviour as a *pir* compared to his wild exemplar Ahmad 'Abd al-Haqq and his inclination towards a 'learned' Sufi life supported by professions of orthodoxy and of dislike of unbelievers. His treatment of yogic ideas and techniques of ecstasy (probably passed on to him in the Rudawli *khanqah*) may be seen as an attempt to regularize an unorthodox, largely non-Muslim tradition within the confines of a learned (though profoundly Indianized) Muslim orthodoxy, the intellectual world of the religious classes patronized by the rulers and high officers of late fifteenth- and early sixteenth-century Hindostan.

'Abd al-Quddus and the Indo-Persian Poetic Tradition

'Abd al-Quddus' poetic tastes were formed in his youth, in a rural and Sufi environment and at a time when his formal education in Arabic and Persian polite sciences had not progressed very far. His taste in Persian verse evidently did not incline towards the refined and ornate classical courtly tradition mainly represented by the *qasida* and the literary rather than didactic *mathnavi*. The Persian verses which he quotes in the *Rushd-nama* and in his letters are usually *bayts* of *ghazals* or of *mathnavis* of which the Sufi interpretation is obvious. The *Rushd-nama* often, though not always, mentions by name the authors of the Persian verses quoted in it; and on some other occasions the *maqta* or a *ghazal* quoted in it gives the *takhallus* or pen-name of the poet. The most frequently quoted verses are those of Mas'ud Beg, a poet of strongly Sufi inclinations of the later fourteenth-century Dehli Sultanate, who enjoyed considerable esteem in northern India until the middle of the sixteenth century, but seems to have passed out of fashion and almost into oblivion at that time.[228] When 'Abd al-Quddus first came to the *khanqah* at Rudawli, Shaykh Piyare was engaged in reciting aloud from the *divan* of Mas'ud Beg.[229] 'Abd al-Quddus was evidently influenced in his poetic tastes by his association with Shaykh Piyare.[230] This, besides the presence of a copy of the *divan* in the Rudawli *khanqah* and the persistent preoccupation of Mas'ud Beg with *wahdat al-wujud*, may account for the frequency with which his *ghazals* are quoted in the *Rushd-nama*, where he is named no less than twelve times.[231] The next most frequently cited poet is Farid al-Din 'Attar who appears by name ten times; in every case the quotations are from his *mathnavis*, not *ghazals*.[232] 'Attar had also been a favourite poet among earlier Shaykhs of the Chishti *silsila* in India. The only other non-Indian Persian poets quoted in the *Rushd-nama* appear to be Sa'di and Rumi (three times each).[233] The remaining verses quoted are probably all of Indo-Persian poets: Muhammad Qalandar (a *ghazal*) of five *bayts*,[234] Nakhshabi (once, a *du-bayti*),[235] Bu 'Ali Qalandar

[228] For a notice of Mas'ud Beg with a few biographical details, see 'Abd al-Haqq, *Akhbar al-akhyar*, p. 164; for a *ghazal* of Mas'ud Beg inscribed in the decoration of a mosque at Dehli dated 900/1494, see S. Digby, 'The Tomb of Buhlūl Lōdī', *JRAS*, 1970 (forthcoming) [this article was eventually published in *Bulletin of the School of Oriental and African Studies*, vol. 38, no. 3, 1975, pp. 550–61. See pp. 560–1 for S. Digby's discussion, transcription, and translation of the *ghazal*. Also to be found in *L&WSD* VI.8. ~DL]; for a *jawab* to this *ghazal* written in Sikandar Lodi's time, see Badayuni, *Muntakhab al-tawarikh*, vol. I, p. 323.
[229] *Lata'if*, p. 9.
[230] See below for Hindi *dohas* probably by Shaykh Piyare.
[231] *Rushd-nama*, pp. 11, 19 (twice), 21, 22, 25, 26 (twice), 27, 29 (twice), 32.
[232] Ibid., pp. 2, 3–4, 4, 5, 7–8, 8, 9, 18, 24, 28–9.
[233] Ibid., pp. 15, 26, 32—Sa'di; pp. 11, 17, 33—Rumi, the quotation on p. 17 being from the *Divan-i Shams-i Tabriz*.
[234] Ibid., p. 2.
[235] Ibid., p. 14.

(once),[236] and Sharaf-i Qattal (once).[237] A *bayt* of a *ghazal* by 'Abd al-Quddus himself, with the *takhallus* Ahmadi (or Ahmada) is also reproduced.[238]

In estimating 'Abd al-Quddus' talents as a Persian poet we are mainly dependent upon the small collection of his poems appended to the *Lata'if*.[239] This contains five *ghazals* with the *takhallus* Ahmadi, a *ruba'i* and some *qit'as* or fragments. The opening piece is a long *ghazal* of twenty *bayts* in a jingling rhyme and metre recalling the weaker portions of Rumi's *Divan-i Shams-i Tabriz*:

ay taliban badanid, ay taliban badanid
man 'ishq-i haqq guzidam, ay taliban badanid.

O seekers know, O seekers know,
O seekers know I have chosen the love of God!

A *qit'a* of six *bayts* is a description of the qualities of a true *darvesh*:

darvesh nest anki bakhuspad khvurad chu kar
darvesh sir-i haqq buvad az ruh paktar.

The darvesh is not a man who sleeps and eats like an ass:
the darvesh should be a divine mystery more pure than the spirit.

The piece was possibly inspired by a *ghazal* on the same theme in a similar metre by Sa'di, to which it is greatly inferior.[240] In both these quotations *haqq* also alludes to the

236 Ibid., p. 18.
237 Ibid., p. 26.
238 Ibid., p. 15.
239 *Lata'if*, pp. 96–9.
240 Sa'di, *Badayi'*, *ghazal* on the theme of the life of the *darvesh*, beginning:

an-ra ki jaye nest hama shahr jayi u-st
darvesh har kuja ki shab ayad sarayi u-st

poet's *pir*, Ahmad 'Abd al-Haqq. In conclusion, a *qit'a* of three *bayts* may be quoted, which probably fairly represents 'Abd al-Quddus' limited achievements as a Persian poet:

darshor-i 'ishq-i jahan ghamha-i har du 'alam
durde-st dard-i ma-ra dar jam-i sir-i 'alam
dar shawq-i dost ya rabb jan bar kanam ba har dam
ta jan-i jan na yabam ba jan u dil banalam
az jan u dil gudhashtam bar sar-i jan baraftam
didim sir-i haqqahaqq ast jumla 'alam

In the tumult of love of the beloved the griefs of this world and the next
are the less for our pain in the cup of the world's secret.
In desire for the friend, O Lord, I uproot my life every moment;
until I find the spirit of life I will cry out with all my life and heart.
I abandoned my life and heart; I went to the limit of life;
I saw that the whole world is wholly the mystery of God.

Once more in *haqqahaqq* there is an oblique reference to his *pir*. The *qafiyya* or rhyme-scheme of the *qit'a* is imperfect, *'alam* being used in the same sense three times. The impression left is of a poet of limited technical proficiency writing in a hackneyed Sufi style. However, aided by the shaykh's powerful charisma, when 'Abd al-Quddus' verses were sung with all the resources of a *qavval* of a Chishti *khanqah*, they may have had a considerable emotive effect upon listeners.

Two *ghazals* reproduced by I. Quddusi from modern oral tradition are of greater verbal felicity than the Persian verses preserved in the *Lata'if*.[241] In the first of these the *takhallus* is not Ahmadi, but Quddusi, and in the second '*banda-i Quddus Gangohi*': this is in itself sufficient to cast

[241] *Shaykh 'Abd al-Quddus*, pp. 404–5.

doubt upon their authenticity. The first of these, which is a fine *ghazal* beginning '*astin bar ru kashida hamchu makkar amade*' (You came like a deceiver, hiding your face with your sleeve), is also found, less the second *bayt* and with a different *maqta'* and *takhallus* in the *Rushd-nama.*[242] The *takhallus* there is Muhammad and 'Abd al-Quddus himself attributes the poem to Muhammad Qalandar.[243] The *maqta'* substituted in the oral version is certainly the best known of all verses attributed to 'Abd al-Quddus and in the early years of the twentieth century a Sufi figure of repute died of ecstasy when listening to it in a *mahfil* in Ajmer:[244]

> *guft quddusi faqire dar fana' u dar baqa*
> *khvud-ba-khvud azad bude khvud giriftar amade*
> Quddusi, a *faqir* in the transient world and in the world eternal, said:
> 'You were free by yourself alone, by yourself you became captive!'

The reference is to the embodiment of the unconditioned Creator in creation. It is sad that this fine couplet must almost certainly be rejected as a composition of 'Abd al-Quddus himself, rather than of any anonymous devotee of the shaykh.

One further aspect of 'Abd al-Quddus' activities as a Persian poet is noteworthy. In his youth he embarked upon a Persian translation of the *Candayan* of Mawlana Da'ud, a late fourteenth-century Avadhi romance.[245] A considerable

[242] *Rushd-nama*, p. 2.

[243] Ibid.

[244] Mawlana Muhammad Husayn Ilahabadi: the event is commemorated in an Urdu *qit'a* of Akbar Ilahabadi.

[245] *Lata'if*, pp. 99–100. For editions of the *Candayan*, see note 81. The *Candayan* describes the adventures of Canda, a beautiful lady who elopes

portion of the translation had been made, when the manuscript was destroyed in the war between Bahlul Lodi and Husayn Shah Sharqi.[246] The *Lata'if* quotes seven *bayts* which had survived this destruction, from which it is clear that 'Abd al-Quddus was adapting the form of the poem, from stanzas of five *caupais* followed by a *doha* in the Hindi original into the standard form of the Persian *mathnavi*. Four of the *bayts* preserved are of a section on the *m'iraj* (ascent of the Prophet) which had been lacking in the original poem and was therefore inserted by 'Abd al-Quddus; the other three *bayts* are a close translation of three *caupais* of the original Hindi, which the *Lata'if* reproduces:

unca birikha phara laga akasas
hatha carhai kai nahin asa
kahu jogita ko banhan pasarai
taravara dali chuai ko parai
rati divas bahuta rakhawara
nayana dekhai jai so mara[247]

A lofty tree, whose fruit is up in the sky;
there is no hope of reaching it with the hand.

---

with the Ahir champion Lor or Lorik. It was composed by Mawlana Da'ud of Dalamau in the UP in 781/1379–80 and was dedicated to the younger Khan-i Jahan, minister of Feroz Shah Tughluq. It is the earliest of the series of verse romances by Muslim poets in Avadhi or Eastern Hindi which has survived. It evidently enjoyed considerable popularity in Muslim educated circles (see Badayuni, *Muntakhab al-tawarikh*, vol. I, p. 250).

[246] See p. 327 above, and also note 39. The translation of the *Candayan*, like the *Rushd-nama*, was a work of the youth of 'Abd al-Quddus.

[247] *Lata'if*, p. 100; Dalama'i, *Candayana*, ed. P.L. Gupta, p. 113; Dalama'i, *Candayana*, ed. M.P. Gupta, pp. 54–5. I have given a transcription agreeing with the form of the verses in the *Lata'if*, which must represent the manuscript reading from which 'Abd al-Quddus was translating.

Say, who has the power to stretch up his arm
to pass on to touch the branches of the tree?
Day and night there are many guards
and he who with his eyes looks up will be killed.

This is rendered into Persian by 'Abd al-Quddus:

shajar i buland ast thamar dar sama
qat'-i ummid ast bar an dast-i ma
zahra ki-ra dast-farazi kunad
shakh-i falak dast-i ki bazi kunad
roz u shab gashta nigahban-i base
kushta shavad chun ki ba-binad kase.

The adaptation or translation of romantic love stories from poetic versions in north Indian vernacular languages into Persian *mathnavis* became popular in the Mughal period, from which scores if not hundreds of such *mathnavis* survive; but if such translations were made in the Sultanate period they appear to have perished[248] and 'Abd al-Quddus must be regarded as an innovator of the tradition.

'Abd al-Quddus and the Hindi Poetic Tradition

'Abd al-Quddus' taste in Hindi is of greater significance than his taste in Persian verse from the point of view of literary history. In the mystical *ghazal* and didactic *mathnavi* he drew upon comparatively well-documented tradition; but in Hindi poetry the fifteenth century is a rather obscure period which preceded the great flowering of devotional verse under the

[248] Amir Khusraw's *Daval Rani Khizr Khan*, based on some kind of narrative written partly (?) in Hindi according to the poet, is not a true example of the genre: *Daval Rani Khizr Khan*, ed. R.A. Ansari, Aligarh: Matba'-i Institute, 1917, p. 41, line 15.

influence of the revival of the Krishna cult and other forms of *saguna bhakti* in northern India in the sixteenth century. The confusion which prevails in fifteenth-century Hindi literary history may be illustrated by reference to our knowledge of its greatest poet, the Muslim weaver Kabir. Kabir is said by his hagiographers to have been born in AD 1398 and to have died in AD 1518.[249] No source earlier than the last years of the sixteenth century appears to attest his historical existence.[250] Apart from the *Adi Granth*, compiled in 1603–4, the manuscript traditions which preserve his verses are preserved in copies dating from the late seventeenth to the nineteenth centuries. Efforts have now been made to isolate a corpus of original verses of a historical Kabir from the accretions and textual corruptions of the differing manuscript traditions.[251] If this is our present state of knowledge with regard to Kabir, we are even worse off with regard to the other *bhagats* of the *nirguna* type who are said to have been Kabir's contemporaries. In these circumstances the *Rushd-nama* of 'Abd al-Quddus, whose composition can be dated to within a few years of AD 1480, provides valuable evidence of types of Hindi verse current at that time as well as of the climate of popular devotion and sensibility.

Metrically, the verses reproduced by 'Abd al-Quddus (with the exception of a single macaronic couplet) are divided by him into *dohra* (*doha*), *caupad*, and *sarod*: by the last term he means a song generally of more than four lines of

[249] Rev. F.E. Keay, *Kabir and his Followers*, Calcutta: Association Press, 1931, pp. 27–8.

[250] 'Abd al-Haqq, *Akhbar al-akhyar*, p. 291.

[251] Dr Parasnath Tiwari's edition of Kabir's *Granthavali* (Allahabad: University of Allahabad, 1961) applies classical methods of textual criticism to the very diverse traditions in which the verses of Kabir are conserved. My friend Mr S.C.R. Weightman, in his forthcoming paper on 'The Thought and Poetry of Kabir' remarks, 'We can say no more than that [this edition] represents a nucleus text of the maximum probability.'

a loose metrical structure, to be sung in a particular *parda* (*raga*). Many verses are reproduced without indication of authorship. The occurrence of the word *piyara, piyare* ('dear') in a number of *dohras* suggests that these are in fact the compositions of Shaykh Piyare, whose influence upon 'Abd al-Quddus and upon his tastes has already been noted.[252] One poem of three *dohras* seems to contain the pen-name Ladhan; and the identification of this poet as Shaykh Muhammad, grandson of Ahmad 'Abd al-Haqq, suggested by the marginal gloss, admirably fits the purport of the verses.[253] A considerable number of the *caupads* and *sarods* bear the pen-name Alakhdas ('servant of the Invisible'), used by 'Abd al-Quddus himself.[254] In their content the Hindi verses of the *Rushd-nama* belong to several recognizable genres or to a mixture of one or more of these genres.

The simple poem expressing human love is clearly one of the bases of the Hindi poetic tradition: but it is stylized in a form somewhat alien to both European and Islamic traditions of love poetry. Even the anonymous early poets of vernacular folk tradition must mostly have been men, but the Hindi love poem expresses the lawful love and passion of the married woman. She longs for her lord in his absence, and in his presence she rejoices and disports herself: she confides her feelings to her *sakhi*, a female companion of

[252] See above (pp. 318 and 378): Shayrani (*Maqalat*, Lahore: Kitab manzil, 1966, vol. I, p. 149) identified the pen-name *Piyara* in these *dohas* with the Shaykh Piyare at Rudawli, but he also attributed the *dohas* with the name *Ladhan* to the same author.

[253] *Rushd-nama*, p. 20, marginal note 8: this reads *Lad* (for *Ladhan*) in both the lithograph and the related Aligarh (Subhan) MS.

[254] *Rushd-nama*, p. 3 (also Aligarh MS) on the first occasion where the pen-name Alakh Das occurs has the interlinear gloss *kinaya az 'Abd al-Quddus*. The number of times that this pen-name occurs and its fanciful resemblance to the second portion of the Shaykh's name can leave very little doubt that the verses so signed are of 'Abd al-Quddus himself.

gentility and intelligence, not unlike the lady's companion of Victorian England, except that both she and her employer or hostess are young and desirable.

Few verses in the *Rushd-nama* belong to this genre in its simple and unadulterated form, in which there is no indication of divine love (*'ishq-i haqiqi* in Persian Sufi terminology) rather than human love (or *'ishq-i majazi*):

ranga bhavana men piya paya rahansi karun badhaya
gaya burhapa bha tarunapa je sain ghar aya[255]

In the pavilion of pleasure I have found my lord: in private I make merry.
Old age has gone, youth is here since my lord came home.

An interesting variant pattern, rare in later Hindi literature, occurs in a *dohra* in which a man speaks of his passion for a woman:

je so nari sulakhati mujhahi dikhlavai mukha
kyon nahin nacun mora jyon bisaren sabha dukha[256]

[255] Ibid., p. 17. The transcriptions of these verses from the *Rushd-nama* (cited with page references to the lithographed edition) are based on the collation of three manuscripts with it, by Mr S.C.R. Weightman, Lecturer in Hindi at the School of Oriental and African Studies, London, and myself and they are a product of our joint labours. The text of these Hindi verses in Arabic script is often in a very corrupt state in the manuscripts (and lithograph) and the readings of the selection of verses presented here cannot be considered definitive, particularly as we were not able to consult all the known manuscripts. In a few instances I have differed from the readings or interpretations which Mr Weightman prefers and take full responsibility for errors; and I certainly could not have undertaken the task of reconstructing the text of the verses without his close collaboration. Mr Weightman is now engaged in producing a full critical edition of all the Hindi verses of the *Rushd-nama*, with linguistic analysis.
[256] Ibid., p. 12.

If that beautiful lady show[s] her face to me,
Why should I not dance like a peacock, all grief forgetting?

However, almost all the love poems quoted by 'Abd al-Quddus show in their text as well as in the use to which he puts them signs of the equation of human and divine love:

jidhara dekhun he sakkhi tidhara aur na koi
dekha bujha bicari main sabahi apan soi[257]

Wherever I look, O friend, there is none other:
after reflecting I realised that everything was Himself.

The love poetry of the *Rushd-nama* differs considerably in content from the Maithili *padas* of Vidyapati which are our principal evidence of the state of development of love lyrics in the north Indian vernaculars in the first half of the fifteenth century.[258] Although Vidyapati's charming poems have later been assumed to be songs of mystical and divine love, in fact hymns of the Krishna-Lila cult, their words give no indication that they are other than poems of mortal love. The Hindi love lyrics and *dohras* of the *Rushd-nama* can be seen as a development rather similar to that which took place in the Avadhi romantic narrative poem in the hands of Jayasi,[259] in which the joys of mortal love are vividly described, but a preoccupation with the parallel of divine love is seldom absent. By contrast, a rather different flavour is found in many *dohas* of Kabir, probably current at the same time as those of the *Rushd-nama*; in these the

[257] Ibid., p. 3.
[258] Vidyapati, *Gita-sangraha*, ed. with English introduction and translation by S. Jha, Banaras: Motilal Banarasidass, 1954.
[259] Malik Muhammad Jayasi, *Padamavati*, ed. V.S. Agravala, Chirgaav, Jhansi: Sahitya Sadana, vs 2012/AD 1955; English tr. A.G. Shirref, Calcutta: Bibliotheca Indica, 1944.

setting of human love is often vestigial, surviving only as a casual appeal to the *sakhi* or friend.[260] Looking towards the future, in the love poems of the *Rushd-nama*, there does not appear to be any close association with the Krishna-Lila, whose participants are never mentioned by name, or with any other aspects of the *saguna* or humanized *bhakti* cults which became increasingly popular in northern India in the sixteenth century. However, such an association is foreshadowed by two songs for the Holi festival by Alakhdas, that is to say 'Abd al-Quddus himself, of which one is reproduced here:

jana ajana saba khelai loi
bina piya khela na khela hoi
janaajana jaga kheli re
ho ho holi re
saba khelanha sakhi mana mahan jana
saraba nirantara piya parvana
jana ajana jaga khelai phaga
kanta bala leun hirdai laga
alakhdasa akhai sunu nanhan
hamatuma khelahin de kara banhan[261]

Knowing and unknowing all the people play;
without my lover the game cannot be played;
knowing and unknowing the world plays;
O, O, Holi O!
Know my friend, that all the plays are in the heart.
My lover is the validator of all without end.
Knowing and unknowing the world plays *phag*.

[260] It is perhaps characteristic of this tendency that in one of the *dohas* quoted below *baun dhani gai hirai* in the *Rushd-nama* has been replaced by *rahya kabira hirai*.
[261] *Rushd-nama*, p. 8: described as a *sarod* in the *parda* (Rag) Maru.

I will take my love close to my heart.
Listen, my Lord!—says Alakhdas—
You and I shall play with our hands and arms joined.

A number of *horis* or Holi songs are also attributed to Kabir. A number of close parallels in *dohas* referring to love attributed to Kabir and those of the *Rushd-nama* can be found.

herata herata he sakhi haun dhani gai hirai
parya bunda samanda manah kaha kyon heri jai[262]

I the lady, O friend, through looking and looking [for my lord] have vanished:
the drop has fallen into the ocean; tell me, how can it be espied?

alakha niranjana mera sain so jo lakha na jai
jina lakhya tina apa ganvaya kahun to ko patiyai[263]

The Unseen Pure One is my Lord, He who cannot be seen:
he who saw Him lost himself: If I were to tell of this who would believe it?

Other *dohras* of the *Rushd-nama* are indistinguishable in type and sentiment from those of Kabir and employ the same homely and vivid similes, for instance:

(1) An incitement to concentration upon the spiritual path:

nihacala rakhau apa syon dhari kai nihacala loi
pithi sabahi pisai kai kanji kyonkara hoi[264]

Keep yourself motionless, having kept your eye without moving:

262 Ibid., p. 8: cf. Vaudeville, *Granthavali* (*doha*) 7–4; p. 17.
263 *Rushd-nama*, p. 17.
264 Ibid., p. 14.

when you have ground up any amount of *pithi* (pulse steeped in water) how can it become *kanji* (rice-gruel)?

(2) A description of guidance along the spiritual path:

jinha gala phansi kanta ki te nij pavahin bata
phansa bihune bapure dubai cambala ghata[265]

Those on whose necks is the halter of the Beloved, they find their proper path;
the unlucky ones without (such) a halter drown at the ford of the Chambal.

(3) A statement of the nature of Creation and the common birth of mankind:

camahin bandhi putali hari bandha guda
ikai nari jaga upanya ko bahaman ko suda[266]

A doll was enclosed in skin, brain was encased in bone:
One woman gave birth to the world: Who is the Brahman? Who is the Shudra?

In one case a *doha* common to Kabir and the collections of verse attributed to other *bhagats*, also found in the *Rushd-nama*, can be traced back to the *dohakosa* of *Saraha*, and therefore appears to be an inheritance from earlier *sahajiya* Buddhist tradition:[267]

ja ka guru jo dubyan cela kain tarahin
andhe andha theliya dou kui parahin[268]

[265] Ibid., p. 23.
[266] Ibid., pp. 8–9.
[267] D.V. Bharati, *Siddha-sahitya*, Allahabad: Kitab Mahal, 1955; Vaudeville, *Kabir Granthavali*, p. 2 and note 9: the *doha* also appears in the works of Dadu.
[268] *Rushd-nama*, p. 5.

How can the *chela*, when his guru drowns, swim across?
The blind man pushes the blind man and both fall into the well.

Kabir's deity is *alakha rama*, Rama invisible or unincarnate. Occasionally he refers to traditional Hindu belief in the incarnation of Vishnu as Rama of Ayodhya, the hero of the *Ramayana*; the golden age to which Kabir occasionally looked back was *raja piyare ram aka*, the reign of the beloved Rama.[269] But it is clear that his concept of God was of Rama, unincarnate, ahistorical, and *nirguna*, without attributes. Kabir's belief in this attributeless deity is superimposed upon yogic cosmogonic and physiological concepts which provided, through the practice of selected austerities, a technique of ecstasy.

By contrast with the verses attributed to Kabir, those reproduced in the *Rushd-nama* mention neither *alakha rama*, Rama invisible nor the quasi-historical Rama of Ayodhya celebrated anew by Tulsi Dasa at the end of the sixteenth century. The theories advanced by Hazari Prasad Dvivedi regarding Kabir also find no confirmation in the *Rushd-nama*.[270] Even if many weavers were Jogis, corrupted into married life and then superficially converted to Islam, the influence of yogic doctrine is no less strong upon 'Abd al-Quddus than it was upon Kabir; yet 'Abd al-Quddus was a man of ancient and learned Muslim descent. Indeed, it can be argued that the yogic influences upon 'Abd al-Quddus are stronger than those upon Kabir. Kabir, in all the variant recensions of his verse, repudiated the cult of Gorakhnath as he did the other competing faiths of northern India. The Gorakhpanthi Jogis were rivals and enemies of the cult of *alakha* Rama which he himself was propagating. In the verses

[269] Vaudeville, *Kabir Granthavali* 24, 26.
[270] H.P. Dvidedi, *Kabir*, Bombay: Hindī Grantha Ratnākara, 1947, pp. 1–21 and passim.

attributed to Kabir there is no direct dependence on hitherto published Gorakhpanthi literary tradition.

'Abd al-Quddus, however, often refers to Gorakhnath in terms devoid of hostility. His Gorakhnath is a historical figure, equated in Rukn al-Din's glosses with the *insan-i kamil*, the *pir* whose distinction from the Divine Nature is minimal.[271] Elsewhere it is clear that 'Abd al-Quddus regards Gorakhnath as a Hindi name for God himself, comparable to Kabir's *alakh* Rama.[272]

jagai gorakha savai papa
alakha niranjana apai apa[273]

Gorakh wakes: sin sleeps:
the Pure Unseen One, alone by Himself.

alakhadasa akhai sunu loi
dui dui mata kaho bhai koi
jala thala mahiyala saraba nirantara
gorakhanatha akela-soi[274]

Alakh Das says, Listen, O people!
Do not speak in terms of two and two, O brother, at all:
in water, on land or in the mountain, all without end—
it is Gorakhnath alone.

Though many verses in the *Rushd-nama* are *caupads* and this appears to have been a favourite metre among Natha-panthi Jogis, there are a few obvious points of

[271] *Rushd-nama*, p. 9: Gorakh Nath interpreted in the interlinear gloss as *ustad-i kamil u wasil bi-haqq*.
[272] Ibid., marginal gloss: *jagai gorakha* interpreted as 'the guardian of the world "who doth not yawn nor sleep" is awake'.
[273] Omitted in the lithograph of the *Rushd-nama* and the Aligarh MS: Tuebingen MS f. 19.
[274] *Rushd-nama*, p. 7.

correspondence with the *Gorakhabani*, the alleged Hindi poetical works of Gorakh. Manuscripts of the *Gorakhabani* older than the seventeenth century are not known, and a number of verses contained in the collection are not likely to be much older than this.[275] Two *caupads* found in the *Rushd-nama* appear in nearly the same form in the *Gorakhabani*, and one other shorter couplet has been expanded into a *caupad* in the *Gorakhabani*. The first of these *caupads* has already been quoted, in connection with 'the place of sleep which is in the head'. The second emphasizes that all spiritual life is contained within the heart:

yaha mana sakti yaha mana siva
yaha mana tina bhavana ka jiva
yaha mana lai jo unmani rahai
tina bhavana ka baten kahai[276]

This *man* (heart, mind, inclination) is *Shakti*: this *man* is *Shiva*:
this *man* is the spirit animating the three worlds:
this *man* is the passion which exists in a state of ecstasy:
what a tale the three worlds are telling!

The remaining couplet in the *Rushd-nama* found in an expanded form in the *Gorakhabani* refers to a dying before physical death, and appears to be an allusion to the suspension of ordinary bodily processes in *Samadhi* and burial alive for subsequent resuscitation:

marahu pandita maranu mitha
ton marana sri gorakha ditha[277]

Die, O learned One, for dying is sweet
when Shri Gorakh has shown the way to die.

[275] Barthwal, *Gorakha-bani.*
[276] *Rushd-nama*, p. 18; Barthwal, *Goraka-bani*, p. 18, no. 50.
[277] *Rushd-nama*, p. 9; Barthwal, *Gorakha-bani*, p. 10, no. 26.

In Natha-panthi literature one *caupad* found in the *Rushd-nama* is reproduced in a work other than the *Gorakhabani.* Although in the *Rushd-nama* it appears with the name of Gorakh himself, it is also found in a collection of *banis* or poetical works attributed to other Nath figures assigned to Charapat Nath.[278] It is a satirical verse describing Natha-panthi Jogis who have not reached any state of spiritual enlightenment:

kanani mudra gale rudrakha
Phiri phiri parhahin bihuni sakha
bolata gorakha suna ho loi
baratana hoi pai joga na hoi[279]

In their ears the earrings and around their necks the *rudraksha* beads.
Roaming around they recite meaningless verses;
Gorakha says, Listen O people!
This is a livelihood but it is not Yoga.

In the *Rushd-nama* a number of gnomic couplets regarding religious life may derive from the Natha-panthis or from some other tradition of the popular religious life of northern India. One of these, like the *caupad* quoted above, satirizes false men of religion:

roti sate gyan bikae
rata kahe dina bisari jae[280]

They trade mystic knowledge for bread:
what they say at night is forgotten the next day.

[278] P.D. Barthwal, ed., *Natha-siddhon ki banian,* Kashi: Nagari Pracharini Sabha, vs 2012, p. 26.
[279] *Rushd-nama,* p. 16.
[280] Ibid., p. 15.

Others of these couplets concern the role of the guru:

bina kauri hata nahin
bina guru bata nahin[281]

Without the cowrie there is no market:
without the Guru there is no path (to salvation).

guru hira guruchara kudara
khodai nikasai hira sara[282]

The Guru is a diamond and his follower is a spade:
if he digs there will come out a wealth of diamonds.

The Persian verse which precedes this in the *Rushd-nama* provides an almost exact translation:

pir zamin-i gawhar ast u murid kulande
gawhar ba dast nayad ta na bakande[283]

The *pir* is a jewel-bearing ground and the *murid* a mattock:
the jewel will not come to hand until you dig.

Verses bearing the name of Alakh Das are invariably *caupads* and *sarods*, never *dohas*. They stem mainly from the Natha-panthi tradition but are influenced by *bhakti*, embodying the idea of a personal God, identified as *piya*, the beloved and *parvana* (Skt. *pramana*), the validator, immanent in the universe. Certain catchphrases, also found in the Natha-panthi collections of *caupads*, are very often repeated, e.g. *papa na puna* ('neither sin nor merit'), *saraba nirantara* ('all continuously'). The two characteristic sets of verses of Alakh Das quoted above may suffice.

281 Ibid., p. 6.
282 Ibid., p. 5.
283 Ibid.

The last important category of verses in the *Rushd-nama* are *dohas* which are likely to be the compositions of other inmates of the Rudawli *khanqah*, whose poetic talents compare favourably with those displayed by ʻAbd al-Quddus himself. As has been mentioned, Shaykh Muhammad bin Shaykh ʻArif bin Ahmad ʻAbd al-Haqq had been identified as the Ladhan of three fine *dohas* which adapt this Hindi verse tradition to the expression of Muslim and Sufi sentiments:[284]

mahmada mahmada jaga kahai cinhai nahim koi
ahmada mima ganvaia kaha kyon duja hoi
mahmada phula anada ka phala bhi apana soi
so kyon janai bapura jinha na caka hoi
mahmada ʻarifa ho rahai ʻarifa ahmada soi
akatha katha yaha ladhana ki bira bujhai koi[285]

The world says Mahmad, Mahmad, but nobody understands.
Ahmad has lost its *mim*[286] tell me, how could there be a second?
Mahmad is the flower of the eternal; he is himself also the fruit;
How can the poor wretch know this who has not tasted it?
Mahmad is becoming ʻArif and ʻArif, he is Ahmad,[287]
This is the untellable tale of Ladhan; there are few who understand.

The *dohas* in which the name of (Shaykh) Piyare appear are of a less obviously Muslim colouring. Their diction shows affinities on the one hand with the *caupads* of Alakh Das and on the other with the *dohas* of Kabir:

[284] See above, note 253.
[285] *Rushd-nama*, p. 20.
[286] *Ahmad* losing the *mim* becomes *Ahad*: 'One', i.e. God. The verses have several different meanings in them which will be examined when Mr Weightman's edition is published. Muhammad is deliberately vocalized Mahmad, in accordance with the textual indications of the manuscripts and lithograph.
[287] The allusion is *inter alia* to the pedigree of Shaykh Muhammad bin Shaykh ʻArif bin Shaykh Ahmad ʻAbd al-Haqq.

eka gusain sabhin mahan so jo lakha na jai
jo usa sisa no nyavai tasa mathe bhaka jai
bajhe piyare saian aur na dekhun cukkha
jidhara dekhaun he sakhi tidhara sain mukka
kyon haun sisa so nyavaun aisa dekhun mai
bahara bhitara he sakhi apana eka khudai[288]

There is one Lord in all, He who cannot be seen:
he who does not bend his head to Him, his forehead will be broken.
I do not see with my eye (?) aught other than my dear Lord:
wherever, O friend, I look, there is the face of the Lord.
Why should I not bend my head when thus I behold, O friend?
O friend, within and without He is Himself, the one *Khuda*.

Finally, there is one couplet in the *Rushd-nama* described as *rekhta*. This is not in archaic Urdu of mixed vocabulary, but is a macaronic verse of which the first line is Persian and the second Hindi:

sadq rahbar sabr tosha dost manzil dil rafiq
satta nigari dharma raja joga marga nirmala[289]

Sincerity is the guide; patience the provision for the journey; the friend our destination; the heart our companion:
truth is the city; righteousness its King; Yoga the pure road.

With this we may suitably come to the end of our own travels in the survey of 'Abd al-Quddus Gangohi's diverse activities as a Sufi shaykh.

[288] *Rushd-nama*, p. 30.
[289] Ibid., pp. 14–15.

Simon Digby: A Biographical Sketch

Richard Harris and David Lunn

Simon Digby was born in Jabalpur, India, in 1932, where his father was a high court judge. His mother, Violet M. Digby, a gifted artist, was also from a colonial family. Simon was educated in Britain, and he received his BA in History from the University of Cambridge, where he was also later registered as a PhD student under the supervision of Dr Percival Spear. Already able to read Hindi and Urdu, it was here that he began to study Persian, and began a long, albeit non-traditional, academic career with a major focus on the history of medieval India.

Digby returned to India regularly throughout his life. His earliest academic article was written at the (then) Prince of Wales Museum in Bombay under the supervision of the director, Dr Motichandra. He travelled extensively across the subcontinent, spending substantial time in Kashmir, Hyderabad (Deccan) and Delhi. His last visit to India was in 2010, where he died after a short illness, and where his ashes were scattered.

*For fuller details of Simon Digby's biography, see the longer piece 'Simon Digby: A Life' in volume I of this series. That account was initially prepared by Digby himself, for the citation of his degree of DLitt (honoris causa) from Jamia Hamdard University in 2003.

From 1965, Digby was registered at London University's School of Oriental and African Studies (SOAS) for PhD research. He was appointed honorary librarian of the Royal Asiatic Society in 1968, where he was involved in cataloguing and preserving the collections—he also later co-edited a volume on the 'history and treasures' of the Society. In 1971, while in Karachi he availed himself of the opportunity to have his first scholarly monograph privately printed (*War-Horse and Elephant in the Dehli Sultanate*, an updated edition of which is in volume V of this series). In 1972, he was appointed to the only formal university post he ever held, in the Department of Eastern Art of the Ashmolean Museum, University of Oxford. He resigned from that role only a few years later—thus able to resume his travels, and dedicate more time to research and writing. He retained an association with the University's Oriental Institute and with Wolfson College, which included supervising and examining research students, until 2000.

Digby's travels helped form and inform his academic interests. While perhaps best known as a historian of Sufism and Sultanate-era north India, some of Digby's earliest published work was on art history. Later, fortuitous discoveries of Indo-Persian texts led him to produce extensive translations, and shaped some of his major academic writings—on the *Malfūzāt-i Naqshbandiyya*, or *Latā'if-i Quddūsī*, for example. His substantial collection of manuscripts—some of them unique—was to prove invaluable for his work; those now reside in the Bodleian Library, University of Oxford.

Digby was the author of a wide range of academic articles and chapters, over sixty of which were published in his lifetime, on topics that ranged from the above noted interests in Sufism and Sultanate-era Indian history, to art, architecture, numismatics, toys and games, travel writing, folklore, and colonial-era English-language literature. On receiving the Burton Medal of the Royal Asiatic Society in 1999, he delivered a paper on 'Richard Burton: The Indian Making of an Arabist', which he later published privately.

A very substantial body of his work remained unpublished at the time of his death in 2010, and much of his earlier work too had become relatively inaccessible. The trustees of his estate decided to auction off his most valuable artefacts—Digby had established himself as a discerning collector, even on a perpetually tight budget—and founded the Simon Digby Memorial Charity to further work in the fields that were of interest to Digby. Through funding a postdoctoral fellowship at SOAS, the charity has enabled the production of this series, bringing Digby's previously unpublished work to completion alongside much of his published material, and making it all available to new audiences.

Bibliography

Abbott, J.E., *The Life of Eknāth*, repr., Delhi: Motilal Banarsidass, n.d.

'Abd al-'Aziz b. Sher Malik, *Ta'rīkh-i Habībī*, Urdu tr. by Ma'shūq Yār Jang, Hyderabad, Deccan: n.p., 1368 Fasli.

'Abd al-Ḥaqq, *Akhbār al-akhyār*, Delhi: Mujtabā'ī Press, 1892 [1309 AH].

'Abd al-Quddus, *Anwar al-'uyun*, Lakhnau: Gulzar-i Muhammadi Press, 1296.

'Abdallāh, Sayyid Abū, *Khulāṣat al-alfāẓ*, Manuscript, Bodleian Library, University of Oxford, MS S. Digby Or. 8, n.d.

Abhayadatta, *Buddha's Lions: The Lives of the Eighty-Four Siddhas*, tr. James R. Robinson, California: Dharma Publishing, 1979.

———, *Masters of Mahāmudrā: Songs and Histories of the Eighty-four Buddhist Siddhas*, tr. K. Dowman, Albany: SUNY Press, 1985.

Abu'l Faẓl, *A'in-i Akbari*, Calcutta: Asiatic Society, 1877; tr. H.S. Jarret and J.N. Sarkar, Calcutta: Asiatic Society, 1948.

———, *Akbar-nāma*, tr. H. Beveridge, 3 vols., Calcutta: Asiatic Society, 1902–30.

'Afif, *Ta'rīkh-i Ferozshāhī*, Calcutta: Bibliotheca Indica, 1890.

Aghnides, N.P., *Mohammedan Theories of Finance*, repr., Lahore: Premier Book House, 1961.

Ahmad, Aziz, 'The Sufi and the Sultan in pre-Mughal Muslim India', *Der Islam*, vol. 38, no. 1–2, 1962, pp. 142–53.

———, *Studies in Islam in the Indian Environment*, Oxford: Oxford University Press, 1964.

Aḥmad, Bashīr al-Dīn, *Waqi'āt-i dār al-ḥukūmat-i Dehlī*, Dehlī: Shamsi Machine Press, 1919.

Ahmad, Iqbāl al-Dīn, *Tadhkira-i Khwāja Gesūdarāz*, Karachi: Iqbal Publishers, 1966.

Aḥmad, Niẓām al-Dīn, *Ṭabaqāt-i Akbarī*, Lucknow: Naval Kishor, 1875.

Allah, Hajji Imdad, *Ziya' al-qulub*, Dehli: Mujtaba'i Press, 1284 AH.

Anon., *Manāqib-i Awḥad al-Dīn*, ed. B. Furuzanfar, Tehran: Bungāh-i Tarjumah va nashr-i Kitāb, 1347 Shamsī.

Aris, M., *Bhutan: The Early History of a Himalayan Kingdom*, Warminster: Aris and Phillips, 1979.

Ashraf, K.M., *Life and Conditions of the People of Hindustan*, Delhi: Jiwan Prakashan, 1959.

Askari, Syed Hasan, *Maktub and Malfuz Literature as a Source of Socio-Political History*, Patna: Khuda Bakhsh Oriental Public Library, 1981.

———, *Islam and Muslims in Medieval Bihar*, Patna: Khuda Bakhsh Oriental Public Library, 1989.

'Aṭṭār, Farīd al-Dīn, *Manṭiq al-ṭayr*, ed. S. Gawharīn, Tehran: Amir Kabir, 1348 Shamsī.

Awrangabadi, Nizam al-Din, *Nizam al-qulub*, Dehli: Mujtaba'i Press, 1309 AH.

Bābur, Ẓahīr al-Dīn, *Bābur-nāma*, tr. A.S. Beveridge, London: Luzac, 1921.

Badāyūnī, 'Abd al-Qādir, *Muntakhab al-tawārīkh*, 3 vols., tr. G.S.A. Ranking, W. Haig and W.H. Lowe, Calcutta: Bibliotheca India, 1884–1925.

Baldick, Julian, *Mystical Islam: An Introduction to Sufism*, London: I.B. Tauris, 1989.

———, *Imaginary Muslims: The Uwaysī Sufis of Central Asia*, London: I.B. Tauris, 1993.

Baranī, Aḥmad, *Sirāj al-Hidāya*, ed. Q. Sajjād Husayn, Delhi: Idarah-i-Adabiyat i-Delli, 1983.

Baranī, Ziya' al-Dīn, *Ta'rīkh-i Ferozshāhī*, ed. Saiyid Ahmad Khan, Calcutta: Bibliotheca Indica, 1862.

———, *Fatāwā-i jahāndārī*, ed. Afsar Salim Khān, Lahore: Idārah-i Tahqīqāt-i Pākistān, Dānishgāh-i Panjāb, 1972.

———, *Ta'rīkh-i Ferozshāhī*, Manuscript, Bodleian Library, University of Oxford, MS S. Digby Or. 54, n.d.

Barasavī, *Savāṭi' al anwār*, Manuscript, India Office MS Ethé 654, n.d.

Barasawi, Muhammad Akram, *Iqtibas al-anwar*, Lahore: n.p., 1895.

Barthwal, P.D., ed., *Gorakha-bani*, Prayag: Hindi Sahitya Sammelan, 1946.

———, *Natha-siddhon ki banian*, Kashi: Nagari Pracharini Sabha, 2012.

Battuta, Ibn, *Voyages d'Ibn Batoutah*, tr. C. Defremery and B.R. Sanguinetti, Paris: Societé Asiatique, 1853–7.

———, *The Rehla of Ibn Battuta (India, Maldive Islands and Ceylon)*, tr. Mahdi Husain, Baroda: Oriental Institute, 1953.

———, *The Travels of Ibn Battuta, A.D. 1325–1354*, tr. Hamilton A.R. Gibb, 2 vols., Cambridge: Hakluyt Society, 1958–9.

Bayley, Edward Clive, *The History of India as Told by its own Historians: The Local Muhammadan Dynasties; Gujarat*, London: W.H. Allen and Co., 1886.

Bernier, François, *Travels in the Mogul Empire*, tr. I. Brock, ed. A. Constable, London: Oxford University Press, 1981.

Bharati, D.V., *Siddha-sahitya*, Allahabad: Kitab Mahal, 1955.

Bilgrāmī, Ghulām 'Alī Āzād, *Rawżat al-awliyā'*, Urdu tr., Hyderabad/Aurangabad: Matba Kareemi, 1345 Faslī.

———, *Sarv-i Āzād*, Hyderabad, Deccan: Kutubkhānah-i Āṣafīyah, 1913.

'Bismil', Munshī Qurbān 'Alī, *Sacchī sawāniḥ-i 'umri kalān, ma'hu malfūẓāt-i Khwāja Ajmērī*, Dehli: Raḥmānī Press, n.d.

Briggs, G.W., *Gorakhnath and the Kanphata Yogis*, Calcutta: YMCA Publishing House, 1938.

Bright, Jagat S., *Muslim Miracle Workers*, Mumbai: Jaico Publishing House, 1984.

Brown, Percy, *Indian Architecture: The Islamic Period*, 2nd edn., Bombay: D.B. Taraporevala, 1946.

Bruinessen, M. van, 'Haji Bektash, Sultan Sahak, Shah Mina Sahib and Avatars of the Running Wall', *Turcica: revue d'études Turques*, vol. 21, no. 3, 1999, pp. 55–69.

Bulāq, Muhammad, *Maṭlūb al-ṭālibīn*, Manuscript, India Office MS Ethé 653, n.d.

Burn, R.C., *Imperial Gazetteer of India: Provincial Series: Punjab*, Calcutta: Superintendent of Government Printing, 1908.

Chishtī, Farīd al-Dīn (pseudo), *Fawā'id al-sālikīn*, Delhi: Mujtabā'ī Press, 1892 [1311 AH].

Chishti, Ilahdiya, *Siyar al-aqtab*, Lakhnau: Naval Kishor Press, 1889 AD [1306 AH].

Chishti, Nur Ahmad, *Tahqiqat-i Chishti*, Lahore: Hamidiyya Steam Press, 1907 AD [1323 AH].

Chughtai, M.A., *A Forgotten Kingdom*, Poona: Deccan College, 1941.

Crooke, W., *The Popular Religion and Folklore of Northern India*, London: Archibald Constable & Co., 1896; repr., Delhi: Munshiram Manoharlal, 1968.

———, *Things Indian*, London: J. Murray, 1906.

Currie, P.M., *The Shrine and Cult of Mu'īn al-Dīn Chishtī of Ajmer*, New Delhi: Oxford University Press, 1989; repr., 2006.

Dā'ūd, Mawlana, *Candāyana*, ed. Parameshvari Lal Gupta, Bombay: Hindi Granth Ratnakar, 1964.

———, *Canadyana*, ed. M.P. Gupta, Agra: Pramanik Prakashan, 1967.

Dehlavī, 'Abd al-Ḥaqq, *Akhbār al-akhyār*, Delhi: Mujtabā'ī Press, 1892 [1309 AH].

———, *Tadhkira-yi Muṣannifīn-i Dehlī*, ed. Shams Allāh Qādirī, Hyderabad, Deccan: Historical Society of Hyderabad/Tarikh Press, n.d.

Desai, Z.A., *Malfuz Literature as a Source of Political, Social and Cultural History of Gujarat and Rajasthan in 15th Century*, Patna: Khuda Bakhsh Oriental Public Library, 1991.

Digby, Simon, 'The Tomb of Buhlul Lodī', *Bulletin of the School of Oriental and African Studies*, vol. 38, no. 3, 1975, pp. 550–61 [*L&WSD* VI.8].

———, 'Anecdotes of a Provincial Sufi of the Delhi Sultanate, Khwaja Gurg of Kara', *Iran*, vol. 32, 1994, pp. 99–109 [*L&WSD* III.9].

———, 'Dreams and Reminiscences of Dattu Sarvani, a Sixteenth Century Indo-Afghan Soldier', *The Indian Economic and Social*

History Review, vol. 2, no. 1, 1965, pp. 52–80 and vol. 2, no. 2, 1965, pp. 178–94 [*L&WSD* I].

———, 'Encounters with *Jogīs* in Indian Sūfī Hagiography', paper presented at SOAS University of London, 1970 [*L&WSD* II].

———, 'Iltutmish or Iletmish? A Reconsideration of the Name of the Dehlī Sultan', *Iran*, vol. 8, 1970, pp. 57–64 [*L&WSD* VI.1].

———, 'Review of W.H. McLeod, *Gurū Nānak and the Sikh Religion*', *Indian Economic and Social History Review*, vol. 7, no. 2, 1970, pp. 301–13.

———, *War-Horse and Elephant in the Dehlī Sultanate*, Oxford: Orient Monographs, 1971.

———, 'Abd al-Quddus Gangohi (1456–1537 A.D.): The Personality and Attitudes of a Medieval Indian Sufi Shaykh', in *Medieval India: A Miscellany*, vol. III, Aligarh: Aligarh Muslim University, 1975, pp. 1–66 [*L&WSD* III.10].

———, 'The Tomb of Buhlul Lodī', *Bulletin of the School of Oriental and African Studies*, vol. 38, no. 3, 1975, pp. 550–61 [*L&WSD* VI.8].

———, 'The Waterseller's Pilgrimage', *Lycidas*, vol. III, Oxford: Wolfson College, 1974–5, pp. 20–1.

———, 'Sufis and Travellers in the Early Dehli Sultanate: The Evidence of the *Fawā'id al-fu'ād*', in *Socio-Cultural Impact of Islam on India*, ed. Attar Singh, Chandigarh: University of the Punjab, 1976, pp. 171–7 [*L&WSD* III.4].

———, 'Muhammad bin Tughluq's Last Years in Kathiavad and His Invasions of Thattha', in *Sind Through the Centuries*, ed. H. Khuhro, Karachi: Oxford University Press, 1979; repr., 1981, pp. 130–8 [*L&WSD* VI.4].

———, 'The Currency System', in *The Cambridge Economic History of India, Volume I: c. 1200–c. 1750*, ed. T. Raychaudhuri and I. Habib, Cambridge: Cambridge University Press, 1982, pp. 93–101 [*L&WSD* V.4].

———, 'Early Pilgrimages to the Graves of Mu'īn al-Dīn and other Chishtī Shaikhs', in *Islamic Society and Culture*, ed. M. Israel and N.K. Wagle, New Delhi: Manohar, 1983, pp. 95–100 [*L&WSD* III.5].

———, 'Qalandars and Related Groups: Elements of Social Deviance in the Religious Life of the Dehlī Sultanate of the Thirteenth and Fourteenth Centuries', in *Islam in Asia*, vol. I, ed. J. Friedmann, Jerusalem: Hebrew University of Jerusalem, 1984, pp. 60–108 [*L&WSD* III.7].

———, 'The *Tuhfa-i nasa'ih* of Yusuf Gada: An Ethical Treatise in Verse from the Late-Fourteenth Century Delhī Sultanate', in *Moral Conduct and Authority: The Place of Adab in South Asian Islam*, ed. Barbara Daly Metcalf, Berkeley: University of California Press, 1984, pp. 91–123 [*L&WSD* III.8].

———, '*Tabarrukat* and Succession among the Great Chishti Shaykhs of the Delhi Sultanate', in *Delhi Through the Ages*, ed. Robert Eric Frykenberg, New Delhi: Oxford University Press, 1986, pp. 62–103 [*L&WSD* III.3].

———, 'The Sufi Shaykh as a Source of Authority in Medieval India', *Puruṣārtha*, vol. 9, 1986, pp. 57–77 [*L&WSD* III.1].

———, 'The Sufi Shaykh and the Sultan: A Conflict of Claims to Authority in Medieval India', *Iran*, vol. 28, 1990, pp. 71–81 [*L&WSD* III.2].

———, 'The Naqshbandis in the Deccan in the Late Seventeenth and Early Eighteenth Century A.D.: Bābā Palangposh, Bābā Musāfir and Their Adherents', in *Naqshbandis: cheminements et situation actuelle d'un ordre mystique musulman*, ed. M. Gaborieau, A. Popovic and T. Zarcone, Istanbul: Isis, 1990, pp. 167–207 [incorporated in introduction to Digby 2001/*L&WSD* VII].

———, 'Hawk and Dove in Sufi Combat', in *Pembroke Papers 1; Persian and Islamic Studies in Honour of P. W. Avery*, ed. C. Melville, Cambridge: Cambridge University Press, 1990, pp. 7–25.

———, 'Anecdotes of a Provincial Sufi of the Delhi Sultanate, Khwaja Gurg of Kara', *Iran*, vol. 32, 1994, pp. 99–109 [*L&WSD* III.9].

———, 'To Ride a Tiger or a Wall? Strategies of Prestige in Indian Sufi Legend', in *According to Tradition*, ed. Winand M. Callawaert and Rupert Snell, Weisbaden: Harrassowitz Verlag, 1994, pp. 99–129 [*L&WSD* III.6].

———, *Wonder-Tales of South Asia*, Jersey: Orient Monographs, 2000.

———, *Sufis and Soldiers in Awrangzeb's Deccan*, New Delhi: Oxford University Press, 2001.
———, 'The North Indian Kissa Tradition and the Nepali *Madhumalatī*', in *The Life and Works of Simon Digby, Volume IV: Tales, Translations, Trajectories*, ed. David Lunn, Delhi: Primus Books, 2025.
———, *The Life and Works of Simon Digby, Volume II: Encounters with Jogīs in Indian Sūfī Hagiography*, ed. David Lunn, Delhi: Primus Books, 2025.
Dutt, Sukumar, *Buddhist Monks and Monasteries of India*, London: G. Allen and Unwin, 1962; repr., Delhi: Motilal Banarsidass, 1988.
Dvidedi, H.P., *Kabir*, Bombay: Hindī Grantha Ratnākara, 1947.
Eaton, Richard M., 'The Political and Religious Authority of the Shrine of Bābā Farīd', in *Moral Conduct and Authority: The Place of* Adab *in South Asian Islam*, ed. B.D. Metcalf, Berkeley: University of California Press, 1984.
Eliade, M., *Yoga: Immortality and Freedom*, New York: Pantheon Books, 1958.
Elwell-Sutton, L., 'The *Darvīsh* in Persian Folklore', *Proceedings of the Twenty-sixth International Congress of Orientalists, New Delhi, 1964*, Poona: Bhandarkar Oriental Research Institute, 1968.
Ettinghausen, R., *Studies in Muslim Iconography: The Unicorn*, Washington: Smithsonian Institution, 1950.
Evans-Wentz, Walter Y., *The Tibetan Book of the Great Liberation*, London: Oxford University Press, 1954.
Ewing, Katherine, '*Malangs* of the Punjab: Intoxication or *Adab* as a Path to God', in *Moral Conduct and Authority: The Place of* Adab *in South Asian Islam*, ed. B.D. Metcalf, Berkeley: University of California Press, 1984, pp. 357–71.
Fakhr-i Mudabbir, *Ādāb al-harb wa ash-shajā'a*, ed. E.S. Khwansari, Tehran: Iqbāl, 1346 Shamsī.
Fani Kashmiri, Muhsin, *Mathnaviyyat-i Fani*, ed. S.A.H. Abidi, Srinagar: Jammu and Kashmir Academy of Arts, Culture and Languages, 1964.
Farīdī, Mawlānā Nūr Ahmad Khān, *Tadhkira-i Shāh Rukn-i 'Ālam Multānī*, Multan: Qasr-i Adab, 1961 [1381 AH].

Farīdī, Muḥammad 'Ālam Shāh, *Mazārāt-i awliyā Dihlī*, Delhi: Kutub Khānah-yi Naẕīriyyah, 1928 [1346 AH].
Fārūqī, Aḥsān al-Ḥaqq, *Sultān al-tārikīn*, Karachi: Dā'ira Mu'īn al-ma'ārif, 1962.
Firishta, *Ta'rīkh-i Firishta*, Bombay: Government College Press, 1833–4.
———, *Ta'rīkh-i Firishta*, Kanpur: Naval Kishor, 1874.
Foster, W., ed., *Early Travels in India, 1582–1619*, Oxford: Oxford University Press, 1921.
Gaborieau, Marc, 'Les orders mystiques dans le sous-continent Indien: un point de vue ethnologique', in *Les orders mystiques de l'Islam: cheminement et situation actuelle*, ed. A. Popovic and G. Veinstein, Paris: EHESS, 1986, pp. 105–34.
Gadā, Yūsuf [Rājū Qitāl, Yūsuf], *Tuḥfa-i naṣā'iḥ*, Manuscript, Bodleian Library, University of Oxford, MS S. Digby Or. 56 [ex-Harley], n.d.
Gēsūdarāz, *Asmār al-asrār*, ed. 'Aṭā Allāh Ḥusaynī, Hyderabad, Deccan: Aẓam Steam Press, 1350 Faslī.
———, *Jawāmi' al-kalim*, Kanpur: Intizāmī Press, 1352 Faslī.
———, *Anīs al-'ushshāq*, ed. M.H.S. 'Ata Husaini, Hyderabad, Deccan: Barqī Press, 1360 AH.
———, *Rūh-i tasawwuf*, Urdu tr. Shabbīr Hasan Chishtī Nizāmī, Dehlī: Zawia Publishers, n.d. [c. 1957].
Ghawthi, Muhammad, *Gulzar-i abrar*, Manuscript, John Rylands Library, Manchester, Lindesiana no. 185, n.d.
Ghaznavī, Sadīd al-Dīn Muhammad, *Maqāmāt-i Zhinda-Pīl*, ed. Hishmat Allah Mu'ayyed, Tehran: Intishārāt-i Bungāh-i Tarjumah va Nashr-i Kitāb, 1961 [1340 Shamsī].
Ghurye, G.S., *Indian Sadhus*, 2nd edn., Bombay, 1964.
Grabar, O. and Sheila Blair, *Epic Images and Contemporary History: The Illustrations of the Great Mongol Shahnama*, Chicago: University of Chicago Press, 1980.
Gramlich, Richard, *Die schiitischen Derwischorden Persiens*, vol. I, Wiesbaden: Harrassowitz Verlag, 1965.
Grierson, G.A., *Bihar Peasant Life*, Patna: Superintendent, Government Printing, 1885; repr., Delhi: Cosmo, 1975.

Grube, Ernest J., 'Fostat Fragments', in *Islamic Painting and the Arts of the Book*, ed. B.W. Robinson, London: Faber and Faber, 1976.

Habib, Mohammad and Khaliq Ahmad Nizami, ed., *A Comprehensive History of India V: The Delhi Sultanate (AD 1206–1526)*, Delhi: Orient Longmans/People's Publishing House, 1970.

Habib, Mohammad, 'Chishti Mystic Records of the Sultanate Period', *Medieval India Quarterly*, vol. 1, no. 1, 1950, pp. 1–42.

———, *Ḥaḍrat Niẓām al-Dīn Auliyā': ḥayāt aur ta'līmāt*, Delhi: Delhi University, 1970.

———, 'Shaikh Nasiruddin Mahmud Chiragh-i Delhi as a Great Historical Personality', repr. in *Politics and Society During the Early Medieval Period: Collected Works of Professor Mohammad Habib*, ed. K.A. Nizami, Aligarh/Delhi: People's Publishing House, 1974.

Habibullah, A.B.M., *The Foundation of Muslim Rule in India*, Allahabad: Central Book Depot, 1961.

Ḥāfiẓ, *Dīvān*, ed. Muḥammad Qazvīnī and Qāsim Ghanī, Tehran: Zavvār, 1320 AH.

Hamīd al-Dīn b. Shāh Budh, *Sharaf al-manāqib*, Urdu tr. Munshi Jagannath, Delhi: Afzal al-matābi', n.d. [c.1885].

Hasan, M. Zafar, *Delhi Province: List of Muhammadan and Hindu Monuments*, Calcutta: Superintendent Government Printing, 1916–22.

———, *A Guide to Nizamu-d Din, Memoirs of the Archaeological Survey of India*, no. 10, Calcutta: Archaeological Survey of India, 1922.

Hasluck, Frederick William, *Christianity and Islam under the Sultans*, Oxford: Clarendon Press, 1929.

Hinz, W., *Islamische Mässe und Gewichte*, Leiden: Brill, 1955.

Hodivala, Shahpurshah Hormasji, *Studies in Indo-Muslim History*, Bombay: Popular Book Depot, 1939.

Hujwīrī, 'Alī n. 'Uthmān al-Jullābī, *Kashf al-maḥjūb*, tr. R.A. Nicholson, Leiden: Brill and London: Luzaq and Co., 1911.

Husain, A.M., *Tughluq Dynasty*, Calcutta: Thacker, Spink and Co. 1963.

Husain, Iqbal, *The Early Persian Poets of India (A.H. 421–670)*, Patna: Patna University, 1938.

Husain, Yusuf, '*Haud al-hayat*: la version Arabe de l'Amratkund', *Journal Asiatique*, vol. 213, 1928, pp. 291–344.

Husayn, M.B., *Fihrist-makhtutat-i Shayrani*, Lahore, 1968–9.

Ḥusayn, Wajāhat ('Andalīb Shādānī), *Rubā'iyyāt-i Bābā Ṭāhir*, Lahore, n.d.

Ḥusayni, 'Alā' al-Dīn, *Khulāṣat al-alfāẓ*, Manuscript, Bodleian Library, University of Oxford, MS S. Digby Or. 8, n.d.

Ḥusaynī, Muḥammad Akbar, *Jawāmi' al-kalim*, Hyderabad, Deccan: Maṭba'-i Intizāmī, 1356 Faslī.

Ibn al-Balkhī, *Fārsnāma*, ed. G. Le Strange and R.A. Nicholson, London: Luzac, 1921.

Ikrām, S.M., *Āb-i Kawthar*, Lahore: Ferozesons, 1965.

'Irāqī, *Kulliyāt*, ed. S. Nafīsī, Tehran: Kitābkhānah-i Sanā'ī, 1958.

'Isāmī, *Futūh al-salātīn*, Madras: University of Madras, 1948.

Jahanabadi, Shah Kalim Allah, *Kashkul-i Kalimi*, Dehli: Mujtaba'i Press, 1891.

Jamālī, *Siyar al-'ārifīn*, Delhi: Maṭba'-i Riẓvī, 1893 [1311 AH].

Jāmī, 'Abd al-Rahmān, *Nafahāt al-uns*, ed. M. Tawhīdīpūr, Tehran: Kitabfurushi-i Saadi, 1958 [1336 Shamsī].

Jāyasī, *Padmāvati*, tr. A.G. Sherriff, Calcutta: Asiatic Society, 1944.

———, *Padmāvati*, ed. V.S. Agravala, Chirganw: Sahitya Sadana, 1955 [2012 vs].

Juzjānī, Minhāj-i Sirāj, *Tabaqāt-i Nāsirī*, ed. N. Lees, Calcutta: College Press, 1864.

Kabīr, *Kabīr Granthāvali*, ed. Pārasnāth Tiwārī, Prayāg: Hindi Parishad, 1908; repr., 1961.

———, *Kabīr Bījak*, ed. Sukdev Sinha, Ilahabad: Nilabh Prakashan, 1972; repr., 1989.

———, *The Bījak of Kabīr*, tr. Rev. Ahmad Shah, [1917]; repr., Delhi: Forgotten Books, 1990.

Kāshānī, 'Imād, *Ahsan al-aqwāl*. Urdu tr., Bombay, n.d.

Keay, Rev. F.E., *Kabir and his Followers*, Calcutta: Association Press, 1931.

Khān, 'Alī Muhammad, *Mir'āt-i Ahmadī*, tr. S. Nawab Ali and C.N. Seddon, Baroda: Education Department, 1928.

———, *Mir'āt-i Ahmadī: khātima [Supplement]*, ed. S. Nawab Ali, Baroda: Oriental Institute, 1930.

Khan, A. Wahid, *Bahmani Coins*, Hyderabad: Government of Andhra Pradesh, 1964.

Khānī, Bihāmad, *Ta'rīkh-i Muḥammadī*, Manuscript, British Library, MS Or. 137, n.d.

Khusraw Dehlavī, Amīr, *Khamsa*, ed. A.A. Ashrafī, Tehran: Šaqāyiq, 1362 Shamsī.

———, *Matla' al-anwār*, Kanpur: Naval Kishor, 1884.

———, *Dawal Rānī Khizar Khān*, Aligarh: Maṯba'-yi Insṭīṭiyūṭ, 1917 [1336 AH].

———, *Laylā Majnūn*, ed. M. Habīb al-Raḥmān Khān, Aligarh: Maṯba'-yi Insṭīṭiyūṭ, 1917.

———, *Ā'īna-i Iskandarī*, Aligarh: Maṯba'-yi Insṭīṭiyūṭ, 1917.

———, *Tughluq-nāma*, Hyderabad/Awrangabad: Maṭba' Urdū, 1933.

———, *Nuh sipihr*, ed. M. Wahid Mirza, Calcutta: Asiatic Society, 1948.

———, *Shīrīn u Khusrau*, Moscow: Izd-vo vostochnoi lit-ry, 1961.

Khwandamīr, *Makārim al-Akhlāq*, ed. T. Gandjeï, London: Trustees of the E.F.W. Gibb Memorial, 1979.

Khwurd, Amir, *Siyar al-awliya'*, ed. Chiranjī Lāl, Dehli: Muhibb-i Hindi Press, 1885 [1302 AH].

Kvaerne, P., *An Anthology of Tantric Buddhist Songs*, Bangkok: White Orchid Press, 1986.

Lāhawrī, Muḥammad 'Alī Ismā'īl (son of?) Mas'ūd 'Alī, *'urf* 'Sajjan', *Asrār al-majdhūbīn*, Manuscript, Private collection of Simon Digby, MS 10, n.d.

Lal, K.S., *Twilight of the Sultanate*, Bombay: Asia Publishing House, 1963.

Latif, Syed Muhammad, *History of the Punjab*, Calcutta: Central Press, 1892.

Lawrence, Bruce B., *Notes from a Distant Flute: The Extant Literature of Pre-Mughal Indian Sufism*, Tehran: Imperial Iranian Academy of Philosophy, 1978.

———, *Nizam Ad-din Awliya: Morals for the Heart*, Manchester: Beacon Books, 1991/New York: The Paulist Press, 1992.

Le Strange, Guy, tr., *The Geographical Part of the Nuzhat al-qulūb*, Leiden: Brill/London: Luzac, 1919.

Lynton, H.R. and M. Rajan, *The Days of the Beloved*, Berkeley: University of California Press, 1974.

Maḥmūd, Bābā Shāh, *Malfuẓāt-i Naqshbandiyya*, Hyderabad, Deccan: Nizamat-i umru Sarkar-i 'ali, 1939 [1358 AH].

Majawī, Fażl Allāh, *Fatāwā al-ṣūfiyya*, Manuscript, Bodleian Library, University of Oxford, Uri 321, n.d.

Makkī, *Ẓafar al-wālih*, ed. E. Denison Ross as *An Arabic History of Gujarat*, London: J. Murray, 1910–28.

Manerī, Sharaf al-Dīn Ahmad, *Mukhkh al-ma'ānī*, Manuscript, Bodleian Library, University of Oxford, MS S. Digby Or. 6, n.d.

Manerī, Shaykh Shu'ayb bin Shaykh Jalāl, *Manāqib al-asfiyā'*, Calcutta: Nūr al-Afāq Press, 1895 [1313 AH].

Maqrīzī, *Khiṭaṭ*, Būlāq: Dār al-Ṭibā'ah al-Miṣrīyah, 1270 AH.

Marshall, N.D., *Mughals in India*, Bombay: Asia Publishing House, 1968.

McLeod, W.H., *Gurū Nānak and the Sikh Religion*, Oxford: Clarendon Press, 1968.

———, *Early Sikh Tradition: A Study of the Janam-sākhīs*, Oxford: Clarendon Press, 1980.

Meadows Taylor, Col. H., *A Noble Queen*, 2nd edn., London: C. Kegan Paul & Co., 1880.

Mirza, M.W., *The Life and Works of Amir Khusrau*, Lahore: Baptist Mission Press, 1962.

Misra, S.C., *The Rise of Muslim Power in Gujarat*, London: Asia Publishing House, 1962.

Moreland, W.H. and P. Geyl, *Jahangir's India: The* Remonstrantie *of Francisco Pelsaert*, Cambridge: W. Heffer & Sons, 1925.

Morris, J., *The Venetian Empire: A Sea Voyage*, London: Faber and Faber, 1988.

Muḥammad, Shaykh, *Ādāb al-ṭālibīn*, Dehli: Mujtabā'ī Press, 1311 AH.

Munawwar, Muhammad b., *Asrār al-tawhīd*, ed. Dhabīh Allāh Safā, Tehran, 1953–4 [1332 Shamsī].

Mundy, Peter, *The Travels of Peter Mundy in Europe and Asia*, London: Hakluyt Society, 1914.

Mushar, Khān Bābā, *Fihrist i kitābhā i chāpī-i farsī*, 2nd edn., Tehran: Chāpkhānah-i Arzhang, 1972.

Mushtāqī, Rizqullāh, *Waqi'āt-i-Mushtāqī*, Manuscript, British Library, MS Or. 1929/MS Add. 11,633, n.d.
Nelson Wright, H., *The Coinage and Metrology of the Sultans of Dehlī*, Delhi: Manager of Publications, 1930.
Neshrī, *Cihannuma*, Ankara: Türk Tarih Kurumu Basımevi, 1949.
Nevill, H.R., *Barabanki: A Gazetteer*, District Gazetteers of the United Provinces, vol. XLVIII, Allahabad: Government Press, 1904.
———, *Saharanpur: A Gazetteer*, District Gazetteers of the United Provinces and Oudh, vol. II, Allahabad: Government Press, 1909.
Nicholson, R.A., *Studies in Islamic Mysticism*, Cambridge: Cambridge University Press, 1921.
Nizami, K.A., *Ta'rīkh-i mashā'ikh Chisht*, Delhi: Nadvat ul-muṣannifīn, 1953.
———, *Some Aspects of Religion and Politics in India during the Thirteenth Century*, Aligarh: Aligarh Muslim University, 1961.
———, 'Early Indo-Muslim mystics and their Attitude towards the State', *Islamic Culture*, vols. 22–4 (1948–50).
———, *The Life and Times of Shaikh Farid-u'd-din Ganj-i-Shakar*, Aligarh: Aligarh Muslim University, 1955.
———, 'The Suhrawardi Silsila and its Influence on Medieval Indian Politics', *Medieval India Quarterly*, vol. III, 1957, pp. 109–49.
———, *Supplement to Elliot and Dowson's History of India, Vol. III*, Delhi: Idarah-i Adabiyat-i Delli, 1981.
———, *On History and Historians of Medieval India*, Delhi: Munshiram Manoharlal, 1983.
Oakley, E.S. and Tara Dutt Gairola, *Himalayan Folklore*, Allahabad: Superintendent, printing and stationery, 1935.
Oman, J.C., *The Mystics, Ascetics and Saints of India*, London: T. Fisher Unwin, 1903.
Page, J.A., *An Historical Memoir on the Qutb, Delhi*, Calcutta: Archaeological Survey of India, 1926.
Pakrasi, Mira, *Folk Tales of Bihar*, New Delhi: Sterling Publishers, 1991.
Pellat, Ch., tr., *Le livre de la couronne*, Paris: Société d'édition 'Les belles lettres', 1954.

Qalandar, Hamīd, *Khair al-majālis*, ed. K.A. Nizami, Aligarh: Aligarh Muslim University, 1958.

Quddusi, I'jaz al-Haqq, *Shaykh 'Abd al-Quddus aur un ki ta'limat*, Karachi: Academy of Educational Research, 1961.

Quddusi, Rukn al-Din, *Lata'if-i Quddusi*, Delhi: Mujtaba'i Press, 1894 AD [1311 AH].

Qureshi, I.H., *The Administration of the Sultanate of Delhī*, 4th edn., Karachi: Pakistan Historical Society, 1958.

Rāwandī, *Rāḥat al-ṣudūr*, London: Luzac, 1921.

Sāmānī, Muhammad 'Alī, *Siyar-i Muhammadī*, Allahabad: Yūnānī Davalkhānah, 1928 [1347 AH] [= Storey no. 1206].

Sarda, Har Bilas, *Ajmer: Historical and Descriptive*, Ajmer: Fine Art Printing Press, 1911; repr., 1941.

Sarfarāz, Shaykh 'Abd al-Qādir, *A Descriptive Catalogue of the Arabic, Persian, and Urdu Manuscripts in the Library of the University of Bombay*, Bombay: University of Bombay, 1935.

Sarre, F., *Die Kunst des alten Persien*, Berlin: Cassirer, 1922.

Sarvar, Ghulam, *Khazinat al-asfiyya*, Kanpur: Naval Kishor Press, 1914 AD [1332 AH].

Sen, S., ed., *Indian Travels of Thevenot and Careri*, New Delhi: National Archives of India, 1949.

Shackle, Christopher, *A Gurū Nānak Glossary*, London: School of Oriental and African Studies, 1981.

Shāh, Mūbad, *Dabistān-i madhāhib*, ed. R. Razāzāde, Tehran: Kitābkhānah-'i Ṭahūrī, 1362 Shamsī.

Shāh, Mūbad, *Dabistān-i madhāhib*, Bombay: Matba'-i Lacchman, 1846 [1262 AH].

Sharma, Y.D., *Delhi and its Neighbourhood*, New Delhi: Archaeological Survey of India, 1964.

Sherwani, Haroon Khan, *The Bahmanis of the Deccan*, Hyderabad: Manager of Publications, 1955.

Sijzī, Amīr Hasan 'Alā', *Fawā'id al-fu'ād*, Lucknow: Naval Kishor, 1894.

———, *Dīwān*, ed. M.A. Maḥvī, Hyderabad: Maktabah-i Ibrāhīmiyah, 1933 [1352 AH].

———, *Fawā'id al-fu'ād*, ed. Muḥammad Latīf Malik, Lahore: Malik Sirāj al-Dīn and Sons, 1966 [1386 AH].

———, *Fawa'id al-fu'ad*, Dehli: Fakhr al-matabi', 1272 AH.
Sikandar, *Mir'āt-i Sikandarī*, ed. S.C. Misra and M.L. Rahman, Baroda: Education Society's Press, 1961.
Simnānī, Ashraf Jahāngīr, *Maktūbāt-i Ashrafi*, Manuscript, British Library MS Or. 267, n.d.
Sirhindī, Yaḥyā bin Aḥmad, *Ta'rīkh-i Mubārakshāhī*, ed. Hidayat Hosain, Calcutta: Bibliotheca Indica, 1931.
Sīvistānī, 'Abd al-Ghafūr bin Haidar, *Tadhkira-yi mashā'ikh-i Sīvistān*, ed. S.H. Rashdi, in *Mehrān*, vol. 23, no. 3–4, 1974.
Snell, Rupert, 'Raskhān the Neophyte: Hindu Perspectives on a Muslim Vaishnava', in *Urdu and Muslim South Asia: Studies in Honour of Ralph Russell*, ed. C. Shackle, London: SOAS, 1989.
Snellgrove, David L. and Hugh Richardson, *A Cultural History of Tibet*, Boston: Praeger, 1986.
Spencer Trimingham, J., *The Sufi Orders in Islam*, Oxford: Oxford University Press, 1971.
Srivastava, A.L., *Akbar the Great*, Agra: Shiva Lal Agarwala, 1962.
Storey, C.A., *Persian Literature: A Bio-Bibliographical Survey*, London: Royal Asiatic Society, 1977.
Stow, A.M., 'The Road between Delhi and Multan', *Journal of the Punjab Historical Society*, vol. 3, no. 1, 1914–15, pp. 26–37.
Subhan, J.A., *Sufism: Its Saints and Shrines*, Lucknow: Lucknow Publishing House, 1960.
Sultān, Muhammad, *Armughān-i Sultānī*, Agra: Maṭba'-i Mufīd-i 'Ām, 1902.
Ṭabāṭabā'ī, *Burhān-i ma'āthir*, Hyderabad: Maṭba' Jami'ah, 1936 [1355 AH].
Tāranātha, Jo Nang, *The Seven Instruction Lineages*, tr. D. Templeman, Dharamsala: Library of Tibetan Works & Archives, 1983.
Tattawī, Muhammad A'zam, *Tuhfat al-Tāhirīn*, ed. Badr Islām Rabbānī, Hyderabad (Sind): Sindī Adabī Board, 1956 [= Storey no. 1370].
Temple, Richard C., *The Legends of the Panjab*, Bombay: Education Society's Press, 1885.

Thanesari, Shaykh Jalal al-Din, *Tahaqquq-i aradi-i Hind*, Arabic text edited with Urdu translation by S.S.A. Nadvi, Karachi: Da'irah-i mu'in al-ma'arif, 1963.

Titus, Murray B., *Islam in India and Pakistan*, Calcutta: YMCA Publishing House, 1959.

Trumpp, E., *The Adi Granth*, London: W.H. Allen & Co., 1877.

Tughluq, Feroz Shāh, *Futūḥāt-i Fērōzshāhī*, ed. S. Abdur Rashid, Aligarh: Aligarh Muslim University, 1954.

Turner, Ralph, *A Comparative Dictionary of the Indo-Aryan Languages*, London: Oxford University Press, 1966.

Uberoi, J. Singh, 'On being Unshorn', in *Sikhism and Indian Society*, Simla: Indian Institute of Advanced Study, 1967.

Varma, R.C., *Saṅkṣipt Hindī śabdsāgar*, Kāshī: Nāgarī Pracāriṇī Sabhā, 1933.

Vaudeville, C., ed., *Kabir Granthavali*, Pondicherry: Institut Français d'Indologie, 1957.

Vidyapati, *Gita-sangraha*, ed. with English introduction and tr. by S. Jha, Banaras: Motilal Banarasidass, 1954.

Vogel, J. Ph., *Indian Serpent Lore*, repr., Varanasi: Prithivi Prakashan, 1972.

Wā'iẓī, 'Abd al-'Azīz b. Shēr Malik, *Risāla dar siyar-i Shāh Ni'mat Allāh Walī*, in *Matériaux pour la biographie de Shah Ni'matullah Kermani*, ed. J. Aubin, Tehran/Paris: Adrien-Maisonneuve, 1956.

Yamanī, Nizām al-Dīn, *Latā'if-i Ashrāfī*, Manuscript, John Rylands Library, University of Manchester. Persian MS 679, n.d.

Yazdani, G., *Bidar: Its History and Monuments*, Oxford: Oxford University Press, 1947.

Yazıcı, T., ed., *Manāḳib-i Jamāl al-Dīn-i Sāvī*, Ankara: Anjuman-i Tārīkh-i Turk, 1972.

Zaydī, Bānū Daktar Shamīm Maḥmūd, *Aḥwāl u āthār-i Shaykh Bahā' al-Dīn Zakariyyā' Multānī u khulāṣat al-'ārifīn*, Rawalpindi: Markaz-i Taḥqīqāt-i Fārsī, 1974.

Index

www.ingramcontent.com/pod-product-compliance
Lightning Source LLC
Chambersburg PA
CBHW050713290426
43912CB00084B/127/J
9789368833673